Emperor with family group (about 1932)

from left to right: Princess Zänäbä Warq, H. I. H. the Crown Prince, H. I. M. Empress Mänän, Princess Tänagnä Warq, Ras Dästa, H. I. M. Emperor Haile Sellassie I, Princess Wällättä Israel, Princess Tsähay, and Prince Makonnen; the two children on either side of the Empress are Princess Aida Dästa and Amha Dästa

The Autobiography of Emperor Haile Sellassie I King of Kings of All Ethiopia and Lord of all Lords My Life And Ethiopia's Progress 1892 - 1937 Haile Sellassie I King of Kings of Ethiopia

Frontline Distribution International, Inc.

Chicago • Jamaica • London • Republic of Trinidad and Tobago

The Autobiography of Emperor Haile Sellassie I

translated from
the Amharic Original

My Life and Ethiopia's Progress
1892 - 1937

TRANSLATED AND ANNOTATED BY
EDWARD ULLENDORFF, F.B.A.

*Professor of Ethiopian Studies
in the University of London*

Volume One

RESEARCH ASSOCIATES SCHOOL TIMES PUBLICATIONS
FRONTLINE DIST. INT'L, INC.
CHICAGO, ILLINOIS 60619

Research Associates School Times Publications
Frontline Distribution Int'L, Inc.
751 East 75th Street
Chicago, IL 60619

First Paperback Edition
Published 1999 by:
Research Associates School Times Publications
And
Frontline Distribution Int'L, Inc.
751 East 75th Street
Chicago, IL 60619

2nd Reprint 2003

first Photographic Reprint ©1997

First published in England by
Oxford University Press 1976
New Preface Copyright ©1997
Professor Edward Ullendorff

English translation and annotations
© Edward Ullendorff 1976

My Life and Ethiopia's Progress
Volume 1

LIBRARY OF CONGRESS
CARD CATALOG NUMBER: 97-65862
ISBN: 0-94839-040-9

English translation and annotations
1999 Professor Edward Ullendorf

BARBADOS • CHICAGO • JAMAICA • REPUBLIC OF TRINIDAD AND TOBAGO

Oppression is, in the Abyssinian dominions, neither frequent nor tolerated; but no form of government has been yet discovered, by which cruelty can be wholly prevented. Subordination supposes power on one part, and subjection on the other; and if power be in the hands of men, it will sometimes be abused. The vigilance of the supreme magistrate may do much, but much will still remain undone. He can never know all the crimes that are committed, and can seldom punish all that he knows.

CHAPTER VIII of Dr. Johnson's
Rasselas, Prince of Abyssinia

CONTENTS

Figures in square brackets at the top of each page refer to the
page numbers of the Amharic original

LIST OF ILLUSTRATIONS

ABBREVIATIONS

AOI	Africa Orientale Italiana
BM	British Museum
BSOAS	*Bulletin of the School of Oriental and African Studies*
Cmd.	Command Paper
Dej.	Dejazmatch[1]
DNB	*Dictionary of National Biography*
DTW	Dästa Täklä Wald
EOT	Ethiopic Old Testament
Fit.	Fitawrari
JA	*Journal Asiatique*
JES	*Journal of Ethiopian Studies*
KBT	Käsate Berhan Täsämma
LXX	Septuagint
NE	*Nouvelles Etudes* (by Marcel Cohen)
RSE	*Rassegna di Studi Etiopici*
SOAS	School of Oriental and African Studies

---

[1] A glossary of Ethiopian titles and terms will be found in Ullendorff, *The Ethiopians*, 3rd edition, pp. 221–4. Most terms are annotated at the appropriate place in this book; cf. index.

TRANSLATOR'S PREFACE

A lecture which I had the privilege to deliver at the Accademia Nazionale dei Lincei at Rome, at the invitation of its illustrious president Enrico Cerulli, is reprinted here and may serve as an introduction to the present volume. It was read at Easter 1974, but in the light of recent events it is relevant to observe that it was written at Christmas 1973.

In that introduction I have endeavoured to explain and to justify the literalness of my translation, partly in an attempt to maintain, or even to mirror, the flavour of the original; partly to aid those future historians of the reign of Haile Sellassie who have little or no Amharic and to whom this 'raw' rendering may be of greater service than a polished version; partly to offer a 'crib' to students struggling with the original; and finally to expose my translation to the critical eye of colleagues who will be able to detect where I have gone wrong or misunderstood the original. None of these purposes could have been achieved with a more fluent and literary rendering which would have blurred the problems and would have taken us even further away from the syntactical intricacies, at times truly remarkable, of the Amharic text.

I am profoundly conscious of the stylistic flaws and general ungainliness of the resultant work, but it does at any rate attain a high measure of faithfulness to the original. It would have required translators of the genius of those of the Authorized Version of the Bible to establish a fair balance between original and version. I have experimented with a translation that might be less graceless than mine, but each attempt has foundered on the horrific abyss and chasm, in feeling and performance, that rent prototype from copy or imitative mould. Some sentences—not many—in the original, even though their general purport may be clear, simply do not construe in any conventional sense, and in most of these cases such anacolutha are allowed to peter out equally aimlessly in the translation.

I also feel apologetic, though much less so here, about the transcription employed. It seemed to me highly incongruous to have recourse to the full inventory of diacritics and thus press into service an intricate apparatus that would satisfy scientific criteria but would be ill-adapted for the audience to which this book is addressed. I have, therefore, avoided all fussiness and used forms that will, I trust, be readily intelligible to the English-speaking reader. There are inconsistencies; some, though by no means all, arising from the variant modes of spelling employed in different sources.

I should emphasize that the footnotes are of an explanatory and informative character only; they seek to throw light on obscurities and to provide factual background. They deal with matters of substance only and are not intended to be critical or to offer comments on views, events, omissions, or manner of treatment. A name or geographical location is usually annotated at its first occurrence only. The index will mark the principal *locus* by use of a different fount. I have not been able to explain a few of the less well-known names. The Emperor had promised me help in the hour of need, but recent events have unhappily rendered this promise incapable of fulfilment. I have, however, been fortunate in being able to call on the wide knowledge of Ethiopian personalities and places possessed by H.I.H. the Crown Prince of Ethiopia. I am also grateful to Prince Zara Yaqob and Dr. Zewde Gäbrä Sellasse.

I have used the conventional terms 'Empire' and 'Imperial' to render *nəgusä nägäst,* though I clearly realize that they bear a connotation in the western context which the Ethiopic original does not possess.

In the Introduction I have referred to the tedium of some speeches and certain documents. All these have been translated from the Emperor's Amharic text, mainly to show what interpretation was placed on them by Ethiopians. I have not used the originals of speeches by King George V or King Victor Emmanuel, etc., even if the resultant version must at times seem more than a little quaint. Where differences of substance are involved, I have briefly commented on these in the annotation.

Unfortunately there is very little in this book about the Emperor's happy family life, but we are given some fresh insights into his relations with his father, Empress Taitu, Ledj Iyasu, Empress Zawditu, and many other personalities. His description of the Italian war and of his decision to go abroad also contains aspects and details not hitherto published.

The second volume of this autobiography was published in June 1974 and takes us from 1936/7 up to the liberation of Ethiopia in 1941. In the likely absence of a sequel it is not my intention to translate this second volume which deals with matters that in one form or another are fairly well documented already.

In reading this autobiography one has to bear in mind constantly that it was written in 1936/7 (though not published until 1972/3) which is not only more than a generation ago but in a world that was totally different in its political and emotional texture from the last quarter of the twentieth century in which it appears in print. Moreover, Emperor Haile Sellassie, with all his enlightened views, cannot help being a product of Menelik's polity into which he was born and in which he grew up. The intricate system of human relationships in the tightly structured and hierarchically integrated Ethiopian society maintains a rigorous hold on all those caught within it. And, despite its many shortcomings, who would be so bold as to assert that that system, with its certitudes and carefully distributed responsibilities and restraints, is inferior to the society in which we live with its dissolution of values and of checks and balances? For two thirds of his life all the problems Haile Sellassie had to face arose from the fact that he was in advance of his time; and it was the tragedy of his reign that during the last third the wind of change in Africa blew so fiercely and so suddenly that it swept away the good with the evil.

It will be clear to the reader that much that is related in this volume (and particularly in the first half), though it occurred only some seventy years ago, could equally well have happened centuries earlier. These are considerations which everyone will have to bear in mind who wishes to make a fair and balanced assessment of this king who dominated Ethiopia's destiny throughout the twentieth century. And although these lines are penned while he is still alive, it may already be said of him, seeing his dignity and pride in this hour of turmoil, that nothing in a long reign of achievement as well as vicissitude became him so well like the manner of his leaving it.

Finally, I ought to explain how I came to tackle this translation. In January, 1973, Princess Hirut Desta, the Emperor's granddaughter, came to see me and asked me, on behalf of His Majesty, to undertake this work. My first reaction was not favourable, but when, a few weeks later, I had to review this book and got immersed in its intricacies, linguistic and otherwise, I changed my mind—not least, perhaps, because I thought that translation on this scale might do some good to my Amharic.

I subsequently saw His Majesty on two occasions in London. At first the idea of an annotated translation did not appeal to him, but he was fully convinced of the need for this procedure when last I was received by him at Addis Ababa on 19th March, 1974.

Since then I have lived with this biographical study (and so has my wife) through the vicissitudes of the last year and the agonies endured by the Emperor and his people. At times, when I worked on the chapters dealing with the Italian war and the exile following it, I felt a *déjà vu* quality about it all; and never more so than when I read this passage in the second volume (p. 72):

'Our life at Bath was very hard. We also encountered great financial difficulties. Some sources of information had spread the rumour that We had taken a great deal of money with Us when leaving the country and they were attempting to make people believe this; but it is a complete lie.'

Plus ça change, plus c'est la même chose.

It is not for me to say what mistakes of policy the Emperor or his government may or may not have made; nor indeed am I qualified to anticipate the verdict of history, in the shaping of which the present volume may play its modest part. I have admired Emperor Haile Sellassie for forty years, from a distance as well as at close quarters, and I may thus be forgiven if I am emotionally incapable of joining the rats which are now forsaking the proud ship as it threatens to founder.

Easter 1975   EDWARD ULLENDORFF

POSTSCRIPT

Since this preface was written, more than six months ago, the death of Emperor Haile Sellassie occurred on 27th August, 1975. While he was denied a proper burial by those who now rule Ethiopia and the place of his interment remains unknown, the serious organs of the world press have published obituaries of a depth and size not previously accorded to any other African leader. A Memorial Evensong and Presentation of Garter Banner, attended by his son and heir and an impressive congregation, took place at St. George's, Windsor Castle, and a memorial tribute was offered by the Earl of Avon.

Thus a life has ended of which (like Moses in Deuteronomy 34) 'no man knoweth of his sepulchre unto this day'. And until his last days 'his eye was not dim nor his natural force abated'. Those of us who really knew the man and the king will long mourn the passing of Haile Sellassie, for there will not arise in Ethiopia anyone quite in his image.

E.U.

November 1975

ACKNOWLEDGEMENTS

I wish to record my gratitude to the Publications Fund of the School of Oriental and African Studies for including this volume in the series of books published for the School by Oxford University Press and for sponsoring its publication. Mr. Martin Daly, the Secretary of the Publications Committee, has at all times assisted me with his expert counsel.

The bulk of the typing was carried out by Miss Helena Roth, Miss Carolyn Beckingham, and by my wife. I am greatly obliged to all three of them for the care they have lavished on the preparation of the typescript. My wife, as usual, has made herself responsible for the compilation of the index and of all the ancillary material. She has also removed many inconsistencies and solecisms. Those which remain have to be laid at my door.

E.U.

TRANSLATOR'S INTRODUCTION[1]

Whatever the future of Africa in general and Ethiopia in particular may hold, the place of Emperor Haile Sellassie in the twilight period of emerging Africa is assured. I do not mean to imply that there will be no argument about the nature of this place, that the verdict of history (whatever this may mean) will be unequivocal, or that even now there are not some among the young urban intelligentsia in Ethiopia who would echo Cromwell's imperious words to the Long Parliament (used so effectively, in 1940, by Leopold Amery in relation to Chamberlain): 'You have sat too long here for any good you have been doing. Depart, I say, and let us have done with you. In the name of God, go!'

But such cries of impatience are not likely to be confirmed by the calm view of a longer perspective; and the appearance of an imperial autobiography is certainly a singular and most noteworthy phenomenon in Ethiopia as well as a literary event of some moment.

For close on 58 years Haile Sellassie has been ruler of Ethiopia and for 44 years her Emperor, the world's senior statesman, aloof and regal, heir to a long tradition of Semitic exclusiveness, yet founder of the Organization of African Unity; approachable as well as withdrawn, imbued with profound mystique, small in physical stature, yet commanding in personality and a symbol of regal strength and enduring power.

During the lifetime of this Emperor greater and more profound changes have occurred in Ethiopia than throughout the previous two and a half millennia of recorded Ethiopian history. With his roots firmly imbedded in Menelik's quasi-medieval polity and his senescence concomitant with the antics of General Amin or Colonel Gaddafi, it is scarcely surprising that Haile Sellassie is now more than a little out of step with his country's impatient and clamorous youth. What is much more astonishing is the continuing firmness of his grip—at the age of nearly 82—which, despite many changes and upheavals, has not been markedly relaxed.

[1] Conferenza tenuta nella seduta del 10 aprile 1974 (written Christmas 1973), Accademia Nazionale dei Lincei, Rome.

The first volume of the Emperor's autobiography—under the title of *həywätenna yä–Ityopya ərməjja,* i.e. 'My life and Ethiopia's progress'—was published in Amharic at Addis Ababa in 1965, Ethiopian era, i.e. early in 1973. It was printed by the Bərhanənna Salam Press in a form which is austere rather than ostentatious and in an edition which is not without external flaws. There are 264 pages plus nine unnumbered pages of ancillary material, such as preface, list of contents, etc. The book is stated to have been written at Bath in England (where the Emperor lived from 1937 to 1940) in Yäkatit 1929 (= February 1937). No names of helpers or secretaries are indicated—except for a mention, on p. 264, of Blattengeta Mahtämä Səllase who is credited with the preparation of the useful, intricate, yet ingeniously arranged genealogy which traces, in a vast circular scheme, most of the descendants of King Sahlä Səllase of Shoa, the present Emperor's great-grandfather. This genealogy is in itself a contribution of some importance.

The same is true of the photographs, nearly fifty of them, taking us from the extremely attractive child Tafari, by way of the commanding figure of the Regent, to the grave and truly charismatic Emperor addressing the League of Nations in 1936. They represent a record of considerable interest. The inclusion of several pictures showing Lidj Yasu, Emperor Menelik's grandson and uncrowned successor, who, in 1916, was deposed by the author of the present autobiography, is not without interest.

In Ethiopia the book sells for 12 Eth. dollars (= approx. £2.25 or Italian lire 3.300), and it is said that the first impression was sold out within a few days.

The present work is expressly described as the 'first volume', but there is no indication whether further instalments will be issued within the foreseeable future. I understand, however, that a second volume is about to be delivered to the press[1] and that a third part is at present under contemplation by the 'highest quarter'. The first volume, now in our hands, takes us from the birth and childhood of Tafari to the famous and poignant speech to the League of Nations forty-four years later.

It is likely that the bulk of the book was dictated by the Emperor during his sojourn at Bath, and it is thought that the first

---

[1] It was, in fact, published in June 1974. It takes us from 1937 to the Emperor's return to Ethiopia in 1941. In the nature of things a third volume is now unlikely to appear.

redactor was Blattengeta Hәruy Waldä Sәllase, the former Foreign Minister, who died in England in 1938.

It is not clear what happened to the manuscript between 1937 and 1972, and there is no express indication whether any changes were introduced in the interval. I have it, however, on fairly good authority (though falling short of certainty) that the tone of the narrative has been softened at many points, particularly in relation to internal events and personalities. Kings and statesmen still in harness will inevitably write with a great deal of reticence and circumspection, and their autobiographies are unlikely to produce any major revelations. Nor are the perspectives of 1936/7 identical—or even remotely comparable—with those of 1972/3. Essentially a work of this kind is bound to be in the nature of an *apologia pro vita sua,* and the present book is no exception.

Many readers will be tempted to read between the lines; and while Ethiopians will liberally indulge in this pursuit, Western students of Ethiopia will find it hard enough to read the actual Amharic lines without delving into the arcana of interlinear conjectures. Yet it is clearly as important to assess what has been changed or omitted as it is to appreciate what has been included. The Emperor was as skilled in those desperate days, more than thirty-five years ago, as he is now in expressing himself with a lofty disdain for specifics and with all the oracular trappings of a papal pronouncement. In his inimitable style and elevated diction he is used to telling us what *he* wishes to convey rather than what importunate foreigners might like to hear. In these aims he is assisted by the full resources of Amharic stylistics which are as apt to aid and abet a desire for almost total opacity as they may illumine complicated thought processes by their marvellous flexibility and clarity of hierarchical structuring.

The Emperor's life between 1892 and 1936, as described in this book, falls broadly into three main periods: his youth and the assumption of ever more important functions of state; the regency and foreign travel as well as relations with the west; the assumption of the crown in 1930 and the growing danger of war leading to the events of 1935-6.

The fifty chapters are arranged in roughly chronological sequence under headings such as 'the story of my childhood up to my appointment as Dejazmatch' or 'from my appointment as Dejazmatch to the death of my father', etc. Other chapters, also within the general chronological setting, deal with one specific event only: e.g. 'Ethiopia's entry into the League of Nations' (chapter 13) or the Anglo-Italian agreement of December 1925 relating to Lake Tana and the projected railway from Eritrea to Italian Somaliland (chapter 22), etc. I notice, incidentally, that in rendering the heading as 'Ethiopia's entry into the League of Nations', I have introduced a subtle deviation from the Amharic original which refers to ... *əndətəgäba səlä madrägaččən*, i.e. 'Our (the royal plural) causing Ethiopia to enter ...'. The Emperor is the actor and motivator throughout; there is no deed or action in his realm without his initiative.

The basically annalistic arrangement may seem somewhat constrictive to the Western reader, yet the total effect—especially in the earlier chapters—is, in fact, rather vivid. It must, however, be conceded that this is true only of the Amharic original; no translation can do justice to the peculiar flavour of the Amharic stylistic *genre*. The most touching aspect of Haile Sellassie's childhood is his close relationship with his father, Ras Makonnen, which is beautifully described. The assumption of ever-increasing responsibilities by the boy of thirteen shows the traditional Ethiopian system at its best: a closely knit society with functions, obligations, and rights (*noblesse oblige* in the truest sense of the word) which devolve quite naturally upon those who have been brought up within this clearly defined hierarchical framework. A particularly fascinating chapter deals with the developing conflict between Lidj Yasu and Tafari, the former's deposition, and the beginning of the regency with all the strains and stresses between the exponents of the rigidly traditional order, symbolized by the Empress Zawditu, and the new ideas, however cautiously expressed, by the youthful Ras Tafari.

I have said that an imperial autobiography is a singular and memorable event in Ethiopian history. True, royal chronicles have long formed part of Ethiopic literature, and the biographical *genre* is by no means unknown in Ethiopia: the *gädl*, originally 'struggle', is the type of 'life and acts' of saints and martyrs so ubiquitous in Ethiopian literary history. But such 'chronicles' and 'acts' are essentially annals which are mostly closer to the hagiographical species than to Western conceptions of historiography. Some of these chronicles and *gädl* are indeed of great significance, and scholars like Conti Rossini and Cerulli and, most recently,

Taddäsä Tamrat have derived a good deal of religious, social, and political history from them. One need only think of the splendid narrative of the victories of the fourteenth-century warrior King Amdä Səyon. Some Ethiopian emperors are even said to have been authors of theological tracts, such as the fifteenth-century reformer King Zär'a Ya'qob to whom various books, notably the *mäshafä bərhan* 'Book of Light' (so well edited by Conti Rossini and Ricci), are attributed. European missionaries and travellers have left us biographical sketches of various emperors—none more vivid or imaginative than the portraits of the royal personages of his day drawn by the great Scots explorer James Bruce.

Since 1855 Ethiopia has, in effect, had only four emperors—leaving aside the two brief interregna associated with the names of Wagshum Gobazye (1868–72) and Lidj Yasu (1913–16); and each of these has been the subject of biographical studies of varying importance, though none till Haile Sellassie has essayed the autobiographical *genre*. The Emperor Theodore (Tewodros, 1855–68), apart from numerous European studies chiefly associated with the Napier Expedition of 1867–8, has been the subject of three useful Ethiopian biographies (not to mention some more recent plays), even though these are rather brief and somewhat incomplete. They were edited by E. Littmann, C. Mondon-Vidailhet, and L. Fusella, respectively. And in 1973 alone there appeared at least two English novels on King Theodore: *The Hammer of God* by Alan Scholefield, and *The Guns of Darkness* by Ann Schlee.

The Tigrean Emperor Yohannes IV (1872–89) had received rather summary treatment by Western and indigenous writers (this applies even to Həruy's Amharic opuscule *Ethiopia and Metemma: A short history of Emperor Yohannes,* 17 pp., Addis Ababa 1917/18) until his great-great-grandson, Dejazmatch Zewde Gäbrä Səllase, produced a fine Oxford doctoral thesis devoted to the reign of his ancestor (now in the press). Menelik II (1889–1913) has fared rather better, both in European and Ethiopian accounts, but especially in the annals by his Minister of the Pen, Gäbrä Səllase (published in French in 1930–2 and in Amharic in 1966–7). Menelik's daughter Zawditu (Empress 1916–30) was a sovereign in name only and was completely overshadowed by her Regent and successor Ras Tafari. Nevertheless, a biographical study of Zawditu would not be without interest.

xxii   TRANSLATOR'S INTRODUCTION

Haile Sellassie I (Regent 1916–30; Emperor since 1930) has not been uniformly fortunate in the innumerable accounts of his life and deeds. Of the more substantial ones, the books by Christine Sandford and Leonard Mosley deserve mention.

The present volume of the autobiography draws on the Emperor's recollections, but the meticulous details as regards dates (often even including days of the week which are *nearly* always accurate), itineraries, etc., show that the narrative must have been buttressed by recourse to archival material. Whether this material accompanied the Emperor into exile (as seems likely) or was subsequently added by his amanuenses, I am unable to say. The precise nature and condition of the Imperial archives are in any event not generally known. The narrative is interspersed with many documents; these are particularly valuable when we are offered Amharic originals, often for the first time. They are much less interesting, at any rate for the Western reader, where we have translations into Amharic, not invariably accurate, from European sources, such as treaties, documents of state, or merely addresses of welcome. These latter have a certain tedium in their inevitably repetitive character.

I have been given to understand that a rough translation into English has been in existence for quite a number of years. I also gather that this translation is currently being revised and improved with a view to early publication.[1] In so far as my views have been sought, I have made it clear, both to His Imperial Majesty himself and to his advisers, that only an annotated translation would make sense in terms of comprehending the nature of this work as well as with respect to successful marketing. I am not sure that this view has found favour in the eyes of those in charge of the project.[2]

In the meantime, I have carried on with my own annotated translation which now covers well over one half of the book, including annotation. I should explain what I mean by 'annotation': here I refer not only to an explanation of the general background, such as Ethiopian customs mentioned in the text, personal and geographical names, etc., but also to historical and linguistic explanations, such as corroboration from other sources or elucidation of complex textual problems. Moreover, in quite a

---

[1] This, I understand, is no longer the case.
[2] See the Preface on this point.

few cases the identification of personal names is distinctly difficult; in a few instances European geographical locations appear to be corrupt in the Amharic original; at times dates cannot be correct as they stand, and errors of many different kinds have crept into the Amharic version. Then there are quite a number of cases where original Amharic documents were misconstrued in the existing western renderings, or *vice versa,* and such discrepancies deserve to be pointed out in footnotes. Some of these divergences are of considerable historical or other interest.

Let me now give you a few examples of what I have in mind:

Some of the most sensitive writing occurs in the early parts of the book where—as I have indicated—the relationship of the boy Tafari to his father is described. One passage must suffice to exemplify this:

'Because my father was on his own after his wife, my mother, Wayzäro Yäshimäbet, had died, he used to neglect his meal times and let them pass. But as there was nobody who would dare to say "Your Highness, meal time has arrived", I would beg him in fear, entering his chamber and saying "meal time has come, so please let it be your wish for dinner to be brought in", and consequently he and the officers would order the meal to be brought in at once with a view to pleasing me; when I saw him eat, I felt a sense of joyful pride in my youthful spirit. And my father used to commend me for doing this' (p. 21).

A dramatic, and indeed tragic, incident is described effectively (perhaps because of what would now be termed its 'low key' narrative) when Dejazmatch Tafari was involved in a boating accident on Lake Harämaya (half-way between Harar and Dire Dawa) and seven of the ten men in the boat were drowned (p. 42). The writing is devised throughout to point the moral, i.e. that Providence had spared Tafari, as he had been chosen for a higher destiny.

The names of his companions involved in this accident are set out in the book, but here and elsewhere I have not yet, owing to my ignorance, been able to identify every person. I am still hopeful that I shall succeed, at any rate in the great majority of cases, before my translation is published.

While on the subject of unidentified names, I should mention that a few of the locations described in the course of the Regent's 1924 tour of Europe have so far defeated me. Thus I do not know where on the outskirts of Paris the Villa ከማስተራ (p. 92) is which Ras Tafari rented during his sojourn in the French capital. Neither contemporary French newspapers nor colleagues who were in Paris at the operative time have so far been able to throw any light on the identity or spelling of that name. Similar considerations apply to the Belgian city of ምሬኅ (p. 95) which the Regent visited during the same period, or the sea-side palace of the King of Sweden called ቶልጋን[1] (p. 97).

Among names which I have been able to identify, although at times somewhat disguised, are Admiral Condouriotes, the then President of the Greek Republic (p. 83), and M. Sophoulis (not Sophalis, a printing mistake which every *éthiopisant* can easily spot—p. 115), the Greek Prime Minister. Sir Ronald Graham, the British Ambassador to Rome, appears oddly enough as Sir Roland (p. 126), and the Secretary General of the League of Nations was, of course, not 'de Rimond' (p. 137) but Sir Eric Drummond. Those in charge of the final editing of this imperial work were occasionally a little careless.

Let me turn to some quite different topics. We are told (p. 21) how Ras Makonnen assigned to his son Tafari a separate establishment, shortly after his appointment to the rank of Dejazmatch at the age of 12 or 13. At that time a German mission, under Dr. Friedrich Rosen, visited Ethiopia and also stayed at Harar. While there, Ras Makonnen asked members of the expedition to visit his son Tafari which they did in January 1905 when the young prince was 12½ years old. The account of their visit to Tafari is highly significant, for it shows that the boy of 12 exhibited then the same dignity, composure, and aloofness which the world has come to expect of the aged Emperor. Court etiquette was formal and strict:

Lidj Tafari is slender and delicate. His features are genuinely Semitic, and his colour is fairly light; both are marks of noble blood in Ethiopia . . . His demeanour was composed and dignified, and conversation was confined to the exchange of courtesies and compliments; it was conducted in Amharic at the Prince's request, although his French is said to be quite good . . . He accepted our presents with gracious thanks but betrayed no outward signs of pleasure, for such manifestations are confined to ordinary people . . . His questions about arms and equipment showed interest as well as understanding. When I

[1] Tullgarn.

tried to take photographs, the Prince asked me to desist, as he had received no instructions from his father on this subject (Felix Rosen, *Eine deutsche Gesandtschaft in Abessinien,* Leipzig 1907, 83–4).

While this passage offers interesting and independent corroboration of what appears in the autobiography, the need for annotation for the benefit of non-Ethiopian readers is clearly demonstrated at many points. Thus we are told that Ras Makonnen married, in about 1876, Wayzäro Yäshimäbet, the future Emperor's mother, as his lawful wife at a church ceremony (pp. 14 and 25). In the first place, it is necessary to know something about Ethiopian marriage customs or, at least, to be given bibliographical references to the different types of marriage practised in Ethiopia. Secondly, Ras Makonnen had been married previously, and his common law wife (this at any rate appears to have been her status; it was scarcely a *qal kidan bäqwərban* marriage, i.e. one sanctified in church by joint communion) is not specifically named (p. 25). In any event, she is the woman who had given birth to Tafari's elder half-brother, Dejazmatch Yilma. The latter was born in 1877 (he was thus 15 years older than Tafari) and died in 1907 at the age of 30. It would appear, therefore, that the dates in the book are not wholly reliable; it seems unlikely in particular that the marriage to Wayzäro Yäshimäbet took place as early as 1876 (p. 14), if Dejazmatch Yilma (who subsequently married Wayzäro Assäl-läfätch, the niece of Empress Taitu) was born in 1877.

I must say a few words on language and style. H.I.M.'s predilections in the stylistic field are, of course, well known from published speeches, admonitions to his people, prefaces to books, etc. The present work contains no surprises, and I have already alluded to the felicities of phrasing, particularly where delicate political matters are involved, as well as to a certain repetitiveness, probably unavoidable, in the case of formal addresses of welcome and other occasions of this character.

When last I had the honour to read a paper at this famous Academy, during the fourth congress of Ethiopian studies in 1972, I spoke on animistic expressions and other aspects of direct speech in Amharic (cf. the Congress report and also *BSOAS,* 1972, 270). I have found at least two further examples of the constructions I had in mind in the imperial autobiography. They are particularly beautiful specimens: የልጅነት ፡ ሥራ ፡ መሥራታቸው ፡ እ ልስቃ ፡ ብለ ቻቸው ፡ (33:25) literally: 'his doing childish deeds

said to him "I have not enough yet" '. This passage occurs in a
message of complaint about Lidj Yasu, addressed to his father, and
means, of course, that Lidj Yasu wanted to continue with his
puerilia (see p. 52 below).

The other example, that of an elliptical conditional clause, is
attributed to Negus Mika'el: **ለእስላም ፡ ንጉሥ ፡ ከልተገዝችሁ ፡**
(35 : 10) 'unless you submit to a Muslim King . . .' where the
apodosis of this uncompleted conditional clause must be envisaged
in terms of 'you will be damned' or words to this effect.

Again, there are other instances where the text appears to be
faulty and where sentences just will not construe. A case in point
is at 104 : 1–3 where a number of accusatives seem to be suspended in the air without a governing verb. Here it would seem that
the insertion of *bämmiqqoṭaṭṭär* after *nṣnč* will remedy the position.
The editors ought not to have allowed this to pass, and no list of
errata is appended to the volume.

Language criteria also throw an interesting light on the official
relationship between Empress Zawditu and the Regent, Ras
Tafari. When the Queen writes or speaks to him she uses the
appellation *lṣjje* 'my son' and the second person singular pronoun
antä 'thou' or 'tu' (pp. 98–9), while Ras Tafari refers to her as
gṣrmawit 'majesty' or *nṣgṣst* 'queen', and these nouns are always
accompanied by the third person plural or polite suffixes attached
to verbs or nouns. It is, incidentally, interesting to note that, when
the Empress replies to the Regent's speeches or addresses, her own
pronouncements are read for her by the *ṣähafe tṣ'ṣzaz*, the so-
called Minister of the Pen (99 : 28/9). She does not speak herself.

Throughout the book personal and hierarchical relationships
are subtly elucidated by the device of using either second person
singular or third person plural and polite forms. When Empress
Zawditu speaks or writes, she refers to herself in the first person
singular, and so does the Regent when he communicates with his
sovereign. Otherwise Tafari does not initiate the royal plural only
with his accession to the throne in 1930, but the *pluralis majestatis*
already appears predominantly, if not consistently, ever since his
elevation to the dignity of Ras, Regent, Heir to the Throne and
lṣ'ulnät 'highness' in 1916.

I should explain—apropos of problems connected with
language and translation—that throughout my rendering of this
autobiography I have endeavoured to do justice to the original,

not of course by trying to imitate the shape of Amharic syntax but by using a similar level of speech. There is a certain awkwardness in the flow of the English translation which is intended to mark it unequivocally as a translation in its archaizing tendencies, in its involved sentences, and in its faithfulness to the 'feel' of the Amharic original. I am not, of course, claiming that I have succeeded in this; I am simply stating my aims. Anyone who has ever tried his hand at translating the highly involved (not to say convoluted) structure of Amharic sentences into a European language will be conscious of the extreme complexity of such an undertaking. It would, of course, be fairly easy to cut up long Amharic periods, with their highly charged logical subordinations and carefully and intricately dovetailed hierarchical structures, and convert them into short and idiomatic English or French or Italian sentences which no longer betray their provenance and origin. There are indeed contexts where such a procedure would be entirely appropriate. But I did not feel that in the case of the present work it was proper to present a translation wholly severed from its indigenous ambience. While it is impossible to imitate Amharic syntax, it appeared feasible, and indeed desirable, to stay close to the sinews and tendons which hold together the framework of an Amharic sentence.

I had meant to give you a few examples of what I have in mind, but I found that such a procedure was not really practicable. Not only would it have occupied all the time allotted to me but, above all, it would have required a large blackboard on which to write, in three parallel columns, the Amharic original, my Amharic-based rendering, and a wholly free translation. I must, therefore, confine myself to describing the aims of my translation in one sentence: to be as faithful as possible and as free as is absolutely necessary; to reflect the original as transparently as can be achieved with the tools of a totally different language; and not to disguise the awkwardness and hesitation of the source by a rendering that is facile and smooth.

There is just one brief illustration I would like to add to this: in the sample passage, which I have adduced earlier on, I have intentionally left the direct speech elements of the original Amharic: 'as there was nobody who would dare to say "Your Highness, meal time has arrived", I would beg him in fear, entering his chamber and saying "meal time has come, so please

let it be your wish for dinner to be brought in" '. . . It would
have been very easy to render this into more 'normal' English
and cut out the awkwardness of the direct quotation, such as:
'as there was nobody who would dare remind my father of his
meal times, I would enter his chamber somewhat hesitatingly and
suggest to him that he should order dinner'.

I think, however, that it will be generally agreed that much of
the flavour and directness of the original would thus be lost; and
it seemed to me preferable throughout to risk some ungainliness,
even clumsiness, of English style, if thereby I would achieve a
greater awareness of the structure of the Amharic original.

In a few instances I have been able to procure the originals or
translations of some passages included in the book, such as treaties,
international agreements, or public speeches. And I have been
surprised how often the European rendering failed to reflect the
Amharic original, or *vice versa*; and these cases range from the
trivial to the crucial clause in a treaty. I have aimed throughout at
translating the Amharic text; where I had access to a European
translation or original, respectively, I have referred to the divergence in the apparatus without allowing this to influence my
rendering of the Amharic version.

One or two brief examples:

In Ras Tafari's complaint to the League of Nations about the
Anglo-Italian Agreement of December 1925 the following
passage occurs which, in my view, means:

It did not seem to Us proper to allow some members of the League of
Nations to conclude an agreement among themselves and to force
another member to accept their plan, even if it did not affect the
national interests of that member
(110 : 22–4).

The official English translation of this clause is as follows:

We were not told that certain members of the League might make a
separate agreement to impose their views on another member even if
the latter considered those views incompatible with its national
interests
(Cmd. 2792 (1927), p. 7).

Leaving aside for the moment the question of the general faithfulness of this translation, the 'even'-clause seems to me rather
illogical; it should surely read 'particularly'. It should, however,

be mentioned that it was the custom in those days for the Ethiopian Government to issue the Amharic text of any note accompanied by a French translation. I imagine the English version is a rendering of the French text (which I have not seen), and I am not, therefore, in a position to say at what point any discrepancies may have arisen.

The opposite process has occurred in a passage where the official Italian version of a letter addressed to Sir Ronald Graham reads:

... il Governo Britannico riconoscerà anche l'esclusività dell' influenza economica italiana ...

(L'Africa Orientale, 1, 336).

The Amharic translation, as it appears in the Emperor's autobiography, can only be understood as:

... the British Government, on its part, will then recognize Italy's special economic influence ...

(107 : 8).

It need hardly be pointed out that the term 'esclusività' differs a good deal from the Amharic yätäläyyä 'special'. No wonder that mistranslations are apt to give rise to international conflicts: traduttore traditore, sometimes even with the best intentions. Incidentally, 'influence' appears in Amharic as səlṭan 'power'; nowadays magəbabat or täṣ'ino would be more common.

I have said earlier on that we possess no clear information about the nature and condition of the imperial archives. Even less do we know which parts of them travelled with His Majesty to Britain between 1936 and 1940. It is, therefore, impossible to explain any discrepancies between Amharic documents published in the autobiography and versions printed elsewhere. A case in point is the proclamation issued by Dejazmatch Tafari in July 1913 when he was governor of Harar province. I have dealt with the text of that proclamation, as compared with the version collected by J. I. Eadie in Ethiopia in 1913, in a collation published in BSOAS 1974/1. Neither H.I.M. nor the late Major Eadie is informative about the provenance of the texts printed in their respective books. The differences between the two versions relate to orthography, punctuation, and textual variants which range from the trivial to distinctions of substance. These textual variants are reminiscent of aspects of text transmission which we encounter in those parts of the Old Testament that are extant in doublets. It would have been interesting to compare the originals on which the two printed Amharic versions are based.

I shall conclude with a few miscellaneous points of general interest.

At one stage in the book the Emperor explains that 'as there existed no railway in those days—as it does today—the journey from Harar to Addis Ababa used to take a month' (p. 17). The distance between these two cities is some 250 to 300 miles, and we know that it was possible to get a message through in two or three days. It was also quite feasible to reach one's destination within a week or so, but when the Emperor says that it used to take a month, he refers to the kind of progress made by Ras Makonnen or himself. A great nobleman was accompanied not only by his retainers but by a veritable army of hangers-on. This inevitably slowed progress considerably. Moreover, at every larger place a stop-over was *de rigueur*, delegations were received, courtesies exchanged, complaints heard, and all the intricate ritual of Ethiopian life and etiquette had to be observed. Later on the railway came to Dire Dawa, and the distance could be covered in a day. Nowadays, it takes an hour by air. And this is the measure of change that has taken place in Haile Sellassie's lifetime where distances of one month have been reduced to one hour.

Explanations of this type have to be included in the annotation. And this annotation also has to make reference to such oddities as the detachment from the Regent's entourage of three personages who accompanied him to Europe, in the summer of 1924, and their despatch to Germany to deliver a letter of friendship to President Hindenburg (p. 113). But the fact is that in the summer of 1924, at the time of Ras Tafari's tour of Europe, Ebert was President of the German Republic, and Marshal Hindenburg did not succeed him till after Ebert's death in the spring of 1925.

It is interesting to observe that the autobiography is exclusively concerned with the life and the activities of its author. There are few reflections or observations of a general kind and certainly no comment whatever on the events and personages of his era. Thus Ras Tafari arrived in France, in May 1924, in the middle of a major government, and indeed constitutional, crisis which early in June led to the resignation not only of Poincaré's government but even to that of the President of the Republic himself. M.

Alexandre Millerand (1859–1943) had been President of the French Republic since 1920, yet when the Regent met him in May 1924, shortly before his withdrawal from the presidency, he is described as the 'new' President (page 90). In fact, when Ras Tafari returned to Paris, in August 1924, the new President, M. Gaston Doumergue, had taken over and M. Herriot had become Prime Minister and Foreign Minister. It was then that the Regent met the truly new President (p. 115). Again, the editors who allowed the first reference to the 'new' President (p. 90) to pass clearly did not discharge their task with the necessary care.

More interesting, however, is the fact that the book has not a single word about the severe crisis which convulsed France when the Ethiopian Regent stepped on French soil. His serene aloofness from events and exclusive preoccupation with the minutiae of etiquette are like an unbroken thread running through the whole course of this work. On this first visit ever to the west by an Ethiopian ruler there are no thoughts on the nature of western society or technological progress, nor are there any comparisons with the conditions in which Ethiopia then found herself. The writing is not philosophical but—as I have indicated—essentially annalistic, enumerative, catalogue-like.

Similarly, while we are given a full list of the princes, noblemen, and officials who accompanied the Regent on his European tour (page 84), no further mention is made of any of them in the course of the narrative. We are not told what they thought of their great experience and whether Jerusalem or Alexandria, Paris or Stockholm, Cambridge or Athens held their attention. We only know from other sources that, while Ras Hailu went on a gay tour of the sights and indulged in a vast shopping spree, the Prince Regent visited schools, universities, and hospitals. There are no references to Ras Hailu's antics as the *enfant terrible* of the party. Thus it is said that King George V asked Ras Hailu whether he knew any English or French or Arabic. When he had to answer all these questions in the negative, he, in his turn, asked the British monarch whether he could speak Amharic or Tigrinya or Galla. The reply was a predictable 'no', whereupon Ras Hailu said to the King, allegedly to the latter's huge enjoyment, 'then, Your Majesty, it would appear that we are both equally ignorant'.

None of this will be found in Haile Sellassie's autobiography; there are no anecdotes, there is no *bon mot,* no wit; its purpose is austerely and severely serious, moralistic, and didactic.

həywätenna yä–Ityopya ərməjja, 'My Life and Ethiopia's Progress', has been issued as a public document and for the official record. Whether there might yet exist a more private and more penetrating record of the Emperor's life is not known to me. Meanwhile we must be grateful for these privileged, if cautious, glimpses into the life of one who would have been adjudged great even if no crown had adorned his head.

MY LIFE AND ETHIOPIA'S PROGRESS

Preface

A house built on granite and strong foundations, not even the onslaught of pouring rain, gushing torrents, and strong winds will be able to pull down. Some people have written the story of my life,[1] representing as truth what in fact derives from ignorance, error, or envy; but they cannot shake the truth from its place, even if they attempt to make others believe it.

At this hour, when I have found occasion and time to write the story of my life, I preface my writing by presenting the following prayer to my Creator and then continue this work.

O Lord, almighty in whom there is no weakness, eternal in whom there is no transience; in admiring Your work as well as Your judgements, a created being, even after much searching, cannot fathom them—except to a limited extent.

It is a subtle secret which a creature, even after much exploring, cannot know but which You alone do know: why in the immediate past as well as now You have made the Ethiopian people, from the ordinary man to the Emperor, sink in a sea of distress for a time, and why You have made the Italian people up to its King swim in a sea of joy for a time.

Since no creature created in Your image and to Your pattern gives up hope that everything he begs of You will be done for him until the day You sever his soul from his body, we beseech You that Ethiopia should not remain with her freedom extinct and prostrate under an alien ruler, so that the mouth of her peoples be silenced for fear of a foreign governor, but rather that You will save them by Your deeds of kindness, lest they remain with their hearts oppressed through being deprived of their own Ethiopian ruler who was leading them towards civilization under a light yoke and with gladness.

O Lord, abode of exiles, light of the blind! Truth and justice are Your thrones. Receive us who have been exiled for our freedom's sake, who have had to leave our country on account of violent

---

[1] I am not clear what works, available in 1936/7, the Emperor had in mind. It should be recalled that at the time of writing (36 years before this book appeared in print in Amharic) the Emperor was only 44 years of age.

assault. In praying to You thus, it is not for our righteousness but for Your great mercies.[2]

And now I am setting out contemplating to write the story of my life from my thirteenth year until this time, on the basis of what You have wrought, making me Your instrument. I pray to You that it may be Your will to let it reach completion. It is right for me to reveal in this preface the reason why I have thought to write this, although from You nothing is hidden.

First, that Your name be praised for all the deeds You do, acting according to Your wishes.

Second, when You make a man rich in the honours of this world and appoint him above other creatures, that it be known that it is not for his merit but only through Your benevolence and generosity.

Third, in every line in this history, where the name of another person is mentioned, it is not through partiality or enmity—save in error—but You know that we are making our heart the judge to write only the truth.

Fourth, although there is nothing that is not written in the Holy Scriptures, if You will enable me to write as I have planned, may our kin and our brothers who will rise up in future take note of the word You have spoken 'for without me you can do nothing'[3] and may their hearts be convinced that with Your help alone will they be able to do anything.

Fifth, unless a man discharges his task by his own resolve and perseverance conscious of being Your tool, whether in times of joy or tribulation, he should realize that he ought to work by his innate ability or by such education as he may have acquired, for his responsibility will not cease even if he acts solely under another man's will.

Sixth, whatever the task may be, let everyone realize and be convinced that it will be accomplished at the proper time and age and that it is impossible to have it fulfilled either by just desiring it or by hurrying it unduly.

I pray to You that all this may be in full accord with Your will.

[2] Daniel, 9: 18.
[3] St. John, 15: 5.

Preface to the 1997 Research Associates \ Frontline Edition

****

The first and principal volume of Emperor Haile Sellassie's Autobiography, taking us from his birth to his exile in Britain in 1937 (thus covering the early and least well known period of his life), was published in Amharic at Addis Ababa in 1973. At His Majesty's request, I translated (and annotated) this work into English; it appeared in 1976, published by the Oxford University Press for the School of Oriental and African Studies, London University. Details of its genesis and travails were set out in a series of prefaces and introductions (pp. xi - xxxii) during the last years of the Emperor's life and its immediate aftermath. The hardback edition was reprinted six times and sold an unexpectedly large number of copies. The last reprint of 1993 was exhausted a little while ago, with quite a few unfulfilled orders having accumulated since then. At this stage it was generally felt that a photographic reprint would be the most suitable way of proceeding henceforth.

In the meantime the Oxford University Press had forwarded to me a number of reprint offers they had received. Among these I selected a proposal by Ras Sekou Tafari of Frontline Distribution International, Inc., and subsequent correspondence and signature of the contract have strongly suggested to me that that choice will prove to have been a very fortunate one. It now seems that the photographic reprint of the xxxii + 335 pages of the original work may appear by or before the middle of 1997.

When the Emperor was deposed in September 1974 and (as far as is known now) murdered by Mengistu in August 1975, Ethiopia suffered what has turned out to be the bloodiest and most traumatic seventeen years of its long history. With Mengistu's ejection and flight from justice, in 1991, there has been a great measure of amelioration. In the twenty three years, since Haile Sellassie's removal from power, an entire generation of Ethiopians, both inside and outside the country, has grown up without much knowledge, if any, of the last reigning King.

That generation, and even their elders, should be reminded of the rich and proud legacy of Ethiopia's progress under Haile Sellassie. Whatever problems may have occurred during those fifty eight years of rule, they will yet be remembered and assessed by future historians against the background of the calamities that were to follow.

I am gratified that this new edition of <u>My Life and Ethiopia's Progress</u> (1892-1937) should see the light of day thanks to the endeavours of a Rastafarian establishment representing people who have done much to keep Haile Sellassie's memory alive and have also so devotedly looked after his grandson.

Edward Ullendorff
Oxford, February 1997

Introduction

WHATEVER the task may be, man may begin it but he cannot complete it, unless God sustains and supports him. If he fails to accomplish the task on which he has set out, having worked to the best of his ability, he is not to be maligned by being called lazy. Thus We Ourselves, by virtue of Our descent from the Queen of Sheba and King Solomon, ever since We accepted in trust, in 1909 (= 1916), first the regency of the Ethiopian realm and later the Imperial dignity, right up to the present, We have set out to the best of Our ability to improve, gradually, internal administration by introducing into the country western modes of civilization through which Our people may attain a higher level; hence Our conscience does not rebuke Us.

In explanation of the notion 'gradually': unless it is through coaxing a child and getting it accustomed, it will not be pleased if one takes from it what it has seized with its hand. When one gives such a baby any sort of food, it will not wish to eat it, unless one shows it to the child and lets it taste it. Unless they give it milk or other soft food until it grows teeth, it will not be able to eat when they place bread or meat before it.

And similarly with people who have lived by custom only, without learning at school, without absorbing knowledge by the ear or observing and searching with the eye, it is necessary to accustom them, through education, to abandon habits by which they have for long been living, to make them accept new ways— yet not by hasty or cruel methods but by patience and study, gradually and over a prolonged period.

In 1901 (= 1908–9) Emperor Menelik[4] fell ill and had to spend his time at home; soon after this Ras Bitwaddäd Täsämma,[5] Ledj

[4] King of Shoa 1855–89; Emperor of Ethiopia 1889–1913. See esp. Gäbrä Sellasse's Amharic history of the reign of Menelik as well as de Coppet's 2 vols. of translation and annotation. Also Afevork's (Afäwarq) *Dagmawi Mənilək* (Rome 1909), and Marcus, *Life and Times of Menelik II*.

[5] Ras Bitwaddäd Täsämma Nadäw: Regent during part of Menelik's illness and guardian of Ledj Iyasu. Died 1911 and buried at Däbrä Libanos. See the bibliography in the previous footnote. Also Heruy, 30; Mérab, II, 67; *JES*, VII, 2, 235; Zewde, *Biographies*.

Iyasu's[6] regent, suddenly died. As a consequence, Ledj Iyasu, who had accepted the authority to guide the government, was for about six years quite incapable of shouldering his responsibility. When I myself took over this responsibility in 1909 (= 1916), it was necessary to correct the chaotic neglect of fully six years and to make a beginning with the work not yet started, i.e. of introducing the new civilization. I spent my time working to the best of my ability, while my own ideas and the people fond of the old customs (particularly as the latter had many supporters) squeezed me like wood between two pieces of iron. There was very little time that I could spend in idle conversations and doing the things that give one pleasure. What I set right in terms of internal administration, initiated already at an earlier stage, the innovations I brought about, and such aspects of foreign-inspired civilization as I introduced into the country, will be found in the following, each at its proper place.

In addition to this, from time to time We encountered some difficulties, internal as well as external, which were spread about by natives or by foreigners and which constituted obstacles to Our work of innovation. It was thus essential to carry out everything patiently, in order to prevent upheavals, bloodshed, and tribal divisions. I was aware, even before I took over the affairs of government, that internal upheaval constituted a useful contribution to the designs of our enemies.

We were particularly convinced, by the policies directed against Us, that the enemy's heart was stricken with envy at Our setting up a constitution to strengthen and to consolidate Ethiopia's unity, at Our opening schools for boys and girls, at Our building hospitals in which Our people's health was to be safeguarded, as well as at all sorts of other initiatives of Ours by which Ethiopia's independence would be affirmed, not only in terms of history but in actual fact. For this reason, while We took great care to prevent any divisions among Our people, We did not wish to take any coercive measures that might appear oppressive to Our people.

While We were engaged upon all this careful work and were beginning to lead Our people on the road to civilization, Our

* Emperor Menelik's grandson and successor (1913–16). Born 1896, the son of Menelik's daughter Shoarägga and Negus Mika'el. Ledj Iyasu died in 1935. For bibliography see note (4) above; also Budge, 542 ff.; Luca dei Sabelli, IV, 48; Heruy, 57–8.

enemy rose up with violence sending to Our country many troops with modern equipment as well as numerous war-planes and tanks, breaking the covenant of the nations and fighting us with machine-guns and artillery and with modern weapons many times superior in quality and quantity to our equipment. We addressed an appeal to the League of Nations and, with Our heart free of panic, We encouraged Our armies. While we resisted firmly and defended ourselves, they poured all sorts of poison and smoke gases upon us which were capable of causing serious damage and which are prohibited by international law. They dropped many bombs on us and even bombarded the International Red Cross doctors together with their medical equipment, thus preventing those injured by bombs and machine-guns or suffocating with poison gas from receiving medical attention or cure. We Ourselves fought for our liberty in battles like any ordinary soldier and mustered the troops like any other officer. On account of Our inability to obtain even a loan for the purchase of arms, We did not have any adequate equipment for defence—except for a few modern weapons. After we had resisted to the best of our ability with weapons forty years old,[7] we were defeated for the time being in no shameful manner. The reason why We returned to Addis Ababa and why We departed from Addis Ababa to go abroad and all other such matters are to be found in the following at their appropriate place.

We would, therefore, remind, confidently and earnestly, all those who are Ethiopian subjects to persist unceasingly, by striving to the best of their ability, in the study of Ethiopia's past from the earliest phases of history lest her freedom be extinguished altogether in the future, particularly as our country of Ethiopia has now been overwhelmed by perils which give rise to anxiety for her independence; and We would equally urge all those who are not Ethiopians, but who hate aggression and love truth and justice, not to withhold their support for the cause of Ethiopia's liberty, the people at large by their counsel and the priests by their prayer.

Bath, England. Written Yäkatit   HAILE SELLASSIE I
1929 (= February 1937).   Emperor of Ethiopia

---

[7] The reference is, of course, to the battle of Adwa in 1896.

Contents

CHAPTER 1

The story of my childhood up to my appointment as Dejazmatch (1892–1906)

MY father, His Highness Ras Makonnen,[1] was the son of the Princess Tänagnä Warq, the daughter of the great King Sahlä Sellasse[2] of Shoa.[3] His father was Dejazmatch Waldä Mika'el Waldä Mäläkot[4] of the Doba[5] and Mänz[6] nobility. He was born on the 1st of Genbot 1844 (= 8th May 1852) at a place called Däräfo Maryam[7] in the district of Gola.[8] Ras Makonnen remained with his father for about 14 years; this was, of course, at a time when Menelik II,[9] the son of Makonnen's uncle King Haylä Mäläkot,[10] was still only King of Shoa. His father, Dejazmatch Waldä Mika'el, then took him to Menelik and said: 'Let this my son, your aunt's offspring, grow up with you in your palace'. And Menelik made Makonnen his special companion—quite apart from the chance fact of their family ties.

Subsequently, since King Menelik had become convinced of Makonnen's loyalty and skill in the service of his government (having tested him many times in various tasks to which he had appointed him), he raised him to the rank of Balambaras when he

---

[1] Emperor Menelik's cousin and right-hand man; grandson of King Sahlä Sellasse; see Pétridès' biography of Ras Makonnen; Heruy, 8–10 (including photograph); Zewde, biographies; *JES*, VII, 2, 222.

[2] 1795–1847. *The Ethiopians*[3], 16, 78; Heruy, 17–18 (incl. photograph); founder of the modern Ethiopian dynasty; Marcus, *passim*.

[3] The heartland of present-day Ethiopia; *The Ethiopians*[3], *passim*; *L'Africa Orientale*, *passim*.

[4] Heruy, 66; de Coppet, 135; Zewde, biographies.

[5] Cf. DTW 328; *Guida*, 400, 402; map 304; KBT 1141. One of the chief centres of the Marabetie region.

[6] Cf. DTW 789; Levine, 28 ff.; *Guida*, 405; highland plateau in N.E. Shoa.

[7] Cf. DTW 390; Pétridès, 28.

[8] Cf. DTW 255; *Guida*, 454 (map, 448): in Harar region.

[9] See footnote (4) in Introduction.

[10] See genealogical table. Son and successor of King Sahlä Sellasse. Died 1855.

was aged 24 in the year 1868 (= 1876). At this time Makonnen married Wayzäro Yäshimäbet,[11] my mother, as his lawful[12] wife.

While Menelik II was still only King in 1879 (= 1886/7), he conducted a military expedition into the Harar[13] region and restored this ancient province to Ethiopia. Since it had become known to him that my father was valorous in battle and a friend and leader of soldiers, he appointed him, at the time of Harar's occupation, Governor of the town and its province as well as Commander-in-Chief with the rank of Dejazmatch. And similarly, after Menelik II had been anointed King of Kings of Ethiopia, he appointed my father to the dignity of Ras in Miyazya 1882 (= April 1890).

When my father conducted military expeditions in the Harar region, he did so leaving behind in Shoa my mother, Wayzäro Yäshimäbet, his lawfully wedded wife whom he had married according to Christian custom.[12] When the war was over and the country began to be pacified, he let her come to Harar.

He then secured the Ogaden[14] region which had not yet been incorporated within Harar province. While temporarily he still had to lay plans of war, he yet continued easing the tax-burdens which weighed heavily upon the population.

I was born on the 16th of Hamle 1884 (= 23rd July 1892), in the year of John,[15] at Ejärsa Goro,[16] not far from Harar. Wayzäro Mäzläqiya, the daughter of my father's sister Wayzäro Ehtä Maryam, had married Dejazmatch Haylä Sellasse Abaynäh;[17]

[11] 'Lady of a thousand'.
[12] See The Ethiopians[3], 172–3; the reference is to a religious and indissoluble marriage.
[13] Guida, 442 ff., incl. maps and plans; Cerulli, La lingua e la storia di Harar, Rome 1936; Encyclopaedia of Islam[2], entry HARAR. The famous walled city and Muslim bastion in eastern Ethiopia.
[14] Guida, 610; Rennell, passim; the Ethiopian Somali region.
[15] cf. The Ethiopians[3], 177; the years are named after the four evangelists.
[16] See Guida (under Giarsagoro), 451 (map, 448); some 30 kms N.E. of Harar.
[17] Dej. Haylä Sellasse Abaynäh (formerly Fitawrari) is, therefore, Emperor Haile Sellassie's cousin by marriage. Throughout his life he was one of the Emperor's closest advisers and friends. He accompanied Ras Makonnen, the Emperor's father, to the coronation of King Edward VII. Later on, in 1924, he went to Europe again in the Regent's suite. He held many senior administrative appointments and fought in the battle of Maytchäw. He spent the years 1936–41 at Jerusalem and returned to Ethiopia after the liberation in 1941. Died in 1952. See photograph in Käbbädä Täsämma, 176; JES, VII, 2, 241–2.

when I was 4 months old she gave birth to Emru[18] (now Ras Emru), and the two of us grew up together as if we were twins. When we were aged seven, my father arranged for a special teacher for us and we began receiving instruction at our home. In our tenth year, three years after beginning our education, we were able to read and write Amharic[19] and Ge'ez.[20] Our upbringing was like that of the sons of ordinary people, and there was no undue softness about it as was the case with princes of that period. My mother, Wayzäro Yäshimäbet, being barely 30 years of age, died on the 6th of Mägabit 1886 (= 14th March 1894) and was buried within the precinct of St. Michael's church[21] at Harar, by the Epiphany water. All this I heard, of course, much later from those in charge of my upbringing.

Many were the months which my father, H.H. Ras Makonnen, had to spend travelling to Addis Ababa[22] and on military expeditions to other provinces of Ethiopia—more, in fact, than he was able to remain in his own governorate of Harar. He also went to foreign countries as envoy of the government.

Here are some of the journeys undertaken by my father: in 1881 (= 1888/9) he was sent to Italy;[23] in 1888 (= 1895/6), during the Alage[24] campaign, he conducted the military expedition as Commander-in-Chief and was accompanied by Ras Wale,[25] Ras Mika'el,[26] Ras Mängäsha Atikäm,[27] Ras Alula,[28]

[18] Emperor Haile Sellassie's second cousin and life-long friend and confidant. One of the outstanding leaders in the Italo-Ethiopian war. A nobleman of well-known liberal and progressive leanings. Cf. photograph in Käbbäda Täsämma, 118.

[19] Ethiopia's national language; The Ethiopians³, 119 ff.

[20] Ethiopia's classical language; The Ethiopians³, 114 ff.

[21] Guida, 448; plan 447, D,4.

[22] Capital of Ethiopia since about 1890; now about half a million inhabitants. Full details and maps in Guida, 474–94. There are also some modern touring maps of Addis Ababa. Cf. Berlan, Addis Abeba.

[23] Pétridès, chapter IX; de Coppet, 285.

[24] Guida, 306–7 (map, 304); de Coppet, 396; Pétridès, chapter XV; November 1895. A vital mountain pass on the Asmara-Addis Ababa road, half-way between Mäqälle and Koräm; scene of many battles.

[25] Ras Wale Betul of Yäjju, brother of Empress Taitu. Fought in the battle of Adwa. Died 1918. See Mérab, II, 71–2; Heruy, 65; JES, VII, 2, 259. He was the father of Ras Gugsa (see chapter 25 below); cf. Zewde, biographies.

[26] Later Negus Mika'el. Of a Muslim family from Wallo. Converted to Christianity by Emperor Yohannes IV. Married Menelik's daughter, Shoarägga. Father of Ledj Iyasu. For his part in the events following upon the deposition of

Dejatch Walde,[29] Fitawrari Gäbäyähu,[30] Fitawrari Täkle,[31] Liqä
Mäkwas[32] Adnäw,[33] and Qägnazmatch Taffäsä;[34] in 1890
(= 1897/8) he undertook a campaign in western Ethiopia, at the
Sudan border, into what is called Arab country; this is the region
nowadays referred to as Beni Shangul.[35]

In 1891 (= 1898/9), since it had been reported that Ras
Mängäsha,[36] the Governor of the Tigre[37] province, had rebelled
against Emperor Menelik, Ras Makonnen was despatched into
Tigre and brought about a reconciliation between Mängäsha and
the Emperor. Subsequently, in order to safeguard the security of
the province—just as he had done when he occupied Harar—he
remained in charge of Tigre for about two years and then
returned. In 1894 (= 1902) he was sent to England for the

his son, see chapter 7 below. Cf. also Mérab, II, 66 ff.; Heruy, 12; Luca dei Sabelli,
IV, 48 ff.; *JES*, VII, 2, 223–4; Zewde, biographies. Died 1919.

[27] Ras (Bitwaddäd) Mängäsha Atikäm, one of Emperor Menelik's earliest and
most faithful followers. Cf. Mérab, II, 72; Heruy, 8; *JES*, VII, 2, 217; Zewde,
biographies. Died 1910.

[28] Ras Alula was one of Emperor Yohannes' most faithful and able generals,
especially distinguished in his fight against foreign encroachment upon Eritrea.
JES, VII, 2, 245–6; Zewde, biographies; Heruy, 47; *Chi è dell'Eritrea;* also Ras
Alula's biography by H. Erlich (London University, SOAS, thesis 1973). Died
1899.

[29] Dejazmatch (later Ras) Walde Ashagre was a close follower of Emperor
Menelik. He served in military commands and district administration. Cf. Heruy,
75; *JES*, VII, 2, 268; Zewde, biographies.

[30] Fit. Gäbäyähu was one of Emperor Menelik's favourite and most renowned
generals. He died in the battle of Adwa in 1896. Cf. Heruy, 88; Pétridès, 135, 153;
JES, VII, 2, 280.

[31] See de Coppet, 182, 779 (index: Teklie); Pétridès, 153.

[32] *Liqä Mäkwas* is a kind of royal military A.D.C.; of old he was attired in
battle like the Emperor, in order to divert the enemy's attention from the sovereign. Cf. Cerulli in Guidi, *Suppl.*, 37–8.

[33] Adnäw Goshu of Bägemeder was a member of Emperor Menelik's household ever since 1865. Cf. de Coppet, 396; Pétridès, 153; *JES*, VII, 2, 254.

[34] Taffäsä Abaynäh grew up in Menelik's palace and served the Emperor
throughout his life. Much renowned for his military prowess. Cf. Heruy, 38; de
Coppet, 396; *JES*, VII, 2, 239.

[35] Designation of population of non-Ethiopian type, adjacent to the Sudan.
Cf. *Guida*, 512; de Coppet, 472, note 3; Pétridès, chapter XX.

[36] The son of Emperor Yohannes IV; 1868–1906. Became prominent after the
death of his brother, Ras Araya Sellasse; father of Ras Seyum. Cf. Heruy, 8; *JES*,
VII, 2, 219; Zewde, biographies, *et passim.*

[37] The great northern province of Ethiopia, the heartland of the Aksumite
Empire. *Guida*, 239; maps 272–3, 304–5.

coronation of King Edward VII.[38] In addition to all this, it was he who had to carry out and to conclude the whole business of relations with foreign countries which is nowadays undertaken by Ministers of Foreign Affairs.[39] And consequently he had to go to and fro to Addis Ababa each year being summoned to consult with Emperor Menelik about every important matter as yet undecided, after correspondence by post and conversations by telephone.[40] As the railway did not yet exist as it does today,[41] the journey by slow march from Harar to Addis Ababa took a month.

Since my father had seen European civilization, having been to Europe twice, and since he was convinced of the value of education, through conversing with some of the foreigners who had come to Ethiopia, he strongly desired that I should learn from them a foreign language. My father had established a hospital in his city of Harar and had brought into his employment a gentleman from the French colony of Guadeloupe, a physician by the name of Dr. Vitalien.[42] With this object in mind, my father arranged that the doctor should teach us French an hour or so a day when he could be spared from curing the sick; and so we began our lessons.

My father had a strong desire to see the people get accustomed to the work of civilization which he had observed in Europe and to make a start in his governorate. It was for this reason that he had established the first hospital in his city of Harar. A year after my father's death the French Government purchased this hospital, by the following accord, from Menelik II for 50,000 francs.[43]

> The Lion of the Tribe of Judah has prevailed.
> Menelik II, Elect of God,
> King of Kings of Ethiopia.

[38] Budge, 537.

[39] About the introduction of departmental ministers into the governmental framework of Ethiopia, see de Coppet, 527 ff.; Perham², 87 ff.; about Ras Makonnen's role as Menelik's chief foreign affairs adviser, see Perham², 60.

[40] Cf. R. Pankhurst, 339–41; Pétridès, 242—as regards the introduction of the telephone.

[41] The Jibuti-Addis Ababa line did not reach the capital until 1917 (Pankhurst, 334). For the time taken to reach Addis Ababa from the coast—in pre-rail days—see op. cit., 304.

[42] de Coppet, index; Pétridès, 233, 286; Pankhurst, 650.

[43] Pankhurst, 650; Mérab, I, 158.

May it reach Dejazmatch Yelma.[44] How are you? Thanks be to
God, I am well. M. Klobukowski,[45] the Special Envoy and
Minister Plenipotentiary in Ethiopia, has acquired, on behalf of
the government of the French Republic, the hospital which Ras
Makonnen had established at Harar and to which the French
Government had brought a doctor to care for the sick of our
country. And, therefore, have the ground-design and dimensions
of this hospital measured and have the title-deeds written out and
consign them to M. Naggiar, the French Consul at Harar.

Given on the 29th Hamle 1899 (= 5th August 1907) at the city
of Addis Ababa.

My father was anxious that I should learn French as quickly as
possible, but because he became convinced that Dr. Vitalien's
lesson of only an hour or so a day would not bring us closer to
this target, he had a word with Abba Andreas[46] who was a
resident in the city of Harar. He sent us an Ethiopian, called Abba
Samuel,[47] who had grown up as a pupil in his mission establishment. He set out to teach us with care and attention. Even so, we
did not give up our daily lessons with Dr. Vitalien.

Abba Samuel, our teacher, was the son of Aläqa Waldä Kahen.
He is the Waldä Kahen who was converted to Catholicism at the
time when Abba Masyas[48] of the Italian mission arrived in Shoa.
It is for this reason that his son Abba Samuel had entered the
Catholic Mission compound and studied there. Abba Samuel was
a good man who possessed great knowledge, who applied himself
to learning and to teaching, who in goodness and humility
gathered knowledge like a bee from anyone, who was devoted to
the love of God and of his neighbour, and who did not strive to
find enjoyment of the flesh but of the soul. I am saying this
because I had known him extremely well while we were together
some ten years.

[44] Emperor Haile Sellassie's elder half-brother. Mosley, 22, 42, 59; de Coppet,
522, note 4. Dej. Yelma (who married Wayzäro Assälläfätch, Empress Taitu's
niece) was born in 1877 and died in 1907. Cf. *JES*, VII, 2, 273.

[45] Pankhurst, 165; de Coppet, 526; Mérab, II, 95; Perham², 151.

[46] Later to become Mons. Jarosseau: Sandford, 27-8; Pétridès, 235; Duchesne-
Fournet, 8 ff.; Pankhurst, 649; see now also Zewde, biographies.

[47] Tafari's revered teacher; cf. Pétridès, 254; he drowned in the Harämaya
accident (see chapter 5 below).

[48] i.e. Cardinal G. Massaia (1809-1889) who spent some 35 years in Ethiopia.
See Zewde, biographies.

As has been observed in the preface of this book, I decided to write a record of my work beginning at the age of thirteen; everything I had done prior to that was under the direction and guidance of my tutor. From the age of thirteen onwards, although my physical strength may not have been great, my spiritual and intellectual powers began to increase gradually and thus had the entrance gate of this world opened. And this was the time at which I started to act on my own will, without being ordered by my tutor, distinguishing good and evil, and conscious that this action would offend others, that action would give pleasure, this being damaging, that on the other hand useful—and thus I began to climb the ladder of introduction to the world.

As the love that existed between H.H. my father and myself was altogether special, I can feel it up to the present. He always used to praise me for the work which I was doing and for my being obedient. His officers and his men used to love me respectfully because they observed with admiration the affection which my father had for me.

I observed H.H. my father striving to fulfil, to the best of his ability, the Christian ordinances enjoined, by giving his money to the poor in trouble and to the church, and by praying at every convenient hour. As I grew up, the spiritual desire was guiding me to emulate him and so to conduct myself that his example should dwell within me. There was no-one who did not know that my father's way of life was as described here above, either in the Palace or among the clergy. Of the great of that period there are still several alive at the time this book is being written, and everyone knows that it is not exaggerated. As my father noticed that all my inclination was directed towards education, his joy was constantly increasing in the measure of his affection.

CHAPTER 2

From my appointment as Dejazmatch
to my father's death
(1906)

BECAUSE of the strength of his love, my father was anxiously
waiting for the time at which I, being sufficiently grown up,
would attain to rank and, when I was 13 years and three months
old, on the 21st of Teqemt 1898 (= 1st November 1905), he
appointed me Dejazmatch in the large region called Gara Mullata.[1] But, according to our country's customs, this dignity of
Dejazmatch was for the sake of rank only. My age did not yet
permit me to sit in judgment in Court or to administer the
governorate or to muster the army in battle order; and, therefore,
my father gave me a chief administrator for all the work, to act as
tutor and deputy, namely his principal trusted servant, Fitawrari
Qolätch.[2]

On the day on which I was appointed to the rank of Dejazmatch, my father's officers and his troops assembled and he
introduced me to them in the great reception hall. After this I
entered into the inner chamber where my father was and, because
he had awarded me this dignity of Dejazmatch, I kissed his shoe
and sat down by his side. Thereupon the officers and all the chiefs
of the army, having been summoned once again, came in; and
when they were standing in front of H.H. my father, he delivered
the following speech: 'All of you are my servants whom I have
raised up and whom I love; therefore I entrust to you, with God,
my son Tafari. His fate is in the hands of the Creator, but I
commend him to you lest you should bear him ill will.' When the
officers and troops heard this speech, they began to shed tears,
saying: 'the fact that our master is making a speech like this about

[1] Region some 20 miles S.W. of Harar. *Guida*, 449–50, map 448; DTW 300;
de Coppet, 246, note 10; Rosen, 54.

[2] Sandford, 28; Rosen 54 ff., 83–4.

the trust seems like a farewell occasion, as if he knew that the time had come for us to be separated by death.'

While I was pleased that my father had bestowed on me this rank of Dejazmatch, yet my joy was mixed with sadness at his delivering to his officers a heartbreaking speech like this. But the thought which my father had with regard to me when he gave me this high rank derived from long, rather than short, deliberations; he had made prior arrangements with a view to my having a separate house for myself alone to live in. He had given instructions, on the morrow of my appointment, to the effect that they should consign the house to me, together with the officers required for each aspect of the work.

While all my father's officers used to like me respectfully also previously, yet afterwards they manifested to me their exquisitely respectful affection, now that I had been appointed Dejazmatch and had a separate household set up for me. Although my age did not yet permit it, I was yet allowed, since my appointment to the rank of Dejazmatch, to be present and to sit down when the great officers came to my father officially for business affairs or for a banquet. I could clearly feel the pleasure of H.H. my father and of the officers when I completed any sort of work which my tender age allowed me to pursue, when I listened attentively to their speech and counsel, and when I spoke or gave answers to questions I was asked.

I thank my Creator as I clearly recall how those of my father's officers who have survived until now sometimes tell me, reviving past tales: 'When at that time you were appointed Dejazmatch, you used to tell such and such; being asked something like this, you used to answer something like that.'

Because my father was on his own after his wife, my mother, Wayzäro Yäshimäbet, had died, he used to neglect his meal times and let them pass. But as there was nobody who dared to say 'meal time has arrived', I would beg him in fear—entering his chamber and saying 'meal time has come, so please let it be your wish for dinner to be brought in'—and, consequently, he would order the meal to be brought in at once with a view to pleasing me. When I saw him and the officers eat, I felt a sense of joyful pride in my youthful spirit. And my father used to commend me for doing this.

H.H. my father had the good fortune to be loved and to be feared. If a man—however great his position might be—was found to be in the wrong, my father would determine the punishment according to the measure of his offence; but because he would not keep silent, they came to fear him. But a few days later he would cause pleasure by sending to the home a gelded ox, honey, and butter, if the convicted person was a great man of position; or a castrated goat and money to buy honey and butter, if he was an ordinary person; indeed, the people would love him for this because there was nothing of actual cruelty in him towards the man against whom he had meted out punishment. Besides, even though no man is perfect and pure before God, since my father's main thought was to please God in every possible manner, he was determined to help with money those in difficulty, to reconcile those who had fallen foul of the Emperor Menelik, to offer prayers at any hour that remained from the work of government in which he was engaged, to assist in their troubles the monks in each of the monasteries and the priests in each of the churches—that he was doing all this was part of his resolve to please God without being vainglorious. He was a fine example of good deeds.

CHAPTER 3

From the death of H.H. my father till my appointment to the governorship of Harar
(1906–1910)

WHATEVER may befall a man in this world, there is no-one who concludes his days entirely in joy or in grief, but pleasure and sadness occur alternately in their turn; hence all my thoughts were floating in a sea of distress as my father, who loved me dearly and was so fond of me, fell gravely ill.

H.H. my father departed from his city of Harar to go up to Addis Ababa on 4th Ter 1898 (= 12th January 1906). At that time he felt a little unwell. On the 9th of Ter (= January 17th) he

camped by the Burqa (Burca)[1] river and, after having spent the
day celebrating the Temqät[2] festival there, he went back, because
the illness took a stronger grip on him, and entered his second
city called Qullebi (Collubi)[3] where he began to be treated by a
doctor. At this time, as my father summoned me in his desire to
see me, I went up to Qullebi. When I entered his bedroom to see
his condition and he saw me standing by his side, he motioned me
with his eyes to sit down, since it was difficult for him to speak
with his tongue on account of the severity of his illness. As I was
convinced that it was his wish that I was not to part from him, I
spent the whole day sitting by his side.

But the hour of the judgement of death decided upon by the
power of God cannot be postponed, even by the love of many—
let alone by the love of one father and son. Thus he died at
Qullebi on the 13th of Mägabit 1898 (= 21st March 1906) and was
buried in the church of St. Michael which he himself had founded
at Harar.[4]

After this my father's officers and troops assembled in full. As,
on one hand, my father had said to them during his life-time 'I
commend to you my son Tafari' and since, in the second place,
they were aware of my father's loyalty to the Emperor Menelik
and his diligent services to his government, they expressed the
hope that he (the Emperor) would not fail to give him (Tafari) his
father's governorate of Hararge. After they had concluded their
consultations saying 'we shall go up to Addis Ababa following the
memorial service (täzkar) customary after 40 days',[5] a letter
reached the officers from Emperor Menelik stating 'Come at
once with Tafari, his son, for it is before me at Addis Ababa that
the lamentations for Ras Makonnen's 40-day mourning are to be
held'.[6]

While my father was still alive he had prepared a present
intended to be sent to the Emperor Menelik; and since it was an
object he had put aside, we took it with us when we departed
from Harar on the 3rd of Miyazya (= 10th April) and set out on

---

[1] Guida, 455 ff.; Rosen, 97 ff.

[2] Epiphany on 11th Ter (= 19th January). See Hyatt, 169 ff.

[3] Guida, 454-5; DTW, 1059; Rosen, 79. Seat of the famous shrine of St.
Gabriel. Cf. Mängestu Lämma, Yalatcha Gabtcha.

[4] About the death of Ras Makonnen see Rosen, 285-6; cf. also Marcus, 226;
de Coppet, 521-2.

[5] Cf. The Ethiopians³, 175.   [6] Cf. Pétridès, 283.

our journey to Addis Ababa. As many people died on us during the trip, grief was heaped upon grief. The reason was that the 'small' rainy season was active and that, because of the multitude of the army, malaria spread in our camp.[7] On the 19th of Miyazya (= 26th April) we reached Addis Ababa.

Emperor Menelik had given orders that tents be pitched, sewn together like a hangar, on a vast field at which he gave a memorial banquet for my father; and there he caused the officers and troops to assemble. While the lamentations proceeded, with the arrivals stationed at one side and the hosts mustered on the other, we were gathered with Emperor Menelik in great mourning.

On the 40th day, i.e. Monday 22nd Miyazya (= 30th April 1906), the priests of the monasteries and churches in Addis Ababa and surroundings, after completing the prayer of absolution proper for Christians, all proceeded to the tent that had been prepared and spent the day at the great banquet arranged for them. The Rases and Dejazmatches, because some of them were his blood-relations and others had grown up with him, entered the appropriate part of the tent, stood there, and observed lest any item of food should be missing. To the poor were given, apart from food, a lot of alms in cash.

On the morrow, according to the custom of our country, on the 40th day after a person's death, lamentations are being held as on the day of death itself. On the vast field, where the big tent had been pitched, the officers and troops assembled. Emperor Menelik himself was seated in the centre, and then the most amazing display of mourning was performed for my father when his ceremonial robes, his Ras's crown, his medals, and his battle arms were carried, and his horse and mules, saddled in golden harness, were paraded in the midst of the army. One of the mourners composed in his honour the following dirge which he recited:

> The telephonist, when he announced his death, was wrong;
> It is not Makonnen but the poor who died.

In the Addis Ababa Palace it was being said that no-one knew an occasion when similar lamentation and mourning had occurred for anyone. After the demonstration of these lamentations had ceased, the ushers informed the assembled army that they should

[7] Literally the 'desert disease', because malaria (usually called *woba*) generally occurred in the desert lowlands only.

go home; they then departed and went on their way. But my father's troops, who had come with me from Harar, had remained there quietly; and when they were asked 'Why do you remain when the entire army has left', they replied 'it is to escort to his camp our master's son, Dejazmatch Tafari.' When the Emperor heard this, he permitted me to go to the camp with my father's troops. When we left, my father's Addis Ababa friends came to join us and to accompany me to the camp; all passers-by on the way stopped and expressed astonishment on account of the extraordinary size of the escort. Owing to this event, other friends of my father's who were living at Addis Ababa—let alone my father's troops—told me they had heard people say among themselves 'the fact that the Emperor is permitting Dejazmatch Tafari to go back with his father's army may be because Menelik is thinking of giving him the governorship of Harar.'

But my elder brother, Dejazmatch Yelma (who had been born to my father before he married my mother, Wayzäro Yäshimäbet), had married Wayzäro Assälläfätch,[8] the daughter of Empress Taitu's[9] sister.

For this reason Empress Taitu, used to supporting all her relatives, was said to be exerting herself with a view to Dejazmatch Yelma getting the governorship of Harar, arguing that, while there is an elder son, the younger son should not be appointed to his father's governorship; and because there had been delay in the announcement, very many people rose up indicating that the governorship of Harar should be mine.

But since, on one hand, Empress Taitu had pestered Emperor Menelik by saying 'Give it to Dejazmatch Yelma for my sake', and because, on the other, the time had not yet arrived at which God had determined that I should become governor of Harar, the matter was decided by saying 'let it go to Dejazmatch Yelma'. The reason why my father's troops and his friends thought that the governorship should be mine was because they were used to me, being constantly in my company, and because my father, when still alive, had said to them 'I commend to you my son Tafari'.

[8] de Coppet, 522; Pétridès, 290; Mérab, 174; DTW, 1179.
[9] Heruy, 97-8, including photograph. Menelik's consort in a childless marriage. Empress Taitu wielded great influence upon Menelik and, during the Emperor's illness, upon the country in general (cf. below). See also the photograph in Budge, 540; Marcus, passim; Zewde, biographies.

After the decision to give the governorship of Harar to my brother Dejazmatch Yelma had been taken, it appeared to be thought that it would upset me and the army if the proclamation were issued while I dwelt in the midst of my father's troops; I was therefore summoned from the camp some eight days before the date of the proclamation and it was arranged that I should stay in a tent prepared for me in the Palace precinct. Then they ordered some of my father's most loyal officers who had shown particular favour and affection to me, Dejazmatch Abba Tabor[10] and Fitawrari (now Dejazmatch) Haylä Sellasse Abaynäh, to stay here at Addis Ababa as suppliants, threatening them for a time with (royal) displeasure and detention. The reason was that Dejazmatch Abba Tabor and Fitawrari Haylä Sellasse had firmly assumed that the governorship of Harar would be mine, and it was rumoured that the advice had been given on the part of Empress Taitu that, if they were now to go back to Harar, they might at every opportunity make things difficult for Dejazmatch Yelma.

Eight days later, on the 2nd of Genbot (= 9th May 1906), the Emperor's proclamation was issued, to the effect that he gave Harar, the governorate of Ras Makonnen, to Dejazmatch Yelma, and Sällale,[11] the governorate of Ras Darge,[12] to Dejazmatch Tafari. As a consequence, my father's army as a whole was distressed. Among them there were many who came to stay with me leaving their home, saying 'We shall not go with Dejazmatch Yelma and abandon Dejazmatch Tafari our master's, Ras Makonnen's, son whom he had entrusted to us.' Among those who remembered me were Fitawrari Qolätch, Ledj (later Dejazmatch) Waldä Sellasse,[13] Ato Dännäqä Gobäze,[14] Ledj Alämayähu Goshu[15] (later Fitawrari), Qägnazmatch Waldä

[10] See Heruy, 51; *JES*, VII, 2, 252. Relative and close companion of Ras Makonnen. Accompanied his master to Europe. Died 1916/17.

[11] Region to the N.W. of Addis Ababa; KBT, 229; *Guida*, 378.

[12] Heruy, 86–7. King Sahlä Sellasse's son and grandfather of Ras Kassa. Zewde and Marcus, *passim*. See the detailed article in *JES*, VII, 2, 277–8.

[13] Käbbädä Täsämma, 54; *JES*, VII, 2, 265. Dej. Waldä Sellasse (Waldä Mika'el) was Ras Makonnen's brother, Emperor Haile Sellassie's uncle and faithful follower. He died in an aeroplane accident, near Dessie, in 1930.

[14] Ato (later Fitawrari) Dännäqä Gobäze. At one time governor of Ogaden; later, during Ras Tafari's regency, he held Palace appointments. Cf. *JES*, VII, 2, 276–7.

[15] Ledj (later Fitawrari) Alämayähu Goshu, of Bägemeder origin. Died fighting in the Ogaden area in December 1934, in the battle of Walwal (see below). Cf. *JES*, VII, 2, 270.

Maryam Abaynäh,[16] Ato Säbsebe (later Bäjerond), Ato Hayle Waldä Rufa'el[17] (later Tsähafe Te'ezaz), Qägnazmatch Defabat-chäw, Ato Täfärra Bäläw,[18] Qägnazmatch Gäbrä Wald,[19] Ato Waqe[20] (later Dejazmatch), Qägnazmatch Därbe.[21]

During the time when I served as governor of Sällale, orders were given to reconstruct the church of the monastery of Däbrä Libanos[22] which had fallen into ruin. Hence, when the foundations were excavated, there was found a ring and a piece of gold which was very fine and which bore an inscription. My deputy, who was carrying out the work there, sent it to me and it reached the Emperor through me; it was thus reckoned to be a great good fortune for me. Having gone, according to the custom of the country, to the governorship of Sällale, the Emperor yet permitted me to stay with my retainers. Since I did not wish to be separated from the Emperor, it was arranged that my deputy should reside in the governorate of Sällale, while I spent the whole day at the Addis Ababa Palace, from 7 a.m. till 8 p.m., eight whole months of attendance at Court.

At that time Emperor Menelik had opened a school for young Ethiopians to study foreign languages and had brought teachers from Egypt. While selecting Ledj Iyasu, Ledj Berru,[23] Ledj Getatchäw,[24] and other sons of the great nobles and placing them

[16] Brother of Dej. Haylä Sellasse Abaynäh.

[17] Born at Tägulät in 1879. At first served in Ras Darge's house and later went into service with Ras Makonnen. During the regency he held a great number of important central government appointments. Following the Italian war in 1935–6 he spent several years at Jerusalem. After the war he was a member of the Crown Council. Died in 1954. *JES*, VII, 2, 244.

[18] Later Qägnazmatch; a descendant of King Sahlä Sellasse; grew up together with Emperor Haile Sellassie; a noted horseman. Cf. *JES*, VII, 2, 237.

[19] A Grazmatch Gäbrä Wald appears in Käbbädä Täsämma, 107.

[20] One of Ras Makonnen's faithful servants; acted as chamberlain in his house-hold; later held similar offices during the regency. Died 1932/3. *JES*, VII, 2, 269.

[21] Därbe Defabatchäw of Mänz; brother of Dej. Wandirad. Servant of Ras Makonnen during his governorship of Harar. Died 1908/9. *JES*, VII, 2, 275.

[22] Ethiopia's premier monastic institution, founded by Abuna Täklä Haymanot. *Guida*, 378.

[23] Probably Berru Waldä Gäbr'el (Fit., Ras). See below, footnote (1) to chapter 29.

[24] Getatchäw Abatä (Ledj, Dej., Ras). Grew up in Menelik's palace together with Ledj Iyasu. Served as provincial governor, Minister of the Interior, and ambassador. Died in 1950. Photograph in Käbbädä Täsämma, 149; cf. *JES*, VII, 2, 287; Heruy, 95.

at that school, he left me out; and this was a matter of great sadness to me. But when I spoke to him, a few days later, revealing my desire to study, he gave me permission and said 'It is because you were a governor that I thought you chose to live like the nobles, but if you wish to study, then go and learn'; thus I began my studies. But, while at Harar, I had learnt French; now at Addis Ababa, since it was not appropriate to take lessons together with the beginners, they began to teach us separately, fixing some hours for us alone. Those of us studying together were Ledj (laster Ras) Emru, Ato Assefaw Bänti,[25] and Ledj Zäwde Gobäna[26] (later Fitawrari). After I had remained for about a year in my appointment over Sällale, I was appointed to the governorship of Baso.[27]

My brother, Dejazmatch Yelma, after having governed for about 17 months following his appointment over Hararge, died at Harar on 29th Mäskäräm 1900 (= 10th October 1907); and when the sad announcement was transmitted by telephone to Addis Ababa and we had grasped it, there was great mourning. Afterwards it again began to be said by the mouth of every man that the governorship of Hararge was to be given to Dejazmatch Tafari. But as I have said before, since the time had not yet arrived which God had determined for me to become Governor of Harar, on 27th Mägabit 1900 (= 4th April 1908) the governorship of Harar was given to Dejazmatch Baltcha,[28] while the Emperor gave me part of the governorship of Sidamo.[29] Therefore I had to abandon my studies and was ordered to proceed, together with the army, to my governorate of Sidamo and to take care of the business of government. It was arranged that some 3,000 men of my father's army at Harar should come to me.

[25] Son of Fit. Bänti, Ras Makonnen's confidant. Sandford, 28; Mérab, I, 156; Pétridès, 153; Käbbädä Täsämma, 105.

[26] Son of Ras Gobäna Datch (cf. Zewde, biographies); died 1916. Cf. Heruy, 79; JES, VII, 2, 272; Käbbädä Täsämma, 44, 56 (photo).

[27] Baso is a locality to the south of Däbrä Marqos (Toponomastica, 52); thus also on the map of the Italian Ministero dell'Africa; see also Käbbädä Täsämma, 289–90. But according to de Coppet (533, note 8) it is north-east of Ankober.

[28] 1863–1936; one of Menelik's ablest commanders; for his relationship with Emperor Haile Sellassie see below chapter 24. Cf. also JES, VII, 2, 14 ff., 231; Heruy, 28; Käbbädä Täsämma, 71–4; Mérab, II, 74.

[29] The southernmost province of Ethiopia and one of its richest; the other part of Sidamo was given to Dej. Nadäw (Mérab, II, 77); Guida, 558–9.

When my departure for Sidamo was decided, it was conceded to me that Dejazmatch Abba Tabor and Fitawrari Haylä Sellasse, who had remained in nominal detention, should go with me. Since Dejazmatch Abba Tabor was alert in everything he did as well as firm in his word and truthful without any falsehood whatever, this was to me a matter of great good fortune. During the period I served in my governorate of Sidamo I had a time of perfect joy, as I encountered no trouble whatever, because there worked for me Dejazmatch Abba Tabor, being responsible for outside work, and my grandmother (my mother's mother) Wayzäro Wallätä Giyorgis, being responsible for the inside work. While I knew that it was proper to exercise judicial functions—a provincial governor, according to local custom, would sit in Court—up to now I had not dared exercising those functions of sitting in judicial assembly, seeing the tenderness of my age. But now, since my appointment to the governorship of Sidamo, I began to pronounce judgment while sitting in Court on Wednesdays and Fridays.

While I divided my own previous servants, those who had come to me from my father's army, and the newcomers, who had entered my service after I had gone to Addis Ababa, into three parts making proper adjustments for each according to their rank and assigning their duties, I remained there very happily for about a year. Then, when I heard in 1901 (= 1908-9) that the Emperor was gravely ill, I asked for permission to come to Addis Ababa. As the Emperor's missive reached me allowing me to come, I went to Addis Ababa in the month of Miyazya (= April 1909) after giving orders to my chiefs in each district that they should carry out their work diligently and that they should guard the country meticulously.

Since the Emperor Menelik was gravely ill, he no longer had the strength to undertake any major work—except to appear before the army by coming out into the palace square; consequently, all the people, great and small alike, felt very grieved. As to all the work of government, it was Empress Taitu who took it on as plenipotentiary. For this reason, as peace became disturbed, many people appeared in the Palace precinct endeavouring to stir up agitation. As all this was going on and while Empress Taitu, acting as plenipotentiary, was carrying out all the work of government, envious men began a conspiracy against her to deprive her of her powers and to evict her from the Palace. When they asked me to join them in the conspiracy, I told them that I did not wish to enter into their plot; and consequently all the conspirators began to look upon me with enmity. When Empress Taitu heard about my refusal to enter into the conspiracy, she told the Emperor and both were very pleased.

Although the Emperor was gravely ill, at that time his mind was still balanced. Nevertheless, he did not find an appropriate occasion to warn and to reproach the conspirators. As to my refusal to join the conspiracy, I did not tell either the Empress or anyone else about it, but those conspirators let out the secret saying 'Dejazmatch Tafari refused when we said to him "join the conspiracy"'. When the Empress repeatedly asked me in order to find out about this matter with certainty, I was firm in my statement that there was no-one who had asked me to join the conspiracy. Therefore she declared that she was very pleased about my not letting out the secret and told me: 'I know the truth. Your refusal to let out the secret is because you are a very discreet man.'

Since Empress Taitu had heard it being reported that it was in the Ministerial Council Chamber that this matter of the conspiracy had been started, she foiled their plot for the time being by causing the Ministerial Council Chamber to be closed. Furthermore, in the previous year three Germans had come on government appointments to an advisership and posts in medicine and education and were working while frequently meeting the Ministers about their respective tasks. Since Empress Taitu entertained some suspicion that perhaps those Germans might have given advice to the Ministers to conspire against her, it was reported that, while seeking some pretext, she made them give up their work.

Since in that year Dejazmatch Abreha,[30] the governor of Endärta[31] in the Tigre province, had rebelled, Ras Abatä,[32] while

[30] Dejazmatch Abreha Araya; son of Ras Araya senior. Born 1872; educated in Italy. His fight with Ras Abatä is described in the present passage. He died in 1916. Heruy, 52; *JES*, VII, 2, 252–3; *Guida*, 302.

[31] A region in the Mäqälle area (*Guida*, 302; map 304).

[32] Ras Abatä was born in 1870 and grew up in Menelik's palace and became, successively, Liqä Mäkwas, Dejazmatch, Wagshum, and Ras. Renowned as warrior. Died 1917. Heruy, 50; Mérab II, 76; photograph in Käbbädä Täsämma, 48; *JES*, VII, 2, 251–2.

he was still Wagshum,[33] attacked Dej. Abreha at the end of Mäskäräm 1902 (= October 1909) and defeated him. It was reported
that other governors of the Tigre province were looking on in
silence without coming to the aid of Dej. Abreha or Ras Abatä.

Emperor Menelik's illness was of the type called paralysis which
prevented him moving all his limbs and carrying out his work;
on the 17th of Teqemt 1902 (= 27th October 1909) at 9.00 o'clock
at night (= 3 a.m.) it suddenly became impossible for him either
to move or to speak; and when the officers and the army heard
about this, there was great sadness in the precincts of the Palace
and in the capital. Yet after a few days the illness seemed to relax
its hold over him and he appeared to be getting better, but it was
not thought that he had many years left till death would overtake
him.

[33] The traditional designation of the ruler of the Wag district (*Guida*, map 304)
in the area of Lake Ashange.

CHAPTER 4

About my appointment to the
governorship of Harar and its province
(1910)

AFTER this, Dejazmatch Baltcha, who was Governor of Harar,
was summoned to Addis Ababa in the month of Tahsas (December
1909/January 1910), and even before he entered Addis Ababa it
again began to be rumoured by the mouth of the people that the
Emperor was about to give the governorship of Harar to Dejazmatch Tafari. When Dejazmatch Baltcha, while still on his way,
heard this, he began to make strenuous endeavours, immediately
on arrival at Addis Ababa, to retain the governorship of Harar by
means of intercessors as well as money. But I was biding my time,
carrying out my other daily duties and thinking that I could not
fail to obtain the governorship whenever it might be God's will
to show me favour.

Later, one day unexpectedly, Ras Bitwaddäd Täsämma,[1] Ras Bitwaddäd Mängäsha Atikäm,[2] Fitawrari Habtä Giyorgis,[3] and Tsähafe Te'ezaz Gäbrä Sellasse Waldä Arägay,[4] while assembled together, summoned me and said: 'Although you are still a youth in age, but because your entire work in governing Sidamo had shown you to be knowledgeable, the Empress has now given you Hararge which used to be your father's governorate.' I bowed and said: 'With your help I will take proper care of the government (of the province), for I know that a great responsibility rests upon me in being Governor of Harar.' The proclamation in my favour was issued in the Great Square on the 24th day of Yäkatit 1902 (= 3rd March 1910); and when I went to my home the people's joy could be seen to exceed all bounds. As the Diplomatic Corps, who had resident consulates at Harar, came to my house informing me of their participation in my joy, they declared: 'We trust that you will govern Harar in the same fine manner as your father.'

Until I could go down to my governorate of Harar, I transmitted orders that Fitawrari (later Dejazmatch) Gäbre,[5] who had been my father's loyal follower, should stay there and protect the country as my deputy. While I was preparing for my journey to Harar, it was suddenly reported that Ras Bitwaddäd Täsämma was once again secretly stirring up a plot against Empress Taitu. Although it was Ras Bitwaddäd Täsämma who was the leader of the conspiracy, Dejazmatch Gäbrä Sellasse,[6] Fitawrari (later

---

[1] See footnote (5) in Introduction.   [2] See footnote (27) in chapter 1.
[3] Born 1851. Grew up as Emperor Menelik's servant. In 1896 he became the Army's commander-in-chief. Thereafter was in charge of War Ministry and became one of the most influential men in Ethiopia. Died 1926. See the detailed article in *JES*, VII, 2, 212–13; Heruy, 4–5; Käbbädä Täsämma, 45–8; Mérab, II, 79; Mosley, *passim*.
[4] Private secretary and chronicler of Emperor Menelik for more than thirty years; 1844–1912. See Bairu Tafla's article in *JES*, V, 2, 133–8. Heruy, 91; Mérab, II, 85, 87.
[5] Gäbre Dällal, one of Ras Makonnen's officers. Served for long periods in the Harar province. Died 1936. *JES*, VII, 2, 285; Mérab, II, 96.
[6] Dejazmatch Gäbrä Sellasse of Tigre. Had an Italian education and was appointed to the Adwa governorate by Emperor Menelik; subsequently became Neburä'ed of Aksum. Spent some time in Eritrea, but returned during Empress Zawditu's reign. In 1924 he accompanied the Regent on his European journey. Died 1930. Father of Dejazmatch Zewde. Heruy, 92; de Coppet, 496, 538, 621, 627; Luca dei Sabelli, IV, 112 ff.; Littmann, *Aksum*, I, 9; *BSOAS*, 1972, 230–1.

Dejazmatch) Wassäne,[7] Dejazmatch Berqe, and Dejazmatch Märed[8] were those who acted as principal supporters. It was said that Dejazmatch (later Ras) Dämes,[9] who was living there after removal from his governorship, was urging things on secretly rather than openly.

A few days after my appointment to the governorship of Harar, all the nobles assembled in the house of the Archbishop, Abuna Mattewos,[10] made various seditious charges against Empress Taitu and proffered advice, expressing their thoughts as follows: 'We do not want you to enter upon the affairs of government, but you should henceforth remain in the Palace looking after the sick [Emperor]'. But Empress Taitu had many partisans and consequently things remained in abeyance, because it caused difficulty to determine the matter. Empress Taitu was strong-willed and an expert in the art of ruling. At that time, I was an admirer of Empress Taitu's regal qualities. Since it was with her help that I had been appointed to the governorship of Harar, the nobles did not dare talk to me about it and reveal the matter.

After things had remained in abeyance, without a decision having been reached, for about 15 days, a meeting was called in the house of Fitawrari Habtä Giyorgis, and all of us were summoned on 11th Mägabit (= 20th March 1910) and went there.[11] Ras Bitwaddäd Täsämma also came, summoned like the (other) noblemen, in order to let it appear that he had not entered upon the matter. Afterwards Fitawrari Habtä Giyorgis, being the spokesman of the meeting, declared: 'We are not pleased about all the work which Empress Taitu is carrying out, and particularly about the appointments and dismissals. Only Dejazmatch Tafari's appointment to his father's governorship in Harar is fine and his alone may stand, but the remaining appointments and dismissals are to be cancelled. In future she is not to interfere with

---

[7] Wassäne Terfe served Emperor Menelik as cavalry commander. Father of Dejazmatch Makonnen Wassäne and of Dejazmatch Mängäsha Wassäne. *JES,* VII, 2, 268; photograph in Käbbädä Täsämma, 50.

[8] Märed Habtä Maryam. de Coppet, 538, note 7; Mérab, II, 90; *JES,* VII, 2, 215.

[9] Ras Dämes, son of Afä Negus Näsibu. Governor of Walläga. Died 1921. Heruy, 85; de Coppet, 461, note 3; Mérab, II, 77; *JES,* VII, 2, 274.

[10] One of the last of the Egyptian Archbishops. Died 1926. Cf. Hyatt, 47-50; Mara, 28; photograph in de Coppet, 188.

[11] For an account of these events see Mérab, II, 230 ff.

us in the business of government.' And the speech finished thus:
'We all say with one voice "let Dejazmatch Tafari's appointment
be valid", but it is proper to cancel the other appointments and
dismissals.'

On the morrow, 12th Mägabit (= 21st March), being all
assembled together, they entered the Palace, approached Empress
Taitu, and said: 'It is our view that the Empress should reside in
the Palace and look after the sick Emperor on our behalf, but the
work of government she should leave to the regent, Ras
Bitwaddäd Täsämma.' When they had finished speaking,
Empress Taitu turned her face towards Ras Bitwaddäd Täsämma
and said: 'Why do you put the blame on someone else when you
know that it is you who has planned and done this whole thing?
I have heard everything for certain; what really saddens me is your
operating by stealth. As for government business, when I told
you some time ago that I would take care of the ailing Emperor
and leave affairs of state alone, you sent Ras Mängäsha Atikäm as
an intermediary, arguing: "While you have been carrying on the
business of government, without initiating us, so what do we
know about it? As for your statement that you will abandon state
affairs, this is tantamount to saying: what do I care if things break
down?" When you said to me: It is by the work you undertake
from now on that you can best show gratitude to Menelik; did I
not say to you in reply that I would help in every way possible if
I can usefully do any work? And again, what is the work that I
have done without consulting you? Come now, tell me frankly
and say: "this I had not heard and that I had not known".' After
having spoken thus, she blamed him for three things: (1) for his
stirring up secretly the conspiracy; (2) for his sending an intermediary demanding that she should carry on the work of government; (3) that she had not been doing anything without informing
and consulting him.

After this, as Ras Bitwaddäd Täsämma and the other noblemen
were ashamed about the matter, they bowed and said 'forgive us'.
But since Empress Taitu was very distressed about it, she gave no
answer whatever as regards (the request for) forgiveness—except
to weep silently. Nevertheless the business of government—in
accordance with the decision taken in the house of Fitawrari
Habtä Giyorgis—was transferred in full into the hands of Ras
Bitwaddäd Täsämma and began to be carried out by him.

It had appeared to me proper for this reason that I should wait before going down to my governorate of Harar, but when things were settled I asked Ras Bitwaddäd Täsämma's permission to depart but was told to wait. The reason why I was told to wait was that rumours began to circulate outside to the effect that some monks, who claimed to have seen a dream-vision, told him 'If Dejazmatch Tafari goes down to Harar, it may become very dangerous to the government of Ledj Iyasu.' On the fourth day after Ras Bitwaddäd Täsämma had become regent plenipotentiary, he immediately arrested Fitawrari Tayye Gullelate[12] claiming that he was an adversary of Ledj Iyasu; and consequently there was for a time a good deal of anxiety on my part. But since man cannot avert what God has willed, it was Ras Bitwaddäd Täsämma's plan to cause Ledj Iyasu and me to enter into a covenant and thus to prevent anything from happening that might be an obstacle in his work. Thus he took me and my father's senior officers to the house of the Archbishop, Abuna Mattewos, and all of us entered upon the following covenant with oaths and invocations:

(1) That I would not seek, by trickery or rivalry, Ledj Iyasu's throne.

(2) That my officers would not give me bad advice to seize Ledj Iyasu's throne.

(3) That Ledj Iyasu, looking upon me with eyes of rivalry, would not depose me from my father's governorate of Harar.

(4) That Ras Täsämma, by giving bad and deceitful advice to Ledj Iyasu, would not dismiss me from the governorship of Harar and would not bring about my destruction on account of my (alleged) rivalry.

Since I was subsequently permitted to go down to Harar, I took leave of the great men of rank to whom it is proper to say good-bye by going to each of their houses. Although it was a very delicate time for taking leave of Empress Taitu, I felt that my conscience would reproach me if I went without saying good-bye; hence I went to the Palace, took my leave, and set out on my journey.

[12] Later Dejazmatch. Born 1886. Descendant of King Sahlä Sellasse. Following upon the Italo-Ethiopian war in 1935-6 he spent several years in exile in Italy. Died at Addis Ababa in 1965. Cf. Heruy, 37; *JES*, VII, 2, 237.

At that time the railway from Addis Ababa to Dire Dawa[13] had not yet been built, and the journey was extremely tiring for me. We reached Harar towards the end of Miyazya (early May). While my deputy at Harar had been awaiting the day of our entry into the city, having prepared a big banquet, it so happened by coincidence that on the day on which I reached Harar it was reported that the English king H.M. Edward VII had died on 28th Miyazya 1902 (= 6th May 1910). Consequently we gave orders that the planned reception in our honour be cancelled and that the flag be flown at half-mast; we then informed the English Consul at Harar of our participation in the grief. That we felt a special grief was because, at the time of King Edward VII's coronation as King of England and Emperor of India, my father H.H. Ras Makonnen had gone there as principal envoy of Emperor Menelik and used to tell me, at that time, of the honour with which he had been received by the English royal house. As my father reached London for the coronation and heard of the postponement of coronation day on account of King Edward's sudden illness, he went to Westminster Abbey and gave—according to the custom observed in our country Ethiopia—to the church, as a votive offering, a large golden cross and said: 'Coming to London and finding the King in great danger, if I were to return to my country with the celebration of the coronation not taking place I would be considered the harbinger of bad luck; therefore, my God, let your trust [King Edward] recover for my sake.' My father had told me about this and I also know of the existence there of the cross from a similar encounter: When I came to visit London in 1916 (= 1924)—King George V having done me the honour of inviting me—the then Archbishop of Canterbury, the Rt. Hon. Randall Thomas Davidson, when showing me Westminster Abbey, pointed out to me this golden cross and said: 'It is the one which your father, H.H. Ras Makonnen, had given as a votive offering for the illness of King Edward.'

Seven days later the entire ceremony of festive welcome was happily completed, and we set out on the task of administering the country. What it means to administer a large province can only be appreciated by men who have carried the responsibility of governorship. Even when setting down in writing the affairs

[13] Important centre in eastern Ethiopia, particularly since the construction of the Jibuti-Addis Ababa railway. Cf. *Guida*, 432 ff.; *Encyclopaedia of Islam*[1], II, 317.

of administration, the burdens of the task can scarcely be felt by those who just read about it. It may thus seem a commonplace matter to them. However, I had a heavy and very wearisome burden which was different from that of other provincial governors. The reasons are as follows:

(1) In my father's time the peasants and soldiers had not known another governor and they lived in concord recognizing him alone as master and as father. But since my father's death, because of the gubernatorial tenure of Dejazmatch Yelma and Dejazmatch Baltcha, this state of affairs had changed, and it now fell to me to devise a method by which it was possible to govern by reconciling peasants and soldiers and to please them as in my father's time.

(2) Since my brother, Dejazmatch Yelma, had died shortly after his appointment to Harar and Dejazmatch Baltcha had been appointed Governor in succession, 3,000 of my father's army were given to me; these 3,000 had subsequently gone to Walläga,[14] nominally as Ledj Iyasu's army. Now, therefore, as they were once again returning to me, I had to re-establish quarters for them.

(3) There were many of Dejazmatch Yelma's and Dejazmatch Baltcha's servants who had remained in Harar because they wanted to stay with me, and I now had to give quarters to them as well.

(4) As I informed myself of the Klobukowski accord[15] into which Emperor Menelik had entered with the French Government in 1900 (= 1907–8), concerning all matters dealing with relations with foreigners, I had to operate the yoke of this treaty with which Ethiopia had been burdened.

The great among the noblemen, soldiers, and peasants in each district had assembled and come to participate in my joy at my appointment to the governorship of Harar. We told them that in future we would inform them of everything we were going to do about the administration of the country; and then we dismissed them. We were resolved to set out on the task of administering the province.

---

[14] Province to the S.W. of the Blue Nile and intersected by its tributaries. *Guida*, 506; *The Ethiopians*[3], 192.

[15] The treaty concluded between Menelik and the French, designed to protect French citizens (and other Europeans) from the application of Ethiopian legislation (Perham[2], 151).

At that time we became convinced that the administrative regulations were at present unwelcome to the army. Nevertheless, these regulations will undoubtedly become familiar in the course of time, and so we carried on with our ideas, conscious that it was necessary to do what is to the benefit of good government. While we were seeking to find all the records with which the governors preceding me had been working (thinking that they would assist us in the task), it turned out to be impossible to find them in full, and only a few of the records of my father, H.H. Ras Makonnen, and of my brother, Dejazmatch Yelma, were in fact discovered. It therefore became necessary for us to make enquiries and to ask the elders among those noblemen and peasants who had for long been living in Harar.

Moreover, the problem of accommodation of the army officers and men had become very troublesome for us. The officers' quarters being in one district, while the men's were in another, they met only during military expeditions, but did not always know each other either by sight or in the chain of command. We were convinced that, unless officers and men lived together in one district (uprooting them from their present quarters) and got accustomed to each other by sight and command, it would be very damaging to good discipline for them to meet at the time of military operations only. Consequently, it was necessary for us to know, first of all, the number of the troops and the extent of their quarters, in order to enable us to make proper provisions. We therefore gave orders that men should tour the districts of Harar province, counting the peasants able to pay taxes, and provide this information speedily by going to each district. When the men who had been ordered to count these peasants returned after completing their work within three months, they presented us with written records showing that there were 70,000 inhabitants able to pay taxes.

After this we arranged for the governorate of Harar to be divided into twelve large districts—as follows: Tchärtchär,[16] Qori,[17] Wab-bära,[18] Mietta,[19] Anya,[20] surroundings of Harar, Gara Mullata, Afrän Qalo, Djarso, Jijjiga,[21] Ogaden, Issa[22] and Gorgora.[23]

---

[16] *Guida*, 454, 457.   [17] *Guida*, 471.   [18] *Guida*, 513; DTW, 407.
[19] AOI map I-l.   [20] For many of the following names cf. *Guida*, 436-60.
[21] *Guida*, 438-9.   [22] *Africa Orientale*, 370.
[23] The only place by this name known to me is on the northern shore of Lake Tana—clearly inapplicable in the present context; see, however, attached map.

Over these large districts we appointed several principal chiefs and arranged that in each district officers and men, according to their ranks, be properly organized. Landowners, soldiers, and officers had their names entered in the register, and it was arranged that officers and men should stay together instead of being separated from each other, so that they would be found together at a time when they were called up for any reason. It was also arranged to have courts of justice set up in each district to be responsible for each administrative division. Only as far as the administration of the Church is concerned, was the time not granted to us to complete matters according to our plan; and for the time being we left it as of old.

After my father, H.H. Ras Makonnen, had died, much of the governmental framework which he had established had been destroyed on account of the frequent change of governors of Harar; I therefore felt sure in my heart that the yoke of government was heavy upon the inhabitants, for the provincial governors (Abägaz),[24] the district chiefs (Dämina),[25] and the local headmen (Gärada)[26] did not protect the population with impartiality; consequently, we began to seek an improvement of the situation. The Abägaz is in effect the provincial regent. The Dämina stands between the people in the district and the tax collector, so that the inhabitants pay their taxes on time; he functions as a controller, lest the tax collector should harm the people either by taxes or in other ways. Some Däminas have charge of perhaps from 20 to 300 peasants. The Gärada is a chief who issues orders and acts under the authority of the Dämina. This system is the one which has remained in force up to now, it having become customary at the time when the Turks (i.e. Egyptians)[27] had seized Harar for a short time, for about ten years.

After my father's death, when the administrative framework which he had established was progressively disintegrating, some tax collectors were receiving up to 12 dollars in cash, when it was difficult for the peasant to produce the honey tax payable on his land. We therefore commanded the governors and tax collectors not to harm the peasants by their rule, for they had begun to do other similar things which were harmful to the inhabitants. But unless the people heard of this command in form of a proclamation,

[24] Guidi, 457.   [25] Guidi, *Suppl.*, 187; Cerulli, *Harar*, 40–1.
[26] Guidi, *Voc.*, 729; Cerulli, *loc. cit.*   [27] *Encyclopaedia of Islam*[2], III, 4; 176.

we were convinced that they were not able to dispute impositions of this sort by refusing to pay; and we therefore promulgated the following proclamation:

Proclamation[28]

You who are Abägaz, look out for thieves and brigands in the country which you govern as deputy. If I hear it being said that in a certain province people have been robbed, it is the Abägaz who will pay them. You who have no master and are unemployed, enter the town which I have given to the Abägaz and stay there; but do not disturb the peasants by being in the villages. If the roads in your respective governorates fall into disrepair, build roads in order not to make things difficult for the traders going up and down the country. Hitherto work on the Sabbath was forbidden; now you will, in fact, be punished when found working on the Sabbath. As for you who are liable to honey tax and possess honey, I have indicated to your Abägaz the proper measure; hence render your honey in that measure. But if you do not have honey, then give in lieu of the honey 4 dollars if you are a Gärada, 3 dollars as a Shebäta,[29] two as a tenant and one as a shepherd. If, however, you possess honey and say 'I would rather give cash', then you have to pay double the quantity of honey if you are found selling your honey. You being a Gärada paying the same amount of tax as a Shebäta, spend three dollars, like a Shebäta, for your honey. Gärada, Shebäta, tenant, and shepherd, except if it is difficult for you, your tax is honey; hence hang up your bee hives. And you, Mälkäñña (district collector), do not touch the honey before it is ready; in future, as in the past, work with your Dämina in all the work that is to be done. Previously I told you by proclamation as follows 'having wandered from province to province, yet you have not acquired a new country; hence do not eat up the *kobe basa*'.[30] Now I have heard it being said that you are receiving it from the peasants; therefore return to the peasants this money which you have received beyond the terms of this proclamation. And for the future, you, the Abägaz and Dämina,

[28] Cf. the somewhat different text in Eadie, 183 ff. See also *BSOAS*, 1974, 208 ff.

[29] Probably 'elder', a local Harar term for what appears to be a functionary below the rank of Gärada.

[30] Apparently a local term for taxes? or benefits? said to be levied by a governor newly arrived in his district.

watch lest the Mälkäñña (district collector), going beyond what
has been assigned to them, take away the peasants' money. If the
peasants tell you about the money which has been extorted in
excess and if you persist in not returning it to them, and if then the
peasants do no work and come to me to complain, then the loss is
yours and you will have to pay the money and will then have to
get it back from the person who had taken it from the peasants.
And as for you, peasants, do not come to me before you have
spoken to the Abägaz and the Dämina. For the three annual
festivals, i.e. for Mäsqäl, Christmas, and Easter,[31] receive two
dollars each in lieu of castrated goats, but beyond this you will not
receive anything.

Harar, 13th Hamle 1905 (= 21st July 1913).

When the proclamation had been issued, although the Abägaz
and district collectors were for a time not at all pleased, after a few
months they got used to the new administrative rules and discovered their usefulness. As for the peasants, since the yoke of
government and taxes was lightened for them, they all set out to
do their work with a calm heart.

[31] *The Ethiopians*[3], 101–2. Mäsqäl is the feast of the Cross.

CHAPTER 5

From the time of my marriage up to
my appointment as crown-prince
and regent plenipotentiary
(1911–1916)

WHEN I had been governor of Harar and its entire province for
about a year, stabilizing without mishap the life of peasants and
soldiers, of government and of all else necessary for administration, it was decided, by my wish and by that of my relations, that
I should marry (I was in my twentieth year at the time) Wayzäro
Mänän[1] (now Empress), the grand-daughter of Negus Mika'el.

[1] Empress Mänän was born about 1890 and died in 1962. She had been previously married to Ras Lul Sägäd. By her marriage to Emperor Haile Sellassie she
had three sons and three daughters.

We were married by church ceremony on 23rd Hamle 1903
(= 31st July 1911).

Her character is such that, apart from goodness, there is no evil
or malice in her. Ever since we were married we lived together, by
virtue of her being fertile, in one family sharing joy as well as
sadness.

In saying that we lived together sharing joy as well as sadness,
I cannot omit writing about the first great sadness, as follows:
We were informed at Harar of the death, in 1907 (= 1914/15),
of Ras Haylä Maryam,[2] Wayzäro Mänän's younger brother.
When their mother, Wayzäro Sehin,[3] returned from Wallo[4] to
Addis Ababa, it was decided that, because of her brother's death,
Wayzäro Mänän should go up to Addis Ababa for the joint
mourning. And consequently she set out from Harar on Monday,
30th Genbot (= 7th June 1915). Having accompanied her as far as
Harämaya,[5] we camped by the shore of Lake Harämaya, as We
(i.e. Dej. Tafari) wished to return (to Harar).

In the past there was a boat in which the foreigners living at
Harar and Dire Dawa used sometimes to enter Lake Harämaya for
recreation; we therefore left the tent at 9 o'clock (= 3 p.m.) and
went to the lake. There were ten people who boarded the boat
with us to relax on the lake. After we had embarked we passed
towards the centre and eventually crossed to the other side.
Having stayed a little while on the opposite shore, we entered the
boat once again to return to our camp. But the boat was rather
old and, as we reached the middle of the lake, it was holed and
water began to enter.

As the people in the boat scooped out the water with their hats,
it did not diminish when they poured it out. Once we had become
convinced of the fact that the boat was leaking, that it was
impossible to cross with us inside it, and that we were all of us
sinking with the boat, we began to swim with great difficulty.
But as the lake was wide and it was impossible to cross it by
swimming, the following seven men became exhausted and

[2] Haylä Maryam Assefaw was a native of Wallo, a son of Janterar Assefaw and
Wayzäro Sehin, the daughter of Negus Mika'el; he was born in 1888 and died in
Nähase 1915. Cf. Heruy, 41; JES, VII, 2, 241.

[3] See footnote (2) and Heruy, 22.

[4] The great central province of Ethiopia; Guida, 396 and main map; The
Ethiopians[3], 192.

[5] Or Arämaya; Guida, 436, map 448; Mérab, I, 152; Rosen, chapter V.

drowned: Abba Täsfa, Qägnazmatch Gäbrä Wald, Ato Ayälä Seyum, Kidanä Maryam Manyazäwal, Asämre, Abba Samuel, Paulos. But I and Dejazmatch Haylä Sellasse were going under and coming up again. Dejatch Abreha's servant helped me. As the officers and men who were watching this standing by the shore of the lake became convinced of the shipwreck, all those able to swim threw themselves into the lake; and as they reached us we emerged, having only just escaped from death. As we got out, our soul had barely been prevented from getting separated from our body, but we were unable to recognize anyone or to speak.[6]

It so happened that by chance Dr. Zervos,[7] a Greek who had earlier been a physician, was there at that time and he treated me with medicines as far as possible; and little by little I was able to recognize people's outline.

On the morrow they carried me on a stretcher to Amaressa,[8] and from Amaressa took me down to Harar; and on the twelfth day, being quite well again, I went up to the church of St Michael and gave thanks to God.

Wayzäro Mänän, being shocked on account of my accident, abandoned her journey to Addis Ababa and returned to Harar.

[6] This incident is described, in somewhat different versions, in Sandford, 36, and Mosley, 80. Of the people who died only Abba Samuel is known to me. He was, of course, the Emperor's tutor and close friend; his death was a great shock to him.   [7] Pankhurst, 64, 237, 650.

[8] Amaressa is a river; Rosen, 54; Mérab, I, 155.

CHAPTER 6

The reason why the rancour between Ledj Iyasu and myself began

AFTER my appointment to the governorship of Harar and my marriage to Wayzäro Mänän, I lived happily for about a year. But thereafter, since in this world joy and sadness always alternate, my joy began progressively to change into sadness. The reason for this is as follows:

After the death of Ras Bitwaddäd Täsämma, who had been Ledj Iyasu's guardian and regent of the Empire, no other guardian had been appointed for Ledj Iyasu. But the latter thus sought in everything the company and counsel of worthless men who only wanted their own immediate profit, while the great nobles and ministers became hostile and removed their hearts from him.

Those worthless men whom he had made advisers associated with some foreign traders and said: 'We are importing from abroad commodities like this; we are sending abroad goods like that, hence excuse us customs-duties.' Very few only were those who sought the truth and advised him as follows: 'Quite apart from obtaining permits by fraud, if they do this your government will be harmed; if they do that your government will profit; if they do this rotten thing, the people will be hostile.'

Furthermore, when he claimed, by virtue of his Wallo descent, to be descended from the Prophet Muhammad, counting back some forty generations, and when he worked for a meeting and rapprochement in faith with the Muslims, he would not accept it if anyone tried to advise: 'Lay off, for it is this sort of thing that will bring damage upon your government and upon yourself.' He began to arrange for the Palace arms and all the other excellent equipment to go to Negus Mika'el.

While, in doing all this, he was aware of everybody's hostility, and instead of watching things by being in one place, he did a great deal of roaming about, joyfully invading tranquil provinces and killing people, some time going to Gimira,[1] another to Wallo, yet another to Adal[2] country, and sometimes to Harar. The blood of many was flowing. When he returned from his trips, the nobles and ministers, tendering advice and getting angry, all despaired when they realized their inability to restore his mind to sanity.

There were, however, some who advised him as follows: 'If the honour of the great nobles of Menelik's time were reduced and their rank diminished, then it would be convenient for you to raise to office the humble; it would assuredly result from this that these minor figures will respectfully love you alone, and with their support you will be able to act as you wish and to destroy your enemies.' As this appeared to him to be true, he began to strive to bring this about.

He himself came upon me at Harar in 1907 (= 1914/15), summoned my army's officers and the great among the peasants, and asked at a secret meeting: 'Tell me if there is a wrong that

[1] *Guida*, 542; KBT, 1206; DTW, 277.   [2] *The Ethiopians*[2], 64–72.

Dejazmatch Tafari has done you.' He then granted audiences while giving advice to my detriment, stayed for a few days and then returned. I heard this from men who had actually been questioned.

Afterwards, in Genbot (= May 1916), he summoned me to Addis Ababa; and when we had remained together for about two months, he set out from Addis Ababa by night on 21st Hamle (= 29th July), without informing me, boarded the train at Akaki,[3] and next morning I heard about his descent to Harar.

When I knew for certain that he had gone down to Harar and although he went there without informing me, I thought it should not appear that I was hostile to his journey there because he had not given me prior information (for the title to the Harar governorship was mine), and I therefore wrote him a letter as follows: 'If you are staying at Harar, let me come there; if you are returning to Addis Ababa, I shall return together (with you).' When I had sent him that letter by the hand of my servant Zälläqä Källäla, he wrote back to me on 28th Hamle 1908 (5th August 1916) as follows: 'I had told Bitwaddäd Haylä Giyorgis[4] that he should inform you of the reason why I came to Harar. If you were to come to Harar now and then to return with me to Addis Ababa, the railway deficit would be very great for you, because your army is so numerous; hence stay there. If I were to stay here for a long time, I would write to you again.'

When he entered Harar city, evil men, who came between us and tendered advice that he should dismiss Dejazmatch Tafari from the governorship of Harar and appoint himself, began to press him to put into practice the counsel they had earlier proffered, for now they had Ledj Iyasu to themselves. Therefore, on 7th Nähase 1908 (= 14th August 1916) he summoned my deputy, Fitawrari Gäbre, and gave orders that all the camping places in the hands of Dejazmatch Tafari's servants be seized—apart from those occupied by government troops. He then transmitted the following orders by telegram to Bitwaddäd Haylä Giyorgis: 'I have assumed, with immediate effect, the governorship of Harar.

---

[3] *Guida*, 428.

[4] Under Emperor Menelik the first Trade and Foreign Minister. During Ledj Iyasu's short reign he was, in effect, the principal minister of the realm. Subsequently he lived under restriction and died in 1925. Cf. *JES*, VII, 2, 242; Heruy, 42–3; de Coppet, 527, note 8; Mérab, II, 81–4.

I have given the governorship of Kaffa[5] to Dejazmatch Tafari; let him be told.' He informed me that I was to go to Kaffa at once, as these were Ledj Iyasu's orders.

Subsequently he (Ledj Iyasu) sent me a letter direct, written on the 10th of Nähase 1908 (= 17th August 1916), stating: 'I have appointed Harar my own personal governorate; I have placed under your governorship Kaffa and Maji,[6] and under your authority Gurrafärda.'[7]

When the people at Addis Ababa, great and small, heard this, they declared openly: the fact that he (Ledj Iyasu) is taking away the governorship of Harar from Dejazmatch Tafari is not so much for the governorate but because he has been converted to the Islamic faith and for the sake of further rapprochement to the Muslims.

At the time of the Great World War, when some foreigners presented to him (Ledj Iyasu) their view: 'even though you cannot help the English, the French, and the Italians, who are Ethiopia's neighbours at the frontiers, with armed force, it would be good if you would at least assist with provisions, i.e. with food', yet he did not listen. Instead, he had begun on an exchange of secret correspondence with the peoples surrounding Ethiopia, the Adalites and the Somalis, with a view to resisting the Allies. But as the representatives of the three governments resident at Addis Ababa had discovered this exchange of secret letters, they made an official approach and, it is reported, presented [the correspondence] to Bitwaddäd Haylä Giyorgis.

When the leaders of Ethiopia found out about this whole affair, they became convinced of the need to depose Ledj Iyasu. But as it appeared to them likely that their secret would be betrayed if they were assembled together for consultation, they chose servants as trusted messengers and began to correspond through them as go-betweens. But some met by night at a hidden place and, after talking to each other face to face, separated again. Others again were asking: 'Inform us first about the successor once Ledj Iyasu is deposed'; but the party which approved of Ledj Iyasu's deposition began to grow steadily, since they gladly accepted the opinion when they were told: 'We shall put Emperor

[5] The great province in southern Ethiopia, comprising the old Sidama kingdom. *Guida*, 537 ff. (map 528); Cerulli, *Stud. Et.*, IV.
[6] *Guida*, 544.   [7] *Guida*, 541.

Menelik's daughter, Wayzäro Zawditu,[8] on the throne and shall appoint H.H. Ras Makonnen's son, Dejazmatch Tafari, as Crown Prince and Regent.'

When they asked me to enter upon these consultations, (I replied): When I first departed for my father's governorate of Hararge to take up my appointment, Ras Bitwaddäd Täsamma took us both (Ledj Iyasu and myself) to the house of the Archbishop, Abuna Mattewos, and caused us to enter upon a covenant,[9] by oaths and invocations, that Ledj Iyasu should not depose me from my governorship of Hararge and that I should not seek his throne by foul means. But now Ledj Iyasu has violated the solemn covenant of oaths and invocations, has dismissed me from my governorship of Hararge, and for my part this is sufficient evidence. Furthermore, I said to them: since you have now convinced me of Ledj Iyasu's conversion to Islam, there is nothing in which I differ from you. And they gave me adequate information by reading out everything they had written, so that it be proof to the people for the future.

[8] The daughter of Emperor Menelik by Wayzäro Abetchiw. 1876-1930; Empress 1916-1930. Married first to Ras Araya, son of Emperor Yohannes; after his death, successively to Wagshum Gwangul, Dej. Wube, and, finally, Ras Gugsa Wale.

[9] See pages 18-19 of Amharic text (= p. 35 of translation).

CHAPTER 7

From the deposition of Ledj Iyasu on 17th Mäskäräm 1909 (= 27th Sept. 1916) to the assumption of the crown by Queen Zawditu on 4th Yäkatit 1909 (= 11th February 1917)

WHILE Ledj Iyasu went to and fro between the towns of Dire Dawa, Harar, and Jijjiga, and while he assembled Adalites and Somalis giving them medals and arms, he stayed there declaring: 'I am on your side in respect of religion'; it was then heard that

Muslims were mocking: 'he is neither Christian nor Muslim'. On the 17th day of Mäskäräm 1909 (= 27th Sept. 1916), on the day of the great feast of Mäsqäl,[1] it was arranged that the nobles with the army, and the Archbishop Abuna Mattewos, and the Etchäge[2] Waldä Giyorgis[3] with the priests, should assemble at a prepared place within the precincts of the Palace; and when they had all arrived and taken their seat according to their rank, the following indictment against Ledj Iyasu, which had been secretly prepared, was read out:

'The Christian faith, which our fathers had hitherto carefully retained by fighting for their faith with the Muslims and by shedding their blood, Ledj Iyasu exchanged for the Muslim religion and aroused commotion in our midst; in order to exterminate us by mutual fighting he has converted to Islam and, therefore, we shall henceforth not submit to him; we shall not place a Muslim king on the throne of a Christian king; we have ample proof of his conversion to Islam:

(1) He married four wives claiming: "the Qur'an permits it to me". Of these wives one is the daughter of Abba Jiffar[4] of the Jimma[5] nobility; the second is the daughter of Hajj Abdullahi[6] of the Harar nobility; the third is the daughter of Abu Bakr[7] of the Adal nobility; the father of the fourth, Dejatch Djote,[8] became a Christian and baptized his daughter; while she lived under her baptismal name Askalä Maryam,[9] it was to Dejatch Djote's daughter that he (Ledj Iyasu) later on, after his conversion to Islam, gave the Muslim woman's name of Momina.[10]

(2) He built a mosque at Jijjiga with government funds and gave it to the Muslims.

(3) At that time he sent to Mahazar Bey,[11] the foreign [Turkish] consul resident at Addis Ababa—as he was celebrating the

---

[1] *The Ethiopians*³, 101-2.

[2] *The Ethiopians*³, 63, 103; the prior of Däbrä Libanos and in the past Ethiopia's premier indigenous ecclesiastic.   [3] Heruy, 72-3.

[4] Hereditary ruler of Jimma (1861-1932). Heruy, 51; de Coppet, 45, 171 (6); *Guida*, 526; Zewde, biographies.

[5] *Guida*, 528 ff.; and maps 527/8.   [6] de Coppet, 567, 242-4; *Guida*, 455.

[7] Pankhurst, 99-105; Budge, II, 543-4; Starkie, *Rimbaud, passim*.

[8] Käbbädä Täsämma, 61; DTW, 401; Zewde, biogr.; de Coppet; 390 (10).

[9] DTW, 1171.   [10] مُؤْمِنَة   [11] Budge, II, 544.

Ramadan[12] feast—our Ethiopian flag (on which there was written "The Lion of the Tribe of Judah has prevailed"[13] and adorned with the sign of the Cross) on which he had caused to be written the following words (in Arabic): "There is no god but Allah and Muhammad is the messenger of Allah".[14]

(4) He wore Somali Muslim clothes and the Muslim turban, held the Islamic rosary, and was seen to prostrate himself in the mosque.

(5) He was seen praying and reading the Qur'an having had it transcribed in Amharic characters.

(6) On the headgear of his special guards he had embroidered the legend "there is no god but Allah".

(7) H.H. Ras Makonnen had built a church at Harar and had made the area adjoining the church into a dwelling for the clergy, giving the Muslims a place in exchange; then, 32 years later, he (Ledj Iyasu) expelled the clergy and restored it to the Muslims.

(8) When a girl was born to him he saw to it that she would grow up learning the Muslim religion, and he gave her to the Muslim Madame Hanafi[15] and said: "Bring her up on my be-half".

(9) He despised the descent of Menelik II, which comes direct from Menelik I,[16] and claimed to be descended from the Prophet Muhammad; assembling the great Muslim sheikhs he spent the day convincing them of his genealogical calculations.

(10) The day on which our great king, Emperor Menelik, who had bequeathed him the throne, died, instead of mourning and of arranging lamentations he went out horse-riding to Jan-Meda[17] and spent the day playing combat-games. He forbade Menelik's body to be buried with dignity and thus it has remained up to now.[17a] We possess a great deal of further similar proof (against Ledj Iyasu).

[12] Hughes, *Dictionary of Islam*, 533 ff.   [13] *Rev.* 5 : 5.

[14] لا اله الا الله ومحمد رسول الله

[15] Any connexion with the Hanafi mentioned in Mérab, II, 103?

[16] Menelik I is the putative son of the Queen of Sheba and King Solomon as embodied in the *Kebra Nagast* (*The Ethiopians*[2], 138–9).

[17] The great display-field at Addis Ababa; see DTW, 399–400; *Guida*, map, 490, A4.

[17a] i.e. until the erection of the Menelik Mausoleum.

Therefore, having deposed him (Ledj Iyasu), we have placed on the throne Wayzäro Zawditu, Emperor Menelik's daughter. We have appointed Dejazmatch Tafari, the son of H.H. Ras Makonnen, Crown Prince, with the rank of Ras, and Regent of the Empire.'

When the reading of this proclamation was concluded, all those assembled said with one voice: 'We accept gladly, hence let it be carried out with success.' The Archbishop, Abuna Mattewos, and the Etchäge Waldä Giyorgis spoke the following final words: 'Ledj Iyasu has repudiated the Christian religion and, because he has been converted to the Islamic faith, we have excommunicated him; you will be excommunicated if henceforth you follow Ledj Iyasu and submit to him—instead of living strong in the Orthodox faith and watchful of the freedom of your government'.

Afterwards the proclamation was issued by which the Throne and the Crown went to Queen Zawditu, while the succession to the Throne and the Regency Plenipotentiary went to me; the text of the proclamation was then transmitted by telephone to the princes and nobles and all the provincial governors in the whole of Ethiopia.

As it was about 40 years since Negus Mika'el had been converted from Islam to Christianity, he had been mentioning to some of the nobles his sadness at his son's conversion to Islam; consequently, the text of the proclamation was transmitted to him in the thought that he was bound to be allied with us now as regards his son's deposition.

When Ledj Iyasu, staying at Harar, heard about his own deposition, the enthronement of Queen Zawditu and my appointment as Crown Prince and Regent Plenipotentiary, he collected Somalis and Adalites and arranged for disturbances to be created in the city; as Christians and Muslims were now fighting on separate sides, some 500 men from both sides died. As Dejazmatch Baltcha and Qägnazmatch (now Ras) Emru were at the time at Harar, they were seized; but Ledj Iyasu released Dejazmatch Baltcha under oath that he would not get separated from him. Qägnazmatch Emru, however, he kept under detention.

All my officers and servants—with few exceptions—who were at Harar deserted Ledj Iyasu, departed for a district called Qärsa,[18] and began to wait there in proper battle formation. Qägnazmatch

---

[18] *Guida*, 454, map 448.

Emru escaped from the place at which he had been detained and went out [there].

This is what happened to Ledj Iyasu subsequently: Having collected a regular body of troops, he appointed Dejazmatch Gugsa Alyo[19] as army commander; since it was reported that Ledj Iyasu had despatched him to Awash,[20] we made Dejazmatch Ayalew Berru[21] army commander and sent Dejatch Haylä Maryam Lämma,[22] Dejatch Admasu Berru,[23] Ledj Abäbä Damtäw,[24] Ledj Dästa Damtäw,[25] Fitawrari Mäkuriya Gärmame,[26] and added other regular troops. They encountered each other at a railway station called Me'eso (Miesso),[27] and on the 25th of Mäskäräm (= 6th October) they defeated Dejazmatch Gugsa Alyo. He himself, however, escaped by train and entered Dire Dawa.

When Ledj Iyasu saw that the Christians at Harar and its entire province as well as the Muslims were deserting him, he went down to Dire Dawa and seized about all he could of the money in the treasury; what he could not (take), he sent to Jibuti[28] by the hands of M. Ydlibi[29] and then travelled by way of the Adal desert to reach his father's governorate of Wallo.

[19] Käbbädä Täsämma, 45–6. Served Ras Mika'el and Ledj Iyasu. Died 1934. Cf. *JES*, VII, 2, 286.

[20] *Guida*, 424–5; one of the great river systems in Ethiopia.

[21] For him and the following names, cf. Käbbädä Täsämma, 44. Heruy, 54. Lived 1886–1948. A relation of Empress Taitu. Exiled in Italy during the war. Cf. *JES*, VII, 2, 253–4.

[22] Käbbädä Täsämma, 44, 55. 1890–1929. Descendant of King Sahlä Sellasse. Cf. *JES*, VII, 2, 240.

[23] Heruy, 54; brother of Ayalew. Long-time governor of Yäjju. *JES*, VII, 2, 254.

[24] Later Dejazmatch, brother of No. (25), and father of Crown Princess Mädfäriyash Warq Abäbä; 1892–1948. Käbbädä Täsämma, 130 (photo); *JES*, VII, 2, 251.

[25] Later Ras, husband of Emperor Haile Sellassie's daughter, Princess Tänagnä Warq. Ras Dästa was killed in the Italo-Abyssinian war. Käbbädä Täsämma, 133 (photo); *JES*, VII, 2, 275. His father, Fitawrari Damtäw (Heruy, 86) was Ethiopian envoy to Russia and was eventually killed in the battle of Adwa in 1896; *JES*, VII, 2, 277.

[26] Käbbädä Täsämma, 44, 55; native of Shoa. 1874–1932. Was active in provincial administration. *JES*, VII, 2, 220.

[27] Miesso: *Guida*, 421; railway station, some 35 miles west of Dire Dawa (see main map in *Guida*).

[28] *Guida*, 410 ff., with its excellent and detailed article on this important port.

But a telephone message had been transmitted to Negus Mika'el to the effect: 'As your son has gone over to Islam, we have deposed him, have enthroned Queen Zawditu, and have appointed H.H. Tafari Makonnen Crown Prince and Regent Plenipotentiary.' When Negus Mika'el realized this, he said: 'I had been striving to make my son firm in the Christian faith even to the point of angrily counselling him, but nevertheless I cannot silently look on while they take away from him the throne which his grandfather, Emperor Menelik, had given him.' It was reported then that Negus Mika'el had mobilized his army by proclamation and was marching towards Shoa; therefore, the princes, nobles, and ministers jointly sent him the following message in writing:

'May it reach Negus Mika'el whose authority is written upon his shoulder, King of Zion.

You, the King, know that all the work which your son, Ledj Iyasu, has accomplished from the time he became Crown Prince up to the present was childish behaviour. When we meant to train him with reproachful counsel, we did not find the occasion because, to our chagrin, he never stayed long enough in one place. When at times we managed to find him and tendered advice, he would not accept our view. When we watched him patiently, lest his personality should feel offended, thinking that perhaps one day soon he would become aware of his government's need and of his own rank and honour and perhaps abandon his youthful pursuits, yet he had still not had enough of these puerilia and began striving to establish Islam in our country Ethiopia which had lived steadfast in her Christianity for some 1600 years since Abreha and Asbeha[30] and Sälama,[31] the revealer of the light.

When in the previous year he came to Wallo, you, oh King, know yourself all the things he did together with the Muslims during the rainy season. Again, we have heard of your angry counsel to Ledj Iyasu, when you recognized that his heart had been alienated from the Christian faith, and said to him: "I beg you, my son, abandon this plan of yours!", yet even you, oh King, did not prevail. And now we are sending you, together with

[29] Mosley, 78, 100; Turkish Consul at Harar, a merchant of Syrian origin.
[30] *The Ethiopians*[2], 97; the kings under whom Ethiopia is said to have accepted Christianity. [31] *The Ethiopians*[2], 96–7. Frumentius, Ethiopia's first bishop.

this letter, photographs of him which prove all the things he has been doing jointly with the Muslims when he went down to Harar secretly without informing us.

We had suffered all this patiently, but when all of us together, including the Archbishop and the Etchäge, sent him a letter requesting him to come to Addis Ababa, at any rate for the New Year celebrations, he persisted in not coming. Our anxiety in acting in this manner arises from the thought lest the Christian faith be extinguished and, for this reason, the blood of Christians be shed in vain and our country pass into the hands of foreigners; may the king thus be very mindful of this matter! It is known that the people would not have risen up, unless they had been certain of this. Moreover, we would remind you of the extinction of your name as well, for it is bound to remain recorded in history for future generations: Because of Ledj Iyasu, Negus Mika'el's son, the Christian religion was eclipsed in Ethiopia, and the Islamic faith expanded.

In writing all this to the king, it is not that we have acted thus with the intention that Ledj Iyasu be harmed or, in particular, that the king be antagonized, but it is with the thought that we should act jointly for what is of benefit to our religion and to our government; your plans do not diverge from ours, for we know that you love Emperor Menelik and all of us and are much concerned for the Christian faith.'

24th Mäskäräm 1909 (= 5th Oct. 1916).

After this letter had reached Negus Mika'el, he refused to return in any circumstances; and as our envoys informed us by telephone of his marching forward, we placed the army that was stationed at Addis Ababa at the time under the command of Ras Lul Sägäd[32] and sent him on in advance. When he reached a Shoan district called Tora Mäsk,[33] he suddenly encountered Negus Mika'el's advance troops, and on Tuesday, 7th Teqemt (= 17th Oct. 1916), we heard by telephone of the death in battle of Ras Lul Sägäd, Dejatch Täsämma Gäzmu,[34] Liqä Mäkwas Abäbä Atnaf Sägäd,[35] Fitawrari

[32] Heruy, 5; Sandford, 41; Mosley, 68. Empress Mänän's first husband. Died 1916. See also JES, VII, 2, 16, 214.

[33] de Coppet, 63 (9); Guida, 406 (Tuor Amesc!); Harris, II, 46; situated between Ankober and Däbrä Berhan.

[34] Heruy, 30; Käbbädä Täsämma, 44, 55 (photo); native of Märhabete. Died 1916. JES, VII, 2, 235.

Zäwde Gobäna, Asalafi Abbe,[36] Qägnazmatch Delnäsahu, Asalafi Delnäse,[37] Ato Shäwaye,[38] and other army commanders.

Already earlier on our War Minister, Fitawrari Habtä Giyorgis, had left Addis Ababa on 3rd Teqemt (= 13th October); and when he reached Korämash[39] after a long march, we arranged that he should stay there distributing to each soldier arms from the war material at Korämash. And We Ourselves set out on 9th Teqemt (= 19th October). So that the armed forces from each district should arrive by as rapid a march as possible, We informed the army by the following proclamation:

The text of the Proclamation.

'Listen, people of my country, Ethiopia!
Since Ledj Iyasu, digressing from Emperor Menelik's wishes, had openly shown his adherence to Islam, prostrating himself in mosques together with Muslims and tracing back his Islamic genealogy, while setting aside Menelik's curse against him designed to prevent him committing evil deeds, he was unable to carry on the administration, and we, therefore, had to depose him and placed Queen Zawditu on her father's throne.

While we were thinking that Negus Mika'el was aware of his son's conversion to Islam and that together with us he would be shedding his blood for the Christian faith, he came marching from Wallo to fight us and insisting that we should at once submit[40] to a Muslim king. Therefore, those of you who are men, follow me!'

After We had issued this proclamation, We marched forward. But since bloodshed among Ethiopians themselves is extremely saddening, I arranged that monks and priors from the monasteries of Däbrä Libanos and Zequala[41] and from all the various churches should be selected and come with their crosses to request Negus Mika'el to go back to Wallo without making war. But word

---

[35] Heruy, 49; Käbbädä Täsämma, 44, 55 (photo); brother of Dej. Wube; father of Gen. Abiy. Died 1916. Cf. JES, VII, 2, 251.

[36] Heruy, 51; Käbbädä Täsämma, 44.

[37] Käbbädä Täsämma, 55, 105.   [38] Käbbädä Täsämma, 44.

[39] Käbbädä Täsämma, 53, 116; DTW, 677; (Coromasc), Guida, 409, between Ankober and Addis Ababa in the Bulga region.

[40] For the ካተንዛፕቱ· construction see, BSOAS, 1972, 270, and my 'Animistic expressions and other aspects of direct speech in Amharic' (Accademia dei Lincei, IV Congresso di Studi Etiopici, vol. II, 272-4).

reached us by telephone that Negus Mika'el, far from going back, had in fact seized and arrested the monks who had been sent to bring about peace; we thus became convinced that his decision to engage in battle was now plain and generally known.

On 15th Teqemt (= 25th October) we set out from Korämash and marched on; on 16th Teqemt (= 26th October) our camp and that of Negus Mika'el spent the night opposite each other at a plain of the Tärra[42] district called Sägäle.[43]

On Friday, 17th Teqemt (= 27th October), starting at 7 o'clock at night (= 1 a.m.), he (Negus Mika'el) stationed his army officers on the right and left flanks, and positioned himself in the centre; and when the morning dawned, he began opening fire and launched a surprise attack against our gunners who had been spending the night on guard duty. Thereupon We placed Our War Minister, Fitawrari Habtä Giyorgis, at the front, Ras Kassa[44] at Negus Mika'el's rear, and the remaining Rases and Dejaz-matches on the right and left flanks; when we had joined the entire army at the rear, we engaged the enemy in battle.

When we had fought from early morning for about five hours and when the Shoan army, leaping like a leopard seeing a goat, like a lion seeing a cow, entered in battle formation—swords drawn and fighting hand to hand—Negus Mika'el was defeated and captured. Of his army many died and many were captured, while those who remained fled and returned to Wallo.

When Ledj Iyasu, having to travel by way of the Adal country and marching fast to reach the battle, arrived at Ankober,[45] he heard of Negus Mika'el's defeat; he retraced his steps and got to the Wallo region by the Adal detour.

Although it was generally known that Negus Mika'el had been captured, this was a formality only; in fact, We arranged every-thing befitting his dignity, so that no humiliation whatever should affect him. As for the other prisoners, since we have no other quarrel with Wallo and mindful of the fact that we are all natives of one Ethiopia, we allowed them, by proclamation, to go back to their country of Wallo after their release.

[41] *Guida*, 426. The great mountain with its crater-lake and monastery.

[42] de Coppet, 86 (9).   [43] *Guida*, 396.

[44] Heruy, 63. H.H. Ras Kassa Haylu, grandson of Ras Darge, King Sahlä Sellasse's son. Probably the most important member of the Ethiopian aristocracy; picture on p. 139 of Käbbädä Täsämma. 1880–1956. *JES*, VII, 2, 258.

[45] *Guida*, 407. Former capital of Shoa and situated in the Shoan heartland.

As we announced the story of the victory to Addis Ababa by telephone all the people of the capital, from Queen Zawditu downwards, were overjoyed. When we got back to Addis Ababa, on Thursday, 23rd Teqemt (= 2nd Nov.), H.M. Queen Zawditu, seated in a vast tent at Jan-Meda, and the people of the capital being assembled in full, received us with a great parade, with ululating and with joy.

CHAPTER 8

From the coronation of Queen Zawditu up to Ledj Iyasu's defeat at Wallo and subsequent escape

SINCE it had been resolved in Council that Queen Zawditu's coronation should take place on 4th Yäkatit 1909 (= 11th February, 1917), we began passing on instructions to all chiefs that everything necessary for the celebration of the coronation be prepared. There were invited to come to Addis Ababa for the coronation the governor of Bägemeder[1] and Semien,[2] Ras Waldä Giyorgis,[3] the governor of Sällale, Boräna[4] and Därra,[5] Ras Kassa, the governor of Gojjam,[6] Ras Haylu,[7] the governor of Tigre, Ras Seyum,[8] and other governors of the large provinces. The political atmosphere at that time was grave for invitations of this kind.[9]

[1] Bägemeder is the vast region to the north and east of Lake Tana. *Guida,* 391. map 368–9.

[2] The gigantic mountain massif of central Ethiopia; *Guida,* 251.

[3] 1851-1918. Heruy, 71–2. Grandson of King Sahlä Sellasse; created King (Negus) early in Zawditu's reign (picture in Käbbädä Täsämma, 33); *JES,* VII, 2, 267.

[4] North of Sällale and just to the east of the loop of the Blue Nile. See Käbbädä Täsämma, 416; de Coppet, Atlas, IV.

[5] See previous note which applies in full. Cf. also DTW, 382—adjacent to Marabetie area.

[6] The great province within the loop of the Blue Nile. *Guida,* 375.

[7] Hereditary ruler of Gojjam, but of somewhat erratic loyalty to the reigning house. Photograph on p. 407 of Käbbädä Täsämma; Heruy, 43-4. Died 1951. *JES,* VII, 2, 243. See below, chapter 31.

Respectful invitations to come to the coronation were sent to the governors of foreign countries coterminous with Ethiopia, i.e. the governors of the British Sudan and of British Somaliland as well as the governor of French Somaliland.

When all those invited had arrived, on Sunday the 4th of Yäkatit (= 11th February 1917), in the great cathedral, the Church of St. George,[10] Queen Zawditu was anointed with the oil of kingship at the hands of the Archbishop, the Abuna Mattewos, and wore the Imperial Crown.

After this, according to the law of the Ordinances of Kingship,[11] it was once more proclaimed, in front of those assembled within the precincts of the church, that Queen Zawditu sitting on her father's throne was assuming her reign and I was becoming[12] Crown Prince and Regent Plenipotentiary.

Eight days later, on 11th Yäkatit (= 18th February), Ras Waldä Giyorgis was crowned by Queen Zawditu and proclaimed Negus of Gondar.[13] For the sake of his kingship, authority over the Tigre province was added for his enhancement.

In making once again proper balances and adjustments for provincial appointments and demotions, We gave to Ras Wale his erstwhile governorate of Yäjju;[14] to his son, Ras Gugsa[15] (Wale), the Sayent[16] region; and to Ras Abatä the seven tribes[17] of Wallo, Negus Mika'el's former governorate.

---

[8] 1887–1960. Grandson of Emperor Yohannes IV and father of H.H. Ras Mängäsha Seyum; governor-general of the Tigre province. Heruy, 24. Photo on p. 140 of Käbbädä Täsämma; details in *JES*, VII, 2, 225.

[9] This is probably a reference mainly to the World War then at its height.

[10] *Guida*, 486–7. Architectural details *ibidem*.

[11] For the *ser'atä negs*, see Guidi, *Letteratura*, 114–15.

[12] The unequal grammatical treatment of ዐውግዝ᎑ፎውኅ ፣ and ዐውሥኔ ፣ is puzzling.

[13] *Guida*, 350 ff.; map 368–9; formerly capital of Ethiopia and one of the great historic cities of the Empire.

[14] *Guida*, 316; the principal town is Waldia (map 304–5); de Coppet (Atlas, IV).

[15] Heruy, 95. Son of Ras Wale and nephew of Empress Taitu; husband of Queen Zawditu. *JES*, VII, 2, 286. For his later history see chapter 25 below.

[16] *Guida*, 394; de Coppet, 55 (5): Region between the Bäshello and Abbay rivers (Atlas, IV).

[17] The Wallo are traditionally held to be made up of seven tribes or 'houses' (*säbat bet*); cf. Huntingford, *Galla*, 14.

When Ledj Iyasu heard of the appointments and dismissals that had been made, he hurried down from Magdala[18] and marched to Yäjju; as the news reached us that he had clashed with Ras Wale's (younger) son, Dejazmatch Amäde,[19] defeating and capturing him, it became clear to us that henceforth there could be no peace or security unless Ledj Iyasu were seized. We, therefore, arranged for a large army, under the command of Our War Minister, Fitawrari Habtä Giyorgis, to proceed to Wallo, to search strenuously for Ledj Iyasu and to capture him.

When Fitawrari Habtä Giyorgis reached Wallo, he heard that Ledj Iyasu was collecting an army while roaming the country here and there; he then took the city of Dessie[20] and began waiting for Ledj Iyasu there. The principal commanders with Fitawrari Habtä Giyorgis were Ras Abatä and Ras Kassa; and with them were Dejazmatch Käbbädä Täsämma[21] and Dejazmatch Haylä Maryam Lämma as well as Dejazmatch Mäkuriya Gärmame and other military commanders.

After Ledj Iyasu had collected a sizable army, he appointed his father's army commanders, i.e. Ras Yemär[22] as commander in chief and Fitawrari Serah Bezu[23] as deputy commander. On 21st Nähase 1909 (= 27th August 1917), early in the morning, he launched an attack, joined battle, and fierce fighting took place. Fitawrari Habtä Giyorgis, without leaving his walled emplacement, resisted vigorously and emerged victorious, while Ras Yemär was captured. But Fitawrari Serah Bezu died in the battle. When Ledj Iyasu heard of the capture of Ras Yemär and of the death of Serah Bezu, he escaped galloping off on his horse quite alone and made for the countryside. The news of the victory was transmitted by wire the same day, and there was great rejoicing at Addis Ababa. But since in this world joy and sadness

[18] *Guida*, 394–5; *The Ethiopians*, 17–18, 80–5. Tewodros' fortress and the destination of Napier's expedition.
[19] de Coppet, 623; *JES*, VII, 2, 246. Governor of Yäjju. Died 1919.
[20] *Guida*, 395–402; capital of Wallo province.
[21] See Pankhurst, 113. Not to be confused with the author of የታሪክ ፡ ማስታ ወሻ ። The son of Ras Täsämma.
[22] Ras Yemär Ali, one of Negus Mika'el's principal army commanders. After the battle of Sägäle, he first fled to Magdala but was eventually captured and taken to Addis Ababa as a prisoner. Heruy, 80–1; *JES*, VII, 2, 273.
[23] Serah Bezu Gäbre, another major army commander in the service of Negus Mika'el. Eventually killed in battle in 1917/18. Heruy, 22–3; *JES*, VII, 2, 225.

are mixed, Ras Abatä, who had been ill for some time, rose on the day of the battle, refusing to stay in bed in his tent, and spent the day fighting; as a consequence his illness became worse, and on 6th Teqemt 1910 (= 16th October 1917) he died. When the death announcement reached us there was great mourning. We arranged for his body to be taken to Däbrä Libanos, went down there Ourselves and had him buried with high honours. As a memorial We caused his sword to be buried with his body.

CHAPTER 9

About the dismissal of ministers and the outbreak of an influenza epidemic

ABOUT ten years had elapsed since ministers[1] were (first) appointed. In any event, since the people as a whole were very incensed about the ministers' negligence to carry on equitably the business of government and about the gradual deterioration of every aspect of the work, they rose up in league with each other and indicated that the ministers should be changed for the good of the people. But as it had not hitherto been customary for the authority of the people to intervene in the appointment and dismissal of ministers, We argued on their behalf to the best of Our ability by refusing to dismiss them. In thinking to calm matters, We arranged for the ministers to depart for the time being. Until new ministers could be selected and appointed, the entire work had to be carried out on Our responsibility alone, and this caused great fatigue to Us.

After this, from the 1st Hedar to the 30th (= 10th November–9th December), there broke out at Addis Ababa and in all the other provinces of Ethiopia an influenza epidemic, and in the city of Addis Ababa alone more than 10,000 people died. But I, after I had fallen gravely ill, was spared from death by God's goodness.

The great war that had raged in Europe came to an end in this year, and the Germans and the Turks were defeated by France,

---

[1] Cf. de Coppet, 527–8; Sandford, 34; Mosley, 59; Clapham, 15. See also above, chapter 1, note (39).

England, Italy, and by the other allied governments. Ledj Iyasu had not at that time permitted us to help even by supplying provisions to our neighbours; and, although we had stood apart, the victors were our neighbours and we, therefore, decided to send envoys to them to congratulate them, adding some money for the aid of the wounded. The following were selected for this task:

To the French government: Dejazmatch Waldä Gäbr'el Bäshah[2] as principal, and included in his delegation were Dejazmatch Shebäshi Bäyan[3] and Nägadras Zäwgä.[4]

To England and the United States: Dejazmatch Nadäw[5] as principal, and included in his delegation were Ato Heruy Waldä Sellasse[6] and Käntiba Gäbru.[7]

To the Italian government: Dejazmatch Getatchäw Abatä as principal, and included in his delegation were Fitawrari Mängäsha Webe[8] and Azaj Dägäfe.[9]

They departed from Addis Ababa in April–May (1919) and returned when they had concluded the business for which they had been sent.

[2] 1850–1935. Held high offices in provincial administration, as Minister of the Palace, and on missions abroad. Cf. Heruy, 70; *JES*, VII, 2, 266–7; Mérab, II, 78.

[3] A native of Wallo; a younger brother of Wayzäro Abetchiw, Menelik's wife and Empress Zawditu's mother. Cf. *JES*, VII, 2, 226; Käbbädä Täsämma, 159.

[4] Renowned for his knowledge of foreign languages. Cf. Heruy, 79; *JES*, VII, 2, 272.

[5] Nadäw Abba Wallo. Prominent already during Menelik's reign; later on created Ras. Died 1929. Cf. Heruy, 47; *JES*, VII, 2, 245.

[6] 1898–1938. Emperor Haile Sellassie's future Foreign Minister and a major figure in Amharic literature. Cf. Gérard, 287–94; *BSOAS*, 1972, 233 ff.

[7] Gäbru Dästa (1855–1950). Cf. Bairu Tafla's valuable article in *JES*, VII, 2, 22–31; also *ibid.*, 284; Heruy, 94; *BSOAS*, 1972, 247. Gäbru had a foreign education, had travelled abroad widely on a number of missions, served as *Käntiba* of Gondar, and was an author as well.

[8] Later Bitwaddäd. 1895–1961. President of the tribunal for the freeing of slaves. Ethiopian Ambassador at Rome. After liberation held a number of ministerial appointments. President of the Senate. *JES*, VII, 2, 218; Käbbädä Täsämma, 44, 55, 64.

[9] See de Coppet, 615, fig. 94, where Azaj Dägäfe is described as Minister of Agriculture (on his seal).

CHAPTER 10

About Ledj Iyasu's arrest
in Tigre

LEDJ IYASU, having fought at Dessie with our War Minister, Fitawrari Habtä Giyorgis, and having been defeated, had escaped into the Aussa[1] desert; when he had stayed there for about two years—wandering to and fro—he emerged from the desert and was rumoured to have gone to a place called Qebsya.[2]

The governor of Tigre, Ras Seyum, had for a time tried to make peace with him (Ledj Iyasu). But as it was extremely difficult to say: 'Give up the notion of kingship and crown, and let someone else take them!', he abandoned reconciliation and made him leave his governorate. Thereupon he went away from Ras Seyum's domain and entered that of Ras Gugsa Araya.[3] When We heard of this, We transmitted orders to Ras Gugsa that he should search for him and capture him.

Ras Gugsa indicated as follows: 'I wish to undertake the search, but as Ledj Iyasu had secret conversations with Ras Seyum, I am afraid the latter might come and snatch him away; therefore, let some men come to me as his guards.' We therefore sent to Tigre, for the arrest of Ledj Iyasu, Ledj (later Ras) Dästa Damtäw as internal (personal) guard, and Dejazmatch Getatchäw and Dejazmatch Haylä Sellasse, Fitawrari Waqe, Dejatch Wassäne Terfe, and Dejatch Waldä Sellasse, so that they should act, together with Ras Gugsa, as external guards.

We were at Dessie, having travelled there departing from Addis Ababa on the Thursday after Easter, 27th Miyazya 1913 (= 5th May 1921), in order to listen on all sides. The governor of Gojjam, Ras Haylu, was summoned and we met as he entered

[1] Aussa: *Guida,* 344.
[2] Qəbsya, a monastery in the Seloa region of the Tigre province: Luca dei Sabelli, IV, 122–3; *Guida,* 325 (map 304–5).
[3] Käbbädä Täsämma, 52 (incl. photograph); Heruy, 94. Grandson of Emperor Yohannes. Died 1933. *JES,* VII, 2, 286. As a scion of the Tigrean dynasty and son of Ras Araya Yohannes (1870–88) he carried much prestige. See chapter 37 below.

Dessie in battle order. When Ras Gugsa informed Us of the arrest of Ledj Iyasu after a successful search, We ordered him to come to Dessie at once with the captive, and he brought him along and handed him over.

Ras Seyum was also summoned, and We took away from him the governorship of Adwa as a punishment for sending off Ledj Iyasu without arresting him and gave the governorship to Dejazmatch Gäbrä Sellasse. To Ras Gugsa We gave an additional governorship, on top of his previous one, for capturing and bringing in Ledj Iyasu. We made a number of adjustments in promotions and demotions and gave leave to Ras Haylu to return to Gojjam. We went back to Addis Ababa and got there on 12th Hamle (= 19 July 1921). We despatched Ledj Iyasu to Sällale, to Fitche,[4] and arranged that he should reside there guarded by Our faithful Ras Kassa.

As Ledj Iyasu had remained at liberty for about four years since his deposition in 1909 (= 1916), some idlers had not ceased causing trouble. But following Ledj Iyasu's arrest there had been great benefit to the country in the progressive spread of peace and security.

    [4] *Guida*, 378. An important market town—not far from Däbrä Libanos.

CHAPTER 11

About men who were an obstacle to the work of government by coming between Queen Zawditu and myself

THERE had existed between Queen Zawditu and my father, H.H. Ras Makonnen, a friendship of mutual confidence and consideration, over and above their relationship; and seeing me with my father's eye, she showed for me almost a mother's regard. Moreover, Ledj Iyasu had done us some sort of injustice intending to sadden and to offend both of us. He had forcibly evicted Queen Zawditu, lest she should dwell in her father's capital, Addis Ababa, and sent her to Falle[1] to stay there like a prisoner. Lest I should

    [1] N.W. of Addis Ababa—*Guida*, map, 496.

live in my father's city of Harar or in the capital, Addis Ababa, he had ordered me, by threat of force, to go to Kaffa, pretending it was by way of an appointment. But as God in his goodness had caused Ledj Iyasu to be deposed and us to be chosen, Queen Zawditu to Ethiopia's crown and throne and me as Ethiopia's Crown Prince and Regent Plenipotentiary, we marvelled at this and lived in amity and concord.

Previous to that, on 17th Mäskäräm 1909 (= 27th September 1916), the officers with the troops, the Archbishop and the Etchäge with the priests, being assembled together and proffering advice, while choosing the Queen for crown and throne and me for the succession to the throne and the regency plenipotentiary, had defined for us the following allocation of duties for our establishment and our work:

(1) That the Queen should take the honour of Crown and Throne and be called Queen of Queens;

(2) That I, being called Crown Prince of Ethiopia, should beyond that take the regency plenipotentiary and carry out in full all the work of government;

(3) That I, selecting the officers of the army, should appoint and dismiss them;

(4) That I, sitting in Court, should judge all the civil and criminal appeals which the judges had handed down in the first instance;

(5) That I should conclude by negotiations any matters whatsoever concerning relations with foreign governments.

After we had carried on, for about a year, undertaking in accord the work that had been assigned and given to us, some men who were seeking their own profit alone came between us and set about attempting to destroy our unity and to estrange us from each other. What they told the Queen as principal proof of their contention was that, if appointments and dismissals and all the other aspects of government remained in the hands of the Crown Prince, there would be no-one who would fear and respect the Queen, for it was necessary that the authority of the Queen should enter in the appointment of army officers and ministers, in the balancing of provincial governorships and the establishment of hereditary land-rights,[2] in the allocation of money and in all

2 i.e. *rest;* cf. *The Ethiopians*[2], 181; Hoben, *passim.*

similar matters. They sought to establish that judicial decisions which those who acted as judges had handed down should not, after they had come before me on appeal, be upset against them; they, therefore, told the Queen that it would be good if she sat in Court, pretending that it was for the sake of the Queen's honour. The object of all this was to see that old habits should not be changed and education not be developed.

Apart from this, everything I was doing I intended to be for the dignity of the realm and for the prosperity and welfare of the people—yet they were talking to the Queen by interpreting all this in a bad way and by dissimulating to her.

For example:

(1) When I granted a contract to a French company called Bayard,[2] thinking that it would be of great advantage to government and people if the minerals existing in Ethiopia were extracted by it from where they lie buried, they spread the rumour as if we had by this inflicted damage upon our country;

(2) If aeroplanes were introduced into our country, then it might be with the object of scaring off and frightening some idlers who were disturbing the country's security. When, therefore, I arranged for an aeroplane to arrive that had been purchased from France with the intention that it should expedite the turn-round of postal services and transport of people in each province, they spread it about that this was to destroy by 'plane the entire Queen's party and to deprive her by force of crown and throne. Moreover, I encountered great trouble in setting free the slaves.

As to these men who were speaking to the Queen under false pretences and coming between us, at times she would follow their counsel without examining its uselessness to the government—yet useful to themselves; hence I had great trouble in carrying out the work of government according to my plans. Nevertheless, some great noblemen, notably Ras Kassa, would speak to the Queen, as they were saddened at the work of government being frustrated by the fraudulent advice of a few men and at our remaining behind in civilization; they convinced her of the usefulness for us in carrying out the work of government according to the assignment we had been given when the Queen and I were first chosen; she therefore disregarded most of the advice tendered to her by others.

[2] I am unable to identify this company; see Pankhurst, chapter VI, particularly 235-6.

CHAPTER 12

About the improvement, by ordinance and proclamation, of internal administration and about the efforts to allow foreign civilization to enter Ethiopia

EVER since the 17th Mäskäräm 1909 (= 27th Sept. 1916), when I became Crown Prince of Ethiopia and Regent Plenipotentiary, until now in 1928 (= 1935), when this great danger came upon us by the violent activity which Italy unleashed against us, We did not cease to struggle, to the utmost extent possible, for everything that appeared to Us to render honour to the government and prosperity to the people. Although We appointed ministers for all the work, there was yet a great deal of thought and effort required of Us, since the ultimate responsibility was Ours.

Moreover, according to the custom of Ethiopian kings which has survived from antiquity, We sat in court two days in every week, Wednesday and Friday, as it was a principal aspect of Our work to adjudicate cases on appeal; thus We had no time for respite.

Apart from the minor chores which We carried out daily and apart from what We have forgotten because of the lapse of time, the following is some of the major work which We now remember:

(1) Prior to 1909 (= 1916) ministers had been appointed for all the work of government. But no proper allocation of duties in writing had been given to them for all their work; and as they did not have adequate office accommodation, it was in their private houses that they frequently carried on their ministerial business. But from 1913 (= 1920) onwards the operations of government were gradually straightened out as we imported from Europe regulations and books which were suitable for all their work and as we arranged for offices to be built for each of the ministers and provided them with some foreign advisers whom We assigned to their ministerial activities.

(2) The entire situation in the courts did not work out equitably; but from 1914 (= 1921) onwards We provided each court with written regulations and reference books, and consequently things gradually improved very much. Moreover, by virtue of Our causing to stop the cutting off of hands and feet, which had been laid down in the *Fetha Nagast*[1] and had been customary for a very long time, and of similar cruel punishments, Our whole people were very pleased.

(3) The custom as regards punishment which had persisted since ancient times was that, if a man had committed a criminal act, the judge had the power to do as he pleased: if the punishment was in terms of money he could decrease or increase the fine; if it was in terms of imprisonment he could shorten or lengthen the period of imprisonment, but there was no fixed punishment either in terms of fines or imprisonment. Thus, if the judge thought to benefit his friend by his judgment or to injure his enemy there was no law that would prevent him from doing so; consequently, if two men were caught having committed the same crime, the judge was able, if he so desired, to punish one and to let off the other without punishment.

But since 1923 (= 1930) We had established a criminal code which provided that, every act that was criminal having been laid down in detail, whoever had committed a certain crime would pay such and such a fine or be imprisoned for such and such a period; consequently, We saw to it that arrest and release according to the judge's whims ceased, i.e. that he could no longer benefit his friend and injure his enemy or impose fines as he pleased. Justice now took a road that had honour.

Again, after a murderer had been condemned to death, either by confessing to the murder or by witnesses testifying against him, he used to be handed over to the avenger (i.e. the victim's closest relative) who would, in front of the assembled people, kill him in any manner he wished, by battering him as he pleased and by increasing his anguish.

But now We have set up a special place where a murderer is to die and have arranged that the government executioner alone,

---

[1] The 'Legislation of the Kings', Ethiopia's historic law code; see *The Ethiopians*[3], 147. For the punishments here mentioned, cf. chapter 49 of the *Fetha Nagast*. See also Abba Paulos Tsadua, The *Fetha Nagast*, index under 'mutilation'.

without anyone seeing it, should kill him painlessly with a rifle that possesses a special aim.[2]

(4) With a view to having disputes settled in an improved manner when natives and foreigners were engaged in litigation, We caused, from 1913 (= 1920) onwards, special courts to be established and appointed judges expert in the law. As We assigned to the judges foreign advisers knowledgeable in law and justice, the administration of justice greatly improved. The adviser appointed for this task was a native of Switzerland, M. Auberson.[3] This grave accord[4] affecting the honour of the country had been contained in the treaty which the French envoy, M. Klobukowski, had made with Emperor Menelik in 1900 (= 1907-8).

(5) As there did not exist in Ethiopia anything like an adequate printing press[5] for books, all books had to be written by hand; consequently, all the people had great difficulty in finding and in reading books. The reason was that it was not possible to make available to everybody books written by hand because the price was very high.

From 1914 (= 1921-2) onwards We purchased from our private money two book printing presses,[6] and many books in Ge'ez and in Amharic (with interpretation) were printed; the entire people, therefore, derived much benefit from reading what they could buy at a low price. A weekly paper called 'Light and Peace'[7] and a monthly paper called 'Revealer of the Light'[8] were being printed by these presses. We gave the income of the printing houses as endowment to the Bet Sayda Hospital.[9]

We desired other printing presses to be established with government money, and when it was handed over to the Märha Tebäb[10] Press, many books and stationery for the work of each ministry as well as all similar matters were printed there. The weekly paper called 'Aymero'[11] was also printed at this press.

[2] A more detailed version in Mérab, III, 220 (note).

[3] Pankhurst, 64, 237; Maître Jacques Auberson; Sandford, 61.

[4] See above p. 37; Perham[2], 151: an accord designed to exempt Frenchmen and other foreigners from the application of Ethiopian legislation.

[5] Menelik's first printing press reached Ethiopia in 1906, but its capacity was very limited. See Pankhurst, 677.   [6] Pankhurst, 679-80.

[7] *Berhanenna Sälam*, Pankhurst, 679-80.   [8] *Käsate Berhan*, Pankhurst, 684.

[9] Pankhurst, 651 ff.; Wright, *Incunabula*, 21-2.

[10] Wright, *Incunabula*, 21.

[11] i.e. 'Knowledge', Ethiopia's first paper; Pankhurst, 677, 680, 684.

(6) Prior to 1915 (1922) there were no regulations as regards loans; anyone who possessed money might lend it at an interest rate of 20% to 30%, and when the debtor did not have the money to pay, he would be arraigned before a judge and would be handed over to the lender and be imprisoned until he paid his debt.

But from 1915 (= 1922/3) onwards We ordered that the interest rate should be 9%[12] and that anyone who accepted interest above that should pay a fine. If it turned out that the borrower did not have the money to pay and after it had been ascertained that he did not have cattle or hereditary land that could be sold by auction, We forbade by decree of 1916 (= 1923) that he be handed over to the lender.

(7) At Addis Ababa and in the other principal cities lighting in each house was by gas or tallow or wax candle, but there was no electric light.

The service, which had started to some extent in 1909 (= 1916–17), had by 1915 (= 1922–23) produced excellent electric light[13] in the Palace and in the offices of ministers, in the houses of the nobility and along the sides of the great Ras Makonnen Avenue,[14] in the major churches, and in the cities of Harar and Dire Dawa, and in the government buildings of Dessie and Däbrä Marqos.[15]

(8) Previously the sons of foreign kings and princes used not to come to Ethiopia.

But since 1916 (= 1923–4), because We had directed that foreign civilization should enter the country, the sons of foreign royalty and princes would come to Ethiopia for a visit. Chief among these were the Duke of Gloucester,[16] son of the English king, H.M. George V, the Swedish Crown Prince Gustaf Adolph,[17] the uncle of the Italian king, H.M. Victor Emmanuel, the Duke of Abruzzi,[18] the Savoy Prince da Udine.[19]

[12] Perham[2], 143.   [13] Pankhurst, 710.

[14] At that time leading from Entoto to the market; Mérab, II, 132.

[15] Capital of Gojjam: Guida, 374 ff.

[16] The Duke of Gloucester represented King George V at the coronation of Emperor Haile Sellassie I in November 1930.

[17] Later King of Sweden (Gustaf VI Adolph); he visited Ethiopia in January 1935 (Pankhurst, 714); see chapter 32 below. Lived 1882–1972; King since 1950.

[18] Louis Amadeus, Duke of Abruzzi, was, in fact, a first cousin of King Victor Emmanuel III. He was born in 1873 and led an expedition to the sources of the Webi Shebeli, 1928–9. See R. Soc. Geogr. Ital., L'Africa Orientale, 63–5; Luca dei Sabelli, IV, 200.

(9) Prior to 1915 (= 1922), apart from one motor car,[20] there were hardly any numbers of cars and lorries in Ethiopia. And since, from the Emperor downwards, it was by horse or by mule that the nobles as well as the people proceeded, and as the transport of goods and similar things was carried on beasts of burden, it took a long time to reach a planned destination.

But since 1915 (= 1922) We had seen to it that many cars, motor-cycles, bicycles, and lorries were imported; consequently, operations of all kinds were gradually accelerated.

(10) Up to 1915 (= 1922) the Star of Solomon and of Ethiopia were the only two kinds of medals. But now We caused a gold chain to be made for the Solomon order and it was to be awarded to foreign kings who had the rank corresponding to that of Emperor.

We also had an order with gold chain made called 'The Queen of Sheba Order' which is awarded to the Queen Consort and to foreign queens. In addition to this, We had orders of very high rank made, called The Menelik II and the Trinity Order, as well as a military medal and arts and science medals, in their various ranks; many people were awarded these orders.

(11) There were few people who could speak foreign languages because there was only one school, the Menelik II School,[21] at Addis Ababa [in which instruction in foreign languages was offered].

But since 1917 (= 1924) We established at Addis Ababa and the other major cities schools for instruction in foreign languages; in addition to the schools which existed before, We gave permission and aid to various missions[22] and, consequently, language schools were opened in each province. Furthermore, since many boys whom We had sent abroad had been properly educated, many of them were now able to work in the offices of the various ministries.

(12) As there was only one hospital, called the Menelik II Hospital,[23] in existence at Addis Ababa, it was not sufficient to protect the health of the entire population.

[19] The Prince of Udine was probably Ferdinand, principe da Udine, born 1884.

[20] Possibly a reference to the Imperial car; cf. T. R. Nicholson, *A toy for the Lion*, London 1965. See also Pankhurst, 290.

[21] It was opened in 1908; Pankhurst, 676.

[22] Pankhurst, 676.　　　　[23] It was opened in 1910; Pankhurst, 650.

But from 1915 (= 1922) onwards We had many hospitals established at Addis Ababa and the other major cities; We gave permission and financial aid to various missions and, as hospitals were being built, the health of many people began to be safe-guarded. Furthermore, We had arranged to have the Swedish physician, M. Hanner,[24] appointed to the hospital which We had named Bet Sayda and which We had established at Addis Ababa with Our private money; the hospital's name became well known and widely respected.

(13) In previous times, all men who were soldiers were so only by custom, but there was no military school.

But from 1911 (= 1918/19) onwards We established a military college[25] and saw to it that the soldiers should learn the entire military craft at the college. In addition to this We set up, under the auspices of Our son Makonnen, Duke of Harar,[26] a Boy Scouts[27] movement, so that boys should carry out their duties well.

(14) In the past there was only a flag with a lion and the three colours.[28]

But from 1920 (= 1927-8) onwards We commanded that the Emperor's daily and ceremonial flag, while unchanged in the three colours, should differ in the design of the lion and in the gold ornamentation; that the flag of the Queen and of the Crown Prince, of the army and the postal services as well as for ships should be distinct in ornamentation and shape, while unchanged in the three colours.

(15) At any time foreign national anthems could be heard in Ethiopia on a gramophone, but there was nothing that might be called Ethiopia's national anthem.

But now, since 1920 (= 1927-8), there has appeared a distinct Ethiopian national anthem and march Tafari, a military march;[29] it is to be heard at the Palace and any other appropriate place, when Ethiopian envoys go abroad and a reception or banquet is given in their honour.

[24] Dr. Kurt Hanner; Pankhurst, 651-2, 654. Del Boca, 39.

[25] Pankhurst, 562-3; Perham[2], 165.

[26] The Emperor's second son who was killed in a motor accident in 1957.

[27] Perham[2], 248; Pankhurst, 682.

[28] Green-yellow-red; Chojnacki, JES, I, 2 (1963), 49 ff.

[29] Hammerschmidt, Afrika und Übersee, 56 (1972-3), 238-9.

When foreign envoys come to Ethiopia, We arrange to have their national anthem played at a reception or banquet in their honour.

(16) Since 1900 (= 1907) there had been set up at Addis Ababa the Bank of Abyssinia[30] under the auspices of the National Bank of Egypt,[30] but apart from this one bank there was no other. The excess over and above the profit, stipulated in the treaty when this Bank of Abyssinia was set up, belonged exclusively to the company; consequently, the position was very difficult for the government and the people. Therefore, in 1920 (= 1927–8), We invested Our own private money in shares and made the nobles and the people share-holders as far as possible; We then bought the Bank of Abyssinia, having paid off its entire deficit and, consequently, having designated it the Bank of Ethiopia, there turned out to be great advantage in this move.

(17) Prior to 1920 (= 1927–8) the word aeroplane was not very well known in Ethiopia. But from 1920 (= 1927–8) onwards, some aeroplanes having been purchased, We brought them to Ethiopia;[31] and subsequently many difficulties for government and people were gradually alleviated.

(18) Since there were no Ethiopian Legations or Consulates in foreign countries, a special envoy had to be sent for every matter concerned with foreign governments. Or a foreign representative, having been specially delegated, had to deliver the message.[32] But since 1921 (1928/9) We ordered legations to be established with neighbouring governments and consulates with the far-off ones; all government business was, therefore, despatched without trouble.

(19) As the import of war materials[33] into Ethiopia had been prohibited, the number of worthless idlers[34] in each province increased.

[30] Pankhurst, 494 ff.
[31] See photographs at pp. 193 and 208 of Amharic edition; Pankhurst, 605–6.
[32] Some European powers had already established permanent missions at Addis Ababa in Menelik's post-Adwa Ethiopia, such as Britain, France, Italy, Germany, and Russia (Mérab, II, 95 ff.).
[33] Pankhurst, 605, sets out details of the arms trade and the various accords to control it.
[34] The term *waslata* is probably a euphemism for shiftas and other internal security risks.

But since, from 1920 (= 1927/8) onwards, it was permitted by treaty that We may purchase arms for the protection of the country, security and peace were established in Ethiopia by virtue or Our directions to destroy these faithless men by supplying arms to those protecting the country in each district. We cannot forget, at the time when it was permitted to import these war materials into Ethiopia, the objection of the Italian envoy arguing that the Ethiopian Government should not be allowed war planes. This proves that, having destroyed peace, the Italians have been planning and preparing for a long time to make war on Ethiopia.

(20) As it has been claimed that it is forbidden by law that bishops be appointed, chosen from among the priors who are natives of Ethiopia,[35] Ethiopians still remain in the position of not being appointed.

But since 1920 (= 1927/8) We have emphasized the large number of Ethiopia's provinces and the fact that all believers in Christ are not such by innate distinctness but by virtue of conduct; and because, after discussions, We had succeeded in making this point, We caused the appointment to the dignity of bishop of five priors[36] chosen from among Ethiopian nationals and assigned them to their dioceses.

(21) Previously there had not existed the custom to invite the despatch of special envoys from foreign governments to attend the coronation of the Emperor.

But now that We have seen to it that Ethiopia should progress on the path to ever higher civilization and that she should strengthen the ties of friendship with foreign governments— when, therefore, We were crowned Emperor on 23rd Teqemt 1923 (= 2nd Nov. 1930), the representatives of twelve governments came to Addis Ababa and honoured Our coronation. This proves Ethiopia's ascent to a higher level during Our time.

(22) The Emperor used to carry out, in accordance with his own wishes and directions, any sort of peaceful and military operations, as well as the administration of the country and anything else like this.

But now, on the 9th of Hamle 1923 (= 16th July, 1931), We promulgated a constitution, set up a parliament, appointed

[35] Y. Mara, 30; The Ethiopians[2], 103.

[36] Mara, 33. The terms of the 1929 agreement with the Holy Synod of Egypt are set out in Mara, 31 ff.

Senators and caused Deputies to be selected; We appointed presidents for these and directed that all the business of government should be carried out on the basis of advice (from parliament).[37]

(23) The Emperor or the nobles used to retain a large army-contingent while moving from one province to another; and the people were forced to produce provisions without payment, such as food, forage, and wood.[38]

But since 1923 (= 1930/1) We prohibited by proclamation that the peasants be forced to hand over any of their property, except voluntarily and against payment.

(24) As the number of country-districts, to which telephone and telegraph communications had been extended, was rather small, it took a long time to bring to an end the difficulties which the government, trade, and the people experienced in every province.

Later on, however, because We had directed that telephones be extended to every district and postal communications[39] be established, the difficulties for the government and the people were gradually greatly alleviated.

(25) The places at which criminals were being imprisoned used not to possess the cleanliness corresponding to health requirements.

But since 1925 (= 1932/3) We provided (having built it with Our private money) a house that possessed washing and clinical facilities, corresponding to health requirements, as well as instruction in reading and writing and manual work. The fettering of criminals by iron and chain fixed at their feet having ceased, We ordered that they be guarded by warders.

(26) Every man who possessed land, in addition to the taxes fixed and payable annually, used to be forced to pay additional money on various occasions and to be liable to forced labour[40] without pay.

---

[37] The text of the 1931 Constitution (superseded by the 1955 Constitution) was published at the time of its promulgation and was reprinted during the Second World War. See below chapters 29 and 30.

[38] Pankhurst, 550 ff.; 563 ff.   [39] Pankhurst, 337–41.

[40] Pankhurst, 511–12, where the iniquities of *corvée* obligations are described in detail.

But now, apart from the taxes fixed and payable once a year, We prohibited, by regulation and proclamation, anyone to work forced labour without pay or to render any other excess dues.[41]

(27) Needless to say, in Europe there existed wireless telegraphy; clearly audible wireless services were not known in Ethiopia.

But since 1924 (= 1931) We had given orders for wireless telegraphy[42] to be established at Addis Ababa and other major provinces; hence every aspect of government business, of trade and other matters was speedily accomplished, both inland and abroad. In 1928 (1935/6), at the time when we had to fight against Italy, the service was of great benefit.

(28) Prior to 1920 (= 1927/8) no civil or military uniform indicative of rank had been specified; hence everybody wore the same kind of uniform.

But later on, as We had directed that distinctions of rank be made in civil and military dress, the seniority of rank, civil or military, could be recognized by the uniform.

(29) For the past hundred years or so, if someone was robbed of money or of other possessions and chattels, there were men— from a family related by descent or by marriage—who claimed to be able to find the thief by giving a drink of medicine to a boy under the age of 15; these men used to live, wandering about at Addis Ababa and in all other districts, by seeking thieves, with the permission of the government, administering the medicine, and receiving payment from people who had lost money. They would claim to have found the thief if the boy, to whom they administered the medicine, went and entered a man's house and lay on the bed in a trance, or seized the man hitting him with his knee (or forcefully) and lay upon him. If things were done in this way, the man was seized by force by this procedure alone, without there being any indications or witnesses to the theft, and was under an obligation to make payment to the owner who had lost his property. Since deeds like these were being carried out by lies and fraud, they were in a position to hypnotize the *liebasha*[43] and to introduce him into the house of an innocent man who had not

[41] Pankhurst, 506.   [42] Pankhurst, 341, 606.
[43] The *liebasha* is an attempt to identify the perpetrator of a theft by a form of hypnosis. See *The Ethiopians*[3], 180; Walker, 157 ff.; Pollera, 127 ff.

stolen anyone's property or to arrest and oppress people by causing the boy to hit someone and to lie upon him in a trance.

But afterwards We gave orders for the *liebasha* method to cease, as We were convinced, after proper investigation, of the fact that it was impossible to find a thief by administering medicine, unless a theft like this had been subject to an examination by a judge or proper evidence or witnesses. Consequently, there was great rejoicing in every province, as We had protected the people from the iniquities that came upon them in this matter.

(30) Although in Ethiopia the Emperor was supreme, feudal rule had not ceased.

But from 1910 (= 1917/18) onwards, since We had become convinced that the rule of the landed gentry was detrimental to government and people, We stopped the landed gentry in Wallo, Gojjam, Bägemeder, Yäjju, Walläga, and Jimma and caused other servants of Our government to be selected and to be appointed.

(31) It had remained customary in Ethiopia for all provincial governors to be military chiefs, but there were no civil rulers. Therefore it was not the custom for the whole country to be under the authority of the government and to allocate taxes, collected by civilian officials, to the army and for other government business, but the governors used to pay the soldiers through their own officers and to give them quarters in their governorate.

As We were uneasy about abolishing all at once this custom which had persisted for a long time, thinking that it might provoke disturbances in the country, We arranged to demonstrate this mode of procedure and to make it acceptable in slow stages by placing under the authority of the (central) government the districts of Jijjiga, Tchärtchär, Bale,[44] Walläga, Säyo,[45] and Jimma; and We also saw to it, as an instructive example, that the revenues should be applied to the expenditure on the army and other government business.

(32) Because, until about 10 years ago, roads in the various provinces had not been properly made up, there was inevitably a great deal of wasted time and money in travelling from one region to another.

---

[44] Province in the S.E. of Ethiopia extending to the borders of Somalia. The capital is Goba. Cf. *The Ethiopians*[3], 191; *Guida*, 464–6.

[45] *Guida*, 509, region in the S.W. of Ethiopia, in the Gambela—Gore district.

But for the past 10 years, as We were convinced of the benefit of roads to government and people, We gave orders that the roads leading from Addis Ababa to the east and west, to the north and south, be properly maintained. Hence districts that could previously be reached in ten or fifteen days, can now be reached in two or three days by car and lorry.

CHAPTER 13

About Our pressing for Ethiopia's entry into the League of Nations

WHEN the great world war was over, it was feared that a similarly dreadful war might break out again in future; therefore, if (a league of nations having been established) a quarrel arose between two governments—the wilful waging of war having ceased—the matter about which the quarrel occurred would come before the league. After investigation, judgement would be given by the vote of the league, it having become manifest—in accordance with the importance of the conflict—that a certain government had given offence, while another government had been the victim of that offence. On 28th Säne 1911 (= 21 June 1919)[1] 27 governments had reached agreement and signed the treaty, concurring that it was improper for a strong government wilfully to attack a weak one or to impose financial sanctions on it, but that, if a government transgressed the wishes of the league, it would be the opponent of the entire assembly and they were all to rise up against it in opposition. The league's principal seat was in the Swiss city of Geneva. Some of the foreigners at Addis Ababa, having given Us information by way of friendship, had spoken to Us about the league and We had studied a great deal of the literature about it; consequently, We convened the great nobles and all Our ministers and delivered to them the following speech:

[1] This equation occurs, in this case, in the original and is not the translator's addition. The Versailles treaty was, in fact, signed on 28 June 1919. There is, therefore, a confusion of dates here: the Ethiopian date should read 21 Säne 1911, the figures having been inverted.

It would be of great benefit if Ethiopia were to enter the League of Nations. It is necessary, however, in future to improve gradually our entire machinery of government, and therefore We asked them to let Us know their present thoughts, lest we should experience difficulties in the League if we failed to improve our governmental procedures, once we had entered the League. The nobles and ministers declared unanimously that it was impossible to effect major improvements within one year but that it was their wish to improve the entire work of government year by year in slow stages, and therefore it was right for us to enter the League. Hence the question of our entry was decided.

After this We sent to Geneva a delegation with Our letter, on 1st Nähase 1914 (= 7th Aug. 1922),[2] consisting of Dejazmatch Nadäw as leader, Ato Heruy Waldä Sellasse and Ato Fasika[3] as aides, with instructions that they should sign in Our name as soon as our entry into the League had been granted.[4]

As Our envoys informed Us, there was for a time a little difficulty with regard to the application which the Ethiopian Government had presented in order to enter the League of Nations.[5] But later on the French delegate, M. de Jouvenel,[6] and the former French minister plenipotentiary in Ethiopia, M. Lagarde,[7] helped a great deal and, consequently, the British and Italian delegates declared their goodwill towards Ethiopia's entry into the League. The assembly, therefore, gave full approval, and Our envoys signed the accord and returned. There was great joy at Addis Ababa. The rejoicing was for no reason other than that We thought that the Covenant of the League would protect us from the sort of attack which Italy has now launched against us.

[2] I think the dates should read 1915 and 1923, respectively.

[3] Heruy, 101–2. Ato Fasika was educated at Jerusalem and in Egypt, largely at the expense of the Regent. On his return to Ethiopia he became consul at Jibuti.

[4] Ethiopia's admission to the League of Nations was voted at Geneva on 28 September 1923.

[5] Among a number of member states, reservations were expressed by Britain, Australia, Norway, and Switzerland, largely on the grounds that the application was premature. But after strong pleas by the French delegate, the decision to admit Ethiopia was adopted unanimously. A somewhat one-sided account of these negotiations may be found in Luca dei Sabelli, IV, 182–6.

[6] Luca dei Sabelli, IV, 184; Baer, 65.

[7] Pankhurst, 319–22, 328. Photograph in Amharic version, p. 81. Léonce Lagarde (1860–1936) had a life-long connexion with Ethiopia. Zewde, biographies; Marcus, 75.

CHAPTER 14

About Our efforts to free the slaves and the progressive improvement, year by year, in the struggle for their liberation

It had been customary in the past in Ethiopia, a part of Africa—just as it had been in Asia, Europe, and America—to sell and to buy slaves. Nevertheless, the number of those who arrived by way of sale and purchase was small, for the majority of slaves came through capture in war. The reason is that in Ethiopia, from the 15th to the 18th century,[1] the power of Muslims and pagans had prevailed against her, gradually and little by little, while many of her provinces rebelled against the reign of the Emperor, establishing their own nobility and looting the country. But later on the kings before Us, and in particular Emperor Menelik, conquered these provinces in battle to restore them as of old to the unity of Ethiopia; and as for all those who had come by way of capture in war, it had been the custom that they should live in slavery to their captor—in accordance with ancient usage. Nevertheless, those who had come as prisoners of war were scarcely distinguishable in appearance (except for a few) from other Ethiopians, and therefore it is very difficult to identify them as slaves. Thus the slavery of some was in name only, but in their mode of living they were not much different from their captors. They were able to purchase and to sell *rest* (hereditary land ownership) or, like other people, to have *rest* rights established by the government, to attain officer's or ministerial rank in government service, or in the service of the Church the rank of deacon, priest, monk, or priorship of a monastic order or the deanship of a cathedral.[2]

As they were indistinguishable in appearance and mode of life, they could even be married to their captor or his son or his

---

[1] I think the 16th to the 19th centuries are, in fact, referred to here.

[2] Pankhurst, 75. See his chapter III for many aspects of slavery in Ethiopia.

relations. When their captor died he might leave them *rest* and money in his will, having treated them like his children.

Again, as is the practice all over the world, there are many people in each province who are doing a day's work being taken in service for a wage. Yet, while the Italians knew all this, they spread it about that there were slaves rather than workers employed for a wage in some rich man's house. They spread these rumours exaggerating to the point of perjury.

The story which proves this is that of a rich man who was descended from a Galla[3] family and who lived in the Harar region. This man—by the abundance of his goodness and his conscience—said that it was more useful to give one's money to one's relatives than to give it to alien workers and thus collected the children of his brothers and sisters and relatives and employed them for wages.

But the Italian Consul at Harar, without knowing or examining all this, wrote a report to his government claiming that such and such possessed so many slaves; as this appeared to his government to be true, it preferred an indictment against us and presented it to the League of Nations.

Apart from the slaves who were set free by the proclamation and ordinance which We promulgated as regards the liberation of slaves, We were doing everything possible to set free the slaves by seeking several other opportunities. Thus the governor of the Beni Shangul, Sheikh Hojele,[4] told Us that in his country many slaves had gone free by virtue of the proclamation and ordinance; whereupon We said to him: 'You cannot expect to be praised for those who are set free on the basis of the proclamation and ordinance, but if you release them of your own free will, that will bring you credit.' As he told Us 'it is with my permission that so many slaves go free', he sent them subsequently to Addis Ababa and We informed him that We were arranging for them to receive instruction. When those slaves were sent to Addis Ababa, We gave orders that they should receive a certificate of their liberation. They immediately entered a military school and began to study.[5] Many of them were selected for musical education, and M. André Nicot,[6] whom We had recruited from Switzerland,

[3] The principal Cushitic population of Ethiopia constituting the major single component of the inhabitants of Ethiopia; cf. *The Ethiopians*[3], 39 ff.

[4] *Guida*, 512 (Scec Cogiali); Pankhurst, 237 (Hojali).

[5] Farago, 225 ff. (incl. photographs); Pankhurst, 679, 714; Harmsworth, 149.

taught them music. When they had completed their training, We provided them with a uniform and they lived in clean dwellings which We had constructed for them. All the foreign envoys and consuls at Addis Ababa knew about Our awarding to one of them, who had excelled in knowledge, the rank and uniform of a lieutenant [command of 100] and about Our decorating him with an order; they also knew that others with him had carried out properly their work of musicianship.

Everyone who saw and knew this *shanqella*[7] who had received the rank of lieutenant used to admire him, for his height was 2·10 meters. And now We hear that in Genbot 1928 (= May 1936), when the Italians entered Addis Ababa, they captured him and killed him.

But in view of what We have done for the emancipation of the slaves and for civilizing them through education, it is amazing that the Italians should make representations to the League of Nations to the effect that Sheikh Hojele had sent to the Emperor a special tribute of slaves!

As We have shown above, this slavery problem is recognized in the hearts of men as something that is not preordained by nature in terms of master and slave but had yet remained firmly established by custom; consequently, Emperors Theodore (Tewodros), Yohannes, and Menelik, who reigned in Ethiopia from 1845[8] to 1906 (= 1852/3 to 1913), had promulgated decrees against the sale and purchase of slaves in Ethiopia. But because at that time it was not customary to set up special offices for work of this kind, their intention remained unaccomplished, as it was impossible to observe and enforce the decree on account of the vastness of the country.

But now, since We accepted responsibility for the affairs of government as Regent Plenipotentiary of the Ethiopian realm, We followed on the foundations laid, as regards the liberation of slaves, by the three kings whose names have been mentioned above and let it be known by proclamation, on 22 Mägabit 1916 (= 31 March 1924), that in Ethiopia slaves were no longer to be sold or purchased.[9] We promoted an ordinance by which people

---

[6] This name appears as one word in the Amharic original. Nicot 'der Schweizer Kommandant der Bläserkapelle Haile Selassies' (Jenny, 240).

[7] The negroid population of parts of western Ethiopia; cf. *Guida*, 512; *The Ethiopians*[3], 43.   [8] This should, I think, read 1847 (= 1855).

[9] This proclamation was issued shortly before the Regent's visit to Europe in 1924 (Pankhurst, 114).

were to be punished, who in future were found to be selling or purchasing slaves, and by which slaves were to go free who had come by way of purchase or capture prior to the proclamation. At Addis Ababa and in other regions offices and courts were set up by which the proclamation and ordinance were to be enforced, and for this work We recruited an adviser from England, Mr. de Halpert;[10] as judges and secretaries were appointed and the entire work of administration progressively improved very greatly, many slaves were set free. Their number was above one hundred thousand. The number of those set free each year is to be found in the register of the League of Nations at Geneva.

Again, when in 1923 (= 1931) a delegation, sent by the British Anti-Slavery Society,[11] came to Addis Ababa, We informed them orally and in writing, after a great deal of discussion, that We shall see to it that within fifteen or, at most, twenty years from now all slaves would go free and that slavery would be totally eliminated from Ethiopia. But in any country a few offenders must always be expected, and if some men are found transgressing the proclamation that has been promulgated, all the foreign envoys know that We have punished them even with the death penalty. Therefore, Our conscience does not rebuke Us, for We have done unceasingly everything possible as regards the liberation of the slaves.

[10] Frank de Halpert (Perham[2], xiii). See also Pankhurst, 122.
[11] Pankhurst, 121-2. The British Anti-Slavery Society's delegation consisted of Lord Noel-Buxton, Lord Polwarth, and the Hon. Grizel Hepburne-Scott.

CHAPTER 15

About the honour of invitations extended to Us to visit Europe

ETHIOPIA is a realm which has lived steadfast in her independence for more than three millennia. But in the early sixteenth century Ahmad Grañ[1] emerged from the east of Ethiopia, from Zeila,[2] penetrated into central Ethiopia, and fought with Emperor Lebnä

[1] The 'left-handed', the great Muslim conqueror of the 16th century (*The Ethiopians*[3], 69 ff.).   [2] Or Adal (*The Ethiopians*[3], 64 ff.).

Dengel;[3] the latter struggled retreating towards northern Ethiopia, while Grañ set fire to all the palaces and churches; apart from a few books which had remained hidden in caves and islands, he burnt the majority of works of history and culture.[4]

Nevertheless, if anyone seeks to know Ethiopia's antiquity, there exist many books which discuss Ethiopian history written in Greek, Latin, Portuguese, and Arabic, and by reading these he will be able to inform himself of her great age. It is a fact that many people had come to Ethiopia, before the birth of our Lord, from Jerusalem, Greece, Arabia, and Egypt. After the birth of our Lord, from the fifteenth century to the eighteenth, visits by some foreigners to Ethiopia were fairly continuous [the reference is again no doubt to the 16th–19th cent.].

It is only in this[5] 19th century that the Italians have begun to cast their eyes upon Ethiopia.

There are many who went abroad on the part of the Ethiopian clergy. On the part of the government, however, my father H.H. Ras Makonnen had gone to Italy in 1881 (= 1888/9) and to England during the reign of H.M. King Edward VII in 1894 (= 1902). In the same year he had visited France *en route*. Other leaders had gone on missions to Germany, Russia, France, and Turkey.

Since for this reason Ethiopia had become known throughout Europe and since Emperor Menelik had concluded treaties of friendship and commerce with various governments, the countries mentioned above had begun to establish consulates and legations at Addis Ababa on account of the many foreign traders and travellers arriving in Ethiopia.

Later, in 1909 (= 1916), when Queen Zawditu sat on the throne, she being without son and heir, I was chosen, by the will of God and by the wish of the people, as Crown Prince and Regent Plenipotentiary of the Ethiopian realm; and, consequently, I gave full expression to the desire that the friendship with European governments, begun in Emperor Menelik's time, be progressively widened and strengthened to the utmost. Because the European governments had heard from their envoys at Addis Ababa and had become convinced of the fact that this my desire

---

[3] Reigned 1508–40 (*The Ethiopians*[3], 68 ff.).

[4] See, however, *The Ethiopians*[3], 144.

[5] This demonstrative pronoun is clearly inappropriate.

was real and true, they extended to Us the honour of an invitation to come to their respective countries to see the prosperity of their country, the good fortune and riches of their people, the beauty of their cities, and the wisdom and knowledge of their scholars. The first invitation was from the President of the French Council of Ministers, M. Poincaré;[6] this was followed by invitations from the King of the Belgians, H.M. Albert,[7] from the Italian king, H.M. Victor Emmanuel,[8] from the King of England and Emperor of India, H.M. George V,[9] from the King of Egypt, H.M. Fuad I,[10] from the President of the Greek Republic, Admiral Condouriotes,[11] and from the Duchess Charlotte of Luxembourg.[12]

As We have shown above, some nobles had gone to Europe on various missions, yet it was not customary for the Crown Prince and Regent Plenipotentiary of the Realm to go abroad; and, therefore, this distinguished invitation which the European governments had extended to Us was a strange thing for all the princes and nobles and the army; they had thus great difficulty over this matter. When We heard this, We gave instructions to have the princes and nobles convened in a great assembly. In the end, they all accepted the matter with pleasure, because We had convinced them that, by Our planning to go on extending our friendship with the governments of Europe, We were causing people to meet in trade and in work and getting to know each other as a sign of friendship; that for this main purpose kings and princes were being brought closer together in mutual direct discussions and that this would induce them to come and visit our country.

After the question of Our journey had come before the assembly and had been decided, We gave orders that everything necessary for Our travel be prepared. We gave instructions that, while Our War Minister, Fitawrari Habtä Giyorgis, carried the principal responsibility for the affairs of the government, each minister was to be responsible for the work of his department and that all of them should report to H.M. Queen Zawditu on everything they had done.

---

[6] R. N. L. Poincaré (1860–1934), Prime Minister of France at various periods; President of the Republic 1913–20.   [7] Albert I, reigned 1909–1934.
[8] Victor Emmanuel III, reigned 1900–46.   [9] 1865–1936; reigned 1910–36.
[10] 1868–1936; Sultan 1917–22; thereafter King.
[11] Paul Condouriotes, born 1855, Regent of Greece, and from April 1924 President of the Greek Republic.   [12] Grand Duchess from 1919.

I had the hope and conviction that my journey to Europe would give me three benefits: (1) to see with my own eyes European civilization and the beauty of the cities of Paris, London, Rome, Brussels, Athens, and Cairo about which I had read in books, first at school and later on in office; (2) when returning to my country after my visit to Europe, I thought it would be possible to initiate some aspects of civilization I had observed with my own eyes, although it would be impossible to carry this out all at once and in full; (3) to find a sea-port; prior to Our journey We had received some encouragement from France and Italy as regards access to the sea.[13]

Afterwards, on Thursday,[14] 8th Miyazya 1916 (= 16th April 1924), We set out from Addis Ababa and went down to Jibuti.[15] Here are the names of the princes and nobles to whom it had been granted to accompany Us: Ras Haylu Täklä Haymanot, Ras Seyum Mängäsha, Dejazmatch Nadäw Abba Wallo, Dejazmatch Gässäsä Waldä Hanna,[16] Dejazmatch Gäbrä Sellasse Barya Gaber, Dejazmatch Mullugeta Yegäzu,[17] Dejazmatch Haylä Sellasse Abaynäh, Ligaba[18] Wädaje Webe,[19] Blatta Heruy Waldä Sellasse, Ledj Makonnen Endalkatchäw,[20] Dejazmatch Wand Bäwassän Kassa,[21] Ato Sahle Tsädalu.[22]

[13] Ethiopia was land-locked at that time: Eritrea, with the ports of Massawa and Assab, was an Italian colony, while Jibuti was (and remains) in French hands.
[14] 8th Miyazya 1916 = 16th April 1924 was, in fact, a Wednesday.
[15] Cf. chapter 7, footnote (28).
[16] Of Semien and Yäjju; nephew of Itege Taitu. Died 1926. Cf. Heruy, 88; JES, VII, 2, 279.
[17] Later Ras and War Minister. A relative of Emperor Menelik. At first Minister of Finance, later provincial governor. Killed at Hayo in the course of battle (1936). Cf. Heruy, 11; JES, VII, 2, 223; photograph in Käbbädä Täsämma, 85.
[18] Master of ceremonies; chamberlain.
[19] 1869–1938. Early in his life served in the Palace; later on promoted Dejazmatch. Captured Negus Mika'el in the battle of Sägäle. Subsequently Crown Prince Asfa Wassän's representative in Wallo. Died as a result of fall from his mule. Heruy, 76; JES, VII, 2, 269; photograph in Käbbädä Täsämma, 102.
[20] 1891–1963. Ras Bitwaddäd and Prime Minister of Ethiopia. Grew up in the Palace and was one of the first pupils in the French School. During the Italo-Ethiopian war fought on the Ogaden front. Spent the five years of exile in Jerusalem. After liberation served in the highest posts in the government. He was also a noted and prolific author. JES, VII, 2, 221; photograph in Käbbädä Täsämma, 411; obituary in The Times, 5/3/63.
[21] 1903–36. Eldest son of Ras Kassa. For many years governor (in his father's place) of Bägemeder at Däbrä Tabor. Continued the fight in the resistance after

When We reached Jibuti, the governor M. Julien received Us with honour, and after that, on 12th Miyazya (= 20th April), We embarked on the Messageries Maritimes Company's boat 'Porthos' and travelled to the Suez Canal.

As we reached the Suez Canal, an envoy of H.M. King Fuad arrived and transmitted to Us the King's greetings. The Patriarch Abuna Qerillos sent Abuna Yohannes, who became Patriarch later on,[23] and gave Us his blessing.

When We reached Kantara,[24] We travelled to Jerusalem on the special train which H.M. King Fuad had arranged for Us. At Jerusalem the British High Commissioner, Sir Herbert Samuel,[25] and the bishops of the various churches came to the railway station and did Us the honour of welcoming Us.

As by the chance of good fortune the festival of the Resurrection (Easter) was approaching, We thanked God for granting Us to see the light of the Easter festival. Afterwards, as We toured Jerusalem and its districts, We visited and kissed all the holy places, including Bethlehem where our Lord was born, Nazareth where he grew up, the Jordan in which he was baptized, Cana of Galilee[26] where he did miracles, the Sea of Tiberias where he taught, and the neighbouring Capernaum,[27] Beth-Saida,[28] Magdala,[29] as well as Hebron where Abraham, Isaac, and Jacob are buried. Although a beginning had been made in discussing the affairs of our sanctuary at Jerusalem with our Coptic fathers in faith, the matter had remained unresolved, and therefore We informed the Coptic Archbishop at Jerusalem, Abuna Timotewos,[30] in writing that he should persist pondering on Our proposals, for We had suggested that we should conclude the

the occupation of Ethiopia in 1936 and was killed in December of that year. *JES,* VII, 2, 268.

[22] Graduate of Menelik School. Served in Foreign Ministry. Spent some time in France about 1920. Heruy, 19; Pankhurst, 682. As Blattengeta Sahle he was in charge of Ministry of Education after coronation of Emperor Haile Sellassie.

[23] Abuna Qerillos, who died in 1927 at the age of 105, was succeeded as Patriarch by his secretary, Abuna Yohannes (Yohannes XIX, 113th Patriarch). Cf. Mara, 28–9.

[24] al-Kantara, 'the bridge', on the Suez Canal (Budge, *The Nile,* 385, 388).

[25] Later Viscount Samuel, the Liberal statesman, 1870–1963.

[26] St. John, 2 : 11.   [27] St. Matthew, 4 : 13.
[28] St. Mark, 8 : 22.   [29] St. Matthew, 15 : 39.
[30] See Abuna Philippos, *Know Jerusalem* (On the Patrimonial Rights Ethiopia has in the Holy Land), Addis Ababa 1972, p. 26.

matter, after friendly discussion, upon Our return from Europe. He wrote to Us the following reply: 'I have already made known your intentions to the Coptic community.'

Afterwards, as We had heard that the Greeks possessed an area of many chambers in Golgotha, We requested the Greek Orthodox Patriarch in Jerusalem, Abuna Demyanos,[31] through the intermediacy of Dr. Zervos, the Greek Consul General at Addis Ababa, that he should give one room to the Ethiopian monks as a patrimony for the celebration of holy mass. When he replied that they would give one room as patrimony in the Monastery of Abraham,[31] We said that We on Our part would assign a benefice to the Greek monastery in Ethiopia; after reaching agreement and accord on the proposal, We signed the following written convention:

'The Ethiopian Crown Prince and Regent Plenipotentiary, Tafari Makonnen, one one hand, in the name of the Ethiopian people, and Patriarch Demyanos of Jerusalem, on the other, in the name of the Greek Orthodox Community, have agreed and contracted as follows:[31]

First: His Beatitude Demyanos, in his capacity as Greek Orthodox Patriarch of Jerusalem and all Palestine, on the occasion of the visit of pilgrimage to Jerusalem of the Ethiopian Crown Prince and Regent Plenipotentiary, while desirous to manifest his great good intentions for the Ethiopian people and the staunch friendship which has existed for a long time between the Ethiopian people and the Holy Church in Jerusalem, has assigned to the Ethiopian people as outright patrimony a room in the Holy Monastery of Abraham near the Church of the Holy Sepulchre.

The length of the room is 18·70 metres. Its width is 8·95 metres, and its height 4·95 metres. The room, being the basement underneath the dining hall of the Fathers, has a strong vaulted ceiling;[32] its ancient door leads to the place where the Holy Cross was found. This room has been given for the requirements of the service of the Ethiopian clergy.

Second: This room is to be connected by a door to Deir el-Sultan.[33] It shall be the duty of the Ethiopians to have the opening

---

[31] *Op. cit.,* 24.

[32] The word ባራ ፡ appears after ቅስት ፡ in the version printed in *op. cit.,* 28 (Amharic text).

made. The Patriarch will extend his help so that this door be opened.

Third: The two front doors leading to Abraham's Monastery shall be closed, but the windows are not to be blocked.

Fourth: It is not permitted to sell, to exchange, or to mortgage this room or to assign it to any other purposes except to the service of the clergy mentioned above.

Fifth: Before this room is redecorated, it is necessary to inform the Patriarch. He will send a person expert in this kind of work.

Sixth: If someone else comes along laying claim to the room given to the Ethiopian community, H.B. the Patriarch accepts responsibility to argue the case.

As the Crown Prince of Ethiopia and Regent Plenipotentiary, H.H. Tafari Makonnen, desires that the friendship which exists between the Ethiopian people and the Patriarch be strengthened, he has granted permission that a representative of the Patriarch should permanently reside in Ethiopia, that the following gift be handed over and that the deed be inscribed in the (land) register in the name of the Patriarch in accordance with the custom of the country.

The gift is as follows:

(1) Five *gashas*[34] of arable land for the church and residence of the clergy, located no further from Addis Ababa than a day's journey;

(2) He will provide one *gasha* of land, for the building of the convent and the church, in the neighbourhood of Addis Ababa, in the Gulläle[35] or Shola[36] regions. These six gashas of land, it has been agreed, are not to be transferred for whatever reason to a non-orthodox community or a non-orthodox church.

Seventh: The two parties who have made these mutual gifts have caused this convention to be made out in two equal copies and have set their seals and signatures to it. Written in the holy city of Jerusalem on 16th Miyazya 1916 (= 24th April 1924).'[37]

[33] See the two sketch maps at the end of *op. cit.*; Cerulli, *Etiopi in Palestina*, II, 169 ff., 239 ff., *et passim*; Zander, *Israel and the Holy Places*, 213 ff.

[34] One *gasha* is equivalent to about 30–35 hectares = approx. 75 acres. Cf. Hoben, 213 ff.; see also Pankhurst, *JES*, VII, 1, 53.

[35] In the N.W. part of Addis Ababa (*Guida*, 483 and following map).

[36] In the eastern outskirts of Addis Ababa (see also Pankhurst, 291).

[37] The dates do not appear to be entirely accurate (those in Abuna Philippos' *Know Jerusalem* (footnote (30) above) are in some confusion: April 17th 1924–

But as it was not God's will, this treaty never came into force.[38]

After We had concluded Our business at Jerusalem, We went to Cairo by train on Miyazya 23rd (= 1st May 1924). At Cairo H.M. King Fuad received Us with honour at his palace. Our pleasure was exceedingly great when both of us expressed the wish in our discussions to go on in future developing the friendship which had remained firm between our two governments since ancient times.

On the next day the Patriarch, Abuna Qerillos, informed Us of his intention to hold mass and prayers in Our honour in the Church of St. Mark and We went to the church. The Patriarch, suffering from the weariness of old age,[39] was seated on his throne by the altar and gave Us his blessing. As the Churches of Egypt and Ethiopia were in a relationship of mother and child and because the Patriarch had for long had the desire and intention of coming to Ethiopia to see his children in faith, he spoke at length of his sadness at his continued inability to come on account of the distance, while at the same time revealing the fulfilment of his desire and thought at seeing, with his own eyes, Our arrival at Cairo today.

Afterwards, while We were in the church, the Patriarch entered the reception hall for guests at one side—We having brought him, in order to honour our father in faith, a golden crown and golden cross, a golden staff, a silk tunic embroidered with gold, and a cape. He was, therefore, waiting for Us wearing the crown and cape, holding the golden cross in his right hand and the golden staff in his left; he was thinking to please Us, although because of his great age and weariness he was not really capable; as We entered the hall from the Church he attempted to receive Us standing, but he was not able to do so. Although We were pleased in Our heart at seeing His Holiness in this dignity, We felt much grief at thinking of his old age and weariness.

The following are the sights which We visited during Our stay at Cairo and which have remained memorable to Us: the pyramids and the Sphinx, the great museum of antiquities, the

p. 29 of Amharic version, and p. 25 of English transl.), as on April 20th the Regent was still at Jibuti.
  [38] The reasons are set out in Zander, *op. cit.*, 216, and are connected with the mandatory government's anxiety not to infringe the *status quo*.
  [39] He was said to be 102 years old at the time (Mara, *loc. cit.*).

great schools and hospitals of the government and of the Copts, the old churches of early times, the antiquities of Luxor and the tomb of Tutankhamun which had been discovered at the excavations near-by, as well as great mosques and the famous Islamic college called Al-Azhar.[40] Subsequently, when We saw four students from Ethiopia, We were pleased as their teacher said that they would return to Ethiopia within two years upon conclusion of their studies.

From Cairo We went to Alexandria and paid homage at the tomb of St. Mark; We then saw the school at which they are teaching more than 4,000 boys and which had been instituted, near the Church, by Abuna Yohannes, the deputy Archbishop of the See of St. Mark. After this We visited Victoria College[41] which had been built at a place called Ramleh[42] near Alexandria and where some boys from Ethiopia were studying. The headmaster of the school, Mr. Reed, was like a father particularly to the boys from Ethiopia, and We had heard[43] of his gentle treatment and of his teaching; and among the boys there We met Sirak Heruy.[44] Our heart was touched with joy when We saw them face to face. The son of Ras Mullugeta, Asratä, and a boy called Gäbrä Mädhen Awwäqä had come with Us in order to study at this school, and We handed them over into the headmaster's care and trust.

[40] *Encyclopaedia of Islam*², 813 ff.

[41] *BSOAS*, XXXV, 2 (1972), 238; Perham², 248.

[42] On the eastern outskirts of Alexandria.

[43] 'We were hearing ...' Cohen, *Traité*, 177–8; *NÉ*, 174–5; Goldenberg, § 234.

[44] Later Blatta Sirak, son of the Foreign Minister Blattengeta Heruy; alumnus of Victoria College and Brasenose College, Oxford; writer, and translator of Dr. Johnson's *Rasselas*.

CHAPTER 16

About Our Journey from Alexandria
to Paris

ON the first of Genbot (= 9th May 1924) We embarked on a
boat called 'Cordillère',[1] and when the ship began its journey a
farewell salute was fired by cannon.

On the 6th of Genbot (= 14th May), when we had passed
Corsica and came within view of the great fortifications at
Toulon, a warship came to receive Us. From there until we
approached Marseilles, many aeroplanes were hovering in the air.
As five warships passed on the right and left of our ship, they
fired their guns.

As We disembarked from the ship, the Prefect of the district of
Marseilles and the Mayor of the city, together with many
officials, received Us. Among these We were very pleased to see
and to meet M. Lagarde who, since the days of my father H.H.
Ras Makonnen, had been the friend of Ethiopia and Ourselves and
had formerly been France's Envoy Extraordinary and Minister
Plenipotentiary in Ethiopia.

After We had rested a little in the Marseilles government
buildings, the officers of the warships came and took Us to sea
once more in order to show Us the warships. Thus We saw the
strength of the construction and the size of the guns and then
returned greatly impressed.

On the morrow, 8th Genbot (= 16th May), in the evening, We
departed by train for Paris; and when We reached Paris at 4.30 in
the morning (= 10.30 a.m.), the new President of the Republic,
H.E. M. Millerand,[2] and the Prime Minister, M. Poincaré, all the

---

[1] I am greatly obliged to my friend, Professor C. F. Beckingham, for checking
this information.

[2] Alexandre Millerand (1859–1943); President of the French Republic from
1920 until his resignation shortly after the elections on May 11th, 1924. He was,
therefore, scarcely the 'new' President; and, in fact, the Ethiopian Regent had the
misfortune to arrive at Paris in the middle of a major government and indeed

ministers in full, Marshal Foch[3] and many other generals received Us with great honour. It was in the Quai d'Orsay, in the palace of the Foreign Ministry, that quarters had been prepared for Us and, seated with the President in an automobile, we proceeded along the parade.

After We had rested a little in the palace, We went on a return visit to the President of the Republic at the Elysée Palace, and subsequently returned.

The programme had laid down that afterwards We should visit the Paris Municipality (Hôtel de Ville), and at the appointed hour We proceeded there. When We arrived, We found assembled there the President of the Republic and all the ministers, army officers, and the city's notables. When we entered the great hall, the Mayor (Président du Conseil Municipal), M. Juillard,[4] and the President of the municipal councillors made a speech of friendship, which greatly touched Our heart, and they expressed to Us their pleasure.

All the amazing things which We saw in Paris and its surroundings were very numerous. Of the many sights We saw during Our stay at Paris, the following are the principal ones: The tomb of Napoleon (Invalides), the airport and an aeroplane display, a tank parade and movement exercise, the Opéra, Notre Dame de Paris, the Palace of Justice, the Mint (this is the place where the coins were struck on which the effigy of Menelik II appears), the offices of the Légion d'honneur, the Eiffel Tower, the Palace of Versailles, the Palace of Fontainebleau, the Radio assembly hall in St. Elysée(?) [perhaps St. Assisse?], the artillery college and artillery range.

It was quite impossible to express in words, on account of the abundance of joy in Our heart, the pleasure We felt until the official visit ended, when We were hearing speeches of friendship which were delivered at receptions and banquets, beginning with the President of the Republic, H.E. M. Millerand, and including the Prime Minister, M. Poincaré, and other French authorities, and also when We inspected the various palaces which We have enumerated above.

constitutional crisis which, early in June, led to the resignation not only of Poincaré's government but of the President of the Republic himself.

[3] Ferdinand Foch (1851-1929), Marshal of France, and Generalissimo of the Allied Armies in 1918.

[4] Hippolyte Juillard, Préfet de la Seine.

When Our official visit was over, We thought of staying on here in Paris in order to have friendly discussions about some matters with the French Government and with the Franco-Ethiopian Railway Company;[5] and, secondly, as We were desirous to rest here in Paris on Our return at the conclusion of each of the official visits to the other governments who had done Us the honour of an invitation, We told Our friend, M. Lagarde, that he should seek and arrange for Us a rented rest-house. When he let us know of the readiness of a house on the outskirts of Paris, called 'Villa Camasterand'(?),[6] We went there now at the conclusion of the official visit and took up residence. As soon as it was known that the official days were over, the Ethiopian boys whom We had sent to France for their studies assembled and came to meet Us. Andarge Massai[7] who was among them made the following speech of thanks in the name of all of them:

'Your Highness! We feel pride in our heart when we read, and when we find it written by foreign historians, that our Ethiopian forefathers in ancient times excelled the whole world in wisdom and in strength, and that they were honoured and feared as they made their power known as far as the land of Egypt by establishing their cities in Meroe and Napata.

But as it is in the Ge'ez language that all our books in our country were written and as the skill of printing did not exist, it makes us very sad that, apart from a few scholars, the people as a whole do not know the history of the country.

But now, through Your goodness and Your endeavour, the whole world has been impressed by Your sending us abroad for study, thinking that Ethiopia will be civilized in wisdom and in knowledge as of old and that she will open her eyes; the whole world has been impressed by Your founding of schools at Addis Ababa and in other provinces, by Your establishing a printing press and causing ancient books, which had been written in Ge'ez, to be translated into Amharic and to be printed, as well as bringing good fortune to the people.

---

[5] Compagnie Chemin de Fer Franco-Ethiopien.
[6] See Makonnen Endalkatchew, የኢሳም ፡ ፉጫ ፡, 52.
[7] Now Ras Andargatchäw Massai, who married the Emperor's eldest daughter, Princess Tänagnä Warq. At one time the Emperor's Representative in Eritrea and holder of other senior positions.

We, Ethiopia's sons, remain unceasingly grateful to You because you have made us study, helping all those of us in difficulty, so that we should follow European civilization and should know Ethiopian history.

But now, the distinguished invitation which the European governments have extended to You, and not to any of the kings of Ethiopia in the past, has come because they know that under Your excellent guidance You will cause Ethiopia to be civilized; and Your arrival has made the name of Ethiopia heard all over the world.

Ethiopia has the duty to thank You, for her joy is not only for the present moment but will be lastingly transmitted from generation to generation. And we in Paris are convinced of our good fortune in seeing our three-coloured flag fluttering suspended on the masts. Therefore, the whole Ethiopian people, the dead ones in heaven, the living on earth, are in duty bound to give praise', he concluded speaking at length.

In support and encouragement of the speech which had been delivered, We reassured them in the following peroration:

'Our thought, as We are helping everybody to the best of our ability, is not only for the few of you here but for all the sons of Ethiopia who should have the opportunity of acquiring education and knowledge. We pray to God that He may grant you to serve your country Ethiopia by persevering in education and by acquiring wide knowledge. For the future, have courage, for We shall help you to the best of Our ability, so that you should not have any sort of financial difficulty until you finish your studies.' They expressed to Us their heartfelt joy at what We had said to them.

As the official visit ended and We were staying in the specially arranged accommodation, important Frenchmen, who had been friends of the Ethiopian government and in particular of H.H. my father as well as of myself, began to arrive and to pay Us visits. After this We requested an appointment with the Prime Minister, M. Poincaré, in order to discuss amicably several matters; and on the appointed day We went to the Foreign Ministry.

What We had intended to discuss was that the French should give us a free gateway to the sea at Jibuti, and prior to Our departure from Addis Ababa, as We informed the French Minister that this was a matter We particularly wished to discuss, some hope had been given to Us; consequently, if they agreed to do this, they should let us know what it was the French government wished to have in exchange for this from Us.

Secondly, the treaty of friendship between the Ethiopian and French governments, referred to as the Klobukowski treaty, and in particular the judicial matters laid down in paragraph 7, were extremely irksome to us and, without abrogating the treaty, the two governments, while maintaining its usefulness, might cause a few improvements to be effected.

When We informed M. Poincaré of these Our intentions, he gave Us his word that he would present Our plan to Parliament and that they would think about it in the most friendly possible manner.

CHAPTER 17

About Our journey from Paris to Brussels

THE Belgian Ambassador in Paris had informed Us that on 14th Genbot (= 22nd May) the King of the Belgians, H.M. Albert,[1] would officially receive Us, and therefore We departed from Paris towards evening and went to Brussels.

At the railway station H.M. King Albert, together with his ministers and his army officers, did Us the honour of an unforgettable welcome.

It was in a wing of the main palace building in which H.M. lived that quarters had been prepared for Us; We went there and rested a little. Afterwards he introduced to Us H.M. Queen Elizabeth and Prince Leopold, his crown prince who later on became king, and his daughter, Princess Marie José.[2]

At the banquet His Majesty assured Us of his complete desire that the firm friendship between the Belgian and Ethiopian governments should in future continue to grow.

[1] Albert I, 1875–1934.
[2] Later the wife of Crown Prince, subsequently King, Umberto of Italy.

Of the things We saw at Brussels and in other Belgian provinces during Our stay in the country, the following remain vividly in Our memory: The Brussels Municipality, horse racing, the Bank of Brussels, the Congo Museum, crop improvement and cattle breeding stations, Waterloo where Napoleon was defeated, the city of Ghent and its match factory, the city of Liége and its munitions factory, the city of Antwerp, the city of Maurage(?); We also saw coal mines and other similar industrial establishments.

FROM BRUSSELS TO LUXEMBOURG

The Grand-Duchess Charlotte of Luxembourg, when she heard of King Albert's invitation to Us to visit Brussels (still before Our departure from Addis Ababa) informed Us through the Belgian Minister at Addis Ababa, M. Gérard, that We should visit her country during Our journey, as Luxembourg was very near to Belgium. We had, therefore, accepted her invitation and now proceeded from Brussels to Luxembourg. At the railway station the Grand-Duchess' husband, Duke Felix,[3] received Us with a large guard of honour and after that took Us to the Palace. But it so happened that on the day We reached Luxembourg the Grand-Duchess gave birth to a son; she therefore informed Us by letter of her regret at being unable to sit next to Us at the luncheon party. We told Prince Felix that it would remain in Our heart as a remembrance of joy that on the day of Our arrival in Luxembourg the Grand-Duchess should give birth to a male child.

The Prince assured Us repeatedly of his pleasure at Our visit to Luxembourg, and after taking Our leave of the Grand-Duchess by message, We returned to Brussels.

As Our official visit to Brussels was completed, We took Our leave of the King and Queen on 23rd Genbot (= 31st May) and returned to Paris.

OUR JOURNEY TO STOCKHOLM, THE CAPITAL OF SWEDEN

Having come to Europe, We had the intention of visiting the countries of Europe as a whole, even though not officially. But because the time was approaching for Us to return to Our country, and although it was impossible to visit all the European countries, We made a firm resolve to visit at the same time the

[3] of Bourbon-Parma.

countries in Northern Europe which it was convenient for Us to inspect, i.e. Holland, Germany, and Sweden. But as We were planning to stay at Stockholm, the Swedish capital, for about three days, We informed the Swedish Minister in Paris; and after he had notified his government and obtained permission he arranged for everything on our journey to go smoothly.

Subsequently, on 29th Genbot (= 6th June) We departed from Paris and reached Amsterdam by way of Brussels and after seeing the Dutch cities of Rotterdam and the Hague.[4] As Our train stopped for about three hours at Amsterdam, We made a tour of inspection of the city by car. From there We travelled through the whole night and at dawn We reached the German harbour-city of Hamburg; after touring the town for about an hour We set out for Sweden. After crossing the water called North Sea[5] which lies between Germany and Sweden, We arrived at Stockholm on 1st Säne (= 8th June) at 3 o'clock in the morning (= 9 a.m.).

When we reached Stockholm, H.M. King Gustaf Adolph[6] had not yet returned from his country home where he had gone for vacation. We therefore put up at the Grand Hotel Royal.

On this day was Pentecost,[7] and, therefore, the Archbishop of Uppsala, Nathan Söderblom,[8] sent an envoy and told Us: 'Because of the feast of Paraclete (Pentecost) we shall be holding prayers and a sermon towards evening and we beg that it may be Your wish to attend.' We departed from Stockholm at 9 o'clock (= 3 p.m.) and reached Uppsala at 10 o'clock (= 4 p.m.). The provincial governor and the Archbishop received Us at the station. Up to the time when the prayers and sermon began We inspected the University of Uppsala and the Library. In the Library We were very pleased to see some Ge'ez and Amharic books.

When the hour of the prayers and the sermon came, We went to the church. The Archbishop, being at an elevated place,[9] read the appropriate extracts for Pentecost from the Bible and gave a long sermon. After this he spoke about Ethiopia as follows:

[4] The Hague appears here in the French form of La Haye.
[5] The reference is no doubt to the Baltic Sea.
[6] This is, in fact, King Gustaf V (1858-1950); reigned 1907-1950.
[7] The festival of Paraclete, the Holy Spirit.
[8] 1866-1931, Lutheran Archbishop of Uppsala and chief promoter of the 'Life and Work' Movement (see *Oxford Dictionary of the Christian Church*).
[9] Pulpits are not known in Ethiopian churches.

'It is a fact that Ethiopia accepted Christianity a long time prior to us. It is only after the steadfast Christians who live upon those heights of Africa that we Swedes, having accepted Christianity, became families and communities of Christ. And now it is an unforgettable experience for us to be hosts, with friendly greetings, to the Crown Prince of Ethiopia and Regent Plenipotentiary who has come from those elevated parts of Africa.' When he had finished speaking at length, my heart was touched with joy at his truly inspiring address, and I therefore replied as follows:

'Your Beatitude!

All the Christians in the world, although they may be divided in some minor matters, yet in essence there is no-one who does not know that there is one Christ only. In former times, on account of the geographical distance, Sweden and Ethiopia did not know each other even by reputation. But now, ever since some Swedes had begun to come to Ethiopia and had recounted in words the beauty of their country and demonstrated by their work the goodness of the people, many Ethiopians wish to see Sweden and to meet the people.

There are many who do not know Ethiopia's history and her acceptance of Christianity 1600 years ago. But you, knowing her history and by your kindness and sincerity acknowledging Ethiopia's acceptance of Christianity even before Sweden did so, have spoken with conviction; and, therefore, I wish to thank you in my own name and in that of the whole people of Ethiopia. Today, on this great day of Pentecost, having made the acquaintance of the Swedish people, I express the hope that this may be an omen of the progressive strengthening and widening of the friendship of the two realms.' When I had finished speaking, all the people assembled there, beginning with the Archbishop, expressed to Us their heartfelt pleasure.

We subsequently returned to Stockholm. Since Our visit to Stockholm was private and not official, We had not had any thought of meeting the King. But as soon as the King heard of Our arrival at Stockholm, he sent a message that it would give him pleasure if we could meet now that We had come to Stockholm. We accepted his unofficial invitation and went to the seaside palace called Tullgarn.[10] The King, together with his

[10] A royal residence south of Stockholm.

courtiers, was awaiting Us standing by the gate of the palace, and we met with warm affection and friendship. When We had rested a little in the great hall, a festive luncheon was served. After lunch we remained talking about the means by which the friendship between the two governments might progressively develop and by which the peoples of the two realms might get much closer to each other. Towards evening, about 5 o'clock, We returned to Stockholm.

Of what We saw at Stockholm and surroundings the following recollections remain in Our heart: the new telephone exchange with 80,000 lines, the iron industry, schools, hospitals, and Uppsala University library.

Afterwards, on the 6th of Säne (= 13th June), We set out from Stockholm, crossed the North Sea,[11] and when We reached the German city of Hamburg, We disembarked from the train and toured the city by car for about three hours; and on the following day, 7th Säne (= 14th June), We re-entered Paris.

[11] See note (5) above.

CHAPTER 18

About Our journey from Paris
to Rome

W E left Paris on 9th Säne (= 16th June) and reached Rome on the 11th (= 18th June). The King of Italy, H.M. Victor Emmanuel, and the leader of the government, Signor Mussolini, with a guard of army officers, received Us with honour at the railway station, thus causing much pleasure. It was in the Quirinale, previously the Pope's palace, in which His Majesty lived that accommodation had been prepared for Us; and We proceeded there.

When We appeared together with the King standing on the upper balcony to salute the people, all the crowd assembled in the square began shouting with one voice joyfully: 'Long live Italy! Long live Ethiopia! Long live H.H. Crown Prince Tafari!' (When they think of this today, how extraordinary must this appear to them?!).

At the banquet H.M. the King of Italy delivered the following speech:

'Your Highness!
It has given me great pleasure to welcome Your Highness to the city of Rome with sentiments of amity. Your arrival today recalls to me the visit, a long time ago,[1] of your father, H.H. Ras Makonnen. It is my sincere wish that the government, which God by his desire has given in your hands, may continue to prosper.

Your Highness' prudence has already done a great deal for the country's prosperity and expansion. Your visit to Italy now will, I believe, progressively strengthen the friendship and mutual benefit between the two governments.

The deeds of kindness which you did for Italy during the Great War will never be forgotten. We on our part have greatly assisted Ethiopia to enter the League of Nations.[2] Therefore the friendship which exists between the two governments will be of mutual benefit.' He then concluded by saying: 'I pray that God's blessing may descend upon Ethiopia.'

I then delivered the following speech:

'Your Majesty!
Having come all the way from Ethiopia, my joy is abundant in seeing Your Majesty, your beautiful country, and your beloved people. I am indeed fortunate in coming to Rome to bind together the ties of friendship between the two governments which were established a long time ago. I am very pleased about your recalling the name of my father, H.H. Ras Makonnen. All the people who heard my father tell of the glorious welcome given to him when he came to Italy during the reign of King Umberto, your father, were greatly impressed. And now that I have arrived here I am very pleased about the marvellous reception which Your Majesty has extended to me. Henceforth it is my entire intention to have our affection strengthened and our friendship extended, and I believe that Your Majesty's intention is likewise.'

We Ethiopians consider the speech of the king of a great country to be like a pledge given under oath, and the words spoken by H.M. the King of Italy (as cited here above) seemed to

---

[1] See chapter 1 (p. 15 above), note (23). Ras Makonnen's visit to Italy took place in 1889 when Victor Emmanuel was Crown Prince and aged 20.

[2] Mosley, 128–9; Luca dei Sabelli, IV, 182 ff.

Us to augur a stable peace and amity between the two governments; and it did not appear to Us a matter of deceit.

On 12 Säne (= 19th June) We paid a visit to the leader of the government, Signor Mussolini, having requested an appointment to discuss, in a friendly manner, a number of matters. The subject which We planned to discuss was concerned with the amicable granting to Ethiopia of a gateway to the northern parts of the country from the port of Assab³ which had originally been under Ethiopian rule and was now an Italian colony.

After we had met at the appointed hour, I said to him that it would give Us pleasure if he were willing to discuss the amicable cession to us by the Italian government of a part of the port of Assab as a free zone.⁴

After Signor Mussolini had listened attentively to this request, he said that he was willing to discuss the matter and that, after conversations with the Director of Political Affairs, Contarini,⁵ the latter would let me know the answer. Contarini having been summoned immediately, we were introduced to each other.

After We had had meetings and lengthy discussions with him (Contarini), he told me that he would report to Signor Mussolini everything that we had spoken about and that the reply would reach me tomorrow by the hands of Conte Colli;⁶ we then parted.

On the morrow, Conte Colli, the Italian Envoy Extraordinary and Minister Plenipotentiary in Ethiopia, came and submitted to Us a draft treaty, explaining that this was his government's proposal concerning my request as regards the port of Assab.⁷ The following is the text of the draft treaty:

First: Since it is the determined wish of the Italian Government to strengthen progressively the ties of friendship which exist

---

³ *Guida,* 338; Luca dei Sabelli, IV, 197. The nature of the proposed arrangement is described in these two works from the Italian point of view.

⁴ See also the entry 'Cora, Giuliano' in *Chi è dell'Eritrea,* p. 90.

⁵ Salvatore Contarini, Secretary General of the Ministry of Foreign Affairs (Kirkpatrick, *Mussolini,* 193).

⁶ Conte Giuseppe Colli di Felizzano (1870–1937), served in Eritrea and Ethiopia, some time Italian Minister at Addis Ababa. See *Chi è dell'Eritrea,* 87.

⁷ Cf. Luca dei Sabelli, IV, 197. The *convenzione stradale* as regards Assab, annexed to the 1928 Italo-Ethiopian Treaty of Friendship (text in *L'Africa Orientale,* I, 343-9), is *not* identical with—or even very close to—the draft text published here.

between the Italian and Ethiopian governments, and for the financial and political benefit and prosperity of Ethiopia, the Italian Government consigns to the Ethiopian Government, for a period of 99 years, an access point to the sea at Assab and a place suitable for a railway from the sea up to the Ethiopian frontier, as well as all the localities and houses which are the property of the Italian Government and are situated within the town which hitherto had been in the hands of the Italian Government. Until the period of this treaty expires, the Ethiopian Government has full sovereignty over the access point to the sea at Assab and over the road to the frontier which it has received from the Italian Government.

Second: Experts whom the Italian and Ethiopian governments will choose are to determine the boundaries in the surroundings of the sea-port of Assab, including the houses that have been built, and the ground required for the construction of the railway from the access point at Assab up to the Ethiopian frontier; and they shall determine the boundary, *in situ*, having regard to what is needed for access to the sea and for the trade of Assab.

Third: The Ethiopian Government, being very desirous to strengthen progressively the ties of friendship which exist between Italy and Ethiopia, will not give economic or political benefit to the citizens of any other government—except to Italian citizens— in the seaport and localities mentioned, as has been agreed in the treaty. All things being equal, precedence shall be accorded to Italian citizens. But the Ethiopian Government, if it wishes to employ people in the area, can do what it likes.

Fourth: If the Italian Government requires a place at which to deposit goods at the gateway to the sea at Assab, the Ethiopian Government will let it have a demarcated area.

Fifth: When Italian merchants cause merchandise to pass through the Assab free zone they shall pay customs duty at the same rate at which Ethiopian merchants have to pay.

Sixth: The Ethiopian Government shall assign the construction of the free maritime zone and of the railway from Assab to the Ethiopian frontier to Ethiopian and Italian companies. When these companies are established, the Ethiopians shall pay two parts of the money and the Italians one part. But if the Ethiopians are unable to raise two thirds of the money, then the two parties alone, without bringing in any foreigners, may form a company and pay the money half and half.

Seventh: If the Ethiopian Government in future concludes a maritime access treaty with another government, and if it finds a location or part thereof that is a free zone at whatever other maritime access point, and if it obtains there genuine advantages, then the Italian Government agrees, by redrawing this maritime access treaty, to extend the advantages for Ethiopia.

Assuming the Ethiopian Government concludes a maritime access treaty with another government and if that other government obtains advantages by the treaty, then the Italian Government may well derive benefit from redrawing this maritime access treaty.

Eighth: With regard to the entire question of frontier treaties previously concluded by the Ethiopian and Italian governments, the two parties agree that border problems be finally settled as soon as experts have been selected from both sides. Furthermore, the Ethiopian Government undertakes to assist to the utmost extent possible those Italian companies who had accepted the previous treaty obligations as regards agriculture, commerce, public works, and minerals, lest they should encounter difficulties.

Ninth: As regards the waters of the Juba[8] and Webi Shebeli[9] rivers, the Ethiopian Government enters into a contractual agreement not to shut off completely those waters preventing them from flowing to Italian Somaliland by offering their benefit to foreign interests—notwithstanding anything required for Ethiopia's own benefit.

Tenth: The Italian Government enters into treaty obligations not to demand any money from the Ethiopian Government for granting it a maritime access point at Assab and adequate ground for the construction of a railway to the Ethiopian frontier—together with all the houses and ground at Assab.

After We had studied this draft treaty, We became convinced of the need to inform the Council[10] upon Our return to Addis

[8] *Guida,* 585 and map *ibidem.*
[9] *Guida,* 463 (map 576), the major river in the horn of Africa.
[10] At that time, the Council, before the promulgation of the 1931 and 1955 Constitutions, was an informal body with no clearly defined powers (see Perham[2], 87–8).

Ababa; We therefore told Conte Colli to inform Signor Mussolini of this Our intention. But for a variety of reasons the draft treaty never came into force.

On 14th Säne (= 21st June) We had been given an appointment to visit the Pope of Rome, Pius XI, and at the appointed hour We met at the Vatican Palace. The Pope spoke expressing his pleasure at the fact that Catholic missions were now residing in Ethiopia in peace and security and that religious freedom was now permitted in Ethiopia, contrary to earlier practice. When we came to take leave of each other, he pronounced a prayer: 'May God bless the land of Ethiopia, its kings and its people.'

When We emerged from there, We entered the church of St. Peter and paid homage at the sepulchre; after We had seen the beauty of the church, We went to inspect the near-by monastery of St. Stephen which had been given to the Ethiopian monks. From the earliest times Ethiopian monks possessed a strong desire to see and to pay homage at Our Lord's sepulchre at Golgotha and the sepulchre of St. Peter and St. Paul at Rome; but when they came to Rome from Ethiopia, they had difficulty in finding lodgings, and it is said that when the Pope who reigned in 1464[11] saw their plight he gave them this monastery saying: 'This monastery of St. Stephen shall be a resting place for Ethiopian monks.'

As We toured every corner of the church in this monastery, We saw the hewn stones on which the names of the seven[12] Ethiopian monks had been incised. When We were seated in one of the rooms in the monastery, the seven Ethiopians who had come here to study approached and expressed their joy to Us by referring to the antiquity of Ethiopia and the strength of her kings and by rendering thanks to Us.

The following are some of the recollections that have remained in Our heart of what We saw at Rome and in the provinces during Our stay there: the Quirinale Palace, the mausoleum of the kings, the motor-cycle races, the Rome Municipality, the

---

[11] The Pope in question was Sixtus IV (1471–84); the year was probably 1481. It was Pope Paul III Farnese who assigned, between 1539 and 1548, the building (subsequently known as 'Santo Stefano dei Mori') to the Ethiopians. See Conti Rossini, *Storia*, 10; *Debre-Keddus Estifanos*, Città del Vaticano, 1971, 35-6.

[12] Until the completion of the present large building of the Pontificio Collegio Etiopico in 1930, the maximum number of students who could be accommodated in the old building was about seven or eight.

Vatican and the church of St. Peter, the convent of St. Stephen where Ethiopian boys are studying, the church of St. Paul and St. John, the church of Our Lady Mary and of Jesus, the palace of the ancient Caesars, the theatre in which the ancient Caesars made Christians fight with wild beasts and slaves fight each other, the Victor Emmanuel II Monument, the military parade at Centocelle,[13] the Rome museums, the cannon-firing at Bracciano,[14] the military hospital called Celio, the ships at Spezia, the city of Turin, the Fiat car factory, and the royal mausoleum at Turin.

When the days of the official visit were over, We thanked H.M. King Victor Emmanuel for the friendly reception he had arranged for Us, took Our leave, and returned to Paris on 25th Säne (= 2nd July).

[13] Is this the ancient Centum Cellae, now Cività Vecchia, the seaport 35 miles N.W. of Rome?
[14] A town and lake 25 miles N.W. of Rome.

CHAPTER 19

From Paris to London

ON 30th Säne (= 7th July) We set out from Paris and travelled to London. When We reached Calais, We boarded a British ship; and as We began the journey two warships, bedecked with the Ethiopian and British flags, sailed to the right and left of our boat. Having crossed the sea We reached Dover and a twenty-one gun salute was fired.

From Dover We travelled by train, and when We reached Victoria Railway Station in London the son of His Majesty King George (now himself king but at that time styled Duke of York), together with many officers and guards of honour, bade Us a distinguished welcome in the name of his father. From there We went to the residence which had been prepared for Us in a house called 'Albert Gate' near Hyde Park and Knightsbridge.

On the morrow, 1st Hamle (= 8th July), so H.H. the Duke of York informed Us, was to be the audience granted by His Majesty King George; and at the appointed hour We went to the meeting.

I delivered to His Majesty the following speech:

'Your Majesty!
It has given me great pleasure to see Your Majesty and Her
Majesty the Queen in your great capital of London which was
founded a long time ago. Your Majesty is aware that the firm
friendship between England and Ethiopia has been established for
a long time.

For the future it is the wish of Her Majesty Empress Zawditu as
well as my own that the friendship of the two governments
should progressively develop and strengthen, and We believe
that Your Majesty's intention and wish are likewise.

When my august father, H.H. Ras Makonnen, came to London
during the reign of your august father, King Edward VII, I was
greatly impressed when I heard him tell his officers about all the
acts of friendship which had been done unto him.

And I, his son, having come to London, derive great pleasure
from seeing Your Majesty, your honoured people, and your
beautiful capital, and this joy will remain in my heart as a constant
memory.

Your Majesty! I would assure Your Majesty of my heartfelt
wish that there may be long life in health for Your Majesty, Her
Majesty the Queen, and the entire Royal House, peace and
blessing for your people, prosperity and development for your
country.' When I had finished speaking, His Majesty replied with
the following speech:

'Your Highness!
I thank you from my heart, for I am exceedingly pleased
having heard the words of friendship which Your Highness has
now spoken. I and the Queen are very pleased at your safe arrival
in the capital of the British realm and at our meeting face to face.

I express the hope that the friendship which has existed between
the two governments for so long may by Your Highness' arrival
be progressively developed and strengthened in future.

I recall the visit of H.H. your father, Ras Makonnen, as representative of Emperor Menelik at the coronation of my father His
Majesty King Edward. I know full well that Ras Makonnen
possessed enduring thoughts of friendship for my country.
Likewise I do not doubt that the same thoughts will for ever be
with his son.

While Your Highness is here, arrangements have been made for you to see, without inconvenience, everything you may require to inspect in my country. Again, while you are with us and enjoying an agreeable and useful time, I hope that, when you return to your country, everything you have seen in England will remain a pleasant memory.

Now, in thanking Your Highness once again, I would assure you that it is my intention to consolidate our friendship. I would request Your Highness to transmit, upon your return to your country, my cordial and respectful greetings to Her Majesty Queen Zawditu. I express to you my wholehearted wish that the Ethiopian realm may have happiness and prosperity, blessings and development.' He thus concluded his speech.

We subsequently returned to Albert Gate and, about two hours later, His Majesty came to Albert Gate on a return visit.

On the 4th of Hamle (= 11th July) an appointment was arranged to discuss some governmental affairs with the Prime Minister, Mr. Ramsay MacDonald, and at the appointed hour we met at the Foreign Office.

After Mr. MacDonald had spoken at length about the disturbances which had occurred at the frontiers between the subjects of the two governments,[1] We replied to him as follows:

'The border settlement has been made on paper only, and the engineers selected by the governments of both sides according to the provisions of the treaty[2] have not delimited the frontiers by a visit on the spot and no marks have been put in the ground; this is the reason why Our subjects and yours have come to blows at the borders; it would, therefore, be better if in future we carried out what is required as soon as possible, i.e. determining the frontier

---

[1] The nature of these particular troubles is not specified, but we may assume that they were part of the then recurrent frictions along the Ethiopia-Sudan and Ethiopia-British Somaliland frontiers. See esp. Perham², 333, which refers to complaints by the Sudan Government in 1923 and which may well have been the cause of Mr. MacDonald's démarche.

[2] Again, the treaty referred to is not identified, but we may surmise that the Regent was thinking of the 1897 Treaty between Great Britain and Ethiopia regulating the eastern frontiers of Ethiopia (Edward Ullendorff in *RSE*, XXII, 1966-8, 116-34) and the 1902 Treaty with Britain designed to determine the frontiers between Ethiopia and the Sudan (Edward Ullendorff in *BSOAS*, XXX, 1967, 641-54).

and marking it properly.' We told him that there could be no doubt that, once this had been carried out, the two sides would observe their boundaries. Mr. MacDonald agreed with this proposal and said that he would arrange that the matter of the frontier determination be begun at once. When We got back, We saw to it that the work of border delimitation was carried out.

The second matter is concerned with the Lake Tana barrage.[3] Mr. MacDonald asked that the Ethiopian Government should grant permission to the British Government to construct the Lake Tana dam. We replied to him as follows:

We ourselves shall cause the Lake Tana barrage to be built; we can, however, talk about the setting up of a company. Once we had completed the construction of the dam, We told him that we would then lease the water to the Government of the Anglo-Egyptian Sudan.

We concluded by saying that we should transmit details to each other in writing, as we had agreed about the proposal in principle.

After this, having asked permission to point out some difficulties on our part, We submitted to him the following requests:

In the past, in Emperor Menelik's reign, a treaty had been concluded that the Ethiopian Government, having purchased the arms it considers necessary for itself, should not be impeded conveying those arms to the country.[4] But now, since the Great European War, We were prevented carrying arms which we had purchased, and We asked the Prime Minister to permit us the purchase and conveyance of arms as of old. He replied that the British Government were unable to resolve the matter on their own, unless they settled this position on the arms embargo in conjunction with the French and Italian Governments;[5] and that after consultation among the three governments about this they would let us know the answer.

[3] This scheme had been mooted on many occasions over a long period; see Cheesman, 4, 21, 161; Luca dei Sabelli, IV, 189 ff.; Perham[2], 8, 63, 389–90.

[4] Ullendorff, *RSE*, XXII (1966–8), 121, 130: article V of the 1897 Treaty between Great Britain and Ethiopia which expressly sanctions the transit of fire arms destined for the Emperor of Ethiopia, subject to the conditions of the 1890 Brussels Conference (to the provisions of which Ethiopia had acceded—Pankhurst, 599).

[5] A convention for the control of arms was signed in 1919 by Britain, France and Italy, and further restrictions were proposed in 1923 (Pankhurst, 605).

Secondly, We had experienced great difficulty because the Ethiopian Government did not possess a sea-port[6] which would bring about contact with foreign countries. It is a fact that skill and wealth are acquired when trade expands as one nation meets and encounters others by sea and by land. The entire object of the Ethiopian Government for the future is to get very close to foreign countries by undertaking the tasks of civilization. Indeed, our accession to the League of Nations last year proves our intention to work for civilization and to develop our country. Therefore, if the British Government were to give the Ethiopian Government a sea-port as patrimony, there would be eternal and unshakable friendship. Hence I said to the Prime Minister that it would give Us pleasure if he would let Us have a definite answer before Our departure from London.

Mr. MacDonald replied: 'I had not heard about this matter until now; I am not able to give you the answer immediately, since this has not been debated and determined by Parliament, and I on my own am not in a position to decide this. I shall, however, see to it that the matter be submitted to Parliament at the appropriate time, so that its advice can be obtained.'

On the same day the Archbishop of Canterbury, the Most Reverend Randall Davidson,[7] gave a dinner party for Us, and We left Albert Gate at seven o'clock[7a] to go to Lambeth Palace. After a very pleasant banquet in Our honour the Archbishop made the following speech:

'Your Highness!
It gives me very great pleasure to welcome Your Highness to Lambeth Palace which is the main centre of the English Church. From time to time I receive those who are the important representatives of the branches of the Church of Christ. But there has never before visited Lambeth anyone whose church stands, in terms of antiquity, in first place among the Christians of the world.

---

[6] Access to the sea was clearly prominent in the Regent's mind, for he referred to it in his discussions with the French (Jibuti, p. 93), Italian (Assab, p. 100), and British governments.

[7] 1848–1930.

[7a] The Amharic text appears to be faulty at this point, as it refers to a lunch party at 7 o'clock, Ethiopian time (= one o'clock, Europ. time) 'in the evening'.

Your Highness! Your Church has an ancient history of about 1600 years. Its beginnings approach the even earlier period of the apostles of Our Lord. Your Church has a history which is related to the time of Athanasius and his companions. Your Highness is not only holding on to ancient traditions, but it is your glory to develop Christian civilization for the future and to spread the Christian scriptures among your people.

From your printing press issue not only ancient and modern religious books. But you yourself are an active participant in the work. The Ethiopian books which Your Highness has caused to be printed have an introduction by you: Everyone who studies the books of Chrysostom and of the monk Mar Yeshaq[8] will derive much benefit.

It is not to be doubted that the main object of your present journey is to acquaint yourself with the modern western world. Be it in spiritual or in secular terms, your visit is to all of us a perpetual joy. I feel assured that your country's spiritual and secular wellbeing is well placed in your hands and that there is due to you every possible assistance for your beneficent endeavours.'

He concluded by saying: 'With cordial friendship and high hopes we wish that everything for which you have come here may prosper.'

On the 5th of Hamle (= 12th July), as the official visit ended, We went to Buckingham Palace and took leave of H.M. the King and H.M. the Queen. During the farewell visit H.M. King George made the following speech:

'Your Highness has given me great pleasure by your visit to England to develop and strengthen the friendship of our two governments. Hence, so that you may have a constant memorial of your visit to London and of your meeting with us, we are returning to you the crown of Emperor Theodore[9] which the commander of the British army at the time of the Magdala campaign[10] had brought back.'

---

[8] Both of these works, dealing with homiletics and monastic life, respectively, were published by the Regent's newly established press in 1922/3 with prefaces by H.H. Ras Tafari (see S. Wright, *Incunabula*, 29; Guidi, *Letteratura*, 56–7; Cerulli, *Letteratura*[3], 140).   [9] Budge, II, 516–17.

[10] The British military expedition of 1867–8, under Sir Robert Napier, to free the European captives held by the Emperor Theodore at Magdala.

Although the capture of Emperor Theodore's crown and its removal to England in no way affected Ethiopia's independence, yet to have it said 'this crown was the crown of an Ethiopian Emperor' and to have it appear in a foreign country did not please me. Hence H.M. King George's gracious permission that this crown of Emperor Theodore now be returned to Ethiopia was, I was convinced, a great mark of friendship; and since I felt very pleased, I expressed to the king my profoundly sincere gratitude.

On 11th Hamle (= 18th July) We departed from London at 4 o'clock in the morning (= 10 a.m.) to visit Cambridge University. Before coming to London, while We were still at Rome, the Vice-Chancellor had asked Us in writing to be gracious enough to visit the University. After We had reached London, he informed Us of his proposal through the Foreign Office, and We, therefore, went to carry out this engagement.

After all the professors of the University had given Us a respectful welcome, the University's Vice-Chancellor approached and said: 'Your Highness! As we have heard of your initiative and perseverance in leading your country Ethiopia in wisdom and knowledge, we bestow upon you the honorary degree of Doctor of Law.'[11] He then gave me the appropriate robes.

Immediately afterwards they arranged for Us a great luncheon banquet. At the banquet the Vice-Chancellor, Dr. E. C. Pearce,[12] made the following speech:

'Your Highness!

The poet Homer says the Ethiopians are blameless. Herodotus says the Ethiopians are long-lived because they do not drink wine at all.

It is a fact that the Ethiopians refused to pay tribute to Cambyses and to the Persian king(s).[13] Subsequently, they turned back victoriously all who came to take their country by force.[14] Who

[11] The Cambridge degree in 1924 was the first of many honorary degrees bestowed upon the Emperor (cf. *Academic Honours of H.I.M. Haile Sellassie I*, Addis Ababa, 1964).

[12] Dr. Edmund Courtenay Pearce was Master of Corpus Christi College.

[13] In the text printed in *Academic Honours* (see note (11)), the word *negus* 'king' is omitted which corresponds to the original English version.

[14] The English original adds: 'a race very jealous of its freedom' which is rendered in the Amharic version published in *Academic Honours*, 13, as:

አሳባቸው ፡ ሁሉ ፡ ነጻነታቸው ፡ እንዳይነካ ፡ ነው ።

does not know that the Queen of Sheba, having heard of Solomon's fame, came by camel bearing spices, gold, and gems to try the king with riddles? Who does not know that she returned to her country to be the mother of all the kings? Who does not remember, as the centuries unfolded, their descent from David? Who does not know of their being of the family of Queen Candace?[15] All this proves the establishment of their Christianity over the whole of Ethiopia and their possession of an ancient faith over a long history.

A man who had studied at Christ's College in Cambridge University has, in recent years, revealed to the English people the literature and law books of Ethiopia.[16]

Today there is amongst us Tafari Makonnen, Ethiopia's Crown Prince. He follows in the footsteps of his ancestors and possesses knowledge exceeding that of orientals and Egyptians. He explores ancient and modern knowledge. He has studied all the ancient Christian traditions. He endeavours to acquire modern science. H.H. Tafari Makonnen is the first Ethiopian Crown Prince who has gone up in an aeroplane.

He has caused the books of John Chrysostom and of Mar Yeshaq[17] to be translated from Ge'ez into Amharic and had them printed at his own press. These books can be found in the Cambridge University Library. Furthermore, he has built a school for the children of Ethiopia.' He ended by saying: 'We therefore make known to all of you here Ethiopia's great Crown Prince and Regent, H.H. Tafari Makonnen, the hope of Ethiopia, who is descended from ancient kings.'

We replied with the following speech to that delivered by the University's Vice-Chancellor:

'It gives me great pleasure to visit Cambridge University where the fount of learning and wisdom for so many different peoples rises. I thank you for receiving me with manifestations of such great pleasure and cordial friendship. Moreover, my joy is immense when you speak of Ethiopia's history proving the existence since earliest times of her independence and the people's adherence to Christianity.

[15] *Ethiopia and the Bible*, 9–11.
[16] The reference is, of course, to Sir E. A. Wallis Budge (1857–1934).
[17] See note (8) above.

Perhaps there remain some people who do not know that the Ethiopian realm possesses great antiquity and that it was established a long time ago. But if they study Ethiopian history carefully, they will be able to convince themselves of the firm existence of the Ethiopian realm prior to the Greeks and the Romans. Our country was well known even at the time of David and Solomon.[18]

Since Ethiopia entered the League of Nations last year, it is appropriate for her to draw closer to the nations of Europe. As we have sent Ethiopian youths to study in Europe and in other countries and as they are very diligent in their studies, I hope that in a few years' time they will come to Cambridge for their university education and then serve their country when they return after graduation.' Upon completing my speech, we took our leave and returned to London.

Everything I saw in London was truly amazing. The following sights are a perpetual memory engraved in my heart: Buckingham Palace, the Tower of London, St. Thomas's Hospital, the Houses of Parliament, the Zoological Garden in which many different wild animals can be seen, the High Courts of Justice, St. Paul's Cathedral, the Wembley Exhibition, the Foreign Office, Lambeth Palace, the residence of the Archbishop of Canterbury, the British and Foreign Bible Society, the Bank of England, and Windsor Castle.

There remains with me a great admiration for the goodness of the people in terms of innate character and habit rather than political motivation. Afterwards, on 14th Hamle (= 21st July), We returned from London to Paris.

Subsequently, having come as far as Europe, I felt I could not return to my country without seeing Geneva where the League of Nations, on which world peace is founded, was established and of which we had become members. So, on 21st Hamle (= 28th July) I went from Paris to Geneva. But as this was the holiday season, the Secretary General was not there, and therefore the Secretaries who were there at the time received Us with pleasure and showed Us all the offices with their various departments. From there We visited the Swiss capital, Berne, and then returned to Paris.

While it was my determined wish to visit Berlin, the capital of Germany, privately and quite unofficially, I was sad at my

[18] The English version printed in *Academic Honours*, 16, is materially different.

inability to go to Berlin in view of the approach of the time at which I had to return to my country. I therefore arranged that Dejazmatch Haylä Sellasse, Sahle Tsädalu, and Täsfaye Tägägn,[19] among the officials who were with me, should go to Berlin, taking with them a letter of friendship and, after meeting the President, Marshal Hindenburg,[20] they were to return.

In the treaty with the Franco-Ethiopian Railway Company there were, in some passages, matters which at times gave rise to dispute; We, therefore, had friendly discussions and agreed, without difficulty, on nine paragraphs and had much pleasure in putting Our signature to it together with that of the President of the Company, M. Maxime Getten.

While We had indicated to M. Poincaré, the Foreign Minister,[21] during the period when We first came to Paris, the need to find a free access point to the sea at Jibuti, it so happened that there occurred ministerial changes in the presidency[22] and the Foreign Ministry. Yet M. Poincaré had given Us hope explaining that they would let Us have the reply at another time;[23] and when We asked that they should give Us the answer, as We were now returning to Our country, the following letter was written to Us by the Foreign Ministry:

---

[19] Later Ethiopian Ambassador to France. Cf. NÉ, XVI; Steer, Sealed and Delivered, 198.

[20] This is puzzling, for in the summer of 1924 Ebert was President of Germany, and Hindenburg did not become President till after Ebert's death in the spring of 1925.

[21] It has already been pointed out (note (2) in chapter 16) that the Regent's stay in France happened to coincide with an exceptionally difficult period in France, leading not only to the resignation of Poincaré's government but even to the withdrawal of the President of the Republic himself. When Ras Tafari arrived in May 1924, M. Millerand was President of the Republic and M. Poincaré Prime Minister (= President of the Council of Ministers) as well as Foreign Minister. At the time of these renewed negotiations (August 1924), M. Doumergue was President of the Republic and M. Herriot Prime Minister and Foreign Minister.

[22] Though there also occurred a change in the presidency of the Republic (note 21), the reference here is no doubt to that in the presidency of the Council of Ministers (= Prime Minister).

[23] See pp. 93–4 above. See, however, Luca dei Sabelli, IV, 186–7.

13th Nähase 1924[24]
Paris

To H.H. Tafari Makonnen, Crown Prince of Ethiopia and Regent Plenipotentiary.

'Your Highness!

Since Your Highness has asked for access to the sea for the purposes of your country's trade, it would have given me pleasure to convey to Your Highness, prior to your departure from here, the terms on which the governments of the two countries might reach agreement and to conclude the investigation of the matter based on the firm desire of the Government of the French Republic to grant to the Ethiopian Government the access which you have requested.

But with the delay of the President of the Council to return speedily from the country to which he has gone, and since the agreement to be concluded is a matter of importance, the whole Government of the French Republic must of necessity deliberate on the matter. Therefore the agreement has not yet been drafted. The matter which you have requested cannot fail to come about, so as to strengthen the friendship of the two governments and likewise the ties of amity which for long have historically bound the French Government to that of Ethiopia. I would respectfully inform Your Highness by declaring that, once the matter has again been urgently raised, it will conclude—with the firm desire that exists—in a written agreement.

The time has hitherto remained unpropitious to expedite the entire agreement upon the basis of the benefit which these two friendly and neighbouring governments attribute to it. But in the accord which will undoubtedly be concluded in future Your Highness will find a distinct remembrance—based on your visit to France—which justifies the trust you repose in the people's profound friendship. Nothing will be forgotten to bring about what is necessary, so that the recollection of the friendship and mutual benefit of the two countries will continue to flourish.

I would request Your Highness to make known, on our behalf, to the Empress of Ethiopia, H.M. Zawditu, the good wishes and goodwill which the Government of the French Republic cherishes for her and her people's prosperity.' (signed) René Renoult.

[24] This is the Gregorian date; hence 13th Nähase is likely to mean 13th August and not 19th August (this is clear also from the dates mentioned subsequently).

Although the draft agreement remained unwritten for the time being, yet We were glad when We read this letter, for its wording gave hope that an accord would be concluded within the near future. Since We were convinced that the time was approaching when We had to return to Our country, We gave orders that the new medal, called Menelik II medal, be struck and also that the Menelik II statue be constructed and sent to Addis Ababa, that the new stamps, with the effigy of Queen Zawditu and Ourselves, be printed, and that the books required for the ministerial departments be purchased.

CHAPTER 20

From Paris to Athens, the Greek capital

W E had not yet made the acquaintance of the new President of the French Republic, H.E. M. Doumergue,[1] and We therefore met by appointment at the Château de Rambouillet; at the same time We took Our leave, and on 7th Nähase (= 13th August) We set out for Marseilles on Our way to Athens. The French authorities and Our old friend, M. Lagarde, who escorted Us as far as Marseilles, were with Us.

From Marseilles We embarked on 9th Nähase (= 15th August) on a small ship called 'Amboise'. On the fourth day, when We reached the Greek harbour town of Piraeus, they received Us with great honour—aeroplanes hovering in the air, and in the sea warships firing their guns. When, proceeding from there, We reached the town of Phaleron, the Greek Prime Minister, H.E. Monsieur Sophoulis,[2] with ministers and army commanders, bade Us welcome. From there We travelled by train to Athens.

---

[1] M. Gaston Doumergue (1863–1937) had been elected on 13th June 1924 in succession to M. Millerand who had resigned. He was President of the Republic till 1931.

[2] Sophoulis (1890—) had only very recently become Prime Minister and lasted for a very short time only. Themistocles Sophoulis was Prime Minister twice after the Second World War.

At the railway station the President of the Republic, H.E. Admiral Condouriotes,[3] together with the country's dignitaries and foreign diplomats, received Us. We immediately went to the principal church at Athens where Archbishop Chrysostomos pronounced a prayer of blessing, and after that We proceeded to the palace where lodgings had been prepared for Us.

At the banquet in the evening, the President, Admiral Condouriotes, spoke of the friendship which had remained steadfast for a very long time between the two countries as well as of the closely knit history of the two peoples.

We on Our part told him that from time immemorial Athens had been the source of wisdom and knowledge, that We had discovered and read in our history of the goodness of the Greek people, and We declared Our intention henceforth to render assistance to all Greeks living in Ethiopia.

On the next day We visited the Acropolis, the ancient sanctuary of gods and idols. When We returned from there, We went to see the Academy and various museums. On the 13th Nähase[4] (= 19th August) they showed Us various displays of gymnastics at a place called the stadium as well as several kinds of military parades.

Towards evening We went to see Athens University, and the head of the University, Monsieur Dimetri Papapouleas, standing at an elevated place, made the following speech:

'Your Highness!

It is in the midst of Athens University that the soul of Greece is being revealed. This evening we are pleased to welcome the representative of a people tied to Greece by inseparable ties and by a friendship that is based on ancient historical traditions.

Your Highness' presence amongst us is apt to strengthen and to renew those memories of 1600 years.

Two Greeks, the sons of Meropius the merchant, Frumentius and Aedesius,[5] were taken prisoner at the Ethiopian seaboard and thus entered the country. They founded the Church of Ethiopia by teaching the country's inhabitants and by becoming apostles of the faith.

[3] Cf. chapter 15, note (11).
[4] If the Regent left Marseilles on 9th Nähase and reached Piraeus 'on the 4th day', this cannot have been before Nähase 12th; if 'on the next day' he visited the Acropolis, etc., the visit to the stadium cannot have been earlier than Nähase 14th.
[5] See Synaxarium for 26th Hamle (ed. Guidi), pp. 411 ff.

Your Highness, the affection which binds the two countries together began at that time. In the year 325[6] Athanasius, the great bishop of Christian Greece, bestowed at Alexandria the name of founder of the Church of Ethiopia upon Frumentius and did so with great glory. And he also anointed him bishop of the Ethiopian Church.

Again, in a different context, Heliodorus of Emesa[7] refers to these historical memories in the book of romance which he wrote. In this book he presents the Ethiopian king's daughter as beautiful and comely.

The Ethiopians were very well known to Homer and to Herodotus who refers to them in his history and to Strabo who speaks about them a great deal in his geography.[8] By virtue of these old traditions the kings of modern Ethiopia have always cultivated true friendship with Greece. Above all, Emperor Yohannes[9] and Emperor Menelik have uttered words of sincere affection for our country in exchanges of letters with the Greek Government.

Your Highness! Our brothers who live in your country are always telling us with feelings of deep gratitude of the welcome and friendship they have encountered among your people. This goes so far that it is virtually granted to them to be like brothers. We are very glad, therefore, to receive today as guest amongst us the representative of this people.

Greek writers, who have described the details of their journeys and whose books are read with benefit, have emphatically shown the extreme natural beauty of Ethiopia. They have described the different kinds of air currents, trees, and leaves as well as the beauty of the sun which, through its light, reveals the beauty of the country.

Your Highness! For a long time now the Greeks have considered everything that is good for your country as their own advantage. Each time they find an opportunity they affirm the

[6] The date of the Council of Nicaea.

[7] The third century writer of the romance *Aethiopica*, the oldest and arguably the best of the Greek romances that have come down to us. The daughter of the Queen of Ethiopia was born white through the effect of the sight of a marble statue upon the Queen during her pregnancy.

[8] Conti Rossini, *Storia*, 56 ff.; Ullendorff, *Ethiopia and the Bible*, 5.

[9] Reigned 1872–89 when he fell in the battle with the dervishes at Metemma. The last Tigrean Emperor. *The Ethiopians*[3], 85–7; Zewde, *Emperor Yohannes*.

thoughts of friendship which they have for the kings of Ethiopia and for the people.

This feeling does not only arise from the friendship which you have for us. What we have achieved in our past history and by our character is due to our respect for the supremeness of learning and complete love of freedom to the point of heroism. Therefore, it is not at all a strange thing for us to consolidate our friendship for the Ethiopian people through the study which our history affords us.

We are aware that Ethiopia's success in guarding her independence at all times arises from the mountains which have been given to her by nature and which separate her from all the other African countries. It is proper to say that Ethiopia has been the bastion of Christianity for more than a millennium among the savages and pagans in the arid desert. Homer said of the Ethiopians that they excelled above others.[10] Diodorus[11] speaks of their virtue. He admires their fight for their freedom.

At the time of Alexander the Great and his heirs Greek culture had entered Ethiopia and had opened a new road of civilization. It left written monuments (a map) which demonstrate its progress. The Ptolemies and the Byzantine kings desired the Ethiopian people to establish a basis and to extend their rule up to the Red Sea. When Byzantium fought with the Persians, it threw into the battle the might of the Ethiopians. Your Highness' country was a crossroads and meeting point of the civilized nations in the Mediterranean and Indian areas. Since the Greeks were at that time held in great honour in Ethiopia, the Ethiopian kings are said to have known the Greek language.

According[12] to those who have studied the history of the Ethiopian Church, in the fourth century this Church, strong in its faith, was doing everything that was necessary to enable the Christian religion to spread over all the distant lands in Africa. But the rise of Islam and its constant and progressive growth greatly weakened the strength of the Ethiopian people as Islam defeated, by the force of the sword, the countries in North Africa. But eventually, defending themselves with the heroism which derives from their nature, the Ethiopians overcame the might of

[10] This is probably a reference to the 'blameless Ethiopians' in Iliad, I, 423.

[11] Diodorus Siculus, 1st cent. B.C. Greek historian. Conti Rossini, *Storia,* 57–8.

[12] This sentence does not seem to construe properly in Amharic.

the Muslims. They built once again the Church of Aksum at the place to which the Muslims had set fire. It may be said that the rebuilding of this Church is a great good fortune and luck for Ethiopia.

By the intelligence of its kings and rulers since the last century, this country has once again taken the road of renewal. It is this road of renewal that is leading this beloved and courageous people towards national unity in equality.

The University of Athens, at this place where the leaders of the Greek people are assembled, greets the courageous ruler of the Ethiopian people, the son of Makonnen.' He concluded by saying:

'The Greek people request that you will accept their best wishes for the prosperity of the Ethiopian people as well as their firm resolve for a progressive strengthening of the ties of friendship which exist between the two nations.'

We were pleased to hear these words of friendship gleaned from ancient history and expressed Our profound gratitude; We then returned to the palace.

On the morrow We went to visit, together with Archbishop Chrysostomos and with other scholars very knowledgeable in history, the Areopagus where St. Paul instructed the Athenians. The place is in the vicinity of the Acropolis. The Archbishop spoke at length about the history of this locality, citing the Acts of the Apostles.[13]

We had, of course, frequently read in history-books of Athens as the fount of wisdom and learning and now We were glad to see it with Our own eyes.

Of all the things We had seen at Athens, the following are the main memories We have retained in Our heart:

The temples of gods and idols of the Acropolis, the Areopagus, the Academy and various museums, the Library, the University, the gymnastics displays and the military parade at the Stadium, the theatre of Herodes Atticus by the ruins of the Acropolis, and the fireworks projected into the air, by the seashore at Phaleron, spread out in the sky in the shape of the Ethiopian flag.

<hr>

[13] *Acts*, 17 : 19 ff.

CHAPTER 21

Returning from Athens
home to Ethiopia

SINCE it had been Our long-standing concern that the problem
which had arisen between us and our fathers in faith, the Copts, as
regards the place of our Jerusalem Convent, should be resolved in
a friendly manner, We had made written submissions to the
Archbishop at the time of Our visit to Jerusalem. He had given
Us the reply that he would reflect upon the matter, and We
therefore decided to go from Athens to Cairo in order to ascertain the outcome of the problem, in case he had perhaps been able
to consider it already. On the 15th Nähase (= 21st August) We
set out from Athens and travelled to Alexandria by a ship called
'Hesperia', for We meant to discuss this problem of our convent
at a meeting with the Patriarch, Abuna Qerillos.

From Alexandria We went to Cairo, and after We had met the
Patriarch, Abuna Qerillos, We were told that the deliberations
about the problem of Our Jerusalem Convent had not yet been
concluded by the counsellors of the synod, and therefore We felt
very distressed. But the time had definitely come for Us to return
home; consequently, We left someone behind who would
convey to Us the news, once he had heard the outcome of the
matter; We then informed the Patriarch of Our intention to
depart, took Our leave, and subsequently travelled to Suez. On
Nähase 21st (= 27th August), We embarked at Suez on a ship of
the Messageries Company called 'Chili' (?) and reached Jibuti on
Nähase 25th (= 31st August).

Dejazmatch (now Ras) Getatchäw and Qägnazmatch (now
Dejazmatch) Amde,[1] and Bäjerond Sahlä Dengel,[2] who had come
as emissaries from H.M. Queen Zawditu to welcome Us at
Jibuti, boarded the ship, and after meeting Us handed to Us a
letter from Her Majesty Queen Zawditu. Its text was as follows:

---

[1] See below chapter 36, footnote (4).
[2] Served in Emperor Menelik's household; later treasurer; died 1927/8.

The Lion of the Tribe of Judah has prevailed.[3]
Elect of God, Zawditu
Empress of Ethiopia

May it reach my son, H.H. Tafari Makonnen, Crown Prince of Ethiopia and Regent Plenipotentiary. How have you been? I, thanks be to God, am well.

While I was distressed about your toiling in strange and hot countries, when you were thinking only of our country's freedom, respect, and honour, I am now very pleased about your safe return. Thanks are due to God for your return, alive, to Ethiopia, your heritage, after visiting all the countries we had proposed. Moreover, as this your present journey to Europe was a first-time experience, we had been very anxious, but now, with your safe return, the entire Ethiopian people must be pleased. Having arrived thus in peace, may He grant that we may soon see each other with our own eyes. Dejazmatch Getatchäw, Bäjerond Sahlä Dengel, and Qägnazmatch Amde have come as our emissaries to welcome you.

Written at Addis Ababa on 19th Nähase 1916 (= 25th August 1924).

We departed from Jibuti on Nähase 26th (= 1st Sept.), paused for a day at Dire Dawa, and entered Addis Ababa on the 29th (= 4th Sept.).

At the railway station, the foreign diplomatic corps in full, Archbishop Abuna Mattewos together with the hierarchy, ministers and army officers, and the people of the city, pressed for space, were waiting and received Us with joy as the gun announcing Our arrival was fired.

When We entered the Palace, We presented to H.M. Queen Zawditu Our affectionate and respectful greetings; and afterwards We delivered the following speech:

Your Majesty!
When we explore Ethiopian history, the writings of great historians convincingly prove to us that Ethiopia has greater antiquity than most countries and that she was honoured for wisdom and learning.

Our *Kebra Nagast*[4] testifies that, when the Queen of Sheba went to Jerusalem to hear Solomon's wisdom, she presented to him various gifts she had brought. This proves to us Ethiopia's antiquity and her wisdom.

Again, the fact that our fathers, the kings of Ethiopia, having crossed the sea, were governing the Arab country called Yemen[5] demonstrates that, according to history, Ethiopia was a powerful nation.

But because wars with the pagans living all around Ethiopia developed from time to time to Ethiopia's detriment, she failed to find propitious opportunities to get markedly closer to foreign governments.

His Majesty, your father, the great Menelik II, together with the mighty ones who supported his throne, conquered once more all the territories that had been lost and made Ethiopia as far-flung as she had been in the past. He did everything possible to bring about a rapprochement with foreign governments.

His choice for this task, in the first place, of my father, H.H. Ras Makonnen, who was his brother[6] and servant, shows us that there was great mutual trust between the two.

And now, when Your Majesty was meaning to manifest to the whole world Ethiopia's independence, the whole world was impressed by your wish that I, your son,[7] should go to Europe and meet its kings and draw closer to them. You could not fail to have heard the news that on these occasions Ethiopia was greatly honoured and that Your Majesty's name was much praised.

I express the hope that henceforth Ethiopia, in educating and civilizing her sons, will attain as high a level as she had in her past. I have to inform you that the kings and presidents of Europe have requested that I should present to Your Majesty their greetings coupled with their gratitude.

After this the Tsähafe Te'ezaz,[8] on behalf of H.M. the Queen, read the following speech:

'Oh Crown Prince my son!

We took leave of each other with grief and tears when you left to meet the kings of Europe for the sake of the prosperity of our

[4] The Ethiopian national saga; cf. *The Ethiopians*[3], 138–9.
[5] *The Ethiopians*[3], 53–4.   [6] i.e. cousin.
[7] i.e. a reference to the filial relationship and affection as well as difference in age.
[8] 'Scribe of orders', secretary; Minister of the Pen.

country and the benefit of our people. But now that you have returned safely and I have seen your face, I present thanks to God. Let this day be blessed.

Although our country Ethiopia is ancient, it is true that she remained distant from the kings of foreign countries because for much of the time she was surrounded by pagans. But later, when my father Menelik II had concluded the conquest and pacification of the surrounding territories which his fathers had already initiated, he intended to draw closer to foreign governments. He therefore selected your father, Ras Makonnen, from among the princes and nobles and sent him to countries which he did not know. Ras Makonnen established friendly relations with their kings, carried out the wishes of Menelik II, and then returned home.

And you my trusted son went, like your father, to countries you did not know and patiently endured the turbulence of the sea and the heat of the sun, carrying out the plan which we had devised for the prosperity of our country and the good fortune of our people; you extended the friendship and affection of kings which had existed of old, and now I am very pleased about your return after carrying out my wishes.

Ethiopia presents her joyful thanks to God. Praise be to God, for all of you, princes and nobles, who travelled together have now safely returned without anyone of you missing.' He[9] concluded by saying: 'I beg our Creator that henceforth He should assist you to think about and to persevere in everything that is proper for the benefit of our people and for the prosperity of our country—as indeed you have witnessed abroad.'

After this We went to Our home; and as We found all Our family safe and well, We presented thanks to God.

[9] i.e. the Tsähafe Te'ezaz reading the speech on behalf of Her Majesty.

CHAPTER 22

About the convention for mutual assistance between the British Government, as regards the barrage at Lake Tana, and the Italian Government, as regards the construction of a railway from the border of Eritrea, cutting through the middle of Ethiopia, to Italian Somaliland[1]

THE British Government, in 1895 (= 1902) despatched Lt. Col. John Lane Harrington[2] as special envoy, and, in an accord[3] between the British Sudan Government and Emperor Menelik, it was agreed that the Ethiopian Government would not permit obstructing the flow of the Sobat[4] river and other small rivers entering the Abbay, i.e. Blue Nile.[5] Because Emperor Menelik had approved this accord, the envoy had given written assurances (by letter only) to the effect that the British Sudan Government would pay the Ethiopian Government annually 10,000 guineas. And subsequently they said: 'May permission be granted to us to regulate the flow of the waters by building a barrage at Lake Tana, for the waters of the Nile are low in the summer and plentiful in the winter.'[6] Once permission had been granted to

[1] For the background to this episode, see Luca dei Sabelli, IV, 188–95 (though in some respects a somewhat biased account); Mosley, 135 ff. Texts of the 1925 Anglo-Italian exchange in *L'Africa Orientale*, I, 330 ff.

[2] Sir John Harrington, previously Governor of Zeila, was British representative in Ethiopia from 1898–1908.

[3] See Ullendorff, 'The Anglo-Ethiopian Treaty of 1902', *BSOAS*, XXX (1967), 641–54.

[4] *Guida*, 510 (called Baro in Ethiopia).

[5] Article III of the Treaty. Perham[2], 389.

[6] Paradoxically, the Nile waters in the upper reaches are low during the rainy season (summer) and high during the dry season (winter), as it takes a fairly long

them they promised to send engineers, lest the waters—having increased with the building of the Lake Tana barrage—should perhaps drown the islands and the churches situated in Lake Tana; they would then present a report to the Ethiopian Government; and the engineers were indeed sent in 1899 (= 1906).

Subsequently, after the Great War in 1912 (= 1919), the Italian Government despatched envoys to London and presented a proposal for mutual assistance in connexion with the British Government's Lake Tana dam and the Italian Government's construction of a railway from the border of Eritrea and cutting through the centre of Ethiopia. But as the British Government had begun to negotiate direct with the Ethiopian Government, the proposals which the Italian Government had presented to it remained for the time being unacceptable.

Later on, in 1916 (= 1924), when We came to London as guest of H.M. King George V, We had discussions at an interview with Mr. MacDonald, the Prime Minister, in order to conclude negotiations over some matters of concern to both governments. When the Prime Minister presented to Us a request to the effect that he would welcome it if We allowed the Lake Tana dam scheme[7] to be carried out (which the British Sudan Government had previously initiated), We explained to him Our proposal that, once *we* had *ourselves* caused the Lake Tana dam to be constructed by well-known engineers, it seemed to Us a good thing if we were to lease it to Britain, embodying it in a treaty in which the interests of both governments would be firmly safeguarded.

When Mr. MacDonald said 'It is our pleasure to accept this proposal of yours, provided you inform us in advance from which country you will appoint the engineers and allow us to make the choice'—adding at once 'won't you appoint engineers from the United States of America?'; We accepted with pleasure and agreed orally on the main matters; and a few weeks later We confirmed this to him in writing. But when the Italian Government heard of the decision as regards the Lake Tana dam, after direct discussions between the British Government and Ourselves, it pressed the British Government once again in 1918 (= 1925) not to lose sight of the proposal that the British Government should

time for the Nile to fill. The highest flow is during October-December after the end of the rainy season.
    [7] See above p. 84 of Amharic text (= p. 107 of translation).

assist the Italians to build the railway from the border of Eritrea, cutting through the middle of Ethiopia, up to Italian Somaliland; and as a result the Italian Government negotiated and agreed with the British Government, at Rome, that the proposal which it had previously initiated in 1912 (= 1919) be implemented; an exchange of correspondence ensued which embodied the text of the agreement. The two governments arranged for the text of the agreement, though allegedly only an exchange of correspondence, to be registered with the League of Nations at Geneva. While they did this, they did not inform, even by a single word, the sovereign Ethiopian Government. The following is the text of the letters of agreement which were exchanged.

Sir Ronald Graham[8] to M. Mussolini.
Rome 20th[9] December 1925.

Your Excellency cannot fail to be aware of the very great benefit for Egypt and the Sudan in preventing an interruption in the flow of the water, and indeed in bringing about an increase in the flow as far as possible, because the water from the White and Blue Niles and their tributary streams is necessary for irrigation. Various proposals which had previously been decided upon with this end in view are now being carried out; and others are being given consideration.

Your Excellency is aware of the talks which the British Government has initiated at Addis Ababa, in view of its fiduciary responsibility for Egypt and the Sudan and mindful in this respect of the value to Egypt. The basis of the discussions is to collect the waters by building a dam, under concession from the Ethiopian Government, at Lake Tana and its shore and to supply this water to the White[10] Nile. Up to now these talks have remained without any result.

In November 1919 (= Hedar 1912), when Italian envoys were in London, they had presented an offer of help, which the Italian Government would extend in regard to this matter, in the following terms:

---

[8] Sir Ronald (not Roland—as the Amharic text has) Graham was H.B.M. Ambassador to Italy from 1921 to 1933. Cf. *DNB*.

[9] The date should be 14th December.

[10] The English original (see Cmd. 2680, 1926) has *Blue* Nile.

'When the British Government, mindful of the great value of the waters of Lake Tana, requests a concession from the Ethiopian Government for the construction of a barrage at Lake Tana, in the part given over to Italian interests,[11] the Italian Government will support Great Britain. This is pending the delimitation of the zone given over to British interests and pending a full investigation of the reservation[12] which Italy requires under the terms of the Tripartite Agreement.[13]

When the British Government asks the Ethiopian Government for a concession to construct a motor road from Lake Tana to the Sudan, it may request the Italian Government to support it.[14] This[15] railway, according to the Tripartite Agreement, will pass to the west (sic) of Addis Ababa.[16] All the works necessary for the construction of this railway shall have a free passage across the above mentioned motor road.

Italy requests Britain to support with the Ethiopian Government all requests which she may submit for exclusive economic rights in the west of Ethiopia and in the territory through which

[11] The original has 'within the Italian sphere of influence', but the Amharic translation of these letters is neither very literal nor always very accurate. The phrase 'Italian sphere of influence' cannot refer to the Lake Tana region in particular but must be a hint to a long-standing British acquiescence in Italy possessing a predominating interest in the area of Ethiopia.

[12] The term 'reservation' in this context bears almost certainly the connotation of a reserved tract of land.

[13] The Tripartite Agreement is the Anglo–Franco–Italian accord of December 1906 under which the three governments pledge themselves to maintain the *status quo* in Ethiopia, while recognizing a predominant British interest in the waters of Lake Tana and the Blue Nile, a vital Italian interest in the area connecting the colonies of Eritrea and Somalia, and a predominating French interest in the hinterland of the French Somali coast (Luca dei Sabelli, IV, 100 ff.).

[14] The tenor of the original is somewhat different and refers to an Italian offer of such support. In the following divergences will only be pointed out if they are of great significance.

[15] A whole sentence, essential to an understanding of the context, has been omitted here in the Amharic translation. It reads in the original: 'Italy requests the support of Great Britain in order that she may obtain from the Ethiopian Government the concession to construct and to run a railway from the frontier of Eritrea to the frontier of Italian Somaliland' (Cmd. 2680 of 1926, p. 2).

[16] This shows the vast extent of the projected Italian sphere of influence. If the words 'west of Addis Ababa' did not clearly appear in article 4 of the 1906 Agreement, one might have thought that this was a simple error for 'east'. Luca dei Sabelli's comment (IV, 101) that this amounted in effect to a partition of Ethiopia is scarcely exaggerated.

the aforementioned railway will pass and for obtaining economic concessions in the Italian zone.[17] She reserves the right to present the identical request to France.'

The above proposal was not found acceptable at that time. The chief reason was that a strong objection arose against any one foreign government whatsoever controlling[18] the source of rivers so vital to the prosperity of Egypt and the Sudan and indeed to their very life. But by virtue of the fortunate existence of mutual trust between our two governments, H.M.'s Government desire to apply this to other matters as well. Therefore H.B.M.'s Government have examined the problem once more.

The British Government is convinced that the proposal which Italy has submitted does not conflict with the provisions of the agreement concluded in London on 13th December 1906 (= 4 Tahsas 1899), since its object was to maintain the *status quo*[19] in Ethiopia on the basis of the international treaties noted in article I[20] of the agreement as well as to protect the respective interests of the signatory governments, lest they should suffer damage on their part.

Consequently, H.B.M.'s Government would welcome the offer of support made by Italy, provided there remain unaffected the waters in which Egypt and the Sudan have such an interest and which the Ethiopian[21] Government has long recognized.

Therefore, I have the honour to request Your Excellency, on behalf of His Majesty's Principal Secretary of State for Foreign Affairs, to support and to assist the request with the Ethiopian Government at Addis Ababa to grant a concession and to permit H.B.M.'s Government to construct and to maintain a motor road on which to transport equipment and personnel and the like from the Sudan border up to the barrage.

---

[17] No such zone had ever been requested, defined, or granted.

[18] It appears that a verb such as በማጽዳትና ፡ must have dropped out after ምንም ፡

[19] The term *status quo* is neatly rendered into Amharic as 'so that Ethiopia should remain as she was'.

[20] That article re-affirmed the common Anglo-Franco-Italian interest in maintaining the integrity of Ethiopia, in preventing changes in the political conditions, and to consult each other in case of such alterations (Luca dei Sabelli, IV, 100).

[21] The English original at this point does not read 'Ethiopian' but 'Italian'. It is odd how the Ethiopian translator could have misread the unequivocal original text.

In return for this, H.B.M.'s Government are prepared to support the request which the Italian Government will submit to the Ethiopian Government to obtain a concession to build and to extend a railway from Eritrea to the frontier of Italian Somaliland. This railway, as well as all the operations necessary to construct and to extend it, may cross freely the above mentioned motor road.

Therefore, in order that both the British and the Italian Governments should simultaneously obtain the concessions which they are seeking as regards Lake Tana and the railway link from Eritrea to Italian Somaliland, it is necessary that identical instructions be despatched to the British and Italian representatives in Ethiopia that they should collaborate and consult together. If one of the two governments obtains the concession it seeks and the other remains unsuccessful, the government which has obtained its aims would unceasingly strive with all vigour that the other should likewise succeed.

If H.B.M.'s Government, with the valued assistance of the Italian Government, obtain the desired Lake Tana concession, then they are prepared to recognize that Italy shall be the economic beneficiary in western Ethiopia and the aforementioned area.[22] Furthermore, since H.B.M.'s Government undertake to support all Italian requests to obtain economic concessions in the above-mentioned zone, the Italian Government on its part, while recognizing the hydraulic rights which Egypt and the Sudan possess, enters into an obligation not to construct a dam upon the sources of the White and Blue Niles or on the sources of their tributaries, nor to carry out any work that would impede or diminish the flow of the waters into the main river. Notwithstanding this, the inhabitants in those regions may utilize the water, construct pools to collect the water, receive anything for drinking or agriculture or foodcrops for the local inhabitants, construct dams for hydroelectric power or utilize the waters in minor tributaries.

H.B.M.'s Government take this opportunity of assuring the Italian Government that the Lake Tana barrage and the hydraulic work will be carried out, as far as possible, with locally recruited labour and that the collection of water by the barrage will not exceed the amount collected hitherto [in the lake] during the

[22] It seems that the word ከፍል ፣ has dropped out after የተባለው ።

rainy season. H.B.M.'s Government are, therefore, convinced that the construction of this dam, quite apart from being of benefit to Egypt and the Sudan, will also increase the prosperity of the region and will progressively help to enrich economically the local inhabitants.

(signed) R. Graham.

Rome, 20th December 1925[23] (= 11th Tahsas 1918)

To H.E. the Special Envoy, Sir R. Graham.
I have received and attentively studied the letter which Your Excellency, under instructions from your government, wrote to me on 5th Tahsas (= 14th December, 1925) concerning the irrigation of Egypt and the Sudan as well as the matter which has remained hitherto unaccomplished owing to inertia on the part of the Ethiopian Government, i.e. to cause a fuller flow of the Blue Nile by the construction of a barrage on Lake Tana.

Your Excellency is not unaware of the proposals which the Italian envoys presented in London in November 1919 (= Hedar 1912) for a friendly Anglo-Italian co-operation in regard to this, but these remained unacceptable at that time because they raised concern over permitting a foreign power to exercise control over rivers and sources so very essential to the prosperity of Egypt and the Sudan and indeed even to their very existence.[24]

Your Excellency further informs me that H.B.M.'s Government, after studying this request more profoundly, accept that there is nothing in the Italian proposals which contradicts the agreement concluded in London on 13th December 1906 (= 4th Tahsas 1899)[25] under which the signatory governments are agreed to maintain the *status quo* in Ethiopia, without abandoning the basis of international law as indicated in article 1 of the accord, and to protect their respective interests. For this reason the British Government, adhering to the Italian proposals, accept Italian

[23] This date-line belongs to the following letter by Mussolini and not (as printed in the Amharic text) to Sir Ronald Graham's missive. See footnote (9) above.

[24] At this point a clause is omitted which appears in the Italian original and which reiterates Ambassador Graham's assurance of the existence of greater mutual trust at the present time (cf. p. 104, lines 3 ff., of Amharic text = p. 128 of English translation).

[25] Cf. footnote (13) above.

support with pleasure. This support in no way affects the existing principal hydraulic interests of Egypt and the Sudan which the Italian Government itself has recognized. Thus Your Excellency, upon instructions from your[26] government, requests that the Italian Government should assist and support the British Government in its demand of the Ethiopian Government to construct a barrage upon Lake Tana and a motor road from the Sudan border to the dam for the transport of food, equipment, workmen, and all similar things. Your Excellency informs me that, in exchange for this action by the Italian Government, the British Government in its turn will assist the Italian Government when it requests the Ethiopian Government for an extension, for its own benefit, of the railway from the frontier of Eritrea to that of Italian Somaliland as well as for a treaty which provides for free transit, across the aforementioned motor[27] road, for everything needed for the construction of the railway and its proper use. With this end in view, the necessary identical instructions have been transmitted to the British and Italian representatives in Ethiopia.

Your Excellency informs me that it is essential that the British and Italian Governments should undertake to request the Ethiopian Government upon the matter on which they are both agreed, i.e. as regards Lake Tana and the railway linking Eritrea and Italian Somaliland.

In case one government obtains the concession it seeks, while the other fails to do so, the successful government shall extend all possible help, without relaxing its efforts, to the unsuccessful one until it likewise achieves its purpose.

Furthermore, Your Excellency informs me that, if H.B.M.'s Government is able to obtain, with the assistance of the Italian Government, the concession which it seeks from the Ethiopian Government as regards Lake Tana, the British Government, on its part, will then recognize Italy's special[28] economic influence in western Ethiopia and in the entire area which the aforementioned railway traverses. In addition the British Government will

[26] Read ከመንግሥትዎም ፣ as elsewhere and in conformity with the Italian original.

[27] The Italian original and the context make it clear that the word በትC ፣ at this point is erroneous. The Amharic translator did not always adhere closely to the original text.

[28] The Italian original has here the much stronger 'l'esclusività'. The Italian 'influenza' is interestingly rendered by ሥልጣን ፡

support every request which the Italian Government makes in the aforementioned zone as regards economic concessions.[29] Nonetheless, this agreement and negotiation will come into force only on the understanding that the Italian Government, while recognizing the longstanding assignment of waters to the Sudan,[30] will enter into an obligation not to construct on the sources of the Blue and White Niles and their tributaries any kind of work that might impede their flow into the main river. Your Excellency informs me that, notwithstanding any of the conditions outlined above, the local inhabitants may make use of the waters to a reasonable extent for anything required for drinking, domestic needs, or agriculture as well as storing waters for harnessing electric power or similar essential purposes.

Furthermore, Your Excellency, upon instructions received from your[31] government, informs the Italian Government that for the construction of the barrage and the road the labour employed will as far as possible be locally recruited and that the level of the lake will not be allowed to exceed the previous maximum attained during the rainy season. Finally, the British Government is convinced that the construction of this dam will be beneficial not only for Egypt and the Sudan but will bring prosperity and economic development to the people of the region.

In reply to the above clarifications and requests which Your Excellency has made to me, and since the British Government recognizes it now being opportune to extend to the aforementioned question the principle of friendly co-operation which has become so precious in all other areas, I would inform Your Excellency that, while the Royal Government is very happy to accept the proposals, I consider that this agreement will be the more useful the more widely applied it is.

The Royal (Italian) Government considers it firmly established that H.B.M.'s Government is now convinced that the (Italian) proposals presented in November 1919 (= Hedar 1912) do not contradict the wording of the agreement reached in London on 13 December 1906 (= 4 Tahsas 1899)—as indeed Italy has always firmly maintained— it being the main aim of these proposals to

---

[29] The Amharic በት ፡ for 'concessioni' would suggest that the translator was thinking of economically advantageous places.

[30] The Italian original refers to Egypt as well.

[31] Read ከመንግሥትዎ ፡ and cf. note (26) above.

maintain the *status quo* in Ethiopia on the basis of international
instruments embodied in article I of the agreement, while the
signatory governments were collaborating lest anything should
adversely affect their respective interests.

This being so, although the proposals presented in London in
November 1919 and outlined above are reckoned to be part of a
wider agreement of a colonial nature deriving from the treaties
signed in London in December 1906[32] and although there were
only a few points of this agreement that have been effectively
carried out, the Royal Italian Government is willing to raise the
matter once again, particularly since the British Government
desires to apply the principle of friendly co-operation, a desire
which Italy shares. Furthermore, we are hoping that the interests
of Britain and Italy in Ethiopia will be properly developed and
protected without transgressing the treaty concluded in London
in December 1906, a treaty which forms the basis of this agreement. To this end the Italian Government will assist the British
Government when it requests a concession to construct a barrage
at Lake Tana and a motor road from the Sudan frontier to the dam
for the transport of food and equipment.

Furthermore, the Italian Government takes firm note of the
offer of help by the British Government as regards the former's
request of the Ethiopian Government to extend the railway from
the frontier of Eritrea to Italian Somaliland and to build stations (?)
as well as to obtain free transit for everything required for the
construction of this railway across the aforementioned motor road.

To this end the Italian Government will transmit the necessary
instructions to its representative at Addis Ababa, coinciding with
the instructions given to its representative by the British Government, so that the concessions which the British and Italian
Governments are seeking as regards Lake Tana and the rail link
between Eritrea and Italian Somaliland be granted to them both
together. In case one government obtains the concession it seeks,
while the other fails to do so, the successful one shall press its
assistance unceasingly until the other achieves satisfaction, so that
both obtain their concessions together, if at all possible.

If H.B.M.'s Government succeeds in obtaining, with the aid of
the Italian Government, the concession regarding Lake Tana
which it seeks from the Ethiopian Government, Britain will

[32] The Italian text has 1915 at this point.

likewise recognize Italian economic preponderance in western
Ethiopia and in the above-mentioned area which the railway
traverses; she will also support the Italian Government in all its
requests of the Ethiopian Government as regards concessions in the
aforementioned zone.

The Italian Government, on its part, recognizing the long-
established hydraulic rights of Egypt and the Sudan, enters into an
obligation not to construct any work on the sources of the White
and Blue Niles and their tributaries that might impede the flow
into the main river.

As regards hydraulic interests, I am confident that the British
Government has the firm intention to respect the long-established
state of affairs of the people resident in the adjacent territories
reckoned to be within the sphere of special Italian influence. This
project, to the utmost possible extent and as far as can be reconciled with the principal interests of Egypt and the Sudan, shall be
carried out on the basis of the utmost possible satisfaction of the
economic requirements of these local populations.[33]

Please accept my respectful greetings.

(signed) Mussolini.

When the British and Italian Ministers at Addis Ababa—
according to the instructions which they had received from their
respective governments concerning this matter—presented to Us
jointly the text of the pact about which the two governments had
reached agreement, We were astonished at this and wrote to
them as follows:

Tafari Makonnen, Crown Prince of Ethiopia and Regent
Plenipotentiary, to H.E. Mr. Charles Bentinck,[34] British Minister
Plenipotentiary.
Peace be with you! The letter which you wrote me on 2nd Säne
1918 (= 9th June, 1926) has reached me. This letter is wholly
identical with the missive which H.E. Count Colli,[35] the Italian

[33] The extraordinary repetitiveness of this document is obvious. Its colonial
spirit is in conformity with the sentiments of that era. Among its many oddities
are repeated references to an undertaking by Italy not to construct any obstacles
by the sources of the *White* Nile which were wholly outside Italian control.

[34] Later Rev. Sir Charles Bentinck, K.C.M.G. Bentinck held a variety of
diplomatic posts, both before and after his service as British Minister in Ethiopia,
1925-8. See also pp. 7-8 of Mrs. Margaret Campbell's *Short History of the British
Embassy*, Addis Ababa 1972.

Minister, has addressed to me. It informs me of the agreement between the two of you that the Ethiopian Government should grant you concessions, i.e. for the damming of Lake Tana by the British and for the construction of a railway in Ethiopia by Italy. The fact that both of you have reached agreement and that you have considered it proper jointly to inform Us of this agreement in identical notes, raises some disquieting thoughts in Us, and therefore We shall now, first of all, have to take counsel about this. To this end, it is right to place the matter before the League of Nations, as it requires to be carefully examined in the first place.

8th Säne 1918 (= 15th June 1926).

A note in the same vein[36] was written to the Italian Minister.

Subsequently We wrote the following appeal and presented it to the Secretary General of the League of Nations, M. Avenol:[37]

Our Government has recently received identical notes written by both the British and Italian governments informing Us of their agreement for Britain to dam Lake Tana and for Italy to construct a railway traversing Ethiopia.

We are greatly distressed about this agreement being concluded by the two governments among themselves alone, without informing Us, and then simply sending Us joint notifications.

When originally we were granted admission to the League of Nations, we were told that all governments of the world were reckoned as equal, that the independence of all would be respected, and that the ultimate aim of the League was to extend

[35] Giuseppe Colli di Felizzano (1870–1937) who spent a considerable part of his official career in Ethiopia where he served in a number of important posts, including that of Minister (cf. *Chi è dell'Eritrea*).

[36] The two notes, to the British and Italian Ministers at Addis Ababa, were indeed identical—with the significant exception, however, of one additional paragraph which appears only in the note sent to Britain. Its omission here is curious. In the English translation (not always wholly reliable) that paragraph reads as follows (cf. Cmd. 2792 (1927), p. 5):

'The British Government had already entered into negotiations with the Abyssinian Government in regard to its proposal, and we had imagined that, whether that proposal was carried into effect or not, the negotiations would have been concluded with us: we should never have suspected that the British Government would come to an agreement with another Government regarding our lake.'

[37] In fact, Joseph Avenol was at that time Assistant Secretary General; he became Secretary General in 1933 in succession to Sir Eric Drummond and remained in that office till 1940 (cf. Baer, 101 ff.).

and to strengthen peace among men in accordance with God's will.

It did not seem to us proper to allow some members of the League of Nations to conclude an agreement among themselves and to force another member to accept their plan, even[38] if it did not affect the national interests of that member.

Secondly, it is the case that on one of the subjects, among those on which they (Britain and Italy) have reached agreement, the Ethiopian and British governments have previously held discussions. No definite answer had been given because the matter under discussion had remained inconclusive and because we were still deliberating about it. Having agreed among themselves to hold discussions about this subject, they informed us in joint notes of this their agreement, but the reason that We did not hurry to carry out what they were demanding of us, without giving it due reflection and without knowing whether it agreed with Our people's needs, is that We cannot help considering the proposals as highly disturbing.

Our people are desirous to do right; it is Our constant wish to lead them on the road of civilization and improvement. But what they know of their history is that among the foreigners there are few who do not desire to violate their frontiers and to impair their freedom. With God's goodness and the bravery of our soldiers we have always, whatever the circumstances, been able to remain upon our mountains proud in our independence.

Therefore, when foreigners who wish to establish themselves, allegedly for economic reasons, in our country or in our frontier areas contiguous to their possessions, apply for permission to do so, we have to be very careful that they do not have political aims; and the recent quite unexpected agreement reached by them and the proposals they presented serve, perhaps, as the best proof of all that such caution is justified. Time has not yet permitted us to get accustomed so quickly to entirely new conditions and such like, for, though our past history is glorious, it is not to be forgotten that it is only very recently that We have begun to follow the path of modern civilization. Even creation itself was not created all at once. And where is the country that has changed all its works within one year?

[38] The official English translation of the 'even' clause is neither accurate nor logical (Cmd. 2792 (1927), p. 7). See above p. xxviii.

If the countries whose geographical position has enabled them to out-distance us were to give us friendly advice and the necessary time, then—with our genuine eagerness—Ethiopia would go on improving uninterruptedly to attain a higher level in future just as she had always done in the past. But to make undue haste may bring the danger of accidents.

We should wish to know whether members of the League of Nations desire means of coercion to be used against us which they would undoubtedly dislike if applied against themselves.

I have the honour to inform all the honourable governments who are members of the League of Nations of those notifications which We have received, so that they be apprised of the fact that the proposals are incompatible with Our country's independence, in particular when it is stated that a part of Our possessions is to be given over to the economic influence of a certain great Power.

Since We are aware that economic and political influence are closely bound up together, it is Our duty to present a strong protest, because in Our opinion this agreement is incompatible with the basic idea of the League of Nations.

Addis Ababa, 12th Säne 1918
(= 19th June 1926).

After this note of appeal of Ours had reached the League of Nations and the subject had been studied, the text of the request was sent to the two governments concerned; and subsequently the British Government replied as follows:

London, 3rd August 1926
(= 27 Hamle 1918)

To the Secretary General of the League of Nations.

On behalf of H.B.M.'s Principal Secretary of State for Foreign Affairs I have received copy of the note which the Imperial Ethiopian Crown Prince, Tafari Makonnen, addressed to Sir Eric Drummond[39] as well as your own respected letter of 15th Hamle (= 22nd July) relating to the protest submitted by H.I.H. as regards the agreement between the British and Italian governments of December 1925 (= Tahsas 1918) by which the two govern-

[39] The Amharic version of this name requires correction. Sir Eric Drummond (1876-1951), later the 16th Earl of Perth, was the first Secretary General of the League of Nations (1919-1933) and subsequently served as British Ambassador to Rome.

ments contracted to assist each other when seeking the permission of the Ethiopian Government for certain kinds of work as specified in those notes.

2. Although the British and Italian Ministers at Addis Ababa had given assurances to the Ethiopian Government when they presented the notes about which Britain and Italy had agreed, H.B.M.'s Government regret that the correct version of these notes appears to have been misinterpreted and that intentions appear to have been attributed to the two governments which they did not, in fact, entertain. According to the text of the Ethiopian protest, it would appear that the British and Italian governments, having put their signatures to a treaty, are intent upon forcing their proposals on a member of the League, although these proposals are incompatible with its interests; they, the Ethiopians, have requested members of the League to state whether it is right that pressure should be exerted upon Ethiopia which they would undoubtedly find unacceptable if applied to themselves.

3. There is nothing at all in the British and Italian notes that might suggest pressure or coercion against the Ethiopian Government. In fact, this agreement as such, Sir Austen Chamberlain[40] has stated in Parliament, was never designed to apply pressure against the Ethiopian Government.

In his opinion the agreement as it stood was in the interests of all three governments, but, he added, the Ethiopian Government were perfectly entitled to be the judge of Ethiopia's best interests.

His Majesty's Chargé d'Affaires had telegraphic instructions transmitted to him in July to inform the Heir to the Throne, Tafari, of this statement.

4. I refer in the following to the suggestion which has been made that the British and Italian governments desired to force the Ethiopian Government to answer in haste the request made to it, without affording it the time to consider the interests of its people. In fact, however, Emperor Menelik confirmed in writing the following statement which he had made orally a few days earlier and which is embodied in notes exchanged between the British Minister at Addis Ababa and the Ethiopian Government on 18th May 1902 (= 8th Genbot 1894):[41]

[40] 1863–1937; Foreign Secretary in the Baldwin Government, 1924–9.

'That there shall not be carried out, without consulting the British and the Sudan governments, any sort of work that may affect the flow of the waters of the Blue Nile and of Lake Tana; but if any work of this kind were planned, all other obligations being equal, preference shall be given to the proposals presented by H.B.M.'s Government and the Sudan Government; H.I.M. Emperor Menelik has no intention of giving any concession with regard to the Blue Nile and Lake Tana to anyone except to H.B.M.'s Government or to a subject of either government.'[42]

Since this undertaking proves that Emperor Menelik II had given permission, 24 years ago, for the British Government to construct a barrage at Lake Tana, it is now possible to examine, with the permission and help of the Ethiopian Government, the specific proposals and their realization as regards this project which had been submitted by the British Government on many suitable occasions; and it has become possible to assess the position properly ever since the engineering experts who had been despatched to Lake Tana have returned with their detailed findings.

It does not, therefore, seem equitable to charge H.B.M.'s Government with acting in undue haste as regards the Lake Tana project.

5. In the concluding part of its protest[43] the Ethiopian Government asks whether the Anglo-Italian note affects Ethiopia's independence, especially when it is stipulated that a part of Ethiopia shall be surrendered to the economic influence of a great Power. In particular, Sir Austen Chamberlain desires to make it known emphatically that the Anglo-Italian note does not state that we shall retain a part of Ethiopia for Italian economic influence. It is true that H.B.M.'s Government for their own purposes (and Italy under her treaty obligations) recognize Italy's

---

[41] The date is difficult: in the first place, Cmd. 2792 (1927) reads 18th March (*sic*) which must be an error; secondly, the 18th May is not identical with 8th Genbot (8 Genbot = 15 May). In the 1902 treaty itself (Ullendorff, *BSOAS*, 1967, 647) the date is 15th May; in the Amharic text 7th Genbot!

[42] The English original has 'except to H.B.M.'s Government and the Government of the Sudan or one of their subjects'. The Amharic text makes no reference here to the Sudan Government, and the 'subjects' concerned here must relate to the British and Ethiopian Governments, while the English version clearly envisages British and Sudanese nationals.

[43] በቀረሰው ፡ should probably read በቀረበው ፡

special economic influence in western Ethiopia and in the entire territory which the aforementioned railway traverses (joining Eritrea and Italian Somaliland). But this undertaking does not impose an obligation on anything affecting the dispositions of the three governments[44] just because the British Government has engaged not to do—or support doing—anything in competition with Italy in the area specified in return for Italian assurances as regards Lake Tana.

6.   Sir Austen Chamberlain will be able to submit once again the assurances and proofs which he has given to Ethiopia, so as to enable the League Council to examine, at its forthcoming session, the note which the Ethiopian Government has sent to you.

(signed) John Murray.[45]

Four days after the British Government had sent the above statement to the League of Nations the Italian Government wrote as follows:

Rome, 7th August 1926
(= 1st Nähase 1918)

I am instructed by the Head of the Government and Minister for Foreign Affairs to inform you of the receipt of your letter of 15th Hamle (= 22nd July) last together with the copy, and enclosures, of the protest addressed to you by Ras Tafari Makonnen, Heir to the Throne of Ethiopia, as regards the agreement reached by the British and Italian governments in December 1925 (= Tahsas 1918) to render assistance to each other in requesting the Ethiopian Government to carry out certain works in Ethiopia.

The Royal (Italian) Government greatly regrets to observe that the Ethiopian Government has not properly understood the thinking embodied in the Anglo-Italian agreement—as is indeed shown by the substance of the note which Tafari Makonnen, Heir to the Throne of Ethiopia, sent to the members of the League of Nations. Moreover, what has caused surprise to the

[44] This sentence construes rather badly in Amharic; it also appears to have comprehended the English original only very imperfectly. The latter has: 'This recognition cannot affect the rights of third parties or bind the Government of Abyssinia. It imposes no obligation on anyone except the British Government . . .'

[45] C.M.G., Head of the Egyptian section, Eastern department, at the Foreign Office in 1926.

Royal (Italian) Government is the fact that only a short time ago the Italian representative at Addis Ababa had fully explained to the Ethiopian Government the scope of the matter in question, pointing out the limited object of the discussions between the two governments with a view to co-ordinating some of the economic interests of Britain and Italy; the Italian envoy also made it clear that the realization of the project depended on the wishes of the Ethiopian Government, whether it contributed to the economic development of the country and whether it was in conformity with Ethiopia's best interests.

Following these explanations, the Heir to the Throne of Ethiopia, Tafari Makonnen, wrote a letter, dated 12th Säne (= 19th June), to the Italian minister at Addis Ababa; in this letter he thanked the Head of the Italian Government for the assurances given to him and said he did not doubt Italy's sentiments of friendship and her willingness to honour Ethiopia's independence. The Italian Government considers that there is nothing at all that could justify the fears of the Ethiopian Government that the British and Italian governments are planning, in the note of agreement in question, any acts of coercion or precipitate pressure against Ethiopia. Furthermore, the friendly and explicit assurances previously given to the Ethiopian Government by Italy should have sufficed to convince Ethiopia that there is nothing to bring about such apprehensions.

The treaty in question as regards the cession of economic influence to Italy in certain regions of Ethiopia, having been undertaken specifically by the British Government, is binding solely on the British and Italian governments but does not affect the powers of Ethiopia nor does it limit any future action of disposition by the three governments.[46]

This agreement is a kind of economic guarantee that the work initiated by Italian young men shall be well accomplished and that the resources found in Ethiopia be developed and exploited without competition with British enterprises.

(signed) Grandi.[47]

---

[46] Here again the original refers to 'third parties' which would appear to have a much wider connotation.

[47] Grandi, Count Dino (1895—), at the operative time in 1926 Under-Secretary of State for Foreign Affairs; later Foreign Minister, Italian Ambassador in London, and finally President of the Chamber of Fasci.

After We had seen the text of the replies, which these two governments had made to the enquiries, transmitted to Us through the League of Nations, We wrote once more as follows:

To the Secretary General of the League of Nations.
Peace be with you!
In a letter which I wrote to you on 12th Säne (= 19th June) I had requested you to communicate, on our behalf, to the members of the League of Nations the protest which it had seemed proper to the Imperial Ethiopian Government to submit as regards the agreement which the British and Italian governments had reached on 5th and 11th of Tahsas 1918 (= 14th and 20th December, 1925) with a view to exploiting their interests in Ethiopia.

The Imperial Ethiopian Government was very properly distressed upon learning of the agreement, which these two great Powers had reached, to act as they desired towards a friendly government which, like them, is a member of the League of Nations, without first requesting the permission of that country.

If the Ethiopian Government were to fail to accept, after due examination, that this convention was in the best interests of Ethiopia, it considers that these two Powers would certainly exert pressure to obtain the economic conditions they had requested.

This being so, it was possible to assert with regard to present events that the Anglo-Italian accord was not compatible, at any rate indirectly, with the covenant of the League of Nations, since the British and Italian governments—like all the remaining members of the League—had undertaken not to touch the age-old independence of Ethiopia or to violate her territorial integrity.

According to our opinion, under article 20 of the covenant, it was incumbent upon them not to enter into such an accord. But as it seemed to us that they planned[48] to violate that article, the object of their agreement could have no validity with regard to us and must, therefore, be reckoned null and void. If the two great Powers, on their part, had not officially notified us on the same day, they would not have aroused our anxiety. This joint notification which they presented appeared to us to reveal the first sign of coercion. From then onwards, while the two great Powers

[48] The English translation (official) curiously renders this as 'but as they had, of course, no intention of violating that article . . .' (Cmd. 2792 (1927), p. 13, ult.). It is, of course, also possible that the Amharic original here is corrupt and was intended to read ያለበት ፡

were exhibiting their friendly intentions when replying to our protest, they began to strive hard to allay apprehensions over the Ethiopian appeal. Furthermore, the British Government took the opportunity with regard to this matter of informing us of the explanatory statement which H.E. Sir Austen Chamberlain had made in Parliament. He announced clearly: 'The two governments have no intention of making economic demands[49] upon the country, and there is nothing in their agreement that could be binding upon the Ethiopian Government; there is no plan to coerce the Ethiopian Government, and it is indeed the Government of Ethiopia that must be the judge of Ethiopia's best interests.' The Italian Government notified us in a similar vein.

Apart from this, the British Government announced that the two great Powers intended to deposit the terms of their accord with the secretariat of the League of Nations, and the Imperial Ethiopian Government has learnt that registration has since taken place.

As we are aware that registration in accordance with article 18 of the covenant is for information only, the Imperial Government does not consider it necessary to submit a protest about the implementation of this requirement. But since the Imperial Government intended to fulfil the obligations embodied in the covenant and to establish relations with the nations of the world based on justice and honour, it seemed to us proper and in accordance with the rules to request your assistance in the publication of this letter, together with the said notes, as well as of the reassuring replies to our protests, so that everybody may be aware of the position taken by the Imperial Government.

This being so, the members of the League of Nations will not then entertain any doubt that the Ethiopian Government has any treaty obligation whatever towards the two governments which have earlier declared an interest in the matter and that it possesses full powers—as indeed the British and Italian governments themselves have stated—either to accept or to reject any requests made to it and that, finally, the Imperial Government is the sole judge of what is in Ethiopia's best interests.

Addis Ababa, 30th Nähase 1918 (= 4th September 1926).

---

[49] This is curious: the Amharic text has ለመራለግ ፣ 'to seek', while the British Command paper (2792, p. 14) has 'to divide the country economically' which appears to be the phrase used by Sir Austen Chamberlain. It is just possible that the

As We thought that this affair of the two governments reaching agreement by themselves (without any information being proffered to the Ethiopian Government) had been disposed of by the League of Nations, We did not consider that the discussions We had held with Mr. MacDonald in 1916 (= 1924)[50] should remain unconcluded; We therefore despatched, in 1920 (= 1928), Azaj[51] Warqnäh,[52] whom We had now appointed as Ethiopian Minister in London, as special envoy to the U.S.A. We arranged that he should return after discussions with the internationally renowned White Engineering Company[53] about the damming of Lake Tana. We also arranged that he should discuss this at meetings in Addis Ababa with representatives of the British Government. After they had departed following these negotiations, the White Engineering Company on their part sent, in 1923 (= 1930), a number of engineers who surveyed Lake Tana and then returned.

Later, engineers of the British Sudan and Egyptian governments came together to Addis Ababa, and after we had held extensive discussions about the matter, they made an appointment to meet once more at Addis Ababa in 1927 (= 1935), to draft the details of the contract; they then went back. But when at the time of the appointment We were preparing to transmit a telegram to summon the representatives of the White Engineering Company, the British Minister[54] and the Egyptian Consul at Addis Ababa let Us know that their representatives had deferred their visit to Addis Ababa for the time being. They did not for the moment reveal to Us the reason for this action. But the Walwal[55] disturbances had

Amharic verb here should read either ለመከፈል ፣ or ለመፍለጥ ፣? አያስቡም ፣ should presumably be followed by a särä (semicolon).

[50] See chapter 19 above.
[51] Ethiopian title, 'commander'; cf. Guidi, Vocabolario, 486.
[52] Lit. 'thou art gold'; Ethiopian proper name. Azaj Warqnäh was known to Europeans as Dr. Martin (born about 1865); he had been picked up as a child by members of the Napier expedition, was educated in India and became a doctor. See Sylvia Pankhurst, Ethiopia: a cultural history, 587, note 1; and especially Richard Pankhurst, 648–50.
[53] According to R. Pankhurst, 291, the J. G. White Engineering Corporation of New York was interested, in 1930, in building a barrage on Lake Tana. Cf. Cheesman, index under 'White'.
[54] Sir Sidney Barton, British Minister to Ethiopia, 1929–36. Cf. DNB.
[55] The Walwal incident of December 1934 was ostensibly the beginning of the Italo-Ethiopian crisis; cf. Guida, 609–10; Hardie, 5 et passim. See also below chapter 32 et seqq.

started, and We reckoned that this was the reason. We notified the White Engineering Company not to send their representatives to Addis Ababa. But the Ethiopian Government had earlier given an undertaking to the effect that it would not cut off the flow of the small rivers entering the Blue Nile, nor that of the river Sobat, without the agreement of the British-Sudan Government, and therefore the British-Sudan Government was to pay to the Ethiopian Government an annual sum of ten thousand guineas. When We noticed in Our records the non-payment to the Ethiopian Government of this money by the British-Sudan Government ever since the said treaty had been signed and letters were exchanged, from 1895 (= 1902) until 1924 (= 1931), We wrote to the British Minister at Addis Ababa asking that the money be paid in accordance with the terms of the letter. He claimed that this money was to be paid when permission to dam Lake Tana had been granted, and while he brought up various other excuses and We were engaged in protracted correspondence, Italy meanwhile unleashed a war of aggression against us, and that matter therefore remained in abeyance.

Furthermore, We had not neglected the interests of the Italian Government by possibly using as a pretext the direct negotiations with the British Government concerning the damming of Lake Tana, and when the former asked for permission to build a motor road from Assab to Dessie and to expand trade, We raised no difficulties whatsoever but accorded them permission in a spirit of friendship.

Details of all this will be found presently in connexion with the ceremonial welcome which We prepared when H.H. the Duke of Abruzzi came to Addis Ababa to return Our visit.

CHAPTER 23

About our treaty with Italy concerning port facilities at Assab, the construction of a road, and general amity

WE were frequently distressed about the fact that it was an obstacle to civilization that Our country lacked a sea-port of her own. Particularly since Ethiopia entered the League of Nations and contacts with governments of the world had greatly expanded, We became convinced of the need to find an outlet to the sea; We therefore requested Italy to make available for us port facilities in the Assab region.

Furthermore, We had been reminding the French Minister at Addis Ababa, from time to time, of Our desire to obtain access to the sea in the Jibuti area. The reasons why We were considering obtaining a sea-port at Jibuti were, in the first place, that, when the French Government originally seized Jibuti, it was by agreement with Ethiopia and, in the second place, that it was a French Company[1] that built the railway, under a concession from the Ethiopian Government, connecting us to Jibuti.

Later, in 1916 (= 1924), when We came to visit Paris at the invitation of the French Government, We disclosed to M. Poincaré, the then Prime Minister, that it was Our desire to obtain access to the sea in the Jibuti area. He had given Us a hopeful reply, but when, after Our return to Our country, We repeatedly requested the French Government to confirm the expectation given to Us, they kept Us waiting for about two years with several excuses and without giving a firm decision.

The Italian Government, however, were not pleased at Our discussions with France about obtaining an outlet to the sea.

Afterwards, in 1919 (= 1927), H.M. Victor Emmanuel III sent his uncle, H.H. the Duke of Abruzzi,[2] to Addis Ababa to return Our visit. As soon as he arrived, he informed Us of his instructions to discuss with Us, since he happened to be on the spot, the question of access to the sea and the construction of a road, but we postponed these talks until the official visit had been completed.

It had appeared to Us and to all Our people that the visit to Addis Ababa of H.H. the Duke of Abruzzi was apt to strengthen greatly the existing friendship with Italy. Therefore, ever since We heard officially about his visit, We prepared a big programme suitable for the reception. In particular We put in hand the building of a new palace in which he was to stay, within the precincts of Our palace,[3] and it was completed within a brief

---

[1] Compagnie Chemin de Fer Franco-Éthiopien (Pankhurst, 304 ff.).
[2] He was, in fact, his cousin (see note (18) to chapter 12).
[3] This was, of course, before the construction of the Gännätä Le'ul palace which was not completed till 1934 (since 1960 it has served as the H.Q. of the University), but it was within the same spacious compound.

period. The house was called 'The Duke's House' and used to be known by his name up to the end of the war.[4]

When he was about to return to his country at the conclusion of the official visit, he asked to be permitted to speak about the matter to which he had referred, for he had received instructions from his government to give certain information to the Ethiopian Government. He then declared as follows:

'As my government has heard that you have initiated conversations with the French Government with a view to obtaining access to the sea—conversations which have so far remained inconclusive—it is my government's intention to grant a sea-port in the Assab area and to construct a motor road from the port to Dessie, while the two governments establish a mutual aid company; it is further my government's intention to conclude a treaty of friendship that shall remain in force for 20 years, and I am therefore to enquire as to the wishes of the Ethiopian Government. This matter had already been broached previously when you came to Rome in 1916 (= 1924).' When he explained his government's proposals in these terms, We accepted them as satisfactory, for we would thus obtain, in the first place, an outlet to the sea and, in the second, a period of 20 years without war in which Ethiopia would work hard and reach a high level. The matter then came before the great princes and nobles, and after it had been approved We signed the following treaty:[5]

Treaty

Whereas it is the desire of the Empress of Ethiopia, Her Majesty Zawditu, and of the King of Italy, His Majesty Victor Emmanuel III, to consolidate and strengthen further the friendship existing between the two governments and to bring about an expansion of the economic relations between the two countries; accordingly H.H. Tafari Makonnen, Heir to the Throne and Regent Plenipotentiary of the Empire of Ethiopia, in the name of H.M. Empress Zawditu, in his own name and that of their successors,

---

[4] The war in question is, of course, the Italo-Abyssinian war of 1935–6. The 'Duke's House' was situated in the palace precincts near Sedest Kilo and is now occupied by the Faculty of Law.

[5] During the Duke of Abruzzi's visit in 1927 only general principles were discussed, and the treaty as such was not signed or ratified until 2nd August 1928. For the Italian text of the treaty see *L'Africa Orientale*, I, 343 ff.

and Commendatore Giuliano Cora,[6] Minister Plenipotentiary of the Royal Italian Government, in the name of H.M. Victor Emmanuel III and his successors, having reached agreement have covenanted as follows:

First

There shall be everlasting friendship[7] between the Imperial Ethiopian Government and the Royal Italian Government.

Second

The two governments have entered into a mutual obligation not to do anything for whatever reason that might affect or damage the independence of the other and to safeguard and protect their respective interests.

Third

The two governments have entered into an obligation to extend and to cause to flourish the trade existing between the two countries.

Fourth

Italian native citizens, subjects, and protected persons, while residing in Ethiopia, and Ethiopians, while residing in Italian colonies,[8] as regards their trade and employment, necessities of livelihood and administration, and in anything that concerns the exercise of their professions, their trade and their employment— it is incumbent upon them to observe and to honour the laws of the state in which they are living. Notwithstanding anything stated above, there shall remain applicable to the said Italian subjects and protected persons, while resident in Ethiopia, the provisions laid down in article VII of the treaty between the Emperor of Ethiopia and the Government of the French Republic,

[6] Cora, born in 1884, was a career diplomat and served in Ethiopia in various offices and at different times—culminating in his period as Italian Minister at Addis Ababa, 1926–30, during which time he was closely associated with the drafting and negotiating of the 1928 treaty. He made considerable endeavours in the post-World War II period to re-establish relations with Ethiopia (cf. *Chi è dell'Eritrea*).

[7] The Italian version refers not only to *amicizia perpetua* but also to *pace costante* which does not appear in the Amharic text printed in the Imperial autobiography.

[8] The Italian version has 'in Italia e sue colonie', while the Amharic text omits mention of residence in Italy.

concluded on 1st Ter 1900 (= 10th January 1908),[9] as long as this treaty remains in force.

Fifth

The two governments bind themselves to submit to conciliation or to arbitration–judges any matter arising between them on which they cannot agree and which is incapable of being resolved by the customary diplomatic means—without recourse to the force of arms. As regards the procedure for selecting arbitrators, the two governments shall exchange notes once they have reached agreement.

Sixth

This treaty shall be registered with the League of Nations. The two governments must accept it after ratification. Once proper arrangements have been made, they shall exchange the instruments of ratification at Addis Ababa as soon as possible.

Seventh

This treaty shall remain in force for 20 years from the date of ratification. When this period has expired it shall be renewable annually.

This treaty has been written identically in the two official languages, Amharic and Italian, one copy remaining in the hands of the Ethiopian Government, the other in the hands of the Italian Government.'

26th[10] Hamle 1920 (= 2nd August 1928).

Later on,[11] in 1921 (= 1928–9), H.H. the Duke of Abruzzi returned to Addis Ababa once more. The reason for his visit was, now that the treaty of friendship and road construction had been

[9] This treaty was negotiated, in the form of a convention of friendship and commerce, by M. Klobukowski who, at the same time, also drew up the new treaty regarding the Franco-Ethiopian railway and its extension from Dire Dawa to Addis Ababa (Pankhurst, 165; de Coppet, II, 615). See also Perham², 151. The relevant provision concerns the exemption of foreigners from the application of Ethiopian laws and court procedures.

[10] The Amharic text has erroneously 16th which requires correction.

[11] At this point a paragraph is missing referring to the convention about the construction of the motor road Assab-Dessie (see *L'Africa Orientale*, 346 ff.). That this originally formed part of the Amharic version, at this point, can still be recognized from the wording on p. 123, lines 3 and 16, which speaks of the 'treaty of friendship and road construction'.

signed, to decorate Us with the Grand Order of the Annunziata with golden chain[12] and then to proceed to Mogadishu,[13] having on the same occasion traversed Arussi[14] and explored,[15] from its sources, the great river Webi Shebeli which rises at the meeting point of Arussi and Bale and flows down to Italian Somaliland.

The reason why he wanted to see the sources was, according to the version he told me, that he had founded a large concern with a big agricultural enterprise[16] near Mogadishu and that the water irrigating those plantations was derived from the Webi Shebeli.

We sent with him a number of men as guides, so that no mishap should befall him throughout his journey.

Even though the Duke of Abruzzi was an Italian Prince, We had hoped things would turn out in accordance with his assurance, for he had certainly declared repeatedly that the treaty of friendship which had been signed would remain firm.

While We had every intention of observing our treaty obligations and honouring our undertaking after we had concluded the treaty of friendship and of road construction, We spent a lot of money appointing engineers from Holland and set them to survey the direction of the road to Dessie, in conjunction with our own engineers at Addis Ababa and the people on the spot. After we had completed drawing up the plans and when we were ready to request the Italians that the road works be started, they were not at all intent on the work but rather on inciting quarrels as of old; they thus delayed matters by dragging their feet and by asking that the work be carried out on their engineers' surveys and calculations—criticizing what our own engineers had done by way of surveys and measurements. But in Europe they began to spread the rumour by letting it appear that the Ethiopian Government had violated the treaty by postponing the work. Whatever the damage to herself might be, Ethiopia refrained from spending her money on press campaigns or from spreading mendacious propaganda, like Italy, but stuck to the truth firmly. Yet it

[12] The highest Italian order of chivalry.

[13] The capital of Somalia. For details, incl. map, see *Guida*, 564 ff.

[14] The fertile province in southern Ethiopia. *The Ethiopians*[2], 191; *Guida*, 461.

[15] The well-known expedition of the Duke of Abruzzi in 1928–9; see R. Soc. Geogr. Ital., *Africa Orientale*, 63 ff. Cf. Cerulli, *Etiopia Occidentale*.

[16] The large *Società Agricola Italo-Somala*, initiated by the Duke of Abruzzi and situated on both banks of the Webi Shebeli, was a vast industrial enterprise. It is described in considerable detail in *Guida*, 602 ff.

undoubtedly suited Italy—in spreading this sort of report—to claim that she had to take Ethiopia by war, as the latter was in breach of her treaty obligations. By Italy's own actions all this has become clearly apparent.

CHAPTER 24

About Our receiving the dignity of kingship without ceasing to be Heir Apparent and Regent Plenipotentiary

WHEN Ledj Iyasu was removed from the throne[1] on the grounds of his inability to conduct the government, it was arranged that I should take charge and be responsible for the entire business of government, while Queen Zawditu became Empress with myself as Heir to the Throne and Regent Plenipotentiary. When, by virtue of my office as Regent, I set to work following the ways of modern civilization, I caused some of the nobles, who to their misfortune had been hanging on to the old customs, to give up the plans they had conceived for ruling, just as they pleased, the district to which they had been appointed. They began to feel aggrieved when, as those who had been wronged protested, We meted out impartial justice in regard to them, without paying heed to their high station; when We told them to render to the government the income derived from their governorship in terms of customs duties, telephone charges, and similar revenues; and when We moved them about, in reshuffles, from one province to another. Because they were aware in their heart that everything was being done equitably and that remonstrating would make them objects of shame, they could not openly discuss this matter which caused them such distress; they therefore let this go and decided instead to make Queen Zawditu an instrument adapted to all their designs.

[1] The Amharic text says 'succession to the throne', but this is not strictly accurate, for Ledj Iyasu was Emperor, though never formally crowned, from 1913 to 1916.

For this purpose it was Dejazmatch Baltcha[2] whom at first they made their leader. It was in a district called Agämja,[3] at a distance of four days' march from Addis Ababa, that Dejazmatch Baltcha was born. During a military campaign in the Agämja region, he was still a young boy; in the hour of victory a soldier found him, took him prisoner, and brought him to Emperor Menelik and he grew up in the palace. It was my father, H.H. Ras Makonnen, who became his godfather at the christening.

When he was grown up, Emperor Menelik appointed him custodian of all government finances. Later on, when he fought against the Italians at the time of the battle of Adwa,[4] he showed conspicuous valour and thus began to live in an exalted position. The fact that the Italians killed him now[5] with such cruel violence was additionally an act of revenge for that battle of Adwa—and not only because he struggled against them in heroic guerrilla actions.

While Dejazmatch Baltcha occupied a position of rank and honour in Emperor Menelik's time and Our own, worthless men who rose up to impede Our work seduced him into becoming their leader, and he thus got involved in the matter. But subsequently, when those worthless men were arrested and condemned to punishment, he himself disputed his involvement in the matter and, having escaped punishment, went to his governorate of Sidamo.

As he maltreated the peasants by his mode of governing and the military by his allocation of quarters, worse even than before, they came to Addis Ababa to complain; when We summoned[6] him to submit to arbitration, he let many months pass before he came, pleading delay or illness or fatigue.

[2] See the references given above in chapter 3, note (28). Photograph in Käbbädä Täsämma, 74. Of particular importance is Bairu Tafla's article in *JES*, VII, 2.

For the construction of the cleft clause here, cf. Blatta Heruy, *Addis Aläm*, 30 : 6 : የፌሪሁት ፡ ይህንኑ ፡ አሳባቸሁን ፡ ነበር ። See also Polotsky, *Collected Papers*, 165, note 1. Polotsky (in a private communication) describes this construction as 'entirely normal'.

[3] According to Bairu Tafla, *JES*, VII, 2, p. 14, a district in the Gurage region, south of Addis Ababa.

[4] The battle of Adwa, in 1896, was the scene of a great Ethiopian victory over the Italians. See Ullendorff[3], 88–9; *Guida*, 240 ff.

[5] As a result of guerilla actions led by Dej. Baltcha in 1936—Bairu Tafla, *op. cit.*, 20–1.   [6] For this and what follows cf. Bairu Tafla, *op. cit.*, 18 ff.

After he had turned up he stayed at his house claiming to be ill, so as not to be called to face arbitration and to appear before the tribunal with those who had been wronged. But as We had heard of his attempts to stir up trouble against Us, We had his house surrounded by troops and made him attend by force. When We caused the matter to be investigated, he admitted by his own statement that he had planned to stir up trouble against Us, and since his own servants testified against him he was sentenced, in the month of Yäkatit 1920 (= February 1928), to be deprived of his office and to reside in a specially designated place.

Later on, in the month of Nähase 1920 (= August 1928), some useless and worthless men rose up against Us, making Dejazmatch Abba Weqaw[7] their leader.

Abba Weqaw had earlier been a retainer of Emperor Menelik. But after We had become Regent Plenipotentiary, We nominated him Dejazmatch and made him commander of Our guard. But without thinking of his country, Ethiopia, or his honour, the insurgent sought to raise up commotion against Us by taking counsel with useless and common people. We heard that he was spreading the rumour (with a view to increasing his following) that it was Queen Zawditu who had ordered him to bring about this upheaval; and when We summoned him to tell Us about this in his own words, he bided his time by wandering to and fro within the extensive grounds of the Palace precincts.[8] And when it became dark, he entered the Menelik Mausoleum[9] adjacent to the Palace and stayed there as a rebel. Later on, he sent as intercessors the Etchäge and some priests, lest We should impose the death penalty upon him, and then he surrendered; while he was spared the death penalty, he was sentenced to reside at a specified place under arrest.

Subsequently, the ministers and nobles living at Addis Ababa as well as the army commanders and all men holding office reached

[7] Dejazmatch Abba Weqaw Berru (see the following narrative) was at various times a provincial governor and Commander of the Imperial Guard (see Käbbädä Täsämma, chapter 8, pp. 75 ff., and photograph on p. 416). Died 1941. Cf. *JES*, VII, 2, 252.

[8] The reference is clearly to Menelik's old compound, the present Grand Palace.

[9] The Menelik Mausoleum, adjoining the old *gebbi*, contains the tombs of Menelik himself, his consort Taitu, and his daughter Zawditu (*Guida*, 494; *Africa Orientale*, 81).

agreement unanimously and declared: 'Worthless common people rise up from time to time against our Crown Prince and create upheaval; perhaps on some future occasion, when similar disturbances arise, we may fail to prevent internal bloodshed; it is, therefore, necessary to think of means of restraining such commotion. For this purpose it is best to act as follows: Empress Zawditu should have solely the honour of the Crown and the Throne—as was established when first she succeeded to the reign, leaving the task of government entirely to the Crown Prince, while the latter should carry out on his sole authority the whole business of government (as was defined and initiated on 17th Mäskäräm 1909= 27th September 1916), without consulting the Empress and without obtaining her permission. In order that his authority should possess force and be respected, it would be best for us to arrange that he should attain the dignity of Kingship.' Once they had decided this, they assembled in the wide square within the palace precincts and approached Empress Zawditu in writing: 'May it please you to have H.H. Crown Prince Tafari proclaimed King and have him carry out, on his sole authority, any government business without having to consult anyone.'

Empress Zawditu summoned her special counsellors, and when they proffered her advice it seemed to them an extremely difficult matter. In truth, I myself felt it to be very difficult. For, once proclaimed King of some large part of Ethiopia, I could not go there or else the Empress would need another Regent. As King I could scarcely reside at Addis Ababa, for it was not customary for two Kings to reside in one city. She therefore sent word to them to be given time in which to ponder the matter.

This proposal by the people was awkward not only for Empress Zawditu but even for myself. I therefore summoned three men from the assembled nobles and despatched them to the people with this message: 'It would be good if the idea which you have had that the work of government be accomplished by one man's sole and undivided design could be carried out, but it would be as well if the proposal as regards the Kingship were not raised. Arrange for this matter to be dropped, for it might appear that I had incited you in the desire to become King; it is God alone who knows that I am not involved in this affair but people do not know.' They sent word back to Us: 'We cannot go back on it, for the reason we have acted was that we were mindful of the honour of our realm and the benefit and peace of the people—without favouring anyone.' We therefore kept quiet.

Later on, when they saw the reply which had reached them from Empress Zawditu asking for time to ponder the matter, they presented to her a further written submission which all of them signed and sealed: The fact that Empress Zawditu was asking for time to think about it was simply to obtain time in order to issue a refusal after consultation with her friends who follow her own way of thinking and who do not like modern conditions; or to bring about, on these grounds, a situation in which revolution and civil war would be created. 'However that may be', their submission ran, 'we are determined to do what is necessary, being assembled here and not intending to disperse unless you give us the reply today.'

Moreover, the people of the city did not know the true reason why the ministers, nobles, and army commanders had assembled in the palace grounds, and it needed very little for them to start a revolution.

Empress Zawditu caused the declaration, which had been presented to her with signatures and seals, to be read; and, when she had understood it, she thought it would be preferable to accept their counsel in order to avoid bloodshed. She then directed that the following written announcement be read out to them: 'It is my wish that the Crown Prince be crowned as King on a date determined by you on the basis of the advice tendered by you.' Consequently security and calm returned. Thereupon they pushed each other forward penetrating as far as the internal court-yard and clapped hands with joy. Then they conveyed their thanks saying: 'Long live H.M. the Empress! May Ethiopia live for ever.' They then went back to their homes.

The next morning they assembled once more and claimed that it would be better for this affair of the Kingship to be accomplished within three days, lest second throughts should ruin this matter if further delay were to occur. We convinced them, however, of the impossibility of a thing like Kingship being carried out within two or three days and, furthermore, of the need to inform each of the governments of our neighbours, so that their representatives might come and take part in our joy. It was, therefore, decided that the coronation should take place one month hence, on 27th Mäskäräm 1921 (= 7th October 1928).

As there was rejoicing about Empress Zawditu's approval that We were to be proclaimed King, and since the British, French, and Italians, who possess colonies in our neighbourhood, were delighted, the British Government despatched to Addis Ababa the Governor of Berbera,[10] Mr. Kittermaster,[11] the French Government sent the Governor of Jibuti, M. Chapon Baissac, and the Italian Government the Governor of Eritrea, Signor Corrado Zoli.[12]

When everything that was required for this festival of Kingship had been prepared, the whole great ceremony which is enacted for crowning a King of the Ethiopian Empire took place on 27th Mäskäräm 1921 (= 7th October 1928); We received the crown from the hands of Empress Zawditu, and the festive day passed off with dignity.

[10] The port and capital of British Somaliland (*Guida*, 441).
[11] Sir Harold Baxter Kittermaster, K.C.M.G., Governor of British Somaliland.
[12] 1877–1951. Governor of Eritrea 1928–30 (*Chi è dell'Eritrea*, 303).

CHAPTER 25

About the instigation by the Italians of Ras Gugsa Wale's[1] rebellion

IT is very surprising to observe how the Italians, who were constantly accusing Ethiopia before the League of Nations of being a country without unity, were themselves engaged in propaganda activities with the object of dividing the Ethiopian Empire. It really is astonishing what diligence We had to employ to counteract their propaganda. Yet try as they might, they were unable to bring about internal splits.

Things that have occurred quite recently testify to the fact that Italy's idea of waging a war of oppression against Ethiopia goes back a long time.

They were disseminating propaganda that caused great damage among our people, yet spreading it about—plausibly so to outsiders—that Italy was Ethiopia's friend. We do not doubt that all

[1] Apart from the information embodied in footnote (15) to chapter 8, see Luca dei Sabelli's somewhat biased account in vol. IV, 139 ff.

the diplomats residing in Ethiopia are aware of this, and if We were to write about all the propaganda ruses which the Italians have employed against Ethiopia, many pages would be used up—but We would rather leave it. Nevertheless, the work of deceit and propaganda they carried out with the connivance of Ras Gugsa Wale and Ras Haylu[2] is known all over Ethiopia, and it would therefore be improper for Us to leave it unrecorded.

Ras Gugsa was the son of Ras Wale, Empress Taitu's brother. His father, Ras Wale, nominated him Dejazmatch over a part of his governorate and later on came to Shoa.

Ever since Empress Taitu had got married to Emperor Menelik she had been striving to bring about a rapprochement and much closer relationship of the people of Bägemeder, Semien, and Yäjju, who were her family, with the people of Shoa, and she made it her principal purpose to arrange marriages of her female relations with Shoan nobles and of her male relations with Shoan ladies. She therefore arranged, in 1892 (= 1899/1900), that Dejazmatch Gugsa, the son of her brother Ras Wale, should marry Emperor Menelik's daughter Wayzäro Zawditu, subsequently Empress of Ethiopia. On those grounds he attained the rank of Ras in 1893 (= 1900-1); and when he served as governor of Bägemeder, Ras Bitwaddäd Täsämma, who became Regent Plenipotentiary of the Ethiopian realm after Emperor Menelik's confinement to the palace because of illness, gave the governorship of Bägemeder to Ras Waldä Giyorgis and directed Ras Gugsa to live in confinement. When Ras Gugsa had remained under restriction for about seven years, Wayzäro Zawditu was chosen, on 17th Mäskäräm 1909 (= 27th September 1916), to succeed to the crown and throne of Ethiopia. When Her Majesty reigned as Empress she declared: 'I shall not live with a husband, but I make a vow to live on my own, for God has selected me, a woman, and has let me live for this great crown and throne.' Since she had chosen to live on her own and as Ras Gugsa became aware of the Queen's firm resolve, the instrument of their separation was completed by mutual consent, and We assigned to Ras Gugsa the governorship of Embabo,[3] in Walläga, and Sayent. But a year later, when the

---

[2] In addition to the details recorded in footnote (7) to chapter 8, cf. again Luca dei Sabelli's far from impartial account in vol. IV, 148 ff. See below chapter 31.

[3] Embabo in the Walläga region was the scene of a famous battle in 1882 (Guida, 506; Gäbrä Sellase, chapter 32; Toponomastica Etiopica, 165 [Imbabo]).

governor of Bägemeder, King Waldä Giyorgis, died, We restored to Ras Gugsa the governorship of Bägemeder, and for the time being he was pleased to get his former province back. But the Italians have always been the bane of the Ethiopian people, and some of them, pretending to come for trade or to see the country, went to and fro from Bägemeder to Asmara,[4] met Ras Gugsa and went on sowing dissension in his heart, so that in the end they managed to turn his joy into sadness.

Worst of all was the fact that the Italian commercial agent resident at Gondar made propaganda his main occupation.

The residence of the Governor of Bägemeder is in the town of Däbrä Tabor.[5] But the Italians had received permission from Emperor Menelik and from Ledj Iyasu, before Our time, to establish a commercial agency at Gondar where priests and traders lived and which appeared suitable to them as a base to carry out their propaganda. Afterwards, as Ras Gugsa Wale possessed a hereditament at a place near Gondar, they presented to him the following proposal in writing: 'If you lease to us this hereditament of yours, we shall develop your place for you; afterwards, at the time we leave it, we shall make over to you free of charge any houses we have built there and absolutely everything else.' He gave them permission, as it appeared to him a genuine proposal.

It was a man called Signor Pollera[6] whom they established as commercial agent at this place. Signor Pollera, in order to equip himself for this work of deceit and propaganda, employed an Ethiopian woman for money and, declaring her his wife, had children by her.

Moreover, he was advanced in age, and as it is the custom of Ethiopians to show respect for the elderly, all the people of Gondar honoured him and did not look upon him as a foreigner.

[4] The capital of Eritrea and Ethiopia's second city. See the detailed article, with town plan, etc., in *Guida*, 197–211.

[5] The capital of Bägemeder province, about 30 miles east of Lake Tana. At times (e.g. during the reign of Yohannes IV) the capital of Ethiopia. Map in *Guida*, 368; detailed description in *Guida*, 391.

[6] Alberto Pollera (1873–1939), colonial official and *éthiopisant*, spent nearly his entire life in Eritrea, married Ethiopian ladies, and established a veritable dynasty in Eritrea. Among his more important books are *Lo Stato Etiopico e la sua Chiesa* (1926), *Le popolazioni indigene dell'Eritrea* (1935), *L'Abissinia di ieri* (1940), etc. The last work includes a photograph of the author.

He on his part would offer money when a woman had given birth,[7] or at the commemoration for the deceased.[8] Although he was a Catholic, he would enter orthodox churches and pray as the priests were watching him. On the festival days of the year he would extend invitations to priests and traders, according to the custom of Ethiopian noblemen, and have beer[9] brewed, honey-mead[10] prepared, and oxen slaughtered. For all these reasons he cultivated excellent relations with the local population.

Again, he knew that Ras Gugsa Wale, the governor of Bäge-meder, was firm in the orthodox faith and an opponent of European religion and civilization; therefore he would go to him and argue thus: 'It is best for Ethiopia to live according to ancient custom as of old and it would not profit her to follow European civilization. But it is said that it is the intention of the present Crown Prince and Regent Plenipotentiary to introduce European civilization into Ethiopia. Once European civilization has penetrated Ethiopia, it will inevitably mean freedom of religion. When freedom of religion exists, then the orthodox faith is bound to weaken and the Catholic faith to strengthen and gradually expand; thus it is rumoured that the Crown Prince himself is about to join the Catholic religion. Also, we have heard that from time to time he is issuing proclamations aimed at the eradication of slavery from Ethiopia. But now, once all the slaves are declared free, how are those lords and nobles of Bägemeder to live? Is it that the masters are to plough with their own hands and the ladies to grind with their own hands? Even in Europe, although slavery has ceased ever since all the work has come to be done by machines, yet in the past every man, like you, had several slaves. Now in this country a great calamity will befall you, unless you and the great nobles like you take heed of this.' Pollera spoke to Ras Gugsa in those terms, inciting him to rise up himself on his part against Us with the might of his army, while persuading each of the great nobles to do likewise. He assembled his officers and let them into the secret: 'A friend of mine has advised me in those terms; what had best be done?' Some of the officers who were convinced that it was fraudulent advice sent word to me in secret.

[7] Walker, 1-2; KBT, 1274.
[8] *The Ethiopians*[2], 175; Walker, chapter X.
[9] Ethiopian beer, *tälla*, is a barley brew.
[10] *Tädj* is the Ethiopian national drink.

But We had no doubt that Ras Gugsa Wale was planning evil things against Our government, as he had listened to the deceitful counsel of the Italians. We therefore bided our time in patience with the intention of clarifying matters. In this affair it was also thoughtfulness for Empress Zawditu that impelled Us towards patience.

Moreover, by sheer coincidence a contract was awarded at that period to a foreigner, on the part of the Addis Ababa Municipality, to establish a leather factory at Addis Ababa. Apart from the hides of oxen and goats, he would strip the skin off horses, mules, donkeys, and dogs and take them to the factory for tanning. When the Italians heard of this, they spread a rumour in every province, to the effect that at Addis Ababa donkeys and dogs were being slaughtered and a start had been made to feed them to officers and troops at official banquets; it did not seem impossible for a proclamation to be issued all over Ethiopia that the meat of donkeys and dogs was to be eaten in future. The people of Bägemeder got a heart-felt shock at this news.

In Ethiopia even people who have only very recently accepted Christianity—leaving aside the people of Bägemeder who are of ancient Christian adherence—are known to feel great revulsion when told that the skins of donkeys and dogs are being stripped off for the process of tanning, let alone for eating their meat![11] Perhaps in Europe, too, people are not lacking who feel disgust at things of this sort.

Ras Gugsa Wale, although it was with his consent that he was separated from Empress Zawditu, had begun to speak to some of his friends of his grief at being confined to reside in Bägemeder only, without being able to come to Addis Ababa at this great time of joy. When the Italians heard this, they realized that this was a suitable time to seduce Ras Gugsa. They told him things which entered deep into his heart, such as: 'We are willing to give you the arms you require, and with the aid of the Italian government you may rebel and fight against the present government, and you may be proclaimed King and, together with Empress Zawditu, you may become the ruler of the whole of Ethiopia.' Now, seizing this opportunity, he said that it would be better to die than to abandon our slaves and to live under a government which forces people to eat the meat of donkeys and dogs. He began to

[11] About Ethiopian dietary prescriptions see *Ethiopia and the Bible*, 100-3.

endeavour to bring the whole people of Bägemeder over to his party and to strengthen the might of his forces. He announced all this openly in form of a proclamation.

As those of Our soldiers who guard the border areas of Our Empire in the Dankali[12] and Aussa[13] provinces—being deserts and places of disease—suffer a great deal, they are permitted occasionally to come up to the highlands[14] for a rest. When the Italians received information about this from their spies, they were watching for a moment when the number of troops was diminished and then sent in army engineers to map the mountains and rivers, valleys and escarpment. They supplied arms and money to the Wajjerat[15] and the Raya[16] and Azäbo[17] Galla and advised them by every possible ruse to rebel against Our government. But some of these Wajjerat came and spoke to Us. While We were in the process of causing it to be investigated whether Italy was doing things of this sort, oblivious of the treaty of friendship she had concluded with Us in 1920 (= 1928), We heard that the Wajjerat and Raya and Azäbo Galla, flaunting the arms and the money they had received from Italy, were mounting the highlands killing people and plundering cattle. Therefore, since We knew that Yäjju was the district in which Ras Gugsa Wale had grown up and because of its proximity to Bägemeder, We transmitted orders to him to go to Yäjju making amicable appeals to the Wajjerat and Azäbo Galla and offering them friendly advice as well as urging them to abandon their evil works; but if they refused, he was to fight them by military force. We thought, incidentally, that, if he now tarried with this mission to Yäjju, it would thereby be revealed that everything of which he had been accused, i.e. being in consultation with the Italians, was true.

When Ras Gugsa received the order, he mobilized the Bägemeder army by proclamation and went to Yäjju, so as to let it appear for the moment that he was carrying out orders. But when

[12] The Danakil inhabit the vast arid depression from the Gulf of Zula to the Gulf of Tajura. Cf. *The Ethiopians*[3], 39; *Guida*, 329 ff.

[13] *The Ethiopians*[3], 39, 72; *Guida*, 344.

[14] The Ethiopian terms for the division of their country into three main zones according to altitude and climate are explained in *The Ethiopians*[3], 25.

[15] The area to the east of Mäqälle (map, *Guida* 304/5 and details on p. 305); Tigrinya speakers, known for their raids into Dankali territory.

[16] For the Raya Galla see Huntingford, *Galla*, 14; *Guida*, 315.

[17] Huntingford, *loc. cit.*; *Guida*, 305, 311; *The Ethiopians*[3], 39–40.

he had reached Yäjju, We heard of his return to Bägemeder without accomplishing properly what he had been ordered to do about the Wajjerat and Raya and Azäbo Gallas and that, after reaching agreement, they would, in fact, join him as his support troops; after he had returned he was chiefly occupied with collecting an army and preparing weapons of war. While We were meaning to be very careful lest the blood of brothers be shed in vain and the desire of the Italians thus be fulfilled, We sent word to Ras Gugsa suggesting that we should at any rate meet at Warräyelu[18] and discuss in detail the reason why he had returned from the military expedition as well as every other matter; thereafter he might go back. While he wrote back merely words of deceit claiming to agree and to set out at once, We received information that, in fact, he was tarrying and preparing for war. We therefore despatched troops, under the command of Dejaz-match Mullugeta, who were to keep watch (being stationed at Wadla and Dälanta[19]) in order to prevent Ras Gugsa slipping into Yäjju and linking up with the Wajjerat and Raya—Azäbo Gallas.

As Italy's propaganda agents were seeking out some magicians and dreamers who are to be encountered in Bägemeder, they sent them to Ras Gugsa instigating them to speak to him encourag-ingly: 'The time has come for you to be King, hence have courage and do not fear.' Proof of all this was discovered in Ras Gugsa's portfolio which was captured in the war.

Since some Ethiopians do not possess, apart from religious knowledge, any other education in secular politics, thus when monks or hermits tell them that at a certain time a certain thing will take place, they accept it as true, for it seems to them that such men were sent by God; to profit by this the Italians—since they are acquainted with this fact—make it their chief instrument.

Anxious to ascertain the Italians' involvement or non-involve-ment in this affair, We spoke to the Italian Minister at Addis Ababa: 'Sell·Us one aeroplane for the preservation of internal security and We shall appoint a pilot from among your people.' He told Us that he would inform his government and convey the reply as soon as possible. But he delayed giving Us any answer,

[18] Warräyelu or Warrä-Ilu, important centre some 50 miles south of Dessie (*Guida*, 400).
[19] The great plains of Wadla and Dälanta, in the Waldia-Magdala-Dessie region, are in central Ethiopia near the Gondar-Dessie road (*Guida*, 393–4).

and when there was just one day left before Ras Gugsa's attack upon Our army, the Minister let Us know that they had not succeeded in sending the aircraft from Asmara immediately. Since in Our heart We had known all along that the reply would be thus, it caused Us no surprise whatever.

Having been deceived by lies of this sort, Ras Gugsa decided to make war; he issued a proclamation of mobilization, marched along in a great hurry and, on 22nd Mägabit 1922 (= 31st March 1930), launched an attack upon Dejazmatch Mullugeta at Qwana.[20] When he had fought for about three hours he suffered a defeat.

Thus the deceitful counsel, over which the Italians had toiled for so many years, was demolished in three hours, and Ras Gugsa came to his end. The fact that the majority of the captured arms, found in the hands of Ras Gugsa's troops in the course of this battle, were Vetterli[21] rifles which had come from Asmara made it quite certain to Us that it was the Italians who had helped Ras Gugsa to rebel.

The Empress Zawditu died on 24th Mägabit 1922 (= 2nd April 1930), two days after the death of Ras Gugsa.

Empress Zawditu had for a long time prior to this suffered from diabetes which had been diagnosed by the Swedish Dr. Hanner and the Swiss Dr. Mayberg.[22] As this disease got progressively worse and more virulent every year, she had latterly been very ill. Therefore, she had not been informed of Ras Gugsa's death, lest this news should aggravate her illness. This was because the physicians who were treating her, Dr. Hanner and Dr. Mayberg, had given instructions that she was not to hear the sad news. But the Italians, with the intention of completing the full measure of their deceitfulness, spread the rumour that she died of shock after hearing the news, while in fact there is no prince, noble, or minister at Addis Ababa who does not know that Empress Zawditu died without hearing of Ras Gugsa's death in battle.

[20] Qwana is a district in Bägemeder (DTW, 1080). The place of the battle is usually given as Zebit, just south of the Takazze river on the Bägemeder-Wadla border (*Guida*, 393; Luca dei Sabelli, IV, 141).

[21] The Amharic word *waččäfo* 'rain-cloud' has come to be associated with these Swiss-designed Italian rifles, possibly because of their speed (Guidi, *Suppl.*, 172). See also Armbruster, *Engl.-Amh. Voc.*, 377, and Cohen, *JA*, Nov.-Dec. 1911, 24; Pankhurst, *JES*, IX, 1, 71-2.

[22] Probably the same person as the Dr. Mayenberger listed in Pankhurst, 651.

CHAPTER 26

About Our planning and initiating gradual improvements and reforms in the work of the clergy

SINCE time immemorial the Kings of Ethiopia, just as they were responsible for the entire business of government, were also in charge of the affairs of the church; they would select persons from among the savants and the learned and make appointments to, as well as dismissals from, office at the various churches and monasteries and, in general, have the authority to control all their functions. But with the gradual increase in government business and the occasional waging of wars against the pagans in neighbouring countries, they simply did not have the time to control in full the affairs of the church; consequently, there were many things detrimental to the ordinances of the church which had in error penetrated into the community of the clergy and had by custom persisted.

But now that We had established a constitution[1] and had introduced a legal framework into each ministry and had also arranged for ministers to carry out their respective functions with full responsibility, We brought about a progressive and step by step improvement in the work of the clergy as We were meeting church leaders and priors in the time left over from affairs of state. These improvements were as follows:

(1) Since the people of Ethiopia, great and small, men and women, were firm in their Christianity, they went to Church and heard mass each week on Sunday and on each of the great festivals. Whoever was able to would receive the eucharist. But as holy mass[2] was in the Ge'ez language which not all the people could understand, many would return home without comprehending the words explaining the mysteries—just listening to the sound of

---

[1] This is slightly anticipating and refers to the first (1931) constitution; see chapter 29.   [2] *qeddase*, The Ethiopians[3], 103.

the chants.[3] But now We arranged for holy mass to be translated into Amharic and to be printed, and once it had been distributed in every church, the people began to understand when the text was read out in their own language, even if not all of it, then at least the main part. It was likewise arranged for the gospels, acts of the apostles, and epistles to be read to them in Amharic.

(2) With a view to bringing about a cessation of the quarrels which flare up from time to time, as regards their livelihood, between deans,[4] priests,[5] and church custodians,[6] or abbots,[7] monks, and adjuvants[8] who live in the various large churches and mona-steries, We assembled the savants and the learned and made them bring along the ancient customs and rules of life of each of the churches and monasteries; by getting them to set up new and improved regulations great benefit was attained. Improved and newly established regulations are to be found at Zequala, Däbrä Libanos, Jerusalem,[9] and all other monasteries.

(3) The fact that there is to be found in each church a copy of the *mäshafä täklil*[10] constitutes proof of the existence in Ethiopia in earlier times of a crowning ceremony at the marriage service. However, the ceremonial of the church was progressively diminished and, therefore, marriage by crowning was not very wide-spread, not even among the clergy, let alone among the people; but it is not known whether this happened at the time of the uprising of Ahmad Gran or during the extermination of Christians when Yodit[11] of the Falasha[12] tribe reigned. Nonethe-less, there were many among the clergy and the people who were

---

[3] *zema, The Ethiopians*[3], 164–5.   [4] *aläqa*, i.e. head of a church.

[5] *kahen*; I am not certain whether it is clearly distinguished from *qes*.

[6] *gäbäz* is the custodian of the services and treasures of the church (Habtä Maryam, 300).

[7] *abbä mahbär* is the prior of a monastery, the head of a monastic community (DTW, 70).   [8] *arde'et* are auxiliaries, adjuvants (*ibid.*).

[9] See above notes (30) and (33) to chapter 15; for Zequala and Däbrä Libanos cf. also first reff. above.

[10] Guidi, *Letteratura*, 75; this work contains the ritual for the blessing and crowning of bride and bridegroom. Cf. also BM (Wright) CXXXVII, 2; CXXXIX, 2; KBT, 598. See Makonnen Endalkatchäw, *Yähelm Rucca*, 121.

[11] Yodit = Judith, a perhaps legendary queen ruling Ethiopia in the 10th century (*The Ethiopians*[3], 57–8).

[12] The Falashas are a Judaized community in the Gondar region. Cf. Leslau, *Falasha Anthology; The Ethiopians*[3], 105–7.

strengthening their marriage by receiving eucharist together with their spouses.

But now We have urged the savants and the learned to preach exalting marriage by crowning and, as a result, it has again become customary.

(4) In earlier times, when a person died, his family, in arranging the *täzkar* (memorial service), would prepare *tälla* (beer), *tädj* (honey-mead), and other intoxicating matter and would invite the priests to the house of the deceased; they would offer them food and drink beyond measure and would make them exceed what has been ordained. But now, since We have become convinced that conduct of this kind does not conform to the new era of civilization and is also forbidden by the Holy Scriptures, We have arranged that the *täzkar* should cease consisting of intoxicating drink and excessive amounts of food and that, instead, the relatives of the deceased should have the absolution prayers performed and give, according to their means, some money to the priests for the performance of absolution. It should not, however, be forbidden to offer food and drink to the poor, provided this is done in moderation. We also urged the bishops and priors to preach in this sense.

Intending to be a model and example to the people, when Our daughter, Princess Zänäbä Warq,[13] died, We distributed gifts of money, for the absolution rites, among various churches and monasteries. Many people then began to do likewise.

(5) Since early times it was the custom in some provinces for some of the relatives of a deceased person to manifest mourning by cutting their hair, beating their breasts and by general wailing. But now We have given instructions to the savants to go round the various churches and to preach that the family of the deceased should—apart from wearing a black patch on the edge of the dress as a sign of mourning—cease the cutting of hair, the beating of breasts, and wearing special mourning clothes. Hence, as the savants preached with diligence, the hopeless mourning for a dead person has gradually eased.

(6) As We were convinced that We had the responsibility to protect the church and to see that the laws given to her were

---

[13] She died before the Italo-Ethiopian war, not long after her marriage to Dejazmatch Haylä Sellasse Gugsa.

firmly kept lest her faith be shaken, We granted one day each week on which the savants and doctors might approach Us and draw attention, personally, to all the difficulties of the church; consequently, the problems of the church gradually eased.

Apart from this, while regulations have been drafted, the following matters have for the time being remained in abeyance:

[14]In Ethiopia the number of priests is very large. To all of these the government had allocated as *rest*-land, individually in each province, from one half to one *gasha* of land (i.e. *approx.* 40 to 80 acres). This land, having been assigned as hereditary, passes on to children's children and, therefore, the church is unable to make provisions with regard to it. Furthermore, beginning with the Emperor, princes, noblemen, and all others like them, not even ladies excluded, could assume the duties of church wardens, and in that case the Emperor used to allocate to them hereditary land of between 200 and 700 *gashas*. It was Our intention, however, to bring about a situation where hereditary land should cease to belong to individuals by virtue of this church-wardenship but should become that of the church; that the deans of churches should allocate, from the income of these properties, adequate amounts to the priests, deacons, choristers, and readers for their livelihood; as regards any surplus, the deans of churches should build—after proper consultations and with the government helping them over any deficit that might arise—schools and hospitals, homes for the aged and educational establishments for the children of the poor.

As it would take Us a long time to have these ideas of Ours carried out in the churches all over Ethiopia, We arranged to make a start, by demonstrating the usefulness of the scheme and its working method, in the monasteries of Zequala, Addis Aläm,[15] and Assäbot[16] as well as the churches of Addis Ababa and in the Menelik II Mausoleum church.

[14] The cardinal numeral 'first' at the head of this paragraph appears to be otiose.
[15] Addis Aläm, considered as a possible capital for Ethiopia by Emperor Menelik about the turn of the century, cathedral church and *gebbi*, some 38 miles west of Addis Ababa (*Guida*, 497; map *ib.*).
[16] Mountain (2500 metres) to the N.W. of Miesso (Mehesso), somewhere about half-way between Harar and Addis Ababa (*Guida*, 421).

CHAPTER 27

About Our arrangements for the appointment of bishops chosen from among the savants of Ethiopia

It does not appear to Us likely that anyone doubts that Ethiopia —besides being a very large country—has lived steadfast in her Christianity from the 4th century up to the present time, some 1600 years. In any event, one can be easily convinced of this fact by reading Ethiopia's history.

But when Ethiopia accepted Christianity, the seat of government and the principal city of the realm were at Aksum; consequently, it was to that province of Aksum that one bishop only was appointed by the Archbishop who was the incumbent of the See of St. Mark at Alexandria. When he died, another would be substituted, but never were there appointed several bishops in accordance with the size of the country.

Recently, in 1864 (= 1872), during the reign of Emperor Yohannes,[1] four Coptic (i.e. Egyptian) bishops had been appointed[2] and eventually arrived in 1873 (= 1880/1). The reason was that Emperor Yohannes, having enthroned King Menelik over Shoa and King Täklä Haymanot[3] over Gojjam, had intended to install his son, Ras Araya,[4] as King of Bägemeder. He was then to retain one bishop for himself for the Tigre province and to distribute three bishops to the three Kings. But the fourth bishop died before reaching Aksum, while Ras Araya died before becoming King; so the Emperor divided Ethiopia into three dioceses and assigned them to each of the three bishops. Thus the clergy

---

[1] Tigrean Emperor of Ethiopia (1872–89). See Heruy, *Ethiopia and Metemma: A brief history of Emperor Yohannes* (in Amharic); Luca dei Sabelli, vol. III, chapter VI; and especially Zewde Gabra Sellassie's political biography of his ancestor.

[2] Ullendorff, *Amharic Chrestomathy*, 21.

[3] Hereditary ruler of the Gojjam province; see *JES*, VII, 2, 236. Died 1900/1.

[4] Ras Araya was Emperor Yohannes' son and Empress Zawditu's first husband. He was born about 1870 and died about 1888. Cf. *JES*, loc. cit., 247.

were relieved of a tiring journey to a distant province, where the one single bishop resided, in order to receive ordination as priest or deacon. When two of these three bishops died and were not replaced by others, there only remained Abuna Mattewos for the whole of Ethiopia; and as his residence was in the capital Addis Ababa, members of the clergy, who came from the various provinces of Ethiopia to receive the office of priest or deacon, encountered great inconvenience and lived in a state of some turmoil.

As We were aware of the great difficulties encountered by members of the clergy in this matter, We set down this Our opinion in writing, with proper documentary support, to say that bishops should be appointed from among the savants of the country, to tour their dioceses preaching and conferring the priesthood and deaconship. This was despatched, with the seal of Empress Zawditu and my own, to the Orthodox Patriarch, Abuna Yohannes, at Alexandria.

After Abuna Yohannes had examined the matter with his lucid mind, he was convinced that this was a proper request and consequently sent to Us the following reply: 'If you choose five from among the Ethiopian savants and send them to us, it is our intention to appoint them as bishops. We shall, however, additionally despatch a Coptic (Egyptian) bishop who shall be primus among the Ethiopian bishops, and may you please appreciate this.'

When We informed the princes, nobles, doctors, and savants of this, the majority received the matter with joy. But some members of the clergy, although unable to oppose Our view openly, did not stop trying. This was not because they had investigated the matter thoroughly and understood it but it arose from their subjugation to custom. However, in the course of time We succeeded in convincing them that it would confer great honour upon the church of Ethiopia if this proposal were carried out. They therefore informed Us that they had changed their previous view and assured Us of the acceptance of Our plan.

Subsequently Mämher[5] Dästa,[6] Mämher Haylä Maryam,[6] Mämher Waldä Kidan,[6] and Mämher Haylä Mika'el[6] were selected and We arranged for them to go to Egypt in the month of Genbot 1921 (= May/June 1929).

[5] Mämher is the head of a monastery as well as the general courtesy title applied to learned men.
[6] Details of their episcopal names are given presently; see also Mara, pp. 33–4.

Meanwhile, the Patriarch, Abuna Yohannes, was waiting, having selected Abuna Qerillos,[7] from among the monks of the monastery of Asqetis,[8] whom he was sending as head of the Ethiopian bishops; and as soon as the Ethiopian savants reached Cairo, he immediately and without delay appointed the five of them together as bishops, i.e. on 25th Genbot (= 2nd June).

He (the Patriarch) assigned to them the following names: Mämher Dästa to be Abuna Abreham, Mämher Haylä Maryam to be Abuna Petros, Mämher Waldä Kidan to be Abuna Yeshaq, Mämher Haylä Mika'el to be Abuna Mika'el.[9]

Abuna Petros was the bishop who died in martyrdom at the hands of the Italians when he was captured, in Hamle 1928 (= July 1936), preaching about Ethiopia's freedom. Abuna Mika'el was battered to a martyr's death, at the hands of the enemy, in the town of Gore.[10]

After the bishops had been appointed to their episcopal office, they returned to Ethiopia together with the Archbishop, Abuna Qerillos. Since We were convinced that this was an unprecedented event in Ethiopia, glorifying the Ethiopian Church, We arranged that, upon their arrival at Addis Ababa, the princes and nobles, doctors and savants as well as the priests of the various churches should assemble *en masse*. Cannons were fired and a ceremonial welcome was held in their honour.

Thereupon, because We meant them to begin their work of education by touring their respective dioceses, We made the following dispositions:

The diocese of Archbishop Abuna Qerillos is to include the whole of Shoa, the districts surrounding Addis Ababa, and added to this Harar and Arussi.

For Abuna Abreham, Gojjam and Bägemeder.

---

[7] Not to be confused with the Patriarch Abuna Qerillos referred to in footnote (23) in chapter 15. The Abuna Qerillos mentioned here was the last Egyptian monk to become Archbishop of Ethiopia (Mara, 34–6, *et passim*).

[8] Asqit, i.e. Scyathis or Scete (see Evetts and Butler, *Churches and Monasteries of Egypt*, 245). According to Mara, 33, he was a monk of the Convent of Qusquam.

[9] Abuna Petros and Abuna Mika'el gave their lives during the Italian occupation of Ethiopia, 1936–41. Abuna Qerillos, after an abortive journey to Rome, retired to Cairo. The aged and ailing Bishop Abreham was forced to take Abuna Qerillos' place and to declare the Ethiopian Church independent of Alexandria.

[10] Important centre in S.W. Ethiopia (*Guida*, 516).

For Abuna Yeshaq, Tigre, Lasta and Wag and all the surrounding districts.

For Abuna Petros, the entire provinces of Wallo and Yäjju.

For Abuna Mika'el, the areas called Kaffa, Ilubabor,[11] Walläga, and the whole of western Ethiopia.

The man who had been selected to be the sixth bishop was Etchäge Gäbrä Mänfäs Qeddus[12] of Däbrä Libanos. But as it had been permanently inconvenient for him to travel to Egypt with the savants, it was his good fortune that later on, in Tahsas 1922 (= December–January 1929–30), the Patriarch, Abuna Yohannes, came to Addis Ababa to visit his children in the faith and immediately bestowed the rank of bishop upon Etchäge Gäbrä Mänfäs Qeddus and named him Abuna Sawiros.[13] We assigned to him as his diocese the whole of southern Ethiopia.

It is wonderful that at this time God in his charity wrought two great works of good fortune for the Ethiopian Church:

(1) The appointment of men, chosen from among Ethiopia's own savants, to the office of bishop—something that had never happened in some 1600 years, from the time Ethiopia accepted Christianity in the fourth century up to the present.

(2) The journey to Addis Ababa of the Patriarch, Abuna Yohannes, his celebrating mass in an Ethiopian church and his blessing of the people, while at the same time appointing the Etchäge of Däbrä Libanos to the dignity of a bishop.

[11] The most westerly of Ethiopia's provinces; cf. *The Ethiopians*[3], 191; *Guida*, 517.

[12] He had been too ill to travel to Egypt and, in fact, died not long after his consecration as bishop.

[13] Mara, p. 34.

CHAPTER 28

About Our coronation as Emperor

ON the 17th Mäskäräm 1909 (= 27th September 1916) I was chosen heir to the throne and regent, with Queen Zawditu occupying the throne; and when I had patiently carried out the work of government, for fourteen years, in my office of regent plenipotentiary, Queen Zawditu died on 24th Mägabit 1922 (= 2nd April 1930) and, consequently, on the morrow I was proclaimed Emperor and assumed the throne.

As regards the succession to throne and crown, we have read in history that, at a time when Ethiopia lived in isolation and before she had established relations with foreign countries, the prevailing custom had been, at the demise of the Emperor, for his death often to remain carefully unannounced.[1] They would then place his son and heir on the throne and crown him immediately that very day. Only after the son's reign and coronation had been announced by proclamation, would they give a ceremonial burial to the dead King.

At other times again, at the demise of the Emperor, the officers of the royal household would take him clandestinely and bury him, before anyone could hear about it, and on the morrow they would place his son and heir on the throne; after they had conducted the royal installation service[2] and crowned him, the death of the father and the new reign of the son would be announced by proclamation at the same time.

But now that Ethiopia had concluded treaties of commerce and friendship with twelve foreign governments, had entered the League of Nations, and had established firm friendly relations, We were convinced that it was proper—in accordance with the practice of the most civilized governments in the case of their coronations—to invite to Our coronation the countries which had set up legations and consulates in Ethiopia. But as it would require a long time to despatch the letters of invitation and to await the arrival of the delegates, as well as to make all the necessary preparations for the coronation, We arranged for the ceremony to be postponed for seven months.

After this, letters of invitation were written and despatched to the kings and presidents whose names follow here:

To H.M. George V, King of England, Emperor of India.
To H.M. Victor Emmanuel III, King of Italy.
To H.M. Hirohito, Emperor of Japan.
To H.M. Albert II, King of the Belgians [should read: I].

---

[1] This was still the case when Emperor Menelik died in 1913.
[2] For the *ser'atä negs* see Guidi, *Lett.*, 114–15, 75, note 3, 48, 92.

To H.M. Gustaf V, King of Sweden.
To H.M. Wilhelmina, Queen of Holland.
To H.M. Fuad I, King of Egypt.
To H.E. M. Doumergue, President of the French Republic.
To H.E. Mr. Hoover, President of the United States of America.
To H.E. Field-Marshal von Hindenburg, President of the German Republic.
To H.E. Mustapha Kemal Pasha, President of the Turkish Republic.
To H.E. M. Condouriotes, President of the Greek Republic.

Furthermore, the Polish Government had initiated conversations to conclude a treaty of commerce and friendship with the Ethiopian Government, but by the time Our coronation day came, these negotiations were still not completed. The Poles then demonstrated their good will by declaring: 'Although the treaty is not yet signed, we shall send an envoy to the coronation, since we have mutually manifested our thoughts of friendship.' We therefore informed the President, M. Moscicki[3] that it was Our intention to receive their envoy with great pleasure.

This mark of friendship which the Polish Government had shown Us at that time remained forever engraved in Our heart.

Again, as We have explained[4] before, since in earlier times the coronation was held on the very day the son and heir ascended the throne, there was no time to invite the princes and nobles of each region. But now that We had arranged for Our coronation to be postponed for seven months, letters of invitation were sent all over Ethiopia to princes and nobles and all the headmen, the priors of monasteries and the deans of cathedrals, that they should come and participate in Our joy. A letter of invitation was also written to Abba Amdä Maryam, the Prior of Däbrä Bizän[5] which had remained well known and esteemed in its importance from early times when the Kings of Ethiopia had consecrated it as a monastery, although today it is within the Italian colony [of Eritrea].

As the following months were part of the rainy season, instructions were transmitted to all to stay put in order to prepare

---

[3] Ignacy Moscicki (1867–1946), President of Poland from 1926 to 1939.
[4] The form should no doubt be corrected to አንዳስረጓነው ።
[5] The Ethiopians[3], 101, 103, 104; Guida, 192. This important 14th century monastery was founded by Abba Fillepos and became the principal bastion of the order of Ewostatewos.

for the journey, to set out at the end of the month of Mäskäräm (early October), when the rainy season had passed, and to reach Addis Ababa towards the 20th of Teqemt (= 30th October).

After these invitations had been despatched to the foreign governments and to the great within Ethiopia, arrangements were made for the principal streets of Addis Ababa and the houses along each street to be repaired as well as for electric light to be installed along the main streets and in all the houses by which the guests would pass.

The imperial vestments, the crown and the orb, the imperial sceptre and the sword, the ring and all similar things were specially made of gold and diamonds.

Formerly the only distinctive mark of honour for princes had been their golden headgear. But now We arranged that the golden headgear should be for Rases who had been appointed by virtue of hard work and services, while for the Crown Prince and for princes of royal descent We had made a pearl-studded headgear (coronet), smaller than a crown but excelling the golden headgear in size and in beauty of workmanship; for the ladies of Our family and the wives of princes golden diadems, smaller than those for princes, and corresponding to their rank.

For military commanders (i.e. for Dejazmatches) vestments and headgear were made of lions' manes that were interlaced with gold and embroidered with velvet.

Furthermore, gold medals were manufactured in large quantities on which the effigies of myself and Empress Mänän were engraved together and which were to be given as souvenirs to foreign guests coming to Our coronation, either by invitation or of their own volition, as well as to notables and important persons from within the country.

Subsequently, between Teqemt 8th and 20th (i.e. October 18th–30th), the foreign envoys who had been invited began to arrive at Addis Ababa, each in his turn.

Here follow the names of the envoys:

H.R.H. the Duke of Gloucester, envoy of H.M. the King of England;

H.R.H. the Prince of Udine, envoy of H.M. the King of Italy;
H.E. M. Gérard,[6] envoy of H.M. the King of the Belgians;

[6] Belgian Minister to Ethiopia (see above p. 95).

THE PLATES

Emperor as a child, with his father Ras Makonnen (about 1899)

Emperor, as Dejazmatch Tafari, standing next to Emperor Menelik (about 1905)

Negus Tafari at his coronation as King (1928) (he was crowned Emperor in November 1930)

Emperor at the opening of Parliament (about 1933)

Emperor with some of the principal Ethiopian dignitaries

from left to right in the front row : Ras Gugsa Araya, Ras Kassa, Prince Makonnen, Emperor Haile Sellassie I, Ras Haylu T'äklä Haymanot, Ras Seyum, Ras Getatchäw Abatä

In action during the Italo–Abyssinian war (early 1936)

Arrival in Britain (1936)

The Ethiopian personalities on the right of the picture are: Ras Kassa, Azaj Warqnäh, H. I. H. the Crown Prince, and Tsähafe Te'ezaz Waldä Giyorgis

H.E. Baron H. K. C. Bildt, envoy of H.M. the King of Sweden;

H.E. Jonkheer Hendrik Maurits van Haersma de With, envoy of H.M. the Queen of the Netherlands;

H.E. M. Isaburo Yoshida, envoy of H.M. the Emperor of Japan;

H.E. Muhammad Tawfiq Nasim Pasha,[7] envoy of H.M. the King of Egypt;

H.E. Marshal Franchet d'Esperey,[8] envoy of the French Republic;

H.E. Mr. H. M. Jacoby, envoy of the U.S.A.;

H.E. Baron von Waldthausen, envoy of the German Republic;

H.E. Count P. Metaxaṣ, envoy of the Greek Republic;

H.E. Muhittin Pasha, envoy of the Turkish Republic;

H.E. Count Dzieduszycki,[9] envoy of the Polish Republic.

All these guests expressed to Us their pleasure at the ceremonial reception which We arranged for them upon their arrival.

Furthermore, We had caused to be set up, in the vicinity of the royal church of St. George, a statue of the great Emperor Menelik II. The work was eventually completed and it was then determined that it should be inaugurated on the eve of the coronation. Consequently, after all the guests who had come for Our coronation had arrived with much ceremonial to be present thereat, We made a lengthy speech explaining the propriety of erecting a statue to Menelik II. When We had finished, We gave the honour of uncovering the veil with which the statue had been wrapped to H.R.H. the Duke of Gloucester. He approached the monument, removed the curtain, and when the statue was seen the joy in the hearts of Ethiopians was inestimable.

On this day, towards evening, the Bäjerond (treasurer) placed the Imperial state vestments and the crown, the orb, the Imperial sceptre, the sword, and the diamond ring as well as the Empress's state robes and crown and diamond ring on a chariot and took it in a great parade to the royal church of St. George where he consigned it to the Archbishop and where it remained all night to be prayed over.

[7] Vatikiotis, 269. Several times Prime Minister of Egypt.

[8] Louis Franchet d'Esperey, Marshal of France, 1856–1942.

[9] Many of the names of these foreign envoys are badly mangled in the Amharic text; they are cited in this translation in accordance with the indications kindly supplied to me, at my request, by the embassies of the countries concerned.

We and the Empress, Our family and princes and nobles went to the church at midnight.

It had been arranged that Our foreign guests should only arrive at seven o'clock in the morning and they then took their seats which had been prepared on the right and on the left of the throne according to their rank. The seating order provided that Ethiopian princes and nobles should be interspersed among the foreign guests.

Before the *ser'atä negs* (the royal ritual) began, the Archbishop, Abuna Qerillos, approached with a gospel bound in gold and asked Us to complete the following words of the oath:

(1) That We should strengthen the orthodox faith which had remained steadfast in Ethiopia from the days of the holy kings Abreha and Asbeha and that We should keep, without disturbance, the laws and ordinances which the orthodox Church has laid down.

(2) That in all We are doing, by Our authority and Our power, to the people in the Imperial realm of Ethiopia We should act with consideration for the interests of the people according to law as well as with kindness and with patience.

(3) That We would permanently maintain the laws We had established after submitting them, of Our own free will, to the Council for advice and that We would safeguard the entire Ethiopian realm and people in accordance with established law and the ordinances of the Council.

(4) That We would assist, by Our good will and authority, the establishment of schools at which secular and spiritual education would be developed in Ethiopia and in which the gospels would be preached.

After We had completed the swearing-in ceremony, affirming Our willingness to maintain all that is laid down above, We appended Our signature thereto.

Subsequently, the Archbishop assigned to the six bishops their respective functions in the coronation service, and then prayers were begun. Of these bishops five were Ethiopians. The sixth was Abuna Yosab[10] who had come from Egypt as the envoy of the

---

[10] Later 115th Patriarch of the See of St. Mark (Mara, 61; see also photographs in *op. cit.* facing page 60).

Patriarch of Alexandria, Abuna Yohannes, to partake in the joy of Our coronation and to convey his blessing.

After the Archbishop and bishops had completed the service, performing readings and prayers, with the choir singing, the Archbishop approached and anointed Us with the oil of Kingship and placed the Imperial crown on Us. At this moment Our heir to the throne, H.H. Asfa Wassän, removed the coronet from his head and, when he knelt before Us, the Archbishop approached with a Gospel and asked him to take the following oath:

(1) that he would honour his father with his whole heart and be obedient to him;

(2) that he would not seek, in association with evil men, what We had not given him of Our own will;

(3) that he would keep the laws which We had established after referring them, of Our own free will, to the Council for advice.

After he had sworn to fulfil this, he appended his signature to it.

Subsequently the coronation service of the Empress commenced. The procedure for the enthronement of the Empress is today very different from what it used to be previously. According to Our historical study of the earlier practice, the Empress was not anointed with the oil of kingship on the grounds that she did not share in rulership with the Emperor. The crown, being merely symbolic, was very small. It was in the palace that the Emperor placed the crown on her head and not in church. This occurred on the third day, for it was not permitted for her to be crowned on the same day as the Emperor. But now it was determined after consultation, and was accordingly carried out, that, except for the regal anointing, the Archbishop should place the crown on her and put the diamond ring on her finger and that this should be on the same day jointly with the coronation of the Emperor.

CHAPTER 29

About Our setting up a Constitution

IN former times, when kings ruled the people according to their own will, be it in Europe, Asia, or Africa, there used to be a good deal of upheaval and divergence between the kings and the people as well as members of the royal family. The history of the governance of many countries demonstrates this.

In our country, in Ethiopia, it used to be done likewise. We had, therefore, been contemplating the promulgation of a constitution for Our reign, to bequeath to Our heirs a form of rule that is based on law and to bring Our people into partnership in the work of government; in fact, while We were still Crown Prince and Regent Plenipotentiary of the Ethiopian realm, We had told Queen Zawditu that it would be of great benefit to the government and the people if a constitution were established. But some of the great nobles, to whose advantage it was to rule the country without a constitution, had pretended that it would diminish the dignity and authority of Queen Zawditu if a constitution were set up. For this reason Our plan had remained unfulfilled.

At that time, although We were Regent Plenipotentiary, there were complex circumstances involved. Before tackling any major affairs, I used to inform H.M. Empress Zawditu. If she accepted the matter I arranged for it to be carried out at once. Yet if she did not approve, I did not wish to upset her and do things by force (insisting that I was Regent Plenipotentiary) but rather to convince her by repeatedly reverting to the matter. This arose from the consideration that it was necessary to be careful lest disturbances or bloodshed should occur in the country. Hence I patiently delayed the establishment of a constitution. But after the death of Queen Zawditu on 24th Mägabit 1922 (2nd April 1930) We inherited crown and throne by due process of law and, therefore, decided to set up the constitution We had planned earlier on during Our regency. Hence We examined the constitutions of various countries and chose people who possessed experience and knowledge of foreign countries, as well as those versed in the customs and early history of each province inside the country, and commanded them to select and extract, from the constitutions of foreign countries, what was appropriate for the Ethiopian people—and then to submit recommendations to Us. When these had been set down in writing and had been presented, We examined them and then gave orders to the following persons to make a joint study and to submit them prepared for signature:

From among the nobles:

Ras Kassa Haylu,
Ras Haylu Täklä Haymanot,
Ras Seyum Mängäsha,
Ras Gugsa Araya,
Ras Emru Haylä Sellasse;

From among ministers:

The Minister of War: Fitawrari Berru Waldä Gäbr'el,[1]
The Minister of the Interior: Bitwaddäd Waldä Tsadeq Goshu,[2]
The Foreign Minister: Blattengeta Heruy Waldä Sellasse,
The Minister of the Pen: Tsähafe Te'ezaz Waldä Mäsqäl Tariku;[3]

From among officials:

Dejazmatch Yegäzu Bähabte,[4]
Bäjerond Täklä Hawaryat.[5]

---

[1] See the detailed entry in *JES*, VII, 2, 233-4; Fitawrari, Dejazmatch, Ras; photograph Käbbädä Täsämma, 49. 1890-1944. Early companion of Ledj Iyasu. Successively Governor of Walläga, Sidamo, and Kaffa.

[2] *JES*, VII, 2, 267-8; photograph Käbbädä Täsämma, 50; Heruy, 74-5. Käntiba of Addis Ababa and Gondar. Successively Minister of Agriculture and of the Interior. President of the Senate. Died 1936.

[3] See the exceptionally full entry in *JES*, VII, 2, 260-4; photograph Käbbädä Täsämma, 41; Heruy, 65-6. 1869-1954. Began his career as chief of Ras Darge's office; under Itege Taitu he became Tsähafe Te'ezaz, and subsequently Auditor General, Minister of the Pen, Governor of Shoa, and President of the Senate.

[4] *JES*, VII, 2, 273-4; photograph Käbbädä Täsämma, 166; Heruy, 82. 1879-1942. Nägadras of Harar, Foreign Minister, Minister of Finance, Crown Counsellor.

[5] Heruy, 31-2; photograph Käbbädä Täsämma, 56. One of the early generation of educated Ethiopians; knew French and English; visited Russia and France; and was the principal architect of the 1931 Constitution.

These men who had been instructed to investigate the matter and then to present it ready for signature had remained disunited in their views and had, therefore, spent a great deal of time arguing in Our presence. Ras Emru, alone among the nobles, had shared the opinion of the ministers and officials, while the remaining four nobles were united among themselves in a rather different view.

The opinion of the nobles was that Ethiopia, having been divided into various large provinces, each should be given as hereditary property to the nobles passing on from generation to generation; that their descendants should not be disinherited, unless it were proved against them that they had committed some serious criminal act against the Emperor or the government; that the provincial landowners within their domain, having the region they hold recognized as their hereditary property, should continue to pay taxes to the nobles and remain subservient to them. In general this connotes a feudal form of government.

But the opinion of the ministers and officials was as follows: If Ethiopia, divided into its respective large provinces, were given as hereditary property to the nobles and landowners, passing on from generation to generation, and if it were claimed that appointments were limited to their descendants, how was there to be a rising generation in the future? If a man has studied and given service and yet does not obtain office or an administrative appointment, how can he say 'Ethiopia is my country'? Therefore, let the present nobles and landowners, unless some wrong-doing is proved against them, stay on in their office of governor only; but if they are dismissed for some misdemeanour or die, then let any Ethiopian who possesses the knowledge and ability be appointed to their governorship, for [exclusive] succession within the family is not a proper procedure. But if their sons are found to be like other men in knowledge and in service, then let the Emperor in his wisdom appoint them to their fathers' governorship or other post of rank; yet it does not appear to us proper for it to be laid down in the constitution that their governorship should pass from father to son as hereditary property.

When the nobles saw that the ministers and officials did not accept the opinion they had submitted, they put forward, as an alternative, the following plan under which it would be laid down in the constitution that some districts only, out of the many within their governorships, would pass on as hereditary. But the

ministers and officials refused to accept this view and remained
steadfast in their earlier opinion.

When We heard that the men whom We had selected for this
task remained divided in their opinions, We arranged that both
sides should submit their proposals, together with supporting
evidence, in writing. After We had examined the matter, We
decided as follows: The Emperor may assign hereditary land-
rights[6] and land held as a fief[7] either to nobles or to other servants
of the realm. A paragraph to this effect is to be written into the
constitution and in future things are to be arranged as required,
having regard to their services; but, so We explained to the nobles,
it was no longer proper that, since We were aware that feudal rule
had ceased in the world, We should now once again re-affirm it,
either having it laid down in the constitution or governing without a constitution. Once matters had been clarified, they were to
be written down and prepared for signature.

Afterwards We arranged for nobles and ministers, army
commanders and provincial governors, chiefs, bishops and savants,
for all to assemble at an important ceremony. Then the constitution which had been prepared for signature was read out to
them and all affirmed their view with one voice: 'We like it; let
it be set up.'

Nevertheless, in Ethiopia for some three thousand years, since
the days of Menelik I, the customary method of rule was not a
king who governed by a constitution, having set up a parliament,
but an emperor who governed by his own authority alone. Some
men who were Our particular friends did not understand the
matter and therefore they advised me with sincerity as follows:
How can you, by your own action, hand over to the people your
authority of government? Please cause this to be stopped. When I
explained things to them to the best of my ability, they accepted
the argument. When the 9th day of Hamle 1923 (= 16th July
1931) was fixed as the date for the signing of the Constitution and
the promulgation of the decree, We gave orders to Our Minister
of the Pen to inform the senior officials and to Our Foreign
Minister to notify the foreign diplomats.

The foreign diplomats arrived with great pomp at 4 o'clock
(= 10 a.m.) on the appointed day and stood by their seats according to their rank. We then made the following speech explaining

[6] i.e. *rest* (Hoben, *passim*).   [7] i.e. *gult* (Hoben, *passim*).

the reason why We had thought it right to establish a Constitution.

'We were thinking that it was not enough for Us to thank Our Lord with words alone for the trust We had received from God to guard Ethiopia and for granting Us this high rank of Emperor, nor was it sufficient to appease him with minor deeds and with what was of benefit to Ourselves only; although We were striving to set up a constitution that was of benefit extending to everybody, enduring for ever and being transmitted from generation to generation, this was still not enough to repay the Lord's favour; because We wished to reveal to you Our intention of entrusting to God the fulfilment of the task We had begun, We have assembled you here at this hour in a great gathering.

Nobody will fail to appreciate that law is the greatest benefit to every man. It is from the equity of law that honour and advantage arise; it is from the deficiency of law that distress and damage result; it is through failure to set up law that violence and injury grow.

While God, being above every creature, would not find it difficult to issue orders by His word alone, yet His instituting law is because He knew that law should be the supreme ruler of the whole world.

He who merits being called just among men, in whatever sphere it might be, is the person who strives and endeavours, by the knowledge given to him, to benefit the majority (even though not all mankind as a whole) when pursuing his principal aims.

Although for a number of reasons Our plan had been delayed in its execution, Our entire endeavour, which We had initiated a long time ago, had been to set up a framework of law for the state. Therefore, Our idea which We pursued steadfastly and which We formulated for Ethiopia and Our beloved people is to declare to you now, first, Our granting a constitution to the Ethiopian people and, secondly, Our wish to follow this law meticulously and to maintain it.

In this constitution which We are giving to the Ethiopian people, the principal ideas formulated in it are the following:

(1) It is to bring about that, Ethiopia being one family undivided by sections, the people shall live in unity controlled by one law and governed by one Emperor, and that this power of unity shall

be safeguarded by the interests which bind them permanently together, and, while the interests of the individual shall not be abandoned, the strength of the united community shall be paramount. Without sacrificing the benefits due to individuals or oneself, one is not to seek divisive private interests.

(2) The law, in its function of conferring advantage or punishment, shall be equitable without showing favour to whomever it may be.

(3) By virtue of the fact that in past times the people of Ethiopia remained cut off from other countries and were, therefore, unable to secure the advantages which the great civilizations of today confer, as well as by virtue of adhering to their own age-old civilization, the Kings of Ethiopia, being like good fathers to the people, continued carrying on their work of administration.

But now, since Our people has progressively advanced, in whatever sphere, to a higher level of civilization, time has permitted Us to establish a constitution and to bring the people into partnership in Our toil, so as to accomplish the heavy task of government with which earlier kings have had to struggle on their own.

It is necessary that at the present time the Ethiopian people should join in all the work of government. We have, therefore, set up two chambers of Parliament, so that all persons suitably qualified for this task should become participants in the work.

The counsellors who tender advice in these chambers shall come from each province, being chosen by the Emperor's authority, until the people are able to hold elections on the basis of education and knowledge. The advice, to be decided by majority voting, will come into force when it has been approved by the Emperor.

(4) Once advice has been tendered by Parliament and been approved by the Emperor, it is the responsibility of ministers to apply it to the whole of Ethiopia and to carry on the affairs of the government and the people.

(5) Lest disturbances should break out and cause harm to Ethiopia, it has been determined by law that the Ethiopian imperial dignity shall not at any time secede from the dynasty in respect of which it has been written into this constitution.

(6) The need for law arises so that any condition of life, as it is being improved, shall be on a well-ordered and trustworthy

basis, for it is knowledge that ameliorates and moderates every-thing. So that the administration of Ethiopia in whatever sphere shall be led towards knowledge, it is right that we should always seek the selective acceptance of all knowledge in its various kinds.

(7) This constitution which We have established is not just idle fiction or discordant with the country's customs, for it closely approaches that of the civilized and educated nations; in its preparation We had the help and ideas of Our nobles and Our officials and of other Ethiopian subjects whom We had chosen for their relevant knowledge.

Man makes a beginning, but it is God alone who has the power to accomplish things; We place Our trust in God that He may grant Us to bring into effect this constitution which We have set up.

Your Excellencies, foreign envoys and consuls, We thank you for having come to share Our joy and to honour with us this fortunate day on which We have established and signed the constitution.'

When We had finished this speech, Our Minister of the Pen read out the following text of the proclamation:

'Having been chosen to the Imperial dignity of Ethiopia by God's goodness and the people's united accord, acting under the law and preserving the trust which We have received from God when We were anointed on accepting, by due process of law, the crown and the throne, We have brought about that Our successor should take over from Us by lawful means and operate within the legal framework, establishing regulations by which he will give protection to Our country in honest administration under the law; We have chosen to set up a constitution, explaining and ex-pounding Our ideas, because We were hoping to cause pleasure and to contribute to Ethiopia's prosperity, to the strength of Our government, and to the profit and benefit of Our beloved people.

The basis upon which the Ethiopian realm is to be firmly placed in future and which justifies the establishment of a constitution requires a trusty safeguard, so that the condition of Our state shall forever be stable and firm—it being well known how this is determined by the law upon which this foundation rests and by the strength with which the law is applied.

For this reason, ever since We have occupied the Imperial throne of Ethiopia and received this great trust from the hand of God, We have recognized the duty to decree and to employ means by which Our realm will be strengthened, the standard of living of Our people be improved, and Our population be led on the road to higher civilization and enjoyment, by which they will obtain all the good things which the free and civilized nations have achieved.

The most productive thing necessary to effect this, We have recognized, is to have the entire work of government well organized, after clarifying the need for a future constitution, to ensure an enjoyable standard of living for the people, and to have the state exist in peace and security by which honour will be attained that passes from one generation to another.

As it was Our lofty idea to bring Our realm to the highest level in its long history, We have established, by decree, this constitution of Our own free will, without being requested by anyone, in the 2nd year of Our reign, in 1923 (= 1931), when occupying the Imperial throne.'

Subsequently, the constitution which had been prepared in writing was presented, and after We had signed it first, then, beginning with Our heir to the throne, the bishops and princes, ministers and notables and officials, all appended their signatures to it. The foreign diplomatic envoys signed for the sake of a memento, writing their names in a specially prepared register.

CHAPTER 30

A commentary on the Constitution

ON the side of the officials and the people there were few who knew what the meaning of a constitution was, but since We considered it essential that they should all understand it, We directed, during the week in which the constitution was signed, that all officials and many of the people should assemble; Our

Minister of Finance, Bäjerond Täklä Hawaryat,[1] then addressed them and explained in the following discourse:

'Your Majesty!

The idea which has been realized in Ethiopia this year and the plan which has been initiated is of a kind which has never before been carried out in any country in the world at any time whatsoever.

A level towards which Ethiopia did not progress in two or three centuries has been brought about by Your Majesty in one rapid march forward, thus causing her to reach a high and lofty rank.

The abundant benevolence which you have up to now shown to each one of us has been astonishing. But today's instance, while not excluding anyone, extends to the entire Ethiopian people all at once and is truly amazing.

Because this is being accomplished in our time and He has granted us to see and to hear it, our good fortune will assuredly be well remembered. It can, therefore, not be doubted that it will serve to glorify our time, not only for Your Majesty's sake but even for ours. It will bring honour to future generations that come after us.

Altogether Ethiopia has found a source of life that will secure her existence henceforth and, while her power develops, she is able to give out light uninterruptedly—shining forth like a sun for ever. Therefore all those enquiring into world affairs, both men of the present time and those to arise in the future, are full of unceasing admiration for the kindness—unexampled in the world—which Your Majesty has done to Ethiopia, quite suddenly with no-one expecting it, by Your free will and benevolence, while only Your understanding and study, Your sincere mind and obvious intelligence were guiding You. History will judge you above the good and wise kings.

It is more than three thousand years that Ethiopia has been known in its nationhood. From that time till today Ethiopia has stretched out her hands towards God[2] and has been waiting patiently for some great benefit; and it is only now that God has

---

[1] Täklä Hawaryat ('plant of the apostles'), Minister of Finance and principal draftsman of the 1931 Constitution. Later Ambassador to Paris and League of Nations delegate. See Clapham, 34–5; and reff. in footnote (5) of preceding chapter. Father of Dejazmatch Germatchäw Täklä Hawaryat, author and minister.

[2] Psalm 68 : 32 (LXX and E.O.T. 67 : 32). See my *Ethiopia and the Bible*, 9.

caused her, at Your Majesty's hand, to be favoured by the divine blessing.

It is by His creating the whole world with inviolable and firm laws, determined for ever, that the Creator causes us to believe in His existence and supreme rulership.

It is through manifesting, by thorough study, the Creator's law and through observing it that man's greatness is particularly recognized. In this way he brings honour upon himself and also serves his fellows. To confer suitable benefits upon Ethiopia, nothing better could be done than to set up a constitution. Nobody will fail to appreciate that it was because Your Majesty was above all convinced that no greater benefit appropriate for Ethiopia could be found that by Your own will You established a basis for the foundation of Your government and determined a constitution for the governance of the people—and not on account of some fanciful or other reason.

While all this was planned not only for those of us who are alive now, We realize that it was done with a view to safeguarding the independence of the coming generation; hence our gratitude is sincere.

Since Your Majesty is convinced that laying a foundation for government and setting up a pillar of law is the main consideration required for safeguarding our generation, we natives of Ethiopia and all Your subjects are able to appreciate and to assess the value of this and to recognize the advantages which You have wrought for us; therefore, all Your toil will not be in vain. But for this favour which You have done for us who live at the present time, can we ever know how to make an adequate return? Or can a counter-favour, whatever it may be, ever be sufficient?

Before making the appropriate response to this question which I have posed, may I first request Your Majesty graciously to accept my sincere gratitude which I present before Your throne for having permitted me, Your humble servant, the interpretation of this great concept before this august assembly.

Your Highnesses the Princes, Your Excellencies the chiefs and officials! What I request of you now is to permit me to explain to you the interpretation of the thoughts underlying the decree promulgated on 9th Hamle (= 16th July), so that you may be aware of the profundity and subtlety of the idea, of who is to be the first beneficiary of it, and what we are to do to render adequate return for His Majesty's great favour.

Well then, I will myself provide answer and discussion to the matters I have mentioned above and if, after listening[3] patiently, you find frivolity in what I say, you must chide me; but if you discover matters of substance, you should store them in your heart.

ABOUT THE CONSTITUTION

Your Majesty has graciously caused it to be proclaimed that from now on and forever the governance of Your imperial realm is to be by the determination of the law. Constitution, i.e. the law of the realm, means to set up well, to constitute. It is like setting something up by selecting from two or three things and uniting them into one only. For instance, the 'constitution' of a wall is established by four things: stone, lime, sand, and straight levelling. And similarly, a country, people, king, and law, when united together, form the basis for the establishment of a government, and the concept of their being fused together is called a constitution. It will be found recorded in world history that many great men, in various epochs and in different countries, toiled hard to harmonize, with well-disposed application, the ideas underlying the establishment of a government.

Let us then indicate to you all the various kinds of expositions that have been presented as conditions and principles to be applied to the framing of constitutions in the world.

(1) A king with unlimited powers, in the absence in his country of any special customs or regulations, will do as he pleases, with his caprice as the only principle guiding him from day to day, and bring about fortuitous changes according to his character. He punishes without proper judgement, and kills and hangs people. A government of this kind may be suitable for pagans but it is not appropriate for a Christian people. The word of the Gospels does not permit it. An example of this would be, if a man lived in an accumulation of stones in a field—as in a cavern—and if they suddenly collapsed they could crush him. This would be called arbitrary government. Succession to the throne is according to the chance of time and superior strength and may change frequently and abruptly; each time such a change occurs it splits the people

---

[3] The version printed here seems an awkwardly conflated text made from the original 1932 edition. At this point እደመጣቹኍኝ ፣ appears to have been omitted.

into factions, seeking to annihilate each other and making their fate constant bloodshed and mutual destruction.

(2) A king with unlimited powers, in the absence of properly specified written legislation, proceeds by long-established custom handed down from generation to generation. He is thus able to apply punishment as well as mercy, to appoint and to dismiss as well as to hold court in open assembly, to award honours and to issue clearly drafted proclamations. If suddenly he commits some wrong, no restraint can be placed upon him. Government of this kind has mostly remained to be practised among peoples for whom no constitution has been set up. An example of this would be a house built with natural stone walls without mortar. This would be called a government existing by custom which possesses a measure of tolerance. The succession to the throne is to the faction to which the chance of time may offer it.

(3) A king with full authority may have specially appointed counsellors who prepare legislation for him and work by meeting in special assemblies on specified occasions. The number of persons who are permitted to tender advice is defined and they are selected from among the princes, officials, and people of each part of the country; if the advisory assembly is held in two or three sections, then the chambers are to be organized and divided in accordance with these sections. The persons who are to be counsellors within each section are chosen according to the rank of their respective parties. Parliament is divided into chambers of princes, notables, and the people. But those selected for the people's chamber, it is by the people's choice that they are appointed according to the rules; and consequently they serve as counsellors for a fixed term only, then they are removed again and others are once more elected and substituted for them.

All their deliberations are to be decided by majority vote and are then to be submitted to the king in writing; if the king likes their counsel and accepts it, he then confirms it. He subsequently causes it to be promulgated. Afterwards the ministers, in accordance with instructions under the law, have to see it is carried out. They have to put on trial people transgressing the law and see that they are punished.

Revision or complete change of the law is undertaken after proper consultations about it according to the (existing) law.

Government of this type is called joint rule determined by law. Succession to the throne in no circumstances passes outside the dynasty. It rests firmly upon the words of an oath and threat of excommunication entered into by the king, the princes, the notables and the people. An example of this is a house whose walls are built with stone, lime and sand.

(4) Then there is a republican form of government where the head of the republic is appointed by the will of the people for a fixed period. A government like this is a communal government subject only to the authority of the people.

The president of the republic demits office at the prescribed time and is succeeded by the next one likewise elected by the will of the people. In a republican government, the president of the republic, the ministers and counsellors are elected entirely by the choice of the people. Any proposal that has to be carried out is decided upon by the party with the majority of popular votes. Such a government is called government of the people. Government of this type is not for very uneducated and uncivilized people. Even in civilized countries it often causes great difficulty and leads to bloodshed.

Even if there exists another method of government apart from those enumerated, none has been discovered that is better than these for the condition of man at the present time.

There is no limit to man's desires, and as such desires increase they have no benefit for life but remain mere concepts. I have, therefore, shown you the various kinds of governance that exist in the world and that can be of use to man's life. Well then, it is the third method of governance for which H.M. Haile Sellassie I has opted in the belief that it will be suitable for the conditions in which Ethiopia exists at present, i.e. the government of Ethiopia is for ever to be a government of the King of Kings (= Emperor), with the Emperor possessing full authority and the principal determination of the law being by the Imperial will, while for the necessary matters of detail he is to be advised, for the time being, by the assembly of princes and notables; these matters are to come into force when approved by the Emperor's authority. Later on, when the people have been educated to an adequate standard of knowledge, they will be permitted to elect, on their part, men to whom the privilege of counsellorship is to be given.

This means that for the present the Emperor is appointing the princes, notables, and officials as tutors for the people, so that they should guide the populace towards amelioration.

Thus the constitution given to Ethiopia by H.M. Haile Sellassie I may be briefly defined as follows:

(1) The government of Ethiopia is for ever an Imperial realm. The Emperor possesses full authority, but his rule is subject to legal determination.

(2) The Senate and Chamber of Deputies are firmly established for ever and cannot be removed; the counsellors are to be elected at a predetermined time from each part of the country from among the princes, notables, officials, and people.

(3) The principal laws, by virtue of being based on the Emperor's knowledge, shall remain permanently valid.

(4) Laws concerning matters of detail are to be examined by Parliament and to be decided by majority vote; after they have been ratified by the Emperor's authority, they shall be promulgated.

(5) Ministers are to be responsible for the work of their respective departments and have to see to it that their work is carried out in the whole of Ethiopia.

(6) It is the Emperor alone who is in supreme command of all the armed forces in Ethiopia.

(7) It is the Emperor alone who can award senior authority and rank, office and rights, decorations and honours, hereditary land-rights and fiefs (*rest* and *gult*), as well as major grants of lodgings and maintenance.

(8) The Emperor alone can proclaim war or peace.

(9) After a malefactor has been convicted by due process of law, it is only the Emperor who is able to lighten his sentence or to pardon him altogether.

Now, then, that I have explained the establishment of the basis of government, in its various forms, which is termed 'constitution', may it be your wish to let me expound also the concept of what is called 'law'.

ABOUT THE LAW

The meaning of law is the obligation of government to define every contract made between men, so that security and peace be created for the conditions of life in the world. The meaning of law is also that it should hold responsible any man transgressing a contractual obligation and hand him over to the powers possessing the responsibility of enforcement. This being so, law provides for man a distinct definition of what it permits to him, so that he may fully benefit from it. Furthermore, the law, while warning man of the duties incumbent upon him, orders him to fulfil his obligations. Anything that is permitted to man to benefit by is called the right of exercise of enjoyment. This right of enjoyment is divided into two main parts:

(1) Private privileges are those which are for each person in his individual capacity.

(2) Joint privileges are those which are for the whole people in its entirety and for Ethiopia in her united capacity.

Private and joint concepts may be of three kinds:

(1) The interests of livelihood (worldly goods);

(2) The interests of the mind (knowledge);

(3) The interests of the inner life (love and religion).

Emperor Haile Sellassie I has given laws as regards the general judicial concepts for all these interests, private as well as communal, which have been referred to. But for matters of detail he has set up what is called a constitution as a basis for the establishment of government, so that the counsellors should submit to him (as we have shown above) the legislative proposals they have prepared in Parliament.

Up to now I have spoken in order to expound what a constitution is and also how the determination of laws is to be done. I shall now explain in detail the answer to the questions I have presented to you before.

THAT WE MAY KNOW MUTUAL AID AND UNITY

What Emperor Haile Sellassie I has done for us, other kings have done for their countries. But in other countries improvements of this kind were not carried out by an act of spontaneous generosity but through bloodshed and compulsions and by leaving behind a sense of danger for all.

But in our country, while the educational level of the people is as yet inadequate, our Emperor, in weighing up and estimating the deficiencies and advantages for the future, has been meaning to improve the conduct of our fortunes and has arranged, by his wisdom and his will, that Ethiopia should rise up from the condition of mere custom, in which she had been living hitherto, and pass on to a higher level of civilization. What makes this so very astonishing is the fact that all this is being accomplished in such peace and security, while Ethiopia turns away from the situation in which she had been up to now and makes progress all of a sudden, the Emperor being in accord with his supporters and servants—all in unity, mutual aid, and joy.

This fact is by itself enough to bring honour to Ethiopia and render her an equal with the civilized nations.

In order to repay His Majesty's generosity, we must judge for ourselves and impose an obligation upon ourselves so as to be truly and sincerely submissive. When His Majesty has been graciously pleased to establish for us such an esteemed project, unless we make an equally gracious and willing return for those benefits, we shall give offence to our Emperor, on the one hand, and to most people, on the other, as well as incurring hatred all round; that is, if we are seekers, on the narrow road, of our own interest only and despise our common benefit which ties us to the nation.

The meaning of law is a strong and unchallengeable force which is ordained to exist among men in sanctity, purity, and honour; it is a requirement of peacefulness to be a safeguard of the interests existing among men—properly poised and for ever indestructible. That which safeguards the law itself is its faithfulness in true impartiality and sincerity in the fulfilment of contracts tied to covenants.

This contract attached to a covenant, referred to as law, specifically cautions on every occasion those dwelling in the world, lest they transgress the proper limits in any of their daily occupations; the law defines those limits for them, brings them into harmony, and delivers them from enmity.

Therefore, the law deserves to be honoured—being the supreme power above all. And we, all the natives of Ethiopia, it is our obligation and our desire to live in future with honour for the law, taking great care never to forget that we have entered into this covenant knowingly and willingly.

Anyone seeking to interfere with the mode of living permitted to every man by law or seeking to cause upheaval deserves to be rebuked before the Creator and by the assembly of the people; he also deserves to be punished as an evildoer before the king. Likewise, if a man fails to carry out what the law has commanded him or if he is found transgressing what the law has determined, then he renders himself liable to be punished by that law.

It is the Emperor who has entered into a contract sanctioned by covenant to safeguard with diligence that the people may benefit to the full from every aspect of life which the law permits; and it is up to us to see he succeeds in this.

Again, it is the same Emperor who has entered into a contract sanctioned by covenant to apply force lest anyone should be guilty of a transgression which the law forbids; let us then strive, for his sake, to the best of our ability to bring about success for this as well.

The existence of a binding covenant between the Emperor and the people entails a desire and an obligation for both parties in unison and not for one side only.

Therefore, there is no greater benefit for us than the desire and obligation that is mutual to both sides. By the Emperor's action of giving us the law and by our action of accepting, honouring, and fulfilling it we are able to make our life in this world one of hope and loyalty. As a consequence, all our thoughts will be tranquil and this will let us take care to initiate and to bring to fruition all kinds of important and beneficial deeds.

We are not wrong in considering this the main concept for our country's prosperity. If there were no law we would have no hope amounting to any sort of confidence—but only violence and injury—and our heart would become insensitive. Our life, on account of our unsuccessful plans, would become unsettled and unstable.

Upon such conduct, our world would remain without proper basis, a thing of idle hopes only. When we come to assess the damage of all this, we cannot fail to be very conscious of the gravity of the matter. But by virtue of the fact that it is the Emperor who gives the law and thereby becomes the custodian of the people's benefits and deficiencies, he is given the special privilege of supreme authority and rights. It is of the essence that this should for ever remain his personal prerogative and thus no other man can challenge him. After his life-time it passes by due inheritance to his children and these, in turn, according to precedence will take over and carry on the work of government according to law, but it cannot be turned over to another dynasty. It is all the natives of Ethiopia in their entirety who have entered into a contract sanctioned by covenant to be guarantors of this arrangement.

The principal advantage deriving from this is that it should stop the quarrels and upheavals which arise each time on the occasion of the succession to the crown and throne, and that it should prevent the mutual extermination which the division of the people into factions causes as well as the dismemberment and partition of Ethiopia.

If any man were to oppose or to infringe the Emperor's authority, the people's interests, or the power of the law, then he would, by his own will, have become an outlaw, and no defence whatever could be found for him to save him from punishment.

From now onwards, Ethiopia, by virtue of being protected and rendered tranquil in every respect, will on one hand internally progress in every sphere of her standard of living and continually grow in wealth; on the other hand again, as far as the outside world is concerned, she will be able to conclude treaties, accruing to her benefit and honour, with her neighbouring countries regulating all mutual relations and consonant with Ethiopia's long-term interests.

It is thus not very difficult for us to appreciate that these two methods of amelioration represent something of major value. When a basis for the establishment of government is set up and the law is defined, it is not possible at the same time to discuss precisely and bring about every determination of matters of detail. This is because the people's mode of living is so very variegated in type, extent, and general distinctions. But our hope is absolute that in the course of time, as the need arises, permission is bound to be granted, and this inspires our heart with confidence for the future.

When that time comes, the full extent of His Majesty's generosity will be clearly seen. While it was perfectly possible for him to rule according to his wishes like the kings in the past and to act as his momentary caprice made him, he abandoned all this and, by his own will and generosity, laid a firm basis for the establishment of his government and gave freedom to his people within the framework of the law. When he did this, he did not compel us to choose a particular kind of law and to live under it by simply translating the constitution of one of the civilized nations. If it had been done like this, it would have been to our detriment rather than our advantage. On the contrary, he saw to it that the constitution was in accordance with the country's customs, the people's educational level, the economic difficulties, and with the spirit of the times; he permitted the people themselves to advise on what was suitable for the time being, to be the custodians of the constitution, and to make their views known.

Any proposal that had to be decided upon by majority vote required to be examined by the properly and specifically established parliament, i.e. by the assembly of counsellors specially selected; if the proposal was suitable to become law according to the constitution, it was to be promulgated after ratification by the Emperor's authority. For the present, no better method of legal procedure can be devised for us. After ratification and promulgation by the Emperor, it has been arranged that the ministers who possess full powers shall be responsible for the execution of the law; and no man whatsoever, be he great or small, shall be in a position to transgress the law.

Well now, I have explained to you the road along which Ethiopia is to be renewed and guided as well as the reason for the differences compared with her earlier situation; henceforth things will be different in that Ethiopian legislation is to be devised by the knowledge of indigenous Ethiopians and to be approved by the Emperor—and is no longer to be a matter that is exclusively under the guidance of foreigners.

The authority of ministers will have reference to all matters directly concerning the government and the people; chief among these are agriculture, cattle-breeding, manufacture, trade, the process of justice, and all other similar matters.

From now onwards, no man will be able to extinguish, by power or force, the rights granted to the people, or to infringe their interests, or to cause upheaval in order to bring about change capriciously, or indeed to commit acts of violence and outrage.

From now onwards the law will be a safeguard to ensure that no powerful person or upstart shall subdue the weak or the poor. It has, therefore, been arranged to have a printed version of the law and to make it available everywhere, so that anyone may take note of the law and will thus be able to save himself from oppression under the protection of the constitution.

From now on legal safeguards have been established, so that the verdict of the judges shall be impartially dispensed; and from this the people will be able to benefit very greatly. What is permitted to the people henceforth is personal liberty and enjoyment of normal life, though not freedom of lawless conduct—nor to do anything outside the law. This recognition has been embodied in the law, so that man's intelligence be uncovered and be directed properly, that he be able to profit from his work and not be deprived of his inherited land. But if the law were merely written down and remained thus, it would be like a dead person; hence an observer and promoter has been appointed, so that it be applied properly. The product of all this will be a secure peace, improvement of civilization, and advancement in the standard of living.

When I say that peaceful security will ensue, it is because it has been willed that to live by force and arbitrariness is forbidden and that to live by law alone has become an obligation—and also because everything has been firmly based on unity, so that it be protected with care. Furthermore, it is also because ministries for the successful achievement of work have been specially set up, with the appropriate distribution of their respective tasks, and because they have been given the necessary authority and rightful power to bring about the fulfilment of their respective duties without mutual friction.

If the superior power of the law does not succeed in making everybody responsible to it, then injustice is bound to be done to someone, as one man's injury is another's benefit; therefore, it is essential that the law should be above everybody.

When I say that improvement in civilization will ensue, it is because, when a man is allowed to profit from his work, he is bound to compete and strive to put his inherited propery right and make it prosper, to advance his standard of living by accomplishing things through the skill of his handiwork; he will save time by the knowledgeable use of new instruments and efficient methods and will thus be able to obtain considerable profit with little effort and at little expenditure; in all things of this kind he will engage in rivalry and competition.

When I say that economic advance will ensue, it is because man will now be able to become wealthy if he proceeds along all the roads accessible to him, and everybody is bound to strive to enrich himself by hard work and to advance and to improve his standard of living.

Now that I have assessed, separately, the advantages and disadvantages incurred by the Emperor and the people and have referred to the contractual obligations and wishes, authority and rights, by which the two sides are tied to the covenant, it is proper to recall—lest we forget—the duties incumbent upon us.

While the king and people are bound under the covenant to live by the obligations and requirements which the law commands, we are likewise mutually bound by covenant to assist them, each of us according to his entire ability, through true service and a sincere mind, as well as to join together in all things relating to Ethiopia's unity; I have therefore reminded you of obligations and requirements that cannot be shed by us. Furthermore, since it is necessary for the law to be equal for everyone, it is essential for all natives of Ethiopia, small and great, rich and poor, educated and uneducated, all without distinction, to profit by it according to their fate. Even though a law may be set down in fine words, unless the substance embodied in it is to be truly carried out—as we have just described—or if some individual is able to transgress the law and to act wilfully, then it will remain a mere sham and cannot become the real mode of life suitable for a civilized Christian government and nation.

We have said that Emperor Haile Sellassie I, when defining by law this basis of government which he has established[4] and when graciously granting it to us, has at a stroke raised Ethiopia from the position in which she had been and has managed to place her on the high level which the civilized nations have attained. When our Emperor revealed to us such a lofty thought, intending to hold us up to honour, and if we, on our part, expose him by failing to accept his plans or by refusing, negligently, to extend our help, then this will be testimony against us that we are seeking, by our own doing, a place of dishonour.

As regards this freedom, while some people fail to understand the meaning of the liberty granted to us in terms of lofty thoughts and a fine and genuine intellect, it is our duty to caution our fellow-men close to us lest they be deceived into thinking that it is licence that has been granted to them. Whatever freedom may be permitted, it is necessary for everyone to appreciate that licence is not acceptable.

Lest anything like this should happen, it seems to me superfluous to have to mention that the powers of enforcement of the Imperial government are entirely adequate.

Anything that the law has ordained, only that same law can abolish, through revision and with the Emperor's permission, but no-one else can cancel it. It is needful for us to have patience, for it always takes a lot of time to accomplish a great concept. That means that this entire plan, broadly conceived, cannot be success-fully carried out in a day, and we must appreciate that sufficient time is required for its fulfilment. Hence some people, lacking the patience to wait for the right time, claim that the law has been set down in writing but has not been acted upon; lest they should annoy the people and make them lose hope, it is our duty to explain matters to our friends wherever we go. There is no-one leaving school who has acquired knowledge in a day. All that has been said cannot, it seems to me, cause any displeasure to the hearts of those who love their government and their king.

A wide-ranging concept of this kind is not to be initiated on slight foundations, and the essence of the scheme is to get to know first of all, by careful research, the principal skills with which the initiative is to be successfully accomplished.

If we set to work without assessing and weighing up the profit and loss which this may entail for the people, i.e. if we proceed on the strength of wanton and frivolous plans, not only shall we fail to reach a high level of civilization but we shall, in fact, be bound to degenerate and retrogress towards ignorance. I do not suspect that you, gentlemen, who are here today will make any mistake about all this. But you cannot fail to assess the level of knowledge of perhaps a majority of the people outside this audience, and it is, therefore, essential that you who are, by the Emperor's wish, leaders and tutors should cause them to be patient and to wait until they are able to analyse the advantages and disadvantages.

In order to appreciate the real meaning and value of freedom it is necessary, first of all, to study and to develop an enquiring mind. An educated person will himself be aware and take care to restrain himself from acts of licence. But an uneducated person requires as guides men who possess knowledge and uprightness, so that he may save himself from perdition and be useful to himself as well as to others.

Apart from this, it is your duty and privilege to be of service to our country and to our Emperor to the best of your ability, as you are yourselves an example by which the inferior person recognizes the duty of complete obedience to his superior, and the superior appreciates the propriety with which he is to issue orders to his inferior.

If in these circumstances we were all of us lending a hand, the great burden which has fallen upon the Emperor alone would be eased for him by being shared and by being spread to all of us; and thus the task would be quickly accomplished to the great benefit of the people throughout Ethiopia.

While we thus apply ourselves to our task jointly with our Emperor who is endeavouring to rule with truth and justice, without withdrawing the generosity which so benefits the people, thinking only of the true and lofty concept without fear or favour, and without curbing the duty which is so pleasing to God, let it be our foremost desire and effort that our country, Ethiopia, should attain a higher level and that thereby our entire generation be blessed.

Now, gentlemen, I have spoken thus far to the best of my ability, and if it has been to your satisfaction, then I, on my part, shall always be prepared at any future time it may please His Majesty to explain with my entire mind the proper application of the law.'

Following this, the two houses of parliament were made ready, and the first was called Senate, the second Chamber of Deputies.[5]

Four months later, We arranged that the counsellors chosen from each district should come to Addis Ababa, and parliament was opened with great celebrations on 23rd Teqemt 1924 (= 2nd November 1931), the first anniversary of Our coronation as Emperor.

Since these happenings disturbed the mind of the enemy, and not content with being upset in his heart only, he declared: 'The

---

[5] On the then French model.

initial stages of the present activities of the Ethiopian Government
are very worrying, and it is therefore necessary that we Italians
should now think about it very seriously.' A man who was
friendly with both⁶ sides told us the actual words he had heard
being uttered.

⁶ It is possible, though no more, that the የሁላችንም ፣ here should read
የሁላታችንም ፣

CHAPTER 31

The Italians engage in deceitful propaganda activities with Ras Haylu and cause the escape of Ledj Iyasu from Fitche

RAS HAYLU is the son of King Täklä Haymanot of Gojjam.
When King Täklä Haymanot was still called Ledj Adal,[1] he
married Wayzäro Laqätch,[2] a relative of Emperor Täklä Giyorgis[3]
who reigned in 1861 (= 1868), and then received the title of Ras.
Later on, after Emperor Yohannes had succeeded to the throne in
1864 (= 1872), he gave him the crown and proclaimed him King
of Gojjam in 1873 (= 1881).

King Täklä Haymanot had other sons called Ras Bäzzabeh[4] and
Dejatch[5] Bäläw.[6] After the death of King Täklä Haymanot,
Emperor Menelik assigned the governorship of Gojjam to Ras
Haylu. But at that time he was called Dejazmatch Seyum.[7]

However, from the beginning all his activities had been of a
deceitful nature; since he meant to bring about the downfall of his

[1] Budge, II, 523; Luca dei Sabelli, III, 266-8; de Coppet, I, 127 : 6.
[2] 'She is superior' (= በለጠች ፣); see DTW, 735. Otherwise nothing about
this lady is known to me.
[3] Formerly Wagshum Gobäze, declared himself Emperor during the inter-
regnum (1868-72) between Emperors Theodore (Tewodros) and John (Yohannes).
See de Coppet, I, 118; Markham, passim, but esp. 383-4; The Ethiopians², 85.
[4] Cf. de Coppet, I, 318 : 4; II, 493 : 9; DTW, 158; JES, VII, 2, 229.
[5] Common abbreviation of Dejazmatch.
[6] Cf. de Coppet, II, 493 : 9; DTW, 173; JES, VII, 2, 227.
[7] See de Coppet, II, 493 ff.; JES, VII, 2, 243.

father's officers, he caused imitations of their seals to be engraved[8] and then wrote messages suggesting that they were betraying Emperor Menelik. When he submitted these to Emperor Menelik, the officers denied having done anything of this sort; when, as a consequence of their protest, the matter was investigated, it was revealed to his disgrace that he had treacherously caused these fictitious seals to be engraved. He was, therefore, condemned to imprisonment, but after he had remained at Afqära[9] for 7 years, Emperor Menelik in his goodness released him from prison and restored to him once again the governorship of Gojjam. He subsequently married Empress Taitu's niece, Wayzäro Assällä-fätch,[10] and in honour of the wedding in 1901 (= 1908–9) he received the title of Ras. He then gave up the name Seyum and adopted the name Haylu. Ledj Iyasu, entirely at the request of his father, King Mika'el, married Ras Haylu's daughter, Wayzäro Säblä-Wangel.[11]

Ras Haylu used to prepare a fine welcome for all the Italians passing through Gojjam and to give them an escort. Apart from this, he pretended to be ill and used to travel to and fro to the Italian commercial agents and doctors resident at Dessie or Gondar.

The Italians who were appointed as resident commercial agents at Gondar, Dessie, and Magalo[12] used to be selected for their medical training.[13] The reason was that by being able to meet district governors and the people in the course of medical work they were conveniently in a position to carry on their deceitful propaganda.

We never ceased suspecting all these Italian activities. But, on one hand, We were mindful of Our treaty obligations and, on the other, We felt that, if We forbade the people, living in the districts which had an agent, to go to the agency for medical treatment, the Italians would accuse Us before the world claiming

[8] For details of this story, see de Coppet, II, 494.

[9] Afqära is a fairly inaccessible mountain in the Mänz district of central Ethiopia (KBT, 837); de Coppet, I, 70 : 4; 97 : 10.

[10] It will be recalled that she was the widow of Dej. Yelma, Emperor Haile Sellassie's elder half-brother, who died in 1907.

[11] 'Harvest of the Gospels'.

[12] Situated in southern Ethiopia, important commercial centre and market (Guida, 467).

[13] This claim is corroborated by the Italian Guida, loc. cit., which refers to 'Maggiore Medico D'Agostino' as the commercial agent at Magalo.

that We were impeding civilization; We therefore waited patiently until We discovered major evidence of these activities.

Later on, when Italy made energetic requests to establish a consulate in Gojjam, We granted her permission, as it seemed to Us proper to honour the treaty of friendship; she subsequently set up the consulate.

The reason for which customarily a request was made to appoint a consul was that subjects (of the applicant power) were resident in the area concerned and were engaged in commerce there. But Italy did not possess a single subject or merchant, be he white or black, at Däbrä Marqos, and thus everybody was aware that it was for propaganda purposes only. There, in the consulate compound, the consul established a clinic, and the notables and the people of Gojjam went there for medical treatment.

We did not suspect that Ras Haylu had any thought that the government of Ethiopia should be abolished and become Italian. But after some lapse of time We finally heard that the Italians were telling him that, if he were to cause the escape of Ledj Iyasu from his place of detention, he (Ras Haylu) would, when Ledj Iyasu became Emperor, be proclaimed at least King of Gojjam, his father's governorate, and possibly even King of Gojjam and Bägemeder. His daughter would in that case become Queen consort. They further told him that the Italian Government would assist him in everything he required in bringing this about and in any difficulties he might encounter.

This piece of advice by the Italians had entered deeply into Ras Haylu's heart and he was waiting for a suitable moment to attempt this project; he, therefore, came to Our coronation to Addis Ababa and stayed for about two years; and meanwhile he began scheming in secret, with the help of money and by all other means at his disposal, to bring about the escape of Ledj Iyasu from his place of detention at Fitche. The deceitful plan which had been devised for this was as follows: when Ledj Iyasu had escaped from detention at Fitche, he was to cross the Mugär[14] and meet Ras Haylu at Metcha;[15] he was then to cross the Blue Nile at

---

[14] The Mugär river is a tributary of the Blue Nile; cf. *Guida*, 389; *Toponomastica Etiopica*, 204; Cheesman, 17, 282, and map; de Coppet, Atlas, IV.

[15] Metcha is a region to the N.W. of Addis Ababa; cf. *Guida*, 389; *Toponomastica Etiopica*, 196; de Coppet, Atlas, IV; Duchesne-Fournet, II, map; Luca dei Sabelli, IV, 150.

Gendäbärät[16] or at some other convenient spot, and when he reached Däbrä Marqos he was to issue a proclamation about his emperorship and at once to install Ras Haylu as King of Gojjam; from there he was to cross into Wallo by way of Bägemeder, and when at Dessie he was to assemble by mobilization decree the armies of Gojjam, Bägemeder, Semien, Tigre, and Yäjju; he was then to go to Shoa and, after fighting with Us, was to enter Addis Ababa.

If it were perchance to happen that this plan of Ras Haylu's should come to grief, he had spoken to the Italians about an aeroplane, so that Ledj Iyasu might conveniently and quickly cross into Gojjam by aeroplane. When a certain Baron Franchetti,[17] before departing from Asmara, requested permission through his legation to land in a large field situated between Addis Aläm and the town of Gännät,[18] because there was no sufficiently large field at Addis Ababa on account of the size of the aeroplane in which he was travelling and which had four engines, We had no suspicion of any connexion with the affairs of Ledj Iyasu or Ras Haylu and granted him permission to land near Addis Aläm. But the secret was the plan to engineer the escape of Ledj Iyasu, for Metcha was near Addis Aläm.

When the aeroplane arrived, many people who had gone to receive it noticed that inside it were a machine-gun as well as rifles and many cartridges. After it had remained there, in the vicinity of Addis Aläm, for about ten days, it requested once more authority to move to a field near Addis Ababa where the radio-station is situated nowadays; We granted this permission. Only later on was it revealed that the purpose of this was to take Ras Haylu from Addis Ababa to arrange a convenient meeting with Ledj Iyasu.

However, God's designs prevail over those of man, and the plan by which Ledj Iyasu was to escape from Fitche went wrong and there occurred a delay in his get-away and in issuing any information about his escape. Hence Baron Franchetti, after waiting for a whole month without news of Ledj Iyasu, returned to Asmara with his aeroplane on 8th Genbot 1924 (= 16th May 1932).

---

[16] Gendäbärät or Kutai, mountainous region to the south of the loop of the Blue Nile; cf. *Guida*, 389; Cheesman, 293, 297 ff.; Duchesne-Fournet, II, pl. 12.
[17] Baron Raimondo Franchetti (1889–1935), Italian explorer; cf. *Chi è dell' Eritrea*, 132–3.
[18] Or Holetta, some 8 miles east of Addis Aläm (*Guida*, 496–7, and map).

On the fourth day after Franchetti's return to Asmara, Ledj Iyasu escaped from Fitche; and when he reached Yaya Gulläle[19] he sent a letter to Ras Haylu: 'I have escaped, and now let us meet'. But since all the arrangements Ras Haylu had previously made had gone awry, he was not prepared and quickly despatched the headman of Gendäbärät to acquire some fifty horses for him.

Ledj Iyasu had sent letters not only to Ras Haylu but also to other chiefs; since Ras Haylu meant to pretend that he had not been involved in the matter and thus to escape blame by seductive words, he showed Us the letter which had reached him from Ledj Iyasu and claimed: 'Ledj Iyasu wrote to me in order to seduce me by a ruse, but I have no master or King other than Emperor Haile Sellassie, and You are bound to recognize that I am loyal to Your government.'

But Ledj Iyasu's escape and Ras Haylu's involvement in the entire affair had already been widely rumoured at Addis Ababa, and many indications were discovered which proved his involvement in the matter. When his briefcase which was in his servant's hand was found and when its contents were examined, the code by which he corresponded with Ledj Iyasu was discovered to his discomfiture as well as other signs mutually known only to these two.

When the man whom Ras Haylu had sent to purchase horses was seized and interrogated, he gave evidence against him and confessed that Ras Haylu had instructed him: 'When you have bought the horses and met Ledj Iyasu and heard what he has to say to you, come back!' But in the end the Ras confessed and said: 'It is true that I have done all this, for Satan misled me; only You in Your goodness can do mercy unto me.' A week later he came before the court for judgement to be given when the judges, unanimously, condemned him to death.

But We commuted the sentence of death and arranged that he should stay, with his property confiscated, in confinement at a specified place. When Ledj Iyasu had waited for some time for Ras Haylu in the Metcha and Gendäbärät regions, he heard of his arrest and imprisonment. Thereupon he crossed the Blue Nile, and when there remained a journey of only two days before entering

[19] See also under Gulläle and Sällale. A locality in the Yaya Galla region in Sällale, to the N.W. of Addis Ababa. Cf. de Coppet, 43 : 4, and Atlas, IV; Duchesne-Fournet, II, map, for general orientation.

Däbrä Marqos, the people of Gojjam seized him and handed him over to Dejatch Dästa Damtäw whom We had despatched for this purpose.

In 1909 (= 1916), when Ledj Iyasu was deposed, the Italians had manifested their opposition to him and had spoken to Us in this sense. But now they pretended to be friendly towards him and aided his escape from Fitche; this proves that they were devising plans to take Ethiopia by provoking us to fight each other, while they themselves would not have a single soldier killed in battle.

CHAPTER 32

As regards the visit to Us by the Crown Prince Gustaf Adolph of Sweden and Our ceremonial welcome to him

BEFORE We became Heir to the Throne and Regent Plenipoten-tiary of the Ethiopian Realm, Swedish missions had set up a school at Addis Ababa and had begun teaching the English language and the gospels to Ethiopian children. These missionaries did not get involved in any political matters whatever, either inside the country or outside it, and they were engaged in teaching through goodness and generosity alone. After We had taken on the regency We caused their entire work to be investigated by the Ministry of Education. When We had convinced Ourselves that they had no thought other than teaching languages and religious knowledge, We did Our utmost to give them every assistance in the gradual expansion of their activities. Moreover, apart from extending to them aid at Addis Ababa, We arranged for them to build schools and hospitals at Harar and Läqämte[1] and to help the people living in these regions with educational and medical facilities, while We gave them ássistance with money and land.

[1] Läqämte (here entered under the variant form Näqämte) or Läqämti, Lekemt, etc., the capital of the rich Walläga province, some 330 kms west of Addis Ababa. See *The Ethiopians*[3], 192, and especially the detailed information in *Guida*, 501 ff.

These missionaries lived in harmony with the people at Addis Ababa, Harar, and Läqämte.

Later on, in 1916 (= 1924), when We visited Europe and also went to Stockholm, the capital of Sweden, We mentioned to King Gustaf,[2] in the course of friendly conversations, that the Ethiopian and Swedish peoples could get very close to each other.

On Our return from Europe to Addis Ababa We erected, with Our own funds, the Bet-Sayda Hospital and appointed Dr. Hanner whom We brought from Sweden and who was well-known for his surgical work; in consequence many sick people were treated and restored to health. Furthermore, We arranged that he should purchase, import, and set up the diagnostic instrument called X-ray which had never before been seen in Ethiopia; in consequence the medical work of the Bet-Sayda Hospital became progressively more extensive and successful.

Subsequently, We engaged from Sweden the great scholar Dr. Kolmodin[3] who was to serve as adviser to the Ministry of Foreign Affairs; he proved to be of great assistance to Us, but he died at Addis Ababa and, a little later, We had his remains taken to Sweden. After this We asked for General Virgin[4] in place of Dr. Kolmodin and arranged for him to come to Ethiopia where he was of great assistance to Us. These two Swedish advisers rendered services as if they were Ethiopians, and Our ministers, in their respective departments, expressed their pleasure to Us.

We also brought Captain Tamm[5] and four other army officers, and when We had built barracks at Gännät they offered instruction in military studies and trained for Us many young men.

For these reasons there were many Swedes living in Ethiopia, and consequently We granted permission to establish, at the

[2] This is, indeed, King Gustaf V (who, on p. 74 of the Amharic text, is wrongly described as Gustaf Adolph) who reigned from 1907 to 1950. He was succeeded by his son, Crown Prince Gustaf Adolph (who visited Ethiopia); from 1950 to 1972 King Gustaf VI Adolph.

[3] Johannes Kolmodin of Uppsala first travelled in Eritrea in 1908–9 and subsequently published his valuable *Traditions de Tsazzega et Hazzega* (Uppsala and Rome, 1912–15). Adviser to Emperor Haile Sellassie from 1930 until his death in Ethiopia in 1934. See *Chi è dell'Eritrea*, 175.

[4] General Erik Virgin, Head of the Swedish Military Mission and of the Officers Training College at Holetta (Gännät). Formerly Chief of the Swedish Airforce, and subsequently political and military adviser to the Emperor. See Baer, 55.

[5] Later the senior Swedish military adviser; cf. Del Boca, 89.

request of King Gustaf,[6] a Swedish Consulate at Addis Ababa. Finally, the King informed Us officially in 1927 (= 1934/5) of his wish that his heir to the throne, Gustaf Adolph, should come to Addis Ababa on a return visit for that which We had paid to the King in 1916 (= 1924). We had plans drawn up by European architects for a palace in which We might receive this important guest from a friendly nation, and it was built and completed within a year.[7]

But Italy never ceased to look jealously upon any act of civilization that was being carried out in Ethiopia; and when there remained only some 20 days before the arrival at Addis Ababa of Our guest, it appeared to her that she could prevent the reception of Our guest. On 26th Hedar 1927 (= 5th December 1934) she entered Our realm at Walwal, launched a surprise attack and killed many of our men. There were at once many Italians who spread rumours in the city suggesting: 'In the present troubled times the Swedish Crown Prince will not come to Ethiopia but will turn back from his journey; the war is bound to begin before the new year.' We were very apprehensive thinking that, if this rumour were, perhaps, to be true, it would cause much sorrow to Our distinguished guest and to Ourselves.

Italy interpreted everything We were doing for the sake of civilization by a completely different reasoning, and We were not oblivious of her rumour-mongering before all the world. The story which proves this is that, when We despatched representatives on a return visit to all the governments which had sent envoys to Our coronation held in 1923 (= 1930) and sent Our heir to the throne to England, France, and Italy, as well as envoys to the other governments, one of these countries was Japan where We had despatched, to Tokyo, Our Foreign Minister Blattengeta Heruy. When he returned having accomplished his mission, the Italians began spreading rumours in the newspapers to the effect

[6] The Amharic original has again, erroneously, King Gustaf Adolph—see footnote (2) above.

[7] According to Pankhurst, 714, 'in eight months'. The Palace, designed and built by E. Kametz (Pankhurst, loc. cit.; Guida, 488) was the last considerable building to be completed before the Italo-Ethiopian war and was just ready for the visit of the Swedish Crown Prince in January 1935. The Emperor lived there until the revolt of December 1960 when this Palace and its fine grounds (called Gännätä Le'ul) were handed over to the Haile Sellassie University. The Emperor then moved into the Jubilee Palace.

that Ethiopia and Japan had concluded a separate secret treaty and, apart from this, Ethiopia had granted a concession of 3 million hectares of land to a Japanese company. The Italians were, of course, perfectly aware of the fact that we had concluded no such secret treaty or concession, but their spreading of rumours of this sort was because it seemed to them that the British and the French, who were our neighbours,[8] would be as envious of us as they were. Ethiopia and Japan, apart from concluding, earlier on, a treaty of commerce like other governments, did not even have negotiations—let alone a secret treaty or concession![9] They published an even worse story in the press to the effect that the Crown Prince of Ethiopia was to marry a Japanese princess. For this reason Our Foreign Minister summoned the Italian Minister, Count Vinci,[10] and asked him: 'Why does the Italian press bring out mendacious news of this kind about our heir to the throne? Are you yourself not well aware that our Crown Prince is married to a wife from his own country?'[11] The Minister replied: 'This matter occurred by mistake and I shall, therefore, arrange for this error to be corrected.' A week after this conversation he notified the correction of the mistake.

Our raising this story now is not that We are able to conclude writing about the lying reports the Italians have been issuing against Us but rather because these matters are connected; but let us return to the description of the reception arranged for Our Swedish guest.

Although the Swedish Crown Prince, H.R.H. Gustaf Adolph, had heard about Italy stirring up unrest by launching a surprise attack upon Our territory at Walwal, he did not consider turning back from his journey and arrived at Addis Ababa in the month of Tahsas on the day that had been fixed, i.e. the Ethiopian Christmas.[12]

---

[8] The reference is, of course, to British and French colonial possessions in East Africa, i.e. the British and French Somalilands, the Sudan and Kenya.
[9] For the Italian version of this alleged Japanese deal, see Luca dei Sabelli, IV, 202 ff.
[10] Count Luigi Vinci-Gigliucci, Italian Minister to Ethiopia since 1933 (Baer, 35). Cf. *Waugh in Abyssinia*, 129 ff.
[11] At that time Crown Prince Asfa Wassän was married to Princess Wallätä Israel, daughter of Ras Seyum of Tigre, by whom he has one daughter, Princess Ejjegayähu.   [12] 7th January (1935).

With him were his wife, Princess Louise,[13] his daughter Princess Ingrid, and his son Prince Bertil as well as other persons in his suite.

The princes and notables of Ethiopia, including even the ordinary people, were conscious of the very firm friendship existing between the Ethiopian and Swedish nations and they felt great pleasure at seeing the Crown Prince and his family. After such a ceremonial welcome of profoundly felt friendship had been accorded to him for about a week, he returned to Sweden.

[13] This was the Swedish Crown Prince's second wife, Louise of Battenberg, Lord Mountbatten's sister.

CHAPTER 33

About Our setting up a Red Cross Society

WE had not thought that Italy would violate the obligations upon which she had entered within the League of Nations and break the Kellogg Pact[1] which she had signed, that she would overturn the treaty of friendship she had concluded with us in 1920 (= 1928) to live in peace and to eschew war for 20 years, and indeed that she would wage war against Ethiopia. When she attacked Walwal and killed our soldiers, We notified the League of Nations because it seemed to Us that the League might restrain Italy from waging a major war in future. But Italy, while discounting any sense of shame, chose a momentary advantage above a perpetually honourable reputation and trampled underfoot all the treaties which she had concluded. Our Chargé d'affaires at Rome, Nägadras[2] Afä Warq Gäbrä Iyäsus,[3] informed Us that Italy was unceasingly sending large quantities of material and many soldiers to her two colonies,[4] and consequently We directed that a Red

[1] Named after F. B. Kellogg, the American Secretary of State (1925-9), and signed at Paris in 1928, designed to outlaw war.

[2] Nägadras is a senior official in charge of trade and customs duties.

[3] Afä Warq Gäbrä Iyäsus is a major figure in early Amharic literature (Ullendorff, *Amh. Chrest.*, 4, 12; Cerulli, *Lett.*[2], 183-4; Ricci, *Lett.*, 855-6). An excellent short outline of his life (1868-1947) will be found in A. S. Gérard, *Four African Literatures*, 279-84; *Chi è dell'Eritrea*, 6-7; Zewde, biogr.

[4] The two Italian colonies referred to are, of course, Eritrea and Italian Somaliland.

Cross Society be founded at Addis Ababa on 1st Hamle 1927 (= 8th July 1935) with the object of safeguarding the lives of Our soldiers as far as possible. Following upon this We at once entered the International Red Cross. But the time since the establishment of the Society had been very brief and, therefore, the people had not yet become aware of the usefulness of the Red Cross; and as nobody could be found—apart from a few important people—who was able to offer financial support, We gave assistance by expending for the time being up to 200,000 dollars from Our treasury for the payment of salaries, the purchase of medicines, and all related matters, being conscious that some time would elapse until We were able to explain the matter to the people. However, since it was not only on one front that the Italians had come to wage war but in the east, and north, and south, it was recognized that there was a need for many doctors and a great deal of medical equipment. Our Ethiopian Red Cross Society presented, therefore, a request through the Red Cross Headquarters at Geneva that the various Red Cross Societies in the world should extend all possible help. When the Red Cross Societies in various countries heard about this, they expressed to Us their willingness to help to the utmost extent possible.

Later on, the British, Swedish, Dutch, Norwegian, and Egyptian Red Cross Societies despatched to Us doctors, medicines, medical equipment and anything else that was needed—including entire ambulances.

The Red Cross Societies of France, Germany, Japan, Turkey, America, Russia, Greece, Australia, and of other smaller nations gave Us considerable help by sending, according to the extent of their ability, money, medicines, and medical equipment.

Furthermore, Red Cross Headquarters at Geneva, apart from sending financial support, additionally despatched two men, Monsieur Braun and Dr. Junod,[5] to set about at once to improve the work of the Ethiopian Red Cross Society; and thus the activities of the Ethiopian Red Cross progressively expanded and became more successful.

Some foreigners resident at Addis Ababa, in their distress at seeing Italy waging a war of aggression against us, left their own work and engaged in Red Cross work; all these We thank profoundly.

[5] Dr. Marcel Junod, Swiss surgeon and International Red Cross representative in Ethiopia (Coffey, 307 ff.).

The Ethiopian Red Cross Society was making enquiries about the places at which the fighting was heaviest and then caused doctors to go there, having local people attached to them, lest they should encounter any difficulties on their respective journeys.

It was arranged that the Swedish ambulance should go for medical work to Sidamo and Bale, the British and Dutch to the north where Our headquarters was, the Norwegian and Egyptian to the Ogaden region.

It was arranged that the doctors whom the Ethiopian Red Cross Society had engaged were to go to Tigre, Ogaden, Sidamo, and any other necessary destination in order to lend their aid; and for a time the work began to develop well.

While the doctors were carrying out their work, they kept at a considerable distance from military camps, thus observing the rules of the Geneva Red Cross Society. But as the war which the Italian soldiers waged against Ethiopia was one of shamelessness and of aggression, We shall describe later on at its proper place how they destroyed Red Cross stations by violating international law and by bomb attacks.

CHAPTER 34

Our notification of
Italy's aggression

WE had made constant efforts at the time in requesting to select arbitrators on the basis of what is laid down in article 5 of the treaty we had concluded in 1920 (= 1928),[1] in order to make it possible to settle peacefully the quarrel that had taken place at Walwal. But since Italy's desire tended towards hostilities, We heard that, in neglect of a peaceful solution, she was piling up war material in the vicinity of our borders. We therefore transmitted to Geneva the following message on 8th Genbot 1927 (= 16th May 1935).

[1] See chapter 23 above.

'To the Secretary-General of the
League of Nations, Geneva.

We, Emperor of Ethiopia, request Your Excellency to be kind
enough to cause the following message to be read at the present
assembly at which Ethiopia's request is to be examined.

While we, on our part, did not up to now order the mobilization of soldiers or equipment nor offer any provocation, Italy has
been assembling, since before last September, troops, military
aircraft, tanks, and other war material of all sorts in the vicinity of
our frontiers. Anyone residing in Ethiopia, the subjects of whatever nation, are aware that Italy has been doing this. Ever since
the time of the attack against Walwal, Italy has begun to request
that Ethiopia should pay her compensation for the wrongdoing
which she has not committed, while Italy was seeking, by every
known diplomatic means, to evade her international obligations
upon which she had entered previously and to prevent an impartial examination of all the quarrels that had occurred between the
two of us—it being well known that she was seizing, in an illegal
manner, large tracts of our territory.

Italy has recently established a propaganda campaign to make it
appear that her occupation of a part of Ethiopian territory, her
attack upon Ethiopia, and her desire to seize the people are simply
in order to civilize them properly; and this is what ought to be
done to a pagan population. If Italy has any accusations to present
against Ethiopia or against the government, We are prepared to
give an appropriate answer at the proper time and place. Italy has
just now chosen for the arbitration and conciliation commission
two of her nationals who are her own government employees.[2]
Their selection is apt to prevent an impartial examination of our
affairs or at least is bound to render such an investigation very
difficult.

Apart from this, Italy's restriction of the matters that are to
come before the arbitrators for examination is liable to leave
unresolved the question of the interpretation of the treaty of 8th
Genbot 1900 (= 16th May 1908)[3] which is of major importance

[2] They were Count Luigi Aldrovandi-Marescotti, an ambassador who had
previously served on the Manchurian commission of the League, and Raffaele
Montagna, a former member of the League secretariat (Baer, 147–8).

[3] The 1908 treaty between Ethiopia and Italy was intended to lay down the
general principles defining the border between Ethiopia and Italian Somali-

and which deserves to be determined by arbitration. It has not been possible, nor will it be in future, to set up by agreement a truly impartial arbitration commission, i.e. in Italy's present state of mind and by diplomatic means.

While Italy put the blame on Ethiopia alleging that we refused to accept arbitration, We notified Italy of Our choice of two arbitrators who were not Ethiopian subjects, thinking that We were neglecting nothing to ensure for us an equitable and speedy outcome, lest Italy should find a way that would permit her to shirk the obligations she had accepted by international treaties. Although this government which is our neighbour did not interrupt its warlike preparations and did not cease its incursions into our border areas, We took the most meticulous care lest there should be any frontier clashes and even gave permission to set up a free or neutral zone wholly within Our territory. We earnestly request the Council to cause the covenant of the League of Nations to be fulfilled and to have Italy's military preparations stopped—preparations which are truly not for defensive purposes. We request that, if Italy refuses to accept that the arbitrators should examine and adjudicate upon all the attacks that have been made in the vicinity of the Somali-Ethiopian border since last December and should pronounce upon the interpretation of the treaty of 16th May 1908, the Council itself will take the investigation in hand and resolve matters by a full examination on the basis of article 15 of the covenant.

In submitting this appeal, Ethiopia only seeks a lawful, complete, speedy, and peaceful outcome of the matter.'[4]

Later on, on 11th Hamle (18th July 1935), We communicated this state of affairs to Our people in a speech which We delivered to Our parliament.[4a] The text is set out here below.

'For more than forty years Italy has never at any time ceased to entertain the desire to take our country. This desire, which had always been apparent in various forms throughout these

land. The detailed work of demarcation was never completed (Baer, 45–6). As can be seen from the opening lines of this chapter, the Emperor was anxious to have arbitration based on the explicit terms of article 5 of the 1928 treaty. This was refused by Italy, and the present passage in the Emperor's message is therefore in the nature of a concession to the Italian position.

[4] On the background of the Emperor's message, see Baer, 148–9.
[4a] Cf. Steer, 43 ff.

years, began to be clearly manifested in her actions during last year's (i.e. 1926 = 1934) rainy season.[5] To prove this, last year, in the month of August, without any reason whatever the Italian Government began to pile up war materials *en masse* in the vicinity of our borders.

When We heard this, We instructed Our Chargé d'Affaires at Rome[6] to make enquiries as to the reason for this; in reply they gave a reason that was baseless and mendacious from beginning to end, i.e. that they had made these war preparations because Ethiopia had the intention of making war against their colonies of Eritrea and Somalia. Although We exposed this answer as completely untruthful, from that time onwards Italy's unswerving resolve was embodied in a plan upon which she had decided after lengthy examination, and she never ceased pushing on progressively with her military preparations—while pretending they were for defensive purposes, although it was her absolutely settled intention to wage aggressive war against us.

In order to make such an aggressive design appear proper in the eyes of the peoples of the world, it was essential for Italy to find a useful pretext.

Last November at Gondar there arose disturbances about some woman between Ethiopian subjects who were, in part, employees of Ethiopian factories and others who were servants of the Italian commercial agency. When blood was spilt as a result of this quarrel between these men in their own affair, the Italian Legation at Addis Ababa energetically intervened in the matter in a diplomatic démarche, and Our peace-seeking government directed that the Italian demands should be satisfied, lest any vehement quarrel should develop.[6a] Later on again, there occurred the Walwal incident which is the basis of our present conflict.

Italy, infringing our territorial integrity and violating—instead of respecting scrupulously—our country's independence, has placed troops and much equipment at a place called Walwal which is some hundred kilometres beyond the border which the treaty concluded between the two governments in 1908 had determined.

On the occasion when the border between British Somaliland and ourselves was being delineated, some men had been ordered

---

[5] Between late June and September.
[6] Nägadras Afä Warq Gäbrä Iyäsus.　　　[6a] Jones and Monroe, 176.

by the Ethiopian and British governments to determine, by inspection on the spot, the places where the British Somaliland tribes were putting their herds to pasture—as had been permitted to them by treaty.[7]

When these delegates, whom the two governments had sent out for this task, were carrying out the work they had been ordered to do within our territory, they were given a military escort[8] because it was Our government that had to protect them. As you are well aware, on 26 Hedar 1927 (= 5th December 1934) a surprise attack was launched against these Ethiopian soldiers, and Our brave troops were hit by Italian machine guns, tanks, and aircraft;[9] their death in battle is adequate testimony of the violence which the Italian aggressors have wrought by premeditation.[10]

Having acted in this manner and having attacked Our soldiers within Our own territory, Italy intended to shift the responsibility for the aggression, which her own men had committed, against us and to reproach us. Not content with killing Our soldiers, Italy went so far as to demand that Our government should apologize to her and pay compensation.

Ethiopia's clear conscience was aware of the rights due to her and We, therefore, submitted immediately Our request to Italy to settle the matter on the basis of the text of the treaty, referring to the treaty concluded in 1920 (= 1928), by which Italy had undertaken that peace and friendship should forever persist between us and that, if a quarrel arose between us, this quarrel should have a peaceful outcome on the authoritative verdict of arbitrators. To this request, which We had presented, the reply was an absolute refusal, and Italy revealed her inflexible resolve to have the demands which she had submitted fulfilled in their entirety— without investigation and without adjudication in the proper manner.

We were resolved that our honour was in no way to be impaired, and We were convinced that a government that submits, entirely voluntarily, a conflict of this kind to a proper international tribunal, which judges matters impartially, would exalt rather than debase itself, if it submitted to judgement and were to

---

[7] For details see Baer, 50 ff.   [8] Baer, 50, 52.   [9] Baer, 55, lines 16–20.
[10] Ethiopian losses were 107 dead and 45 wounded; the Italian side suffered 30 dead and about 100 wounded (Baer, 54).

comply with the verdict; We, therefore, made it known publicly that, if Ethiopia were found to be guilty in this matter, she would at once carry out in full the terms of the judgement pronounced against her.

Because it was Our desire that the matter which arose from Italy's unwillingness to submit to arbitration should be settled legally and peacefully, it became necessary, in pursuit of this peaceable avenue, to cause the matter to come before the Council of the League. We notified the King of Italy and the leader of the Italian government, Monsieur Mussolini, in a detailed written submission of the grounds on which We had brought this matter before the League of Nations.

Last January the matter had appeared on the agenda of the meeting of the League of Nations Council, and Italy accepted, albeit reluctantly, the plan to resolve things by arbitration.[11]

But, while We complied with the text of the decisions reached by the League of Nations Council on 11th Ter (= 19th January 1935), it was necessary for Us once again to submit the matter to the League Council in March,[12] because the Italian Minister[13] went on dragging his feet while endeavouring to make us acknowledge wrongdoing, which we had not committed, in the course of the diplomatic talks that had been started in order to choose the arbitrators.

Indeed, while Italy strove by diplomatic means to exert improper pressure upon Our government, the news which came every day over the radio made clear to Us her intention to make war, as We continually heard of Italy's uninterrupted despatch of soldiers, war material, and ammunition to our frontiers at Eritrea and Italian Somaliland.

As a result of our second submission to the League of Nations, it was decided on 17th Genbot 1927 (= 25th May 1935) that arbitrators should definitely be chosen.[14]

Because it was Ethiopia's desire that the judgement to be pronounced should be impartial and on an absolutely legal basis, she on her part chose as arbitrators two men who were legal

[11] The Earl of Avon, *Facing the Dictators,* 196–7; Baer, 104–5. This was the decision of 19th January, 1935.

[11] Submission by Ambassador Täklä Hawaryat on March 17th, 1935, invoking article 15 of the covenant (Baer, 109–11).

[13] Count Vinci, Minister to Addis Ababa (Baer, 110).   [14] Baer, 153–4.

experts, one French and one American,[15] who were very well known for their knowledge and refinement in international law.

Italy on her part selected two Italians from among Italy's government officials.[16]

Although there was nothing for us to oppose on these grounds, yet it seemed to Us proper to bring to mind the Italian Government's unwillingness, in choosing her own nationals, for the dispute to be settled legally and impartially. The reason is that no man should be put under suspicion for pronouncing impartial judgement upon the country which had chosen him to argue in her favour.

As it was causing anxiety that the dispute might not be settled by arbitration on account of the fact that the gentlemen whom the Italian Government had selected did not possess the independence to judge as they saw fit, the British Government, noting that international law was the main foundation of world peace, began to attempt on its part to see whether a way of conciliation could be found, because its principal desire was that peace be firmly established in the world. Although it was not casting doubt on the legal status of the Ogaden province belonging to Ethiopia and although Italy was launching a bad attack upon Our patrimony by aggressive incursion, the idea of conciliation which the British Government presented was that we should give to Italy, by cession, a part of our Ogaden territory and, in exchange for this, the British would cede to us the port of Zeila[17] and a part of its territory.[18] For Our part there was no limit to Our seeking peace and, therefore, We were prepared to examine this conciliation proposal which had been submitted. But even before this compromise proposal had been properly presented, Monsieur Mussolini had already absolutely refused to accept it, and there was, therefore, no need for Us to consider the matter.

[15] Albert de Geouffre de La Pradelle, professor of law in the University of Paris, and Pitman B. Potter, at that time professor at the Graduate Institute of International Studies at Geneva (Baer, 148).

[16] While the Emperor's point is valid, it must be admitted that their credentials as such were impeccable (cf. note (2) above).

[17] Zeila (cf. note (2) in chapter 15), in the north of the then British Somaliland, some 40 miles to the S.E. of Jibuti (*Guida*, 442; *Africa Orientale*, *passim*; I. M. Lewis, *passim*).

[18] For further details of this British proposal, see Baer, 191, 195; Coffey, 84, 89.

It was not now possible for the arbitrators to complete the task for which they had been chosen. The principal leader of the Italian Government curtly rejected the conciliation idea which the British Government had submitted.

The Italians did not interrupt their preparations. The principal leaders of the Italian Government were declaring openly that the main thought in their heart was to take over our country. Hence, from then onwards the hour of war was progressively coming closer.

Last Säne 1st (8th June 1935), the principal leader of the Italian Government stood before 5000 soldiers who had been ordered to Eritrea and Somalia, now newly designated "Africa Orientale", and, while preaching to the Italian people according to his custom, he spoke to incite their spirit of bellicosity and said: "It is for you who are going out there to write the story of supreme heroism in the annals of our history."[19]

As Monsieur Mussolini said, what Italy seeks is to civilize Our people.

From now on Italy ceased to let the matter be settled peacefully. Her idea was to take revenge for Adwa[20] of old, with a lot of blood being spilt.

The Ethiopian people, whose name Italy seeks to extinguish calling it a heathen people, is a nation that honours the word it has given and upholds the treaty it has signed.

Ethiopia does not seek war. But she is bound to defend herself against the invader. Even at the time of Adwa it was not Ethiopia who picked the quarrel. The reason why the war occurred was that the Italians were found beyond their border within her territory. Maybe they will do so again tomorrow.

Although Ethiopia was victorious in 1888 (= 1896), warding off the invader by God's goodness and the heroism of her brave soldiers, she did not demand everything that was due to her; she did not make it an occasion for the expansion of her territory.

When the war comes which appears daily more inevitable, the Ethiopian Government's conscience will not reproach it; it has done everything possible to preserve peace.

Ethiopia has no intention of establishing her authority over other countries; she is prepared to defend her independence up to

[19] Baer, 180.
[20] The battle of Adwa in 1896, at which Italy was defeated, was a watershed in modern Ethiopian history (*The Ethiopians*[2], 88–9; *Guida*, 240 ff., 271 ff.).

the last, while being mistress in her own domain, and her civilization and territorial integrity undaunted.

When the Italian people, which has turned oppressor, arrives with the weapons of aggression which the modern age has produced and claiming that it is to teach us civilization, the Ethiopian people, which is prepared to die for its Emperor and its country, will await the invader mustered in unity.

Soldiers! When it is announced that a respected and beloved leader has died for our freedom in the course of the battle, do not grieve, do not lose hope![21] Observe that anyone who dies for his country is a fortunate man, but death takes what it wants, indiscriminately, in peace-time as well as in war. It is better to die with freedom than without it.

Our fathers who have maintained our country in freedom for us have offered us their life in sacrifice; so let them be an example to you!

Soldier, trader, peasant, young and old, man and woman, be united! Defend your country by helping each other! According to ancient custom, the women will stand in defence of their country by giving encouragement to the soldier and by caring for the wounded. Although Italy is doing everything possible to disunite us, whether Christian or Muslim we will unitedly resist.

Our shelter and our shield is God. May our attackers' new weapons not deflect you from your thoughts which are dedicated to your defence of Ethiopia's freedom.

Your King who speaks to you today will at that time be in your midst, prepared to shed his blood for the liberty of Ethiopia.

Before We conclude, there is one thing We wish to say to you once again. And this is Our earnest striving for peace. We would remind you of the Ethiopian Government's exertions for peace right up to the present time. By diplomatic means it has continually sought a way of reaching accord which is peaceful and in which there is honour for both of us. It has twice asked the League of Nations to get the Italian Government to honour the treaty of friendship and of arbitration which Italy had voluntarily signed.

---

[21] This is a reference to the Ethiopian custom of abandoning the battlefield in the hour of grief for a fallen leader, even at the time of victory. The most famous example of this is the death of Emperor Yohannes in the battle of Metemma (*Guida*, 363) in 1889, when the Ethiopians fled, even though they had been victorious. See also the pertinent remarks in Steer, 46.

Furthermore, as Ethiopia and Italy, together with other governments, had signed the treaty to outlaw war, We recently informed the American Government, because America was the originator of the treaty.[22]

Again, while the arbitrators of our two sides were now in Holland[23] examining our dispute, the Italian arbitrators were causing much difficulty and We, therefore, had to order Our minister[24] in Paris to bring this to the attention of the League of Nations for the third time.

We shall strive for peace till the end. But even if our exertions and our good-will have not achieved any result, at least our conscience will not reproach us. The Ethiopian people, united in faith, stretches out its hand to God that he may strengthen the power of our valiant men truly to defend our country's independence.

11th Hamle 1927 (= 18th July 1935).

Later on again, on 6th Pagumen 1927 (= 11th September 1935), We spoke to the peoples of the world by letting them hear Our voice over the radio. The speech was as follows:

'At the time when, according to the Ethiopian era, the year 1928 (= 1935/6) begins, We wish that this new year may bring the peace which is essential and which Our people and the world desire with a warm heart; and it appears to Us right to remark upon and to recall the principal events which have occurred in the days of the past year.

The clash which took place between Italian soldiers who were found to have entered Ethiopian territory unlawfully, together with much equipment, on 26th Hedar 1927 (= 5th December 1934) at Walwal, in Our Ogaden region, upon Ethiopian soil, and who are still there up to now, and, on the other side, soldiers who

---

[22] This is obviously a reference to the Kellogg Pact (see footnote (1) to chapter 33). The Emperor summoned the American Chargé d'affaires on July 3rd, 1935, and asked the American Government to secure Italy's observance of the Kellogg Pact of which she was a signatory. But Cordell Hull, a successor to Kellogg in the office of Secretary of State, replied on July 5th in terms which were so measured and olympian that neither was Italy discouraged nor Ethiopia comforted (cf. Baer, 221–2; Brice Harris, 32–5, 45–6).

[23] The sessions of the arbitration commission had at first been held at Milan; they were later transferred to Scheveningen (near The Hague). See Baer, 169–71, 208–10.   [24] Täklä Hawaryat.

had been ordered to escort the personnel who were under instructions to delimit the territory of Ethiopia and Italian Somaliland—because this clash was a serious matter according to the basic provisions enshrined in the covenant of the League of Nations, it was proper to settle it at once according to the text laid down in the special treaty which Ethiopia had concluded with Italy on 20th Nähase 1920 (= 26th August 1928).

This Walwal clash, which Our government had demanded to be settled by arbitration as the attack occurred, was recently adjudicated on 28th Nähase (= 3rd September 1935).[25] While Ethiopia was striving to bring matters to this outcome and to settle the Walwal incident by peaceful and legal means, Italy was strongly opposed, and it was therefore necessary to get the League of Nations Council, assembled in session, to institute an investigation on 11th Ter (= 19th January 1935), 17th Genbot (25th May), and finally on 28th Nähase (= 3rd September). The five[26] men, i.e. the two members of the Italian Government together with the other three arbitrators, who had been appointed to examine the Walwal incident reached the following unanimous verdict: neither Ethiopia nor Italy can be held responsible for the attack which occurred at Walwal. As the Walwal incident was thus closed, Italy was made to stop humiliating Our government, by demanding payment of compensation and salute to her flag; and to brand Ethiopia as an aggressor before the world. As it was the Walwal clash which Italy had made the pretext to wage war upon Ethiopia, this pretext has now been removed by the verdict.

The Council of the League of Nations has done everything necessary and possible for the arbitrators to dispose properly of the matter which had arisen between Ethiopia and Italy. Nevertheless, the Italian Government was strongly opposed.

The primary cause of the present conflict between Ethiopia and Italy is that the interpretation of the treaty of 8th Genbot 1900 (= 16th May 1908), concluded between the two governments about the Somali territory, has remained unsettled. At the January session of the League of Nations Council the Ethiopian Government requested that the interpretation of this frontier treaty should be examined, and in particular it asked that the question be

[25] Baer, 299–303.

[26] The fifth man, appointed by the four arbitrators previously mentioned, was Nicolas Politis, Greek Minister to France (Baer, 299).

investigated and decided as to whether Walwal was situated within Ethiopian or Italian territory. The Italian Government, however, opposed this for fear that the arbitrators might find against her. When it was even claimed that the map officially published by the Italian Ministry of the Colonies, showing Walwal to be within Ethiopian territory,[27] was insufficient, this action on the part of the Italian Government was persuasive enough.

By Our Government's firm stand to obtain an outcome through the authority of the League of Nations, by the application of law and by following the path of peace, the clash which occurred at Walwal was adjudicated by arbitration, although Italy had meant to wage war against Ethiopia since August last year—irrespective of the Walwal incident. She now went on realizing the intention she had formed when, five months later, she discovered a pretext in the Walwal clash to make this war. Since Nähase 1925 (= August 1933) Italy had begun sending equipment to Eritrea and her Somali colony, and she continued consolidating her position by despatching uninterruptedly soldiers, material, various war machines, and ammunition. While the Council of the League of Nations and the arbitrators were working to settle peacefully the matters that had arisen between Ethiopia and Italy, the latter never interrupted the despatch of men and material.

Since the Walwal incident has now been settled and Italy is somewhat short of reasons to make war, she has been active in preventing other governments to sell to Ethiopia the equipment she requires for her defence; she is working to make Ethiopia an object of hatred and to cause the peoples of the world to believe that, since Ethiopians are like wild beasts, they need a civilizing agent.

History will judge Italy's behaviour. While Italy claims to be the very essence of civilization, she is making unjust war upon a people that is peaceful, which has first been prevented from obtaining military equipment, and which lives trusting a treaty which Italy publicly signed on 20 Nähase 1920 (= 26 August 1928), so that peace and friendship should persist. Italy, who is planning to incite a future war against the Ethiopian people, with her soldiers being victorious without suffering too many casualties, is seeking to convince everyone that the useless work she is preparing to carry out against Our people is fully justified, while

[27] Baer, 45–6.

she is striving to prevent Ethiopia from obtaining equipment and thus to become weak.

Hence, to the legally well-founded evidence which we submitted, to the effect that Italian soldiers had unlawfully crossed the border and seized our land, the Rome Government gave no reply. It made its representatives accredited to Us give assurances, many times and in public, that Italy had a cordial and inextinguishable friendship for Ethiopia, while for a long time past it had been collecting information which its employees, whom it scattered in some strength over our territory and whom it paid a large salary, were supplying to it. Now, at the last moment, the Rome Government presented its submission to the League of Nations Council.[28]

As the memorandum, with which the Italian Government presented its rude and mendacious accusations to the League Council on 29th Nähase (= 4th September 1935) has not yet reached Us, it is only a very short time since We have become aware of these accusations and, therefore, there is no time now for Us to give a detailed reply. However, Our government is prepared to provide evidence and to return an answer point by point to these accusations which have arrived at the very last moment—as well as the reason for which they have been revealed to the peoples of the world. It is sufficient to announce only that We are transmitting instructions to Our envoys, now at Geneva, clearly designed to request the League Council to set up an international commission to examine the matter.

It is this international commission which We have asked for that will be able to decide by examining the accusations which the Italian Government has submitted and by looking at both cases.

The Ethiopian people emphatically seeks peace. Moreover, it loves its country dearly. Although it does not possess sufficient military equipment and although, through Italian political machinations, it has been prevented from obtaining it, it will resist by defending itself against the enemy, protecting its chest in which there is a proud heart burning with love of country.

Our peasants, who live tilling their land in peace, whose arm is strong, and who are jealous of their freedom, will rise up with

[28] Baer, 310 ff. The voluminous Italian printed memorandum was mainly a record of accusations against Ethiopia's savage backwardness and the need for Italy's civilizing mission.

their spades and lances to wield them quickly, overturning their ploughs to stop the enemy invading their land. We do not like war. But in war we shall not let our enemy pass without defending ourselves fiercely and without strong resistance. As Ethiopia's faith reposes in God, she knows that God's judgement will prevail over that of man. New weapons and guns which man has devised to destroy his kind are not a mark of civilization.

Thanks are due to all the statesmen who, in the troubles which have come upon today's world and despite their vast and boundless work over many months now, have been striving to strengthen peace lest it be extinguished, while Italy, thinking only of herself, rose to destroy peace.

The Imperial Ethiopian Government, the Ethiopian Church, and the people are unceasingly bringing their prayers before God, that He should be their leader and that He should grant a fruitful result to the exertions which all those in government are making to preserve peace.

Ethiopia is always conscientiously honouring and fulfilling any and all the international obligations upon which she has contractually entered, and she is seeking a way of conciliation, consonant with her honour and dignity, so that the conflict which has now arisen between her and Italy may be peacefully resolved. Her conscience will not rebuke her. As this act of aggression which Italy, who is called a great nation, is committing causes anxiety to all governments of the world, great and small, who are putting their minds to this in the conviction that it is peace that will improve living conditions and offer civilization to all mankind, Ethiopia desires and hopes that, with the assistance of the League Council, the quarrel which has broken out between Ethiopia and Italy may be resolved by law and proper judgement in consonance with the League of Nations covenant.'

CHAPTER 35

We proclaim mobilization

In all the civilized world, if one state seeks to wage war against another, it announces its intention of doing so. After such an announcement has been made, the diplomatic representatives of the two sides return to their home countries. If their citizens so desire, they may also leave.

But Italy continued making announcements that she had no intention of making war,[1] while in fact she had long meant to wage war against Ethiopia, and for the past three years had decided upon it and had begun preparations. However, at some time, when the occasion arises, revelations are bound to occur, and so General de Bono[2] has now spoken of it in the book which he has published about the war. And since this has been confirmed by Monsieur Mussolini's signature, it is not possible to claim that it is a lie.

When We heard of the despatch by Italy of war materials and large numbers of soldiers to her colonies of Eritrea and Somaliland, up to the realization of the time-table she had fixed to start the war, We made enquiries through Our Chargé d'affaires at Rome; a reply was then issued which no-one can accept as true, i.e. that it was as a safeguard against a surprise attack the Emperor might be launching against their colonies and that there was no other reason.

Since this was allegedly the reason, We made it known by radio to Italy and the whole world that we on our part were not thinking of a scheme of this kind.

Although We made this announcement, Italy did not interrupt the despatch of military equipment and troops. There were no factories to produce war materials in our country, in order to make preparations on our part. We did not have enough money

[1] Italy continued doing so until shortly before the outbreak of hostilities. Mussolini was in any event opposed to a formal declaration of war (Baer, 370, 374).

[2] Emilio de Bono (1866–1944) was C. in C. during the opening phases of the war in 1935. The book referred to is his *La preparazione e le prime operazioni*, Rome 1937.

to make purchases abroad. When We asked for loans, Italy's resolve to make war being well known, We did not find anyone who would lend to Us. Furthermore, since Ethiopia and Italy had signed, with approval, what is laid down in the covenant of the League which the nations of the world had set up at Geneva, it seemed to Us that, if any kind of dispute arose between us, the matter was to be looked into by the League in accordance with the covenant with a view to being settled peacefully. Over and above this, if a dispute that arose between the two governments could not be settled by diplomatic negotiations on the basis of articles 5 and 7 of the Treaty of Friendship which the two governments specifically concluded on 21st Hamle 1920[3] (= 28th July 1928), then the matter was to be disposed of by arbitrators, but in any event there was to be no war between them for at least 20 years. Italy had claimed to be one of the great civilized nations, and it, therefore, seemed to Us that she would not violate the covenant of the League. Moreover, by virtue of the fact that We did not suspect that Italy would start a war without notifying her decision to engage in hostilities, as the heathen of olden times used to do, We had not proclaimed mobilization from the moment of the Walwal attack, on 26 Hedar (= 5 December 1934), until 22 Mäskäräm (= 3 October 1935) when she began the war with her attack on Adwa.

But the Italians were well aware of the disposition of Our troops, in remote places and in the fringe areas of the country. As We entertained some suspicion that they might await the rainy season, when no-one would be able to march on the roads, and then launch an attack, We directed that a certain number of reserve troops from each unit should come to Addis Ababa.

Because their homes were very far in the West and South of Ethiopia, the rainy season had started by the time they were ready for their journey. As rain and mud made things difficult for them, they began to arrive at Addis Ababa only by the middle of Mäskäräm (late September), although they had set out in the month of Hamle (July).

But while the Italians were offering deceptive words to the League of Nations and pretending, on one hand, to seek conciliation, they despatched, on the other hand, war materials and

---

[3] The precise date of this 1920/1928 treaty is somewhat variable in this book; cf. chapter 23 (and notes thereto) as well as the dates indicated in chapter 34.

troops. After they had completed all their preparations, they crossed the border by aeroplane, on 21st Mäskäräm 1928 (= 2nd October 1935), without informing either us or the League of Nations of their decision to begin the war; they flew to Adwa and dropped bombs on the city, slaying old men and children, women and priests; they also set fire to the principal buildings.

Perhaps thinking of it as a precaution, We had given orders for a Red Cross Society station to be set up at Adwa; and this, too, they set on fire.

In the civilized world of the present time, when one state intends to wage war against another it will not do so without notification. But Italy, without regard to her honour and good name, apart from some ephemeral advantage to her, began the war without any declaration whatever; it cannot be doubted that this will bring shame to her history.

Apart from this, the Italian Minister at Addis Ababa, Count Vinci, caused Us great difficulties. If it were a government like the states of the civilized world, it would have been right for Italy to instruct her Minister to notify her decision to go to war and then to recall the Minister. We would then have informed all Our subjects, via Our Chargé d'affaires in Italy and Our Consul at Asmara, that they should leave Italian territory. Had Italy recalled her Minister without declaring war, it would undoubtedly have been in order to stop us preparing ourselves and proclaiming mobilization, yet we would have recognized that it was for the purpose of war. Or again, if we did not expel her Minister by force and he had been involved in some major incident, it would have been Italy's intention to have us condemned in the eyes of the world, claiming that Ethiopia had acted with violence of this kind against the Italian Minister.

While we had begun to follow the path of international civilization, We were convinced that it would not be proper to engage in lawlessness and to retrogress like Italy; We therefore notified the Minister and consuls, their agents and all their other subjects, to return to their country by the nearest possible route when no harm of any sort would befall them. Hence it was arranged that they should leave by the route nearest to them: those in the east by way of Jibuti, those in the south via Mogadishu and Kenya, those in the west through the Sudan, and those in the north by way of Asmara.

Even if we had detained as prisoners till the end of the war the subjects of a state which had unleashed the violence of war, without a declaration, and infringed the covenant of the League of Nations, we would not have been reckoned wrongdoers. But as We intended to seek peace, We were unwilling to do this. However, although We pursued the path of peace, the (Italian) Minister, without taking this into account at all, refused to depart until the consuls, agents, and Italian citizens who were resident in the various provinces had all left. Thus, to make things really difficult, he summoned the Magalo agent to Addis Ababa instead of going by way of Mogadishu which was not far from him.[4]

Worse than all this, the Italian Minister abandoned his erstwhile habit of going about Addis Ababa by car and now went on horseback instead—having a servant, also on horseback, follow him holding the (Italian) flag and carrying a revolver in his belt. He even started to go on ordinary roads on which no ministers of foreign countries, nor even the important people of our own, would venture. The soldiers who had been ordered to come for protective duties had just begun to arrive at Addis Ababa, and when they saw this Minister of an enemy power going about the capital in such a procession, We heard that their blood was boiling and they began to look upon this with hostile eyes. We were concerned, therefore, that, if by any chance he got involved in an incident, everything We had hitherto patiently endured for the sake of peace would be in vain. We informed him, through an intermediary, that he was to stay quietly in one predetermined place until the agents who had been summoned arrived, and accordingly it was arranged that he should remain at a certain place.[5] But what We had done for the sake of peace and security they interpreted in an unfavourable sense and spread the rumour that we had detained their Minister in prison.

Later on We received reliable information that the Italians had crossed the frontiers in the north and in the south and had dropped bombs on several of our cities, killing people and burning houses. As We felt that it was right for us to defend our country's independence as far as possible, although we did not even possess

---

[4] The reference to Mogadishu here clearly stands for Somalia in general.

[5] Part of the sentence is missing here, probably as a result of haplography. At the beginning of line 9 on p. 192 the following words may require to be inserted between በሆነ ፣ and ባንድ ፣ ። — ባንድ ፣ ሰው ፣ እጅ ፣ አስታወቀነው፡ና ፣ እንደዚህ ።

adequate modern equipment for defensive purposes, We directed the following proclamation of mobilization to be issued on 22nd Mäskäräm 1928 (= 3rd October 1935):

'The Lion of Judah has prevailed.
Haile Sellassie I, Elect of God,
King of Kings of Ethiopia.

People of my country Ethiopia! You know Ethiopia's ancient tradition since the days of Menelik I and that she is well known and honoured for her independence.

Forty years ago today, Italy, boasting of her ability and strength, had wanted to acquire our people as slaves after destroying Ethiopia's independence. When she came into our country to fight us, our God who does not like violence helped us, and when He gave us victory we did not seek to recover our land that had gone. As Italy violated the borders in the Hamasien⁸ and Somali regions and took away our patrimony, your eye can see and your ear can hear the yoke of serfdom which our brothers, who live in the areas she has usurped, have had to bear.

While We are sad at the violence wrought against them and while We do not seek to recover Our lost lands, Italy is now thinking of imposing the yoke of bondage upon the people who live in the whole of Our country. Having brought war, surreptitiously, to the Ogaden region, she is killing Our people who do not seek conflict and she is violating the treaty which we had concluded. We for our part had entered a League of Nations that was established for the sake of world peace and, therefore, We informed the League with the intention that the offender be identified once the Walwal conflict had been looked into by the arbitrators according to the law.

Even before the matter could be examined and adjudicated by the arbitrators, Italy had brought the war close to the frontiers of the Tigre and Ogaden; We, therefore, had to notify the League of Nations once more, and it issued a verdict in our favour, deciding that the matter was to be looked into by the arbitrators. When the latter had investigated the matter, they found in our favour, determining that the Ethiopian Government had done no

⁸ One of the three great highland provinces of Eritrea (together with Akkele Guzay and Seraye), with Asmara as its capital. See *Guida*, 199; map 192.

wrong and carried no responsibility for the attack which had taken place at Walwal. As all this was going on, Italy did not for the time being abandon the continuation of warlike activities in the direction of our borders. While Italy was reckoning to corrupt with blandishments every intention of Ours to have the matter peacefully settled by arbitral verdict, she coveted Our venerable country—meaning to deprive her of her liberty and to destroy it—which was well known for her antiquity and which has lived in freedom for more than 3000 years. I would be very distressed if we were to be thought of as being defeated; therefore, people of my country Ethiopia, help me, you who have strength with your strength, you who lack strength with your sympathy! The reason for which you are to help with strength and with sympathy is that you know it to be for the sake of your religion and your freedom, for your Emperor who, in mutual thought and assistance, is like a father and like a son, and for the sake of your flag which proudly manifests independence.

A nation without freedom is tantamount to a people driven from its land being pushed like cattle by the hand of the enemy, one that lives in bitter affliction and in humiliation as a tenant watching its inheritance in its own country in the hands of other men, which has no control over its possessions and its livelihood, not even over the soil of its grave, and which exists by inheriting serfdom that passes on to the next generation. With other people at least, when a king or a bishop dies—being human—his descendant is substituted for him. But when a country's independence is extinguished there is no replacement; while serfdom passes on from one generation to the next, it is an eternal prisoner living with a name that does not die; and however proud Italy may be of her equipment, she too is known to share in death.

(1) If you withhold from your country Ethiopia the death from cough or head-cold of which you would otherwise die, refusing to resist (in your district, in your patrimony, and in your home) our enemy who is coming from a distant country to attack us, and if you persist in not shedding your blood, you will be rebuked for it by your Creator and will be cursed by your offspring. Hence, without cooling your heart of accustomed valour, there emerges your decision to fight fiercely, mindful of your history that will last far into the future.

(2) Let your levy of troops, without men being separated from their leader and servants from their master, be mobilized on 12th Teqemt (= 23rd October) at Mika'el[7] near Dessie. If on your march you touch any property inside houses or cattle and crops outside, not even grass, straw, and dung excluded, it is like killing your brother who is dying with you; you will then be punished by paying twice over for his property.

(3) You, countryman, living at the various access routes, set up a market for the army at the places where it is camping and on the day your district-governor will indicate to you, lest the soldiers campaigning for Ethiopia's liberty should experience difficulty. You will not be charged excise duty, until the end of the campaign, for anything you are marketing at the military camps: I have granted you remission.

(4) You, country-squire, take your sons who have reached military age and set out with your district-governor, while the deputy district-governor gives you a stand-in who will be responsible for the protection of your land. But you who are unable to go on a military expedition, owing to old age, guard your district; let your sons set out with the district-governor!

(5) Sons of chiefs and soldiers, if you have reached military age and have not hitherto joined a military unit and have not entered the service of a master and remain without taking any work in the country, yet if you possess a rifle I will assign to you ammunition and your provisions; if you do not possess a rifle I shall let you have a rifle, ammunition and your provisions; and then join your district-governor for the military campaign.

(6) All you soldiers who have come back and stay in your respective districts, having left your army unit after enlisting in it earlier on, rejoin your officer and your regiment and go on the military campaign. You servants of noblemen and of soldiers who live in the country, if you stay there because you have quarrelled, make your peace and join your master in the war. But if you claim that you have been gravely wronged and therefore cannot be reconciled with your master, may you then come quickly to Addis Ababa, consigning to your master, before a War Ministry judge, the equipment and any property you had received in the regiment;

---

[7] A church to the south of Dessie (*Guida*, maps 399, 401).

and then get an officer and a rifle from the War Ministry, in order to get back to the military operations.

(7) You, who are peasants and traders, are to obey the orders which the deputy in charge of the district gives you and to assist him in any difficulties he may encounter, having enumerated before your district-governor's village chief and noted down in a register any metal or rifles you possess.

(8) If you are a trader, a peasant, or a priest in your own particular district, I shall pay you the cost of transportation; so bring things to me at the place of mobilization, loading up even what is usually set aside for grain tithe.

(9) After you have been ordered to go to war, but are then idly missing from the campaign, and when you are seized by the local chief or by an accuser, you will have punishment inflicted upon your inherited land, your property, and your body; to the accuser I shall grant a third of your property.

(10) If previously you have murdered someone and fear the avenger, or if you are a brigand and have set a house on fire, or have robbed a man of his money and have fled and now live in the forest or the mountain precipices, I grant you a pardon; so enlist with your superior officer[8] by 5th Teqemt (= 16th October). When you enlist with your officer and as you are inscribed in the district governor's register, I shall entrust you to a mediator *Ligaba*, and with him or with your officer you are to go to war. But if you fail to surrender on the day fixed for you, you will be hanged in the district where you have been apprehended. You who are the family of the deceased, I shall pay you the blood-money; hence excuse your avenger for my sake.

(11) If, after the campaign proclamation has been issued, you are found committing acts of brigandage or supplying to the enemy provisions or anything at all, you will be deprived of your patri-mony and property. You will be punished mercilessly and have the death penalty inflicted on you.'

We arranged the order of battle as is described here below: In the north, Ras Kassa was to be Commander-in-Chief in defence against the enemy coming by way of the Tigre. Under him were

[8] *Šaläqa* = head of a thousand; nowadays equivalent to major.

Ras Seyum Mängäsha, commander of the entire Tigrean army, Ras Mullugeta Yegäzu, Ras Käbbädä Mängäsha,[9] Ras Emru Haylä Sellasse, Ras Getatchäw Abatä, Däjatch Ayalew Berru, Däjatch Mäshäsha Walde,[10] Däjatch Bäyyänä Wandemagägnähu,[11] Däjatch Mängäsha Yelma,[12] Bitwaddäd Mäkonnen Dämsäw,[13] Däjatch Admasu Berru, Däjatch Abära Tädla,[14] Däjatch Awraris Dullu,[15] Däjatch Waldä-Maryam Bäddada,[16] Däjatch Bälaynäh Däbalqäw,[17] the Crown Prince's army commander Däjatch Wädaje Webe, Däjatch Ambatchäw Gässäsä,[18] the army commander of Wag, Däjatch Haylu Käbbädä,[19] Däjatch Wand Bäwassän Kassa, Däjatch Abära Kassa,[20] Däjatch Haylu Täsfaye,[21] Tsähafe Te'ezaz Afä Warq Waldä· Maryam,[22]

[9] Son of Ras Bitwaddäd Mängäsha Atikäm, soldier of great valour. Governor of various provinces, esp. of Wallo. Died 1940. Cf. *JES*, VII, 2, 256; Heruy, 61; photograph in Käbbädä Täsämma, 51.
[10] Son of Ras Walde; governor of Kämbata; killed during the Italo-Ethiopian war. Cf. *JES*, VII, 2, 216.
[11] Born 1875. Held various palace appointments to Menelik and Ledj Iyasu. Killed in the Italo-Ethiopian war in 1936. Cf. *JES*, VII, 2, 230; Heruy, 28; photograph in Käbbädä Täsämma, 143.
[12] Son of Dej. Yelma Makonnen, Emperor Haile Sellassie's half-brother. At one time Director of the War Ministry. Killed in 1936 during the Italo-Ethiopian war. Cf. *JES*, VII, 2, 218.
[13] Son of Ras Dämsäw Näsibu. Born 1890. Minister of Justice. Killed in 1936 in the Italo-Ethiopian war. Cf. *JES*, VII, 2, 223; photograph in Käbbädä Täsämma, 142.
[14] Long-time governor of the Raya and Azäbo Gallas. Killed during the Italo-Ethiopian war in 1935-6. Cf. *JES*, VII, 2, 249.
[15] Of a Mänz family; in government service since the days of Menelik II; fought in the Italo-Ethiopian war. Died in 1943. Cf. *JES*, VII, 2, 253.
[16] Born 1868. Service in the palace and district administration. During Italian occupation he lived in Kenya. Died in Ethiopia in 1942. Cf. *JES*, VII, 2, 265; photograph in Käbbädä Täsämma, 141.
[17] Born 1878. Served as provincial governor. Died 1959. Cf. *JES*, VII, 2, 227.
[18] Born 1899. Grew up together with Ledj Iyasu, as he was a member of Queen Taitu's family. Later served as provincial governor. Died in 1943. Cf. *JES*, VII, 2, 246-7.
[19] A native of the Wag district. Fought in the Italo-Ethiopian war and was subsequently killed during guerilla operations. Cf. *JES*, VII, 2, 243.
[20] Ras Kassa's second son; born 1905; father of Dej. Amha Abära. Served in provincial administration; accompanied Crown Prince Asfa Wassän on visit to Europe in 1932. Killed by the Fascists in 1936. Cf. *JES*, VII, 2, 249.
[21] A native of Adwa; born 1870. Fought in the Italo-Ethiopian war. After the Graziani massacre he was taken prisoner and deported. After the liberation of

Bäjerond Lätyebälu Gäbre,[23] Qägnazmatch Dähne Waldä Maryam.[24]

Ras Kassa had, before the rainy season, gone to his governorate of Bägemeder and had spent the rainy season there; We therefore transmitted to him orders to set out at once and go to join Ras Seyum.[25] We directed that Our War Minister, Ras Mullugeta, should proceed in advance from Shoa, together with the army commanders enumerated here above.

On 8th Teqemt (= 19th October 1935),[26] when he took leave of Us by parading the army in front of Us, We gave him (since he had to proceed with the troops) and the army mustered before Us the following precise orders:

'It gives Us[27] pleasure watching your departure, determined to shed your blood for your country's independence and for Us, your Emperor, and his honour.

Because it is to the servant he trusts that a master[28] commits his property, so have We instructed you to resist the enemy—placing your faith in God, while you take care of Our army and help everyone in whatever their difficulties may be.

The enemy who has now come upon us is not a new or unexpected enemy but he is our mortal foe of old. Everything he has now achieved by virtue of Our refusal to send Our army

Ethiopia he served in the Tigre provincial administration. Died 1946. Cf. *JES*, VII, 2, 242-3.

[23] Born 1867. Grew up in Menelik's palace. Served in battle of Adwa. Succeeded Gäbrä Sellasse as Tsähafe Te'ezaz. Held various ministerial appointments (PTT, agriculture). Died 1955. Cf. *JES*, VII, 2, 255.

[23] A native of Mänz, born 1893. Served Emperor Haile Sellassie in various personal offices; after the war became Prince Makonnen's tutor. Killed during the 1960 revolt. Cf. *JES*, VII, 2, 214.

[24] Born 1883. Held various administrative offices. Banished during Italian occupation. After the war he served as Deputy President of the Chamber of Deputies. Died 1964. Cf. *JES*, VII, 2, 274.

[25] Ras Kassa is here construed with the singular, while Ras Seyum has the polite plural. This reflects the Emperor's personal relationship to these two grandees.

[26] Oct. 17/18—according to Steer, 160 ff., where the scene of this remarkable parade is described in colourful detail.

[27] The mixture of singular and plural suffixes here, referring to the Emperor, is a little disturbing.

[28] The servant here is, of course, Ras Mullugeta, and the Emperor is the master.

preventively to the front—trusting as We did the peace-seeking efforts of the League of Nations—has been through cruelty, not even killing excluded, and he cannot be suspected of tenderness to soldiers, to the old and to women and children. We have already heard about the early stages of his mercilessness to women and children.

As death can in any event not fail to occur, it would be wrong to forget that it is of great advantage having it said that someone died shedding his blood for his country's liberty, his King's honour, and for the good name of his generation rather than that he died of a cough, a head-cold or of typhoid. If someone dies in war he is said to be extraordinary, but to be stunned at someone's death is to debase the dignity of valour.

It cannot be doubted that to a soldier, a peasant, or a trader his country's independence is his greatest pride. It is, therefore, important to convince you to the utmost extent possible that quarrels and deceitfulness amongst you should disappear, that love and unity should spread, and that a servant should acknowledge obedience to his master and a soldier to his officer. If the Italians are proud of their weapons against us, we on our part are proud that our greatest weapon against them is the help of God. Our flag, red, yellow, and green,[29] and our seal with the legend "the lion has prevailed" are the symbol of our independence; lest this symbol of our freedom should perish, it is a great honour for our good name and for our history if we die shedding our blood to the very last drop.

The reason why We have told you this is that it would suit the enemy if you were to enter the war simply in order to die, without taking precautions and like a butterfly in the flame, rather than save Ethiopia from the hand of the enemy as you are fighting a war according to contemporary fashion.

What exactly you should do is set out as follows:

(1) When you set up tents, it is to be in caves and by trees and in a wood, if the place happens to be adjoining to these—and separated in the various platoons. Tents are to be set up at a distance of 30 cubits from each other.

---

[29] This order, instead of the usual green, yellow, red, is curious, for, while there was for long uncertainty about the sequence of these colours, this was scarcely so in 1935. Cf. de Coppet, 616 ff.; Chojnacki in *JES*, I, 2, 49 ff.

(2) When an aeroplane is sighted, one should leave large open roads and wide meadows and march in valleys and trenches and by zigzag routes, along places which have trees and woods.

(3) When an aeroplane comes to drop bombs, it will not suit it to do so unless it comes down to about 100 metres; hence when it flies low for such action, one should fire a volley with a good and very long gun and then quickly disperse. When three or four bullets have hit it, the aeroplane is bound to fall down. But let only those fire who have been ordered to shoot with a weapon that has been selected for such firing, for if everyone shoots who possesses a gun, there is no advantage in this except to waste bullets and to disclose the men's whereabouts.

(4) Lest the aeroplane, when rising again, should detect the whereabouts of those who are dispersed, it is well to remain cautiously scattered as long as it is still fairly close. In time of war it suits the enemy to aim his guns at adorned shields, ornaments, silver and gold cloaks, silk shirts and all similar things. Whether one possesses a jacket or not, it is best to wear a narrow-sleeved shirt with faded colours. When we return, with God's help, you can wear your gold and silver decorations then. Now it is time to go and fight. We offer you all these words of advice in the hope that no great harm should befall you through lack of caution. At the same time, We are glad to assure you that in time of war We are ready to shed Our blood in your midst for the sake of Ethiopia's freedom—as indeed We have explained to you in the speech We delivered on 11th Hamle (= 18th July 1935).'[30]

[30] See above pp. 184-5 of Amharic original (= p. 220 of translation).

CHAPTER 36

Our organization of the southern army

WE organized Our southern army in three parts, right, left, and centre wings.

We made Dejazmatch Näsibu,[1] the representative of the Duke of Harar,[2] Commander-in-Chief of the right wing of the southern army. We attached to him as aides Dejazmatch Habtä Mika'el[3] and Dejazmatch Amde,[4] Dejazmatch Abäbä Damtäw and Dejazmatch Makonnen Endalkatchäw. There was also a Turkish national, called General Wehib Pasha;[5] since he knew about Italy's war of aggression against Ethiopia, he had come to help of his own free will and without any request on our part; We gave him to Dejazmatch Näsibu as adviser in any military matters. With regard to medical work, Dr. Hockman[6] who had been working in the American mission hospital, established at Addis Ababa in the name of Tafari Makonnen, had given notice, through the Ethiopian Red Cross Society, of his wish to go down to Dagahbur[7] to tend to the wounded; for the time being he went on his own. But later on a Red Cross Society had been set up at Cairo, Egypt's capital, for the assistance of the Ethiopian people; and Prince Ismail Dawd,[8] a member of the royal house, had been sent by the Society together with upwards of twenty doctors and

[1] Dej. Näsibu Zämanil was successively Consul at Asmara, Mayor of Addis Ababa, Director of the War Ministry, and the Duke of Harar's representative as governor of Harar province. He died in Switzerland in 1936. Cf. *JES*, VII, 2, 245; photograph on p. 127 of Käbbädä Täsämma.

[2] The Emperor's second son, Makonnen, who was born in 1922 and died in 1957 in a car accident. Cf. *JES*, VII, 2, 221.

[3] Dej. Habtä Mika'el Yenadu served in Emperor Menelik's household. He was born in 1878 and died in 1962. Cf. *JES*, VII, 2, 211. Photograph in Käbbädä Täsämma, 129.

[4] Dej. Amde Habtä Sellasse. Born 1876. Served in provincial administration. He lived at Jerusalem during the Italian occupation of Ethiopia. On his return he became a crown counsellor. Died 1953. Cf. *JES*, VII, 2, 270–1.

[5] Steer, 189; Barker, 266–7.

[6] Dr. Robert W. Hockman, an American volunteer doctor. Cf. Del Boca, 93.

[7] Important market-centre in the Ogaden province, *Guida*, 612.

[8] Del Boca, 38, 94.

auxiliaries; he had arrived with a complete ambulance, and it was arranged that he should assist the right wing of the southern army with medical work.

We appointed Ras Dästa Commander-in-Chief of the left wing of the southern army. As support for him We nominated Dejazmatch Gäbrä Maryam[9] and Dejazmatch Makonnen Wassäne,[10] Dejazmatch Däbbay Waldä Ammanel,[11] and Fitawrari Taddäsä Gännäme.[12] For the medical work Dr. Hockman had been sent down by the Sudan Mission, but when he went to inspect the condition of a bomb and dismantled the screws, it exploded again and hit him.[13] In consequence he died immediately and We had him brought by aeroplane to Addis Ababa where he was buried.

The valiant Grazmatch Afäwarq.[14] the army officer whom We had stationed at Gorrahei,[15] had prepared trenches and had done well digging the ground to make it suitable as a firing position and for defence against bombs from aeroplanes. Hence, when Italian soldiers came there on two occasions, he sent them back defeated both times. And after the Italians had become convinced that they were unable to engage in an infantry battle, having closed in face to face with Grazmatch Afäwarq at Gorrahei, they began unleashing a rain of bombs on the place, returning repeatedly by plane. On one occasion they dropped three hundred bombs there. But they did not cause much damage—apart from killing five men and wounding fifteen who had not observed the instructions to be cautious.

[9] Served Emperor Haile Sellassie in various court appointments. Later on an official in the Ministry of the Interior. Killed in action in 1936. Cf. *JES*, VII, 2, 282; photograph in Käbbädä Täsämma, 134.

[10] Born 1881. Served Emperor Menelik and later on was prominent in the provincial administration of various parts of the country. Following the Graziani massacre he was deported. Cf. *JES*, VII, 2, 222.

[11] Born 1877. Served in Menelik's palace. Fought in the battle of Adwa, and later was active in provincial government. Died 1936. Cf. *JES*, VII, 2, 276.

[12] I possess no information about him.

[13] This incident is described by Steer, 209–10, in some detail.

[14] Grazmatch Afäwarq Waldä Sämayat, posthumously created Dejazmatch for his valour and leadership during the Ogaden battles. Killed 1935-6. Cf. *JES*, VII, 2, 255; Steer, 169–70.

[15] Gorrahei (Qorrahe), village and airport in the Ogaden, scene of fierce battles and air-attacks in the Italo-Ethiopian war. *Guida*, 609 ff. and frontispiece map; Steer, 169–70.

On Teqemt 23rd (= November 3rd) 20 aeroplanes returned and dropped bombs, and while the brave Grazmatch Afäwarq was firing with the Oerlikon[16] and taking aim to bring down a plane, a bomb splinter that had fallen by his side hit his leg and wounded him.[17] As his bravery, after being wounded, inspired him further, he endured the pain of the wound and carried on his work.

But after he had waited a little, he became aware that his strength was flagging and that he was unable to fire; he therefore requested to be carried off and they took him to a place where he could rest. It was only at Dagahbur, at a distance of some 220 kilometres, that the nearest doctor was; and he was concerned that his soldiers might disperse, if he were to go there. As he lay there, he notified the Commander-in-Chief, Dejazmatch Näsibu, by radio-telegram as follows: I am severely wounded and may perhaps die; therefore, please send an army officer quickly to Gorrahei to replace me.

Dejazmatch Näsibu despatched Fitawrari Gwangul Kolase[18] as commander to Gorrahei. As they took Grazmatch Afäwarq Waldä Säma'et to Dagahbur for medical treatment, he died on the journey and they buried him with honour in the church of St. George at Dagahbur.

At this time, a physician of the (Sudan) Interior Mission had offered his help as a volunteer and went to Sidamo. But later on the Swedish Red Cross Society had appointed Dr. Hylander[19] and sent doctors and auxiliaries together with a fully equipped ambulance; it was arranged that they should go to the left wing of the southern army.

To the centre wing of the southern army We appointed Dejazmatch Bäyyänä Märed[20] as Commander-in-Chief and attached to him in support Bäjerond Feqrä Sellasse Kätäma,[21]

---

[16] The suburb of Zurich where these guns were manufactured.

[17] Steer, 172–3.

[18] This officer is known to me only from Steer's account (pp. 175–6).

[19] Dr. F. Hylander, chief of the Swedish medical team; after the liberation of Ethiopia he became chief medical officer of the Ministry of Health (Del Boca, 93, 95).

[20] Dej. Bäyyänä Märed was married to Emperor Haile Sellassie's daughter Romanä Warq. Governor of Bale when the Italians invaded Ethiopia. Died in the 1935/6 war. Cf. *JES*, VII, 2, 230. Photograph in Käbbädä Täsämma, 131.

[21] Formerly Minister of Finance; Cf. Käbbädä Täsämma, 131.

Fitawrari Atnaf Sägäd Waldä Giyorgis,[22] Qägnazmatch Assefaw Waldä Giyorgis[23] as well as Qägnazmatch Sälaba[24] and Qägnazmatch Andom[25] who had joined us, having deserted the Italians, because they refused to fight our country together with the enemy. For medical work, however, no doctor could be found for the time being, so those Ethiopians went who had some knowledge of bandaging wounds only. Later on it was arranged that some of the Swedish doctors who had gone to Ras Dästa should be detached and proceed to Dejazmatch Bäyyänä Märed.

Apart from this, before the beginning of the war, very few soldiers held all the small towns which were in the districts of the right southern front, such as Dagahbur, Bullale,[26] Sasäbäne,[27] Dägahamädo,[28] Burqot,[29] Gorrahei, Haradiget,[30] Gabredarre,[31] Fafän,[32] Cheqo,[33] Webi Shebeli, Burdäde,[34] Tafari Kätäma[35] as well as similar places on the left southern and central southern fronts. We gave orders to all the army officers who were on guard duty to stay in the poitions to which they had been assigned; if the Italians attacked them they were to resist as far as possible, but if the aggression against them became too fierce they were to fall back.

[22] A relation of Empress Zawditu. Was killed in the course of the Graziani massacre in 1936/7. Cf. *JES*, VII, 2, 254.

[23] Later Brigadier-General, commanding the guard of honour (Käbbädä Täsämma, 131).

[24] An Eritrean who deserted the Italians together with his men (Käbbädä Täsämma, 132).

[25] Andom Tesfa-Seyon took a considerable contingent of Eritreans and crossed the lines early in 1936. He was nominated Qägnazmatch by the Emperor and later created Dejazmatch posthumously. See also *Chi è dell'Eritrea*, 16.

[26] Small village in the Ogaden (*Guida*, 611).

[27] Village and river in the Ogaden (*Guida*, 612).

[28] Village in the Ogaden (*Guida*, 438, 611—as Dagamedo); Steer, map, 88.

[29] Small village in the Ogaden (*Guida*, 611—as Birgot); Steer, map, 88.

[30] Haradiget: Ogaden village; map of Min. dell'Africa Italiana (1 : 2.000.000) N-n; Steer, map, 88.

[31] Important centre in the Ogaden (*Guida*, 610); in Amharic Qäbridähar; Steer, map, 88.

[32] Place and river in the Ogaden (also Faf); see *Guida*, 438, 609; Steer, map, 88.

[33] Cheqo: The position of this Ogaden village is not known to me.

[34] Burdäde: Ogaden village; map of Min. dell'Africa Italiana (1 : 2.000.000) N-p; Steer, map, 88.

[35] Tafari Kätäma is a village close to the border of Italian Somaliland; Steer, map, 88.

But the Italians began to fly over in their planes and to unleash a rain of bombs upon all the little towns enumerated here above. But as the soil of the Ogaden province is dusty and sandy, most of the bombs were found buried in the sand—unexploded. Thus on one occasion a bomb that had fallen near Dagahbur was found unexploded.[36]

The Italians again brought along aeroplanes in waves of 20 each time, on 24th and 25th Teqemt (= 4th and 5th November 1935), and totally obliterated Gorrahei with the bombs they dropped.

They killed the Somalis and their animals, who had come to the Gorrahei region to water their herds, and then entered Gorrahei.

Fitawrari Gwangul Kolase who was Grazmatch Afäwarq's replacement had not heard of the Italians' entry into Gorrahei; he thus marched on with some 500 soldiers and reached a place called Hanäley,[37] to the east of Sasäbäne. When he heard gunfire, he ordered his men to scatter quickly and widely amidst the bushes, crevices, and grass.

Having waited a little, they saw Italian soldiers arriving in lorries, followed by quite a number of tanks. They lay silently until the Italians had gone forward. Later on, however, those in the tanks alighted from their vehicles to look at an engine that had broken down—and the men in the lorries got out as well. Gwangul's soldiers were watching right and left, forward and rear, and when he gave them a sign they fired a volley and wiped out the lot. In this astonishing battle only a few of Gwangul's soldiers were killed. But Gwangul himself was injured, and as his men remained there, being unable to push forward, he informed Dejazmatch Näsibu of his victory.[38]

When Dejazmatch Näsibu heard of their brave action, he sent two lorries and arranged for the wounded to be taken to Dagahbur for medical attention.

In this victory there were captured, in addition to some damaged machine guns, four most excellent machine-guns as well as many rifles and bullets, and they were taken to Dagahbur.

---

[36] It is likely that this sentence has been misplaced and that it belongs to p. 199, line 5, of the Amharic text—preceding the passage where a doctor (Hockman) was examining the bomb and was killed when it exploded.

[37] Should read Hamanley, near the confluence of the Faf and Jerrer rivers (*Guida*, 611).   [38] Cf. Steer, 175-7.

After We had heard about the death of Grazmatch Afäwarq and the occupation by the Italians of Gorrahei, news also reached Us that the Italians on the northern front were pushing on from Adwa towards Mäqälle[39] and that the governor of Mäqälle, Dejazmatch Haylä Sellasse Gugsa,[40] had betrayed his mother-country Ethiopia and Us, his Emperor, and had gone over to the Italians. In consequence, We made Dessie Our headquarters. Since We intended to wait while finding out about the position of the armies on the northern and southern front, before proceeding to Dessie We went down by plane to Jijjiga on 9th Hedar (= 19th November 1935).[41]

The next day We conferred the rank of Dejazmatch upon Grazmatch Afäwarq who had given his life with such valour for his country's independence and for the honour of his Emperor.[41] This was intended to be a memorial for future generations and for history. Subsequently We bestowed the rank of officer upon several men. On the third day We assembled the army officers in full and gave them words of advice as to how to guard against bombs from aeroplanes and other dangers. We then arranged for the following written advice to be distributed:

'Since the Italian Government has for forty years now set out to destroy Ethiopia's freedom by aggression, you heroes who are alive now and who were present at that time and those of you who were not at Adwa but whose fathers had been there, they have shown their heroism by shedding their blood and they have saved their country's freedom and their patrimony from the hands of the enemy. Now the Italian Government is preaching to its people to avenge that battle which it lost forty years ago, claiming that in Ethiopia the army was a spent force and that, therefore, they would fight us without difficulty. The Italian Government has begun the war to make you who did not die share the fate of those who did, to destroy your freedom by abasing the well known bravery of Ethiopia's sons which is recorded in world

---

[39] Provincial capital of the Tigre province. Seat of Emperor Yohannes who had his palace built there. See *Guida*, 302–3, and map 304.

[40] Son of Ras Gugsa Araya, a grandson of Emperor Yohannes; Haylä Sellasse Gugsa married the Emperor's daughter Zänäbä Warq. He flirted with the Italians on many occasions, and soon after the Italian invasion in October 1935 he betrayed his country and crossed over to the enemy. After the war he was condemned to life imprisonment (see ch. 37).   [41] Steer, 184.

history, to invade your patrimony and your houses, to acquire as slaves your old parents, to make exiles of your sons, and to reckon Ethiopia's heroes as if they did not exist, and to attack with its army in the north and in the south. All the governments of the world, being aware of Italy's violent onslaught upon Ethiopia, are our supporters. While Italy believes that Ethiopia's heroes have ceased to exist and persists in discounting those who do, the important thing is that it is your duty to revive your valour by defeating the hostile attack launched against your generation and against Ethiopia and by victoriously driving out from our land our enemies who have taken it by violence. Man has not been created to be everlasting. His end is death which severs him from this world. This death may come early or late, but for all mankind it is inescapable. It is man's name alone that remains as a memorial until the world, which appears to hover beyond the grave, passes altogether.

When this our enemy fought us at Adwa, forty years ago, Ethiopia's brave men beat him victoriously; hence their names will remain unforgotten, mentioned forever, not only yours who are alive but even theirs who were lost there. It is the main source of pride for the present generation. Again, even for a young man, as the enemy attacks him robbing him of his country and his patrimony and carrying his family into exile, it is the death that comes upon him in battle which is indeed his greatest wish and source of pride.

Even the hen will struggle to save her chicks from the vulture. This being so, do recognize that it is proper for a man to fight with the enemy, however many thousands of times the latter may surpass him in knowledge and strength!

Since death is thus in the end ineluctable for mankind, how great will be your honour if you lose your life fighting the invading enemy to establish an inextinguishable reputation, to prevent aged parents, wife and children, being exiled and, while today they live in dignity in their free country of Ethiopia, if that liberty were to be destroyed, to prevent them sinking into humiliation and this their dignity being lost. Your glorious name will endure, being praised by your children and your families and being recalled by world history. We have been aware for some time of our enemy's intention to carry through this plan of aggression and We, your Emperor, ruling you in time of peace, have told you of Our resolve to shed Our blood being amidst you in time of war. Thus We are now with you.

Since you know about the multitude of different instruments of war the Italians have been accumulating, they cannot cause you much injury. The thing which is called "aeroplane" is intended to cause shock by the noise of the bombs it drops and to weaken the heart, but other useful things it does not do. While present-day modes of warfare may not cause you much damage, it is necessary to follow the advice We have given you through your respective officers, so as to enable you to attack your enemy. In order to defend your country's independence, We shall not deprive you of Our support to lighten your burdens in terms of money and provisions in all your difficulties which you may encounter in this place at which you are stationed. And now, lest any kind of trouble should befall the kinsmen and families of the heroes who have laid down their lives, while carrying out their duty, for the honour of their country and their families, We shall protect them as Emperor and father. We have, therefore, instructed Our military representatives that their names should come before Us in writing, through their respective commanding officers. We are forever with you until Our life expires.'

10th Hedar 1928 (= 20th November 1935).

As regards the deployment of the army, if they went down to the central Ogaden, the countryside there would be one of severe desert conditions without sufficient water and food for the army or grass and fodder for the animals. We, therefore, gave orders that they should remain reconnoitring in the area from Jijjiga to Dagahbur and that, if the Italian army crossed the desert and made an approach towards them, they should then open hostilities; they should further let us know about everything that occurred at any time by sending messages to wherever Our headquarters will be.

Subsequently We set out by automobile from Jijjiga to Harar; at Harar We arranged a lunch party for Our retinue and then went down to Dire Dawa. On the morrow, 11th Hedar (= 21st November 1935) We returned to Addis Ababa by air.

CHAPTER 37

About Dejazmatch Haylä Sellasse Gugsa's treachery

AFTER the Italians had entered Adwa by dropping bombs from aeroplanes, rather than by valiant battle, they disclosed in their daily communiqués that many Ethiopian nobles had deserted the Emperor and gone over to them. This news was not the whole truth. According to the custom of our country of Ethiopia, when nobles who have been army officers or provincial governors relinquish their appointments, being no longer able to carry out the work owing to advanced age or ill-health, or when some of them are dismissed from their offices owing to some offence having been proved against them, there are many of them who remain on their inherited property engaged in agriculture or trade or being otherwise maintained. When they live in such circumstances, they do not cease to be referred to by their former rank.

The Italians, however, induced these nobles who had retired from government service to go over to them, by force or by intimidation, and began to reveal over the radio that a certain Dejazmatch or Fitawrari or Qägnazmatch had deserted his Emperor and gone over to them: 'The country accepts us, the people like us', they claimed.

But it was not possible to deny and to claim as mendacious the news of the betrayal of Dejazmatch Haylä Sellasse Gugsa, of the nobles of the Tigre.

Dejazmatch Haylä Sellasse is a son of the Tigrean Prince Ras Gugsa Araya. Being the son of a prince he had married Our daughter Zänäbä Warq. But when only about a year had passed since marrying her, by misfortune both his wife and his father had died in quick succession to each other, and he had thus fallen into deep grief. But although his wife and his father had died, We had no thought of lowering him in rank and, in fact, gave him his father's governorate of Endärta, Agame,[1] Bora[2] and Säläwa,[3] as well as authority over Edda-Mähone[4] and the two Awlalo[5] regions; We also directed that he should reside in the chief city of Mäqälle.

His father, Ras Gugsa, and Ras Seyum had lived in mutual envy and distrust about the headship of the Tigre; and now, since he was still young, two small districts from the extensive governorate which his father had held were added to Ras Seyum's domain. He took this as a pretext and progressively made plain his hostility towards Ras Seyum, meaning to carry on the quarrel that had been started by his father.

The Italians had been laying it down in their preparatory planning that they might be able to take Ethiopia, without recourse to military force, by inciting the important men to mutual enmity and by inducing them to desert the Emperor. Thus when they heard about the quarrel that had started between Dejazmatch Haylä Sellasse and Ras Seyum, they began exchanging messages with the former. Some people gave Us this news, but We discounted the reports directed against him and did not suspect that a man who claimed to be a descendant of Emperor Yohannes would betray Ethiopia—whatever the circumstances, for Emperor Yohannes had been an opponent of the Italians.

Lest this calumny that had been rumoured against him should be revealed, he used to write to Us as follows: 'If by any chance the Italians should invade us by military force, I shall resist them to the utmost in my province of Agame—until I die.' He sent further messages to say: 'I have exchanged messages with the soldiers of the Hamasien[6] and have arranged that they should desert and come over to us.' Later he wrote: 'Those soldiers with whom I have communicated have come over to me.' A second

---

[1] Agame is the Tigrean region between Senafe and Adigrat, with the latter as its chief centre (*Guida*, 298; map 272).

[2] Bora is the district between Amba Alagi and lake Ashangi to the west of the Asmara-Addis Ababa road (*Guida*, 324; map 304).

[3] Säläwa (Seloa) is the district to the S.W. of Endärta (main centre Samre) and N. of Bora (*Guida*, 325; map 304).

[4] i.e. Enda Mehoni (also Meconni), district and kinship group between Endärta and Amba Alagi (*Guida*, 307; map 304); Steer, 302; de Coppet, Atlas, IV.

[5] Awlalo, district to the south-east of Agame, reaching almost as far as the salt-flats (AOI map, GH–f).

[6] This can only refer to Eritreans recruited into the Italian forces.

piece of evidence which he offered for his loyalty was concerning his accusation against Dejazmatch Käbbädä Aragaw,[7] his father's brother. The substance of this accusation was as follows:

'Dejazmatch Käbbädä Aragaw is not loyal to our government. The fact which proves this is his constant exchange of correspondence with the Italians. Having discovered a letter by which he entered into such communication, I have been able to lay my hands on it. Further, he sent his two sons to Asmara and arranged that they should receive their education from the Italians. Therefore, please send a plane to me, for it would be best if he were to come to Your Majesty. If not, he will cause me difficulties by making propaganda for the Italians here. The letter which I have obtained I had to purchase for money from the hands of one of his intimates.'

With the intention of ascertaining the truth of this matter, We told him to send the letter to Us; after he had done so, We had Dejazmatch Käbbädä brought to Addis Ababa by plane. By his acting in this manner, it seemed to Us that all the suspicions against Dejazmatch Haylä Sellasse were untrue and We neglected the matter.[8]

But when We were told about the Italians entering Adwa and Agame, We also heard that he had confiscated the weapons of the men from Hamasien who had come over to our side and had arrested them.

Subsequently We despatched to Mäqälle, ostensibly as support for Dejazmatch Haylä Sellasse, Dejazmatch Haylu Käbbädä (as commander), Dejazmatch Bogalä Berru,[9] Dejazmatch Dästa Gwangul, Dejazmatch Alämayähu Dästa, Dejazmatch Täfäri Waldu, Dejazmatch Bälay Maru, Dejazmatch Damtäw Waldä Täkle, Dejazmatch Ejjegu Käbbädä,[10] Fitawrari Mäsfen Zälläqä, Fitawrari Täbäjjä Täkle. They set up camp near Mäqälle and transmitted to Us by telegram the following message:

'To Haile Sellassie I Emperor of Ethiopia. Dejazmatch Haylä Sellasse whom you trusted has betrayed his mother Ethiopia and

---

[7] Dej. Käbbädä Aragaw, whose *gebbi* was in the Maytchäw area (*Guida*, 310), was a younger half-brother (on the mother's side) of Ras Gugsa Araya.
[8] Steer, 144.   [9] I cannot place this and the following names.
[10] Ejjegu Käbbädä: see Käbbädä Täsämma, 386.

his father the Emperor and has made it known by proclamation that he has gone over to the Italians. The army of Wag alone, fighting at Mäqälle, will not be able to repulse the Italian invader who claims that he will take the whole of Ethiopia. It would, therefore, be well if troops, armed as much as possible, were to come to us.'

Many of Haylä Sellasse Gugsa's officers left him at once, declaring: for the sake of our faith and our history we shall not fight our Emperor jointly with the Italians and deliver Ethiopia into the hands of foreigners. By their coming to Us, We were finally convinced of the truth of his treachery. A servant of his, who had deserted him and had loyally come over to Us because Dejazmatch Haylä Sellasse had betrayed his country and surrendered to the Italians, gave Us the following report:

'When my master, Dejazmatch Haylä Sellasse, went to Asmara for medical treatment or in order to go by boat to Addis Ababa,[11] the Italians used to tell him:[12] "We shall wage war against Ethiopia; after destroying Ras Seyum we shall place you on your father's throne and make you King of the whole Tigre."[13] They also used to show him the multitude of their cannons, their machine guns, and their aeroplanes as well as the modern make of their rifles. Thus, on one hand, they would give him hope of obtaining the whole Tigre and, on the other, would make him afraid, in view of his tender age, when he observed the mass of Italian military equipment.'

The fact which establishes the truth of this, together with what We have said above, is that, when Dejazmatch Haylä Sellasse defected and got mixed up with the Italians, General de Bono

[11] 'In 1933 and 1934 Haile Sellassie Gucsa had visited Asmara, for Eritrea with its railway trains, its champagne, its steamer to Djibouti, made an easier route for the Tigrean lords between Addis Ababa and their provinces. To travel in comfort as a rich man should, why take the long caravan road through Central Ethiopia when the Italians smoothed the other way?' (Steer, 145).

[12] While the Emperor uses the third person singular when speaking of this traitor (in contrast to his usual practice of employing the polite plural when referring to the major nobles), the servant is, of course, made to speak of his former master in the polite form (see above, p. xxvi).

[13] It will be recalled that at that time the Tigre province was divided into two governorates, i.e. the western part belonging to Ras Seyum and the eastern portion to Dej. Haylä Sellasse Gugsa.

issued a proclamation in his favour, declaring: By the command of H.M. King Victor and the Duce, Monsieur Mussolini, we have assigned to you the whole of the Tigre up to the Ala[14] water and have nominated you Ras. However, after their designs had been accomplished, they did not even give him Mäqälle, his father's seat, let alone the whole of the Tigre.

After the Italians had accomplished the desertion of Dejazmatch Haylä Sellasse, they believed that other great officers would desert and go over to them and that on these grounds the hearts of Our soldiers would be panic-stricken. But in fact there was no-one, officers or men, who was stunned or made afraid by his treachery—apart from detesting and hating him, declaring: this is the brother of Judas Iscariot!

After he had announced his desertion, Our officers were approaching Mäqälle and, while his chiefs and servants were getting in touch with Our officers, they determined to try to catch him. But when he heard this, he left Mäqälle, at 7 o'clock (at 1 a.m.) during the night of 30th Mäskäräm (= 11th October 1935), together only with up to 50 of his retainers, and joined up with the Italians having gone by way of Edaga Hamus.[15] Those men from the Hamasien, who had deserted from the Italians and whom he had detained in prison at Mäqälle, got out of prison as soon as he had escaped and joined up with Our men.

After he had made common cause with the Italians, he remained, until the end of the war, in fear of his own servants and country-men—going about the country, at times to Mäqälle, another time to Agame or Edaga Hamus, and again to Adwa, taking extreme precautions and guarding himself like a murderer, but in not a single place did he join battle with Our soldiers and fight. We do not think that foreign historians, let alone natives of Ethiopia, will ever forget the story of his treachery. It must not be thought that he who betrays his mother will benefit his nurse.

[14] The Ala is the river just north of Waldia (*Guida*, map, 304).
[15] A well-known village S.E. of Adigrat (*Guida*, 299; map, 272).

CHAPTER 38

We go to Dessie

AFTER We had made the dispositions for the northern and southern armies, it was Our duty to defend Our country's independence in the midst of Our troops. We therefore directed that Our guard of honour (the Imperial guard) should depart in advance, under their commanding officer Qägnazmatch Mäkuriya Bantirgu,[1] as well as the army group called *Mähal Säfari*,[2] under the command of Ligaba Tassäw.[3] We Ourselves set out from Addis Ababa on 18th Hedar 1928 (= 28 November 1935) and travelled to Dessie. Our main purpose was to stay at Dessie as rearguard for the advance corps until the remote border regions were mobilized on the strength of the mobilization decree We had previously issued.

With Us were the following army commanders: Fitawrari Berru Waldä Gäbr'el, Dejazmatch Haylä Sellasse Abaynäh, Dejazmatch Waldä Ammanu'el Hawwas,[4] Dejazmatch Adäfersäw Yenadu,[5] Dejazmatch Wandirad Defabatchäw,[6] Qägnazmatch Bälhu Däggäfu,[7] Qägnazmatch Täklä Marqos Waldä Gäbr'el.[8]

[1] Fought in Italo-Ethiopian war as commander of the Imperial Guard. Thereafter he served with the guerillas and eventually fled to Kenya. He was later created Dejazmatch and became governor of Bale. Cf. *JES*, VII, 2, 219.

[2] A special corps created by Menelik II (Guidi, *Suppl.*, 66).

[3] Born 1901. Service in the palace as well as in provincial administration. Imprisoned during the Fascist occupation. Died 1955. Cf. *JES*, VII, 2, 289; photograph in Käbbädä Täsämma, 147.

[4] Servant of Ras Makonnen; later companion of Ledj Iyasu and hence for some time under surveillance. Killed 1937 in Graziani massacre. Cf. *JES*, VII, 2, 266.

[5] Born 1873. Served in army and provincial government. During the Fascist occupation he lived at Jerusalem. On his return to Ethiopia he was created Ras and became governor of Sidamo; later member of Crown Council. Died 1960. Photograph in Käbbädä Täsämma, 161. *JES*, VII, 2, 254.

[6] Born 1855. After serving in Ras Makonnen's household, he was an administrator in various parts of the country. Reputed to have been very rich. Killed in Italo-Ethiopian war in 1936. Cf. *JES*, VII, 2, 269.

[7] Palace servant. At first went into exile with the Emperor, but later returned to Ethiopia. Killed in Graziani massacre in 1937. *JES*, VII, 2, 228.

[8] Käbbädä Täsämma, 149.

After We had reached Dessie, the Italians thought of lulling us into a false sense of security and, therefore, waited for about a week before coming over in their planes. Even prior to setting out from Addis Ababa We had instructed Our armies to do everything necessary in the way of precautions against aeroplanes, and they had consequently begun to observe these precautionary measures by digging the ground in their various camps and by constructing shelters. Later on, on Friday morning 26th Hedar (= 6th December), 21 aeroplanes suddenly arrived and began to rain bombs on us. We at once transmitted orders that Our troops should quickly enter their shelter, for We were anxious lest they be exterminated for lack of defence. We Ourselves got hold of an Oerlikon anti-aircraft gun and began to fire. But as the planes were flying very high, it was impossible to hit any on that day.

Considering the size and quantity of the bombs they dropped, it was scarcely believable that any human beings survived at Dessie. But the majority of the bombs they dropped failed to explode, and therefore the number of those who died was only about 20 and of those who were injured about 100. Further, some 50 thatched houses were set on fire, but on this day they did not cause much other damage. Moreover, the bombs which fell upon various churches, apart from just rolling down, did very little damage, and all the people were amazed. Subsequently the planes began to come, at times in a regular turn, at other times again only on every third day.

On one occasion, however, on Ter 7th (= 16th January 1936), one large war plane turned up, and as we were watching and expecting it to drop bombs, at first smoke was seen to emanate from it and, subsequently, the plane caught fire. Those inside it came down by parachute, but as they landed on a precipice, they were all found to be dead. The aeroplane itself was burnt out.

While We were at Dessie, the British Minister at Addis Ababa, Sir Sidney Barton, and the French Minister, M. Bodard,[9] presented to Our Foreign Minister, Blattengeta Heruy, the proposals which Laval[10] and Hoare[11] had put forward for the purpose of

[9] M. Albert Bodard, French Minister to Ethiopia. For his role and the entire episode, see the illuminating account in Steer, 207 ff.

[10] Pierre Laval (1883–1945), the French Foreign Minister and Premier. Later convicted of treason and executed.

conciliation, declaring: 'We have been instructed by our governments to show and to present these proposals to the Ethiopian
Government; if the Ethiopian Government so desires it may
accept them, but this is not a matter of compulsion.' Blattengeta
Heruy transmitted them to Us by telegram on the same day.

The plan by Mr. Hoare and M. Laval was as follows:

'(a) Tigre: the region of Eastern Tigre is to be ceded to Italy; in the
South it is to be delimited approximately by the Geba[12] river; in
the west by a line running from north to south and passing
between Aksum[13] (to be assigned to Ethiopia) and Adwa (to go to
the Italian side).

(b) As regards the rectification of the border between the Dankali
country and Eritrea: to be defined by a line which leaves Aussa
and southern Eritrean parts to Ethiopia to provide for necessary
access to the sea.

(c) Rectification of the border between Ogaden and Italian
Somaliland: Starting from the triangle, at which the frontiers of
the three countries (Ethiopia, Kenya, and Italian Somaliland)
meet, the new Ethiopian-Italian frontier is to be as follows: In the
main it is to take a north-easterly direction, cutting the Webi
Shebeli and passing towards Iddidole;[14] leaving Gorrahei to the
east and Warandab[15] to the west, and joining the border of
British Somaliland at a meeting point on the 45th meridian.

The rights which the British Somaliland tribes possess to use
the pastures and waters, within the territories to be assigned to
Italy under this delimitation, are to be safeguarded.

(d) Ethiopia will obtain an outlet to the sea with full rights of
sovereignty. This access to the sea shall be arranged, at a place to
which Italy will agree, on the Assab[16] coast, together with territory that affords access to the port and goes down in a narrow strip
adjacent to the frontier of French Somaliland.

[11] Sir Samuel Hoare (1880–1959) was Foreign Secretary at the time, but had to
resign as a result of public clamour which brought Anthony Eden into the office
of Foreign Secretary.

[12] The Geba river is a major tributary of the Takazze, running from east to
west along a line just south of Mäqälle (*Guida*, map 272).

[13] The ancient capital of Ethiopia and for long its cultural centre (*Guida*, 259 ff).

[14] *Guida*, 473. It would have meant a very marked diminution of Ethiopian
territory.   [15] A small Ogaden village (*Guida*, 611).

[16] See the excellent description of Assab (with plans) in *Guida*, 338–41.

The United Kingdom and French governments will endeavour to obtain a pledge regarding Ethiopia's fulfilment of her obligations in the matter of the traffic of slaves and arms, incumbent upon them, and applicable in the territory which Ethiopia is to acquire.

The limits of this zone[17] were to be thus: in the east, the rectified frontier between Ethiopia and Italian Somaliland; in the north, the 8th parallel; in the west, the 45th meridian; and in the south, the border between Ethiopia and Kenya.[18]

Within the territory here delimited, which would have severed the greater part of Ethiopia, Italy would obtain exclusive economic rights; and the administration in that territory would be undertaken by a company or some other kind of organization. To this company would be assigned the rights of ownership over unoccupied territories (subject to the rights of natives and foreign citizens there), the monopoly of exploiting minerals, forest, and kindred matters. This organization would be obliged to contribute aid to the country's economic structure. From its income it would have to give a proportion to the welfare of the native population, in a manner which is essentially of a social character.

The control of the Ethiopian administration within the enclosed zone would be exercised, under the Emperor's sovereignty, in accordance with the scheme of the services of assistance granted by the League of Nations. The Emperor had already previously accepted this as extending over the whole Abyssinian territory Within these services, however, and under the direct control exercised by a principal adviser, Italy would possess a preponderant influence. The said principal adviser may possess Italian nationality and will be an assistant, as regards the affairs in question, to the Chief Adviser selected by the League of Nations to help the Emperor. The Chief Adviser is [not][19] to be a subject of any of the powers bordering on Ethiopia. It is incumbent upon the employees of the scheme of assistance, in the capital city as well as throughout the reserved zone, to regard it as essential that

[17] One vital paragraph of the Hoare-Laval accord has been omitted here, i.e. the reference to the formation in southern Ethiopia of a zone of economic expansion and settlement for Italy.

[18] The full effect of this plan can be seen on the map printed in Barker, 195.

[19] This is according to the text of the Hoare-Laval agreement. In the Amharic text here the negative does not appear; I suppose it ought to read አይደሉም ።

the life of Italian subjects and the free development of their initiatives be safeguarded.

The United Kingdom and French governments will willingly endeavour to ensure that this organization, whose terms of reference are to be established by the League of Nations, will protect Italian interests in this region in full.'

After We had examined these proposals of Mr. Hoare and M. Laval, We were resolved not to surrender to Italy, of Our own free will, Our country which had remained free for over 3000 years, unless the League of Nations compelled us to accept such a judgement; We therefore had the following protest communicated to the League of Nations through Our Minister in Paris:

'Is it in conformity with the covenant that the government which is in breach of the covenant should be requested by the League: "Please accept, together with executive control, the major part of the attacked party's territory as well as the remaining part—under cover of the League of Nations"? While it is the unshakable truth that it is the enemy's wish to destroy completely the party that has been attacked—as the General Council well knows—is the country which has fulfilled the charter and which is the victim of wrongdoing to be asked by the League to abandon her defence against the powerful enemy who is opposed to her right of freedom and self-government and, for the sake of world peace, to agree to accept her attacker? Is the attacked country to abandon hope of finding a saviour and to nurse the fear of betrayal by the League, thinking that it will really desert us? This matter which is the main problem for future international relations among peoples, whatever their appearance, their race, or their power may be—ought it not, first of all, to come up before the League and to be examined openly with full freedom and before the eyes of the whole world?'

CHAPTER 39

While at Dessie We hear of the dismissal of General de Bono and the appointment of Marshal Badoglio[1]

WHILE Our headquarters was still at Dessie, We heard of the dismissal of General de Bono, who had been Italian Commander-in-Chief, and of the appointment of Marshal Badoglio. The reason was said to be—as We were told by some of the journalists who were with Us at Dessie—that General de Bono had not wished Italy to start the war but rather to adopt a defensive position. And when the order to start the war reached him, he did indeed start it but he did not do so gladly and is said to have neglected the conduct of hostilities.

What proves this to be true is the account which appears in the book[2] written by General de Bono after his return home upon dismissal from his war command. He there says: 'When I asked how I was to act, since the Emperor was said to be engaged in prayer and fasting, being unwilling to be the initiator of the war, orders reached me to the effect that, if the Negus did not wish to start the war, I was to launch the attack and to fight him. I therefore began the war.'

Secondly, General de Bono states that, since he did not intend to open hostilities at once, he reported that he did not have enough money to begin the campaign. He received the answer that the necessary money and troops would be despatched to him. Since Mussolini signed the preface to the book which General de Bono wrote about the war, one cannot deny the account of the Italian side by arguing that it is all lies.

Furthermore, according to what some people told Us, General de Bono held the view that he could beat the Abyssinians by the accustomed means of warfare, i.e. fighting them with cannons, machine guns, and rifles; and that it would destroy the history and

[1] Pietro Badoglio (1871–1956), first Vice-roy of Ethiopia. Premier of Italy for one year after Mussolini's downfall.   [2] See chapter 35, note (2).

honour of the Fascists if they were to gain victory by fighting, with smoke gas and with mustard poison,[3] peoples who possessed no defence against this; and it would therefore be better for the Italians not to do so. It was said that the reason for his dismissal was that he expressed these views.

Later on, all communications with Our northern armies, by telephone and radio, were disrupted by bombs, and We, therefore, lacked news of the situation of Ras Kassa and Ras Seyum on the Tämbien[4] front, of Ras Emru and of Dejazmatch Ayalew on the Shire[5] front, and of Ras Mullugeta on the Alage front; for this reason We decided to push forward. But, as We have repeatedly shown before, We found Ourselves in great difficulty over the matter of weapons, since, on one hand, We wished to maintain world peace and, on the other, We were putting Our trust in the covenant of the League of Nations; in the third place, We did not have enough money to purchase modern war equipment, and when We asked for a loan, it was withheld from Us.

When We made requests to purchase arms with the little money obtained through support from Our own people, all the governments within the League of Nations refused Us, on the grounds that they were not permitted to sell war material from their countries to Ethiopia and Italy.

This was a matter of much astonishment to all who heard of it. Italy possessed factories in which almost all the various arms which she desired could be made. But Ethiopia did not have arms factories. It was therefore not fair for these countries to argue that neither Ethiopia nor Italy, being rivals, could buy war equipment from them.

Moreover, prior to the war We had made an agreement in Paris with Britain, France, and Italy to purchase arms for the maintenance of internal security. For this reason there were some arms which had already been purchased, and We directed that they should now be brought to us in our present troubles. When they reached Jibuti,[6] the Governor of French Somaliland prohibited

---

[3] Steer, 233.

[4] The Tämbien region in the Tigre is somewhat to the N.W. of Mäqälle, south of Geralta (*Guida*, 276 ff.; map, 272).

[5] The Shire region in the western Tigre (*Guida*, 248, where 'orientale' requires correction to 'occidentale') is to the S.W. of Aksum (*Guida*, map, 272).

[6] *Guida*, 410–16.

their being loaded on the train. We asked him to make enquiries in Paris on Our behalf, but because of his delaying tactics, claiming that he had received no reply from his government, We were convinced that they would not get here in time for our present difficulties. We thus abandoned waiting for their arrival and proceeded to Korām[7] where We had to be. But later on, just before the war ended, permission was given to load the arms on the train. When half the transport was still at Dire Dawa and the other half had reached Addis Ababa, it naturally fell into the hands of the Italians and thus ceased to be of any service to us.

[7] Korām (Quoram) is an important centre, a few miles east of lake Ashangi (*Guida*, 312–13; map, 304).

CHAPTER 40

We hear of the rout of the army
on Ras Dästa's front

OUR son-in-law, Ras Dästa Damtäw, whom We had appointed commander of the left-wing southern army, had come close towards Dolo[1] which is situated on the border of Italian Somaliland. When General Graziani,[2] Commander-in-Chief of Italian Somaliland, heard of Ras Dästa's approach to the frontier, he turned towards Ras Dästa the army, tanks, and aeroplanes which he had stationed in the Ogaden and launched an attack against him with all his strength. Ras Dästa was at a place suitable for bomb attacks but unsuitable for infantry; his army was, therefore, unable to withstand the onslaught of tanks and bombs and was defeated.

Furthermore, another reason why Ras Dästa's troops were so stunned was this: When the Swedish Red Cross doctors (stationed—according to regulations—a long distance from the war front) were treating the injured, these troops saw the Italians, clearly aware where the wounded were being looked after,

[1] Situated on the Juba river, frontier post and seat of an administrative subdistrict (*Guida*, 594).

[2] Rodolfo Graziani, Marshal, governor of Somalia in 1935, Vice-roy of Ethiopia 1936–7; joined Mussolini in his republican Fascist government 1943–5.

coming in their aeroplanes and dropping bombs on them, burning their tents, medicines, and all their medical equipment—including even their food supplies.

Of the doctors themselves, one was killed there. The leader of the Swedish medical team, Dr. Hylander,[3] was severely wounded. The wounded patients who were actually under treatment were hit by bombs while being cared for in that tent and many of them died. When it was learnt that Dr. Hylander had been injured, the Swedish physician at the Bet-Sayda Hospital at Addis Ababa, Dr. Hanner, went there by plane and brought him back; he treated him and nursed him back to health. The remaining doctors, as on one hand a hostile attack had been perpetrated against them and, on the other, their medicines and medical equipment had been set on fire, were compelled to go back to Addis Ababa, in order to prepare fresh medicines, medical instruments, tents, and food supplies. So they had to leave all the wounded and had to return. Because time was needed to make all these preparations until they were ready to return, the Italians, on their part, were hurrying on with the war and were exterminating soldiers and peasants with bombs and poison gas; the time was thus propitious for them to push forward. When Ras Dästa realized that the Italians had seized the road which he had built for cars and lorries, he took the troops who had escaped death and, marching fast by routes cutting through deserts, reached Nägälle.[4] Lest the Italians should find all the food and other provisions which he had collected there, he caused them to be set on fire and then left for Wadara.[5]

After the Italians had set on fire the village and church of Nägälle with incendiary bombs, they proceeded towards Ras Dästa's position at Wadara and attacked there. But as the place was wooded and hence not suitable for bombing, there was nothing they could do there. But they discovered a Swedish Red Cross lorry standing at some place there, filled it up with their own ammunition and then began spreading the mendacious rumour all over the world that they had found a Red Cross lorry loaded with ammunition.

[3] The Amharic text is occasionally faulty at this point, reading ፍ instead of ፪, i.e. making Hylander to appear as Flander. Cf. the detailed account in Steer, 242–3.
[4] Nägälle (Neghelli), important centre in the Galla-Sidamo area of southern Ethiopia (*Guida*, 597).   [5] Locality in the same area (*Guida*, 597–8).

After Ras Dästa had resisted the enemy by moving about the Sidamo and Bale provinces, remaining there for a year or so, he entered Arussi province. As General Graziani heard of this, he surrounded him with a large army and fought a big battle in Arussi and Maräqo.[6] Ras Dästa was captured in this engagement and, on 16th Yäkatit 1929 (= 23rd February 1937) he was killed by the Italians for the liberty of his country and the honour of his Emperor. As to the army commanders who were with him and those attached to Dejazmatch Gäbrä Maryam, the Italians themselves reported that they died doing their duty as officers.

[6] Region in the lake Zway area (*Guida,* 555).

CHAPTER 41

We issue a proclamation for further mobilization

WE had heard that, on the war front in Sidamo, the enemy had increased his pressure and, aided by tanks, was beginning to make progress with his invasion of the country in the Nägälle area; therefore, in order to have additional troops progressively organized, We issued the following proclamation to Our people from Our Dessie headquarters:

'The Lion of Judah has prevailed.
Haile Sellassie I Elect of God
King of Kings of Ethiopia.

People of Our country of Ethiopia! Italy has incited a quarrel, broken a contract, violated frontiers and, while disregarding completely treaties which she herself had voluntarily signed and which the League of Nations had approved, initiated destruction by battering peaceful cities, by annihilating children, women, and the aged, by burning churches, by indiscriminately killing with bombs members of the international Red Cross who are helping Ethiopians and Italians without distinction, and by dropping smoke gas which is prohibited by law. And as if this were not enough, you have yourselves seen and heard her attempts in every way possible to drop down—fighting by distributing mendacious pamphlets—words of lies and deceit to shatter the peace in the country and to stir up trouble among ourselves. And there is no-one who is not sad and resentful about this matter, among foreigners even—let alone our own people.

When an enemy soldier wanted to take and rape a woman living in a town undefended by Our Tigrean army, she pierced his heart with his own dagger and disarmed him. When she came to us, the Ethiopian people, men and women alike, were known to be burning with rage at the violence committed by Italy.

Old men, men and women, you who are able[1] to go to war, help me with sympathy and with your money as you have done up to now. While we resist our aggressive and violent enemy, we find in the attack that has come upon us, and even in death, an inestimable recompense in the scales of history and before God.

Our God has proved that he is with us by the strength which he has manifested in Our army which has so far gone out to war. Our enemies, while unsuccessful by force of rifles alone, have not managed to shake the heart or change the mind of Our brave troops, even when those enemies attempted it by intimidating us with concealed weapons and by dropping gas smoke. Up to now Our army has resisted Our enemy with strength and has pushed forward.

As We told you when the war began, with the Ethiopian people united, We set out determined to defend ourselves until the last drop of blood is shed and to share the trials in the midst of Our army; of this not only the Ethiopian people but the whole world is convinced.

Now then, you who are natives of Ethiopia, I will give provisions to you who have none and I will give arms to you who have none; hence stay mustered and registered on the front of each province, and remain prepared to go to war under the army commander I will announce to you.

12th Ter 1928 (= 21st January 1936).'

We likewise transmitted the following advice and order, so that Our Sidamo army which had been attacked and hurt by the enemy's force should be strengthened and that every one who was not yet a soldier should help:

---

[1] I think this should read 'unable', i.e. Amharic የማትችል ፡ instead of የምትችል ።

'As in this world sadness and joy occur alternately, man feels strong one day and weak on another. You who have up to now gone down into the desert, Ras Dästa had told me at the time of your resistance to attack, sickness, and bombs. You who are doing your duty, having survived not only for the sake of your own district but for the rest of the country, is the enemy to enter Sidamo as if there were no men left there? Now, for the future, not only soldiers but also you young men, who have reached arms-bearing age, be mobilized and help as soon as Ras Dästa notifies you.

19th Ter 1928 (= 28th January 1936).'

We directed that this pronouncement be transmitted to Our army in the Bale region.

CHAPTER 42

Our march from Dessie to Koräm

As We set out from Dessie travelling towards Koräm, bombs were raining down upon Us throughout the journey. Moreover, to travel by night was very difficult for Us, as the road went up and down and there was no moonlight.

Before Our troops set out from Addis Ababa, We had made arrangements to have instructions printed and distributed as regards precautions—so far as these were possible—against bomb attacks. Since they travelled by scattering and hiding in the woods, in accordance with the precautionary instructions, the bomb attacks could not hit them. When the Italians became aware of this, they began to drop bombs on the wooded parts and on all sites offering shelter. Nevertheless, even so they were unable to find Our troops and to inflict much harm. For this reason, they changed their tactics and started bombing rural areas and grazing cattle and thus broke the heart of people in the country. Furthermore, the Italians were aware that the Ethiopian people were firm in their Christianity and so, as every Sunday priests and monks, men and women, old and young flocked to church to hear holy mass, they lay in wait for them and set out to exterminate them with bombs. For this reason many churches were set on fire.

Marshal Badoglio knew that the Ethiopian people, being very religious, felt deep grief at the burning of their churches and so, lest the Italians' heathen works should be revealed, he began scattering pamphlets by aeroplane, to say: 'Take courage and do not grieve, for I shall rebuild the churches which have been destroyed and burnt down.'

Apart from killing Christian people and from setting fire to Christian churches, their burning of ancient Ge'ez manuscripts, which, written on parchment, had long been preserved in many churches and represented sources of knowledge and wisdom, caused much distress not only to the Ethiopian people but to scholars all over the world who were researching into this kind of knowledge and learning.

Italy, while claiming to be a Christian state, had her armies set fire to churches and manuscripts and maybe did not realize that in later times this would debase her honour and extinguish her history.

In difficulties of this kind We passed the town of Waldia in the district of Yäjju and reached Koräm. When the Italians realized, however, that on the journey from Dessie to Koräm they had not inflicted much damage on us with the bombs they had dropped from aeroplanes, they began to drop, in casks, the poison gas called yperite.[1] Some casks exceeded one metre in height. And their width was large. As they fell, they would explode like a bomb and the poison would be splashed, killing everybody near-by.[2] It is very distressing that the Italians should come with such new-fashioned cowardly weapons, in order to destroy completely the brave Ethiopian people who had no defence against weapons of this kind.

Although they may destroy the Ethiopian army with this instrument of poison, yet when it is reported in future history that they wiped out with poison a defenceless people, it is not to be doubted that this will forever be a burden of shame and humi-liation for Fascist Italy.

Subsequently, they installed in their planes a mechanism which sprinkled poison like rain and proceeded to pouring it down like rain upon Our troops and peasants, upon cattle and waters, grass

---

[1] This is mustard gas, named after Ypres.   [2] Steer, 278–9.

and foliage, and upon the soil. As the precipitation was extra-ordinarily fine, it was not clearly visible to the eye. We had heard that a poison spray of this kind might be used to kill disease-microbes if a tree or plant disease had infected some tree or plant, but We had not suspected that it would be employed against troops and peasants.

But the Italian aeroplanes, which were spreading this poisonous mist in order to destroy the Ethiopian people as well as animals living on mountains and in fields, were going to and fro from morning till evening and set out to exterminate man and beast. The countryside as a whole seemed as if it had been consumed by fire. It was impossible to find a pure breeze in the air, and men and animals began to die being unable to breathe.

Anyone fleeing from there and taking shelter under trees and in crevices, thinking to be safe there, was unable to escape and thus expired there; the whole place being nothing but corpses, the stench brought us worse troubles. As there were so many who died, it was impossible to bury the corpses.

While We were at Koräm, a messenger arrived giving Us accurate information about Ras Mullugeta's situation; We felt great sadness at what he reported to Us. Since Ras Mullugeta was Our War Minister, he had marched to Mäqälle with an army of some 50,000 and was firmly resolved to oust the Italians from the city of Mäqälle. But the Italians knew about this plan from their spies[3] and, therefore, overtook him at the front, while Ras Mullugeta was still at Amba Aradom.[4] Also, they had given arms and money to the Raya and to other Gallas in that area and had thus caused them to desert Us; they directed them to surround Ras Mullugeta from the rear and to deny him supplies of pro-visions.

Ras Mullugeta was well-known for his probity and valour; when he joined battle on Wednesday, 4th Yäkatit (= 12th February 1936), he fought hard for three whole days; and al-though he could resist the enemy infantry, it was not possible to put up a defence against bombing and machine-gunning from the air; he was, therefore, forced to withdraw to the rear in order to

[3] Steer, 249–50.
[4] Amba Aradom is a vast rock of a mountain, some 12 miles south of Mäqälle and somewhat west of the Asmara-Addis Ababa road. Cf. *Guida*, 303 (map, 304); Steer, 249 ff.

fight from another and improved position. But as his troops were dispersed at various places and the Raya Gallas had surrounded him at the rear, it was just not feasible for him to wage another battle; so he began marching to join Us. On 18th Yäkatit (= 26th February), at a place called Ahyo,[5] a bullet struck him accidentally and he died; the few servants who were with him buried him, and We learnt about it when they arrived.

The army commander at Walläga, Bitwaddäd Mäkonnen Dämsäw, had heard that Ras Mullugeta was surrounded in front and in the rear and rushed to his aid; he came into contact with the Italian army and fought with bravery forcing them to abandon two fortified emplacements at a place called Qäyhata.[6] On the second day of the battle he was injured by a bomb and died on the 8th of Yäkatit (= 16th February); We heard that he had no longer managed to come to Ras Mullugeta's aid. For all these reasons We went forward and, being Ourselves Commander-in-Chief, were resolved to fight and to lead others in battle.

[5] *Guida,* 314 (map, 304): a small place, some 20 miles S.W. of Koräm, on the road to Dildi.

[6] This place is not known to me, but it is said to be in the Amba Aradom area. See also Steer, 263.

CHAPTER 43

Things go well with Our armies in Shire and Tämbien

IT was with Ras Seyum's troops that the Italian military forces first came into hostile contact. Ras Seyum's soldiers were about 30,000. These were not, however, concentrated in one place only but were fighting dispersed over a number of separate positions. We had transmitted orders to Ras Seyum not to engage in face to face fighting but to remain well to the rear. The reason was to prevent any harm befalling him if he were to join battle while on his own before Ras Kassa, commander of the northern army, reached him;[1] a second argument was to induce the Italian troops

[1] This is another example of Ras Seyum being referred to in the polite plural, while Ras Kassa appears in the singular.

to move towards the centre and thus to afford an opportunity of surrounding them.

After Ras Seyum had been waiting, in accordance with the instructions he had received, for some two months, withdrawn towards the rear and in defensive positions, at the end of Hedar (= early December 1935) Ras Kassa caught up with him;[1a] and while they were waiting, Ras Seyum being stationed on the left wing, Dejatch Ayalew at the front, and Ras Kassa in the rear, the governor of Gojjam, Ras Emru, joined them with an army of 10,000 men. It had been arranged that he should look out for any enemy forces coming from the direction of Shire. Of course, by proceeding in this manner We had not been thinking that the Italians would exterminate Our army by smoke gas and yperite poison but rather that they would join battle by frontal attacks and infantry action with machine guns and rifles. The intention was, in fact, to enable Our army which was positioned on the right and left, in front and rear, to surround the enemies and to cut them off, as soon as they entered into the centre (of the trap). We were further contemplating that the army in Ras Kassa's sector was, perhaps, too small and vulnerable,[2] and We therefore issued orders that, from the armies which were with Our War Minister, Ras Mullugeta, the groups under the following officers should be detached and go to Ras Kassa's sector: Dejazmatch Mäshäsha Walde, Dejazmatch Mängäsha Yelma, Dejazmatch Bäyyänä Wandemagägnähu, Fitawrari Zäwdu Abba Koran.[3] On the basis of this pre-arranged plan things had turned out favourably for Our troops in Shire and Tämbien. Among these officers Dejazmatch Bäyyänä Wandemagägnähu, having fought with bravery, was killed.

At that sector it was Eritrean soldiers who fought hard against Our army, but Italian Blackshirts were few in number.

But the Italian Blackshirts were positioned so far to the rear that there was great difficulty finding them. When they saw Our army come upon them face to face with swords drawn, they fled

---

[1a] See footnote (1) page 265.

[2] The lack of concord in number between these two verbs in Amharic is certainly odd.

[3] Later Dejazmatch (1895–1954). Served with great courage in the Italo-Ethiopian war and became a provincial governor after the restoration. Cf. *JES*, VII, 2, 272.

before all else. Thus in general they would not join battle without preparing a route of escape.

Of those of Our soldiers who were holding defensive positions in the Shire and Tämbien regions there were only about 10 per cent who had Mauser rifles. But 90 per cent had rifles more than forty years old, such as *fucile* Gras,[4] Schneider,[4] and similarly antiquated weapons. They did not possess more than 125 machine-guns. As to cannons, they did not have a single one, apart from that captured from the enemy. And that captured gun was not working at all, as it was found that some parts of it were missing.

The lead of the *fucile* Gras bullet is black and soft and, therefore, when it rests against a bone, it expands and rubs against it. If it penetrates through flesh, there is a big and extensive wound where the lead emerges from the flesh. For this reason, when the Italians noticed this, they announced that we were hitting them with dumdum bullets. At Abbi Addi[5] and on the Erba Wayne[6] Our army, under the command of Ras Kassa, fought hard and was victorious. In the Shire area the army which had been sent under the command of Ras Emru also fought valiantly and captured more than a hundred machine-guns and a great deal of military supplies. But Our soldiers, according to their long-established custom, would throw up their rifles and, unless they engaged in a sword-battle at close quarters and face to face, they would not reckon it valorous to kill by shooting with rifles from a distance. Hence it is true that by such actions they suffered heavy casualties.

Apart from the battles at Abbi Addi and Erba Wayne, there was a large-scale engagement at Shum Awre.[7] At the time of this battle the Italians emerged from their fortified positions and the engagement became a face to face fight. There were no planes in the air, and it was a battle of true heroism. The only difference between Our soldiers and the Italians was that Our men possessed

[4] Guidi, *Suppl.*, 170; *ibidem*, 61; Pankhurst, *JES*, IX, 1, 70–3.

[5] The principal town of the Tämbien and for some time H.Q. of Ras Kassa and Ras Seyum. Cf. *Guida*, 281 (map, 272). The Tigrinya words *Abbi Addi* mean 'big country', and the spelling of this name in the Amharic text throws an interesting light on the differing phonetic patterns of Amharic and Tigrinya.

[6] Erba Wayne (or Ruba Wayne) is a river some 8 miles N.E. of Abbi Addi (*Guida*, 282; map, 272).

[7] The precise location of Shum Awre is not known to me.

antiquated weapons only, while the Italians had modern arms. Nevertheless, Our soldiers with their customary agility entered into the midst of the battle, leaping forward like leopards, while the Italian soldiers began to flee leaving behind their machine-guns, rifles, and ammunition as well as their telephone and radio equipment. Thus the hearts of Our troops were increasingly fortified.

To estimate the quantity of captured weapons and equipment it is sufficient to say only that it took many hundreds of soldiers four whole days to go to and fro between the arena of the battle and their encampments. After Our soldiers had brought in the arms and equipment, diarrhoea spread in their camps and caused them a good deal of harm, so that, in fact, the suspicion was aroused that perhaps the defeated and fleeing Italians might have placed some poison upon their equipment.

Although the Italians were superior to us in modern arms, Our soldiers had the advantage in terms of courage. There is therefore no doubt that the Italians suffered heavy casualties at that time.

While Our soldiers, who had won the battles in the Tämbien and Shire regions, were fighting with obsolete rifles like the *fucile* Gras, they yet managed to capture more than 300 machine-guns and many cannons and tanks.

There were very few in Our army who knew the instrument of war called 'tank'. When they set out from Addis Ababa and We gave them written advice about the precautions against tank attacks, there were some who said 'What is a tank?' Subsequently, however, when they had observed, three or four times, the manner of their operation on the battlefield, they got used to them and followed the precautionary counsel; thus they suffered no damage at all from the tanks. Similarly, they would remain hidden in crevices and bushes until the tank had passed; then they would follow and, like a leopard, would leap climbing on top of it and kill the crews by shooting at the various holes. At times, on account of the heat, the Italians would step out of the tanks and sit under the trees; Our men would then emerge from their hiding places and kill the enemy soldiers and capture the tanks. On Dejatch Ayalew's front, a man called Fitawrari Shäfärra[8] captured five tanks in a single day.

---

[8] Shäfärra (or Shefärraw, Shifärraw) was a native of Bägemeder and one of Dejazmatch Ayalew's army commanders (*JES*, VII, 2, 227).

As things had gone favourably for Our army fighting in the Tämbien and Shire area during Tahsas and Ter (December-January), they had been very close to forcing the Italians to abandon Aksum and Adwa and to getting to Mäqälle and cutting it off. Ras Emru, in the Shire region, was watching very carefully to the east and south of Aksum. He gave his soldiers provisions, as he had been ordered to do, before the opportunity had passed; he then calmed their hearts and began the battle. The Italian army on his front was estimated to number some 25,000. On 11th Yäkatit (= 19th February 1936) he detached a part of his army and despatched it towards the Märäb.[9] When they reached the meeting point of the Asmara and Adwa roads,[10] the Italians who were in the fortress of Rama[11] shone a light on them. They at once began shooting, killing five men and wounding a few. The Italians, however, announced that they had killed 45 and wounded more than a hundred.

But Ras Emru's soldiers approached with a mixture of caution and daring and launched an attack upon the enemy; the Italians at Rama, apart only from those killed and injured, fled in haste and escaped.

What was found there included officers' uniforms and rifles, many machine-guns together with a great deal of ammunition as well as provisions lasting for many days. On the morrow they counted up to four hundred Italian bodies who had been killed, but as they were concerned that Italian soldiers might come back and launch an attack upon them, they left the place and returned to Shire. Ras Emru informed Us of this by telegram and We directed that it should be issued as a communiqué. Afterwards, however, the Italians had the road leading from Adwa to Asmara guarded very carefully, and Ras Emru's troops had thus no opportunity of waging a major battle—apart from inflicting some damage by occasional minor incursions.

---

[9] The Märäb (Mareb) is Eritrea's most important river; it formed the border between Eritrea and Ethiopia during the Italian period. Prior to that it gave its name to the province now called Eritrea, i.e. *märäb mällash*, 'the country beyond the Märäb'. Cf. *The Ethiopians*[2], 24; *Guida*, 238-9 (map, 272).

[10] Cf. Steer, 272-3.

[11] or Mequam, 3 or 4 miles south of the Märäb and on the river Mequam (also Cimitero di Mai Lahla). Cf. the account of this battle, from the Italian side, in *Guida*, 239 (map, 272).

When the Italians realized the position and strength of Ras Emru, they detached a contingent from their army at Aksum and directed them to go to Säläqläqa[12] to build fortifications, while Ras Emru, on his part, began taking precautions by having shelters dug in which his soldiers could be protected from bombs. Later on, the Italians clashed with Ras Emru in the neighbourhood of Säläqläqa, and throughout the entire day there raged a fierce battle.

But the Italians possessed guns that could strike from a great distance and so they fired on our soldiers from far away; on top of this they dropped bombs on them from planes and sprayed them with mustard poison, so that Ras Emru was obliged to draw back with his army.

And again on 2nd Mägabit (= 11th March) the Italians followed up their attack and, after another severe battle had been fought, as usual many aeroplanes arrived wiping out the Ethiopian forces by spraying mustard and yperite poison, so that Ras Emru, being almost on his own, had to withdraw to the rear.

Furthermore, the Italians had begun to send out week by week a very large number of planes and to set on fire, with incendiary bombs, provincial towns, such as Dabat[13] in the Semien, Gondar in Bägemeder, and Däbrä Marqos in Gojjam. When the soldiers from these regions who were taking part in the war heard about this, they panicked and felt unable to stay on the battlefield, and so started to return home little by little.

Nevertheless, Ras Emru had remained offering resistance until he had heard about the military situation on Ras Kassa's front in Tämbien, on Ras Mullugeta's front at Amba Aradom and Alage, and on Our front at Maytchäw.[14] But after he had heard about this, he returned to Gojjam with those of his soldiers who had survived the bombs, gas, and mustard poison. When Dejazmatch Ayalew heard of the Italians entering his governorate of Semien, he went to the city of Däbrä Tabor in Bägemeder.

The Red Cross doctors, stationed on the northern front between Koräm and Lake Ashange, were working with all

---

[12] A locality some 15 miles west of Aksum. Cf. *Guida*, 248 (map, 272) and Steer, 274-5.

[13] Some 40 miles N.E. of Gondar; important market centre (*Guida*, 258).

[14] Maytchäw on the Asmara-Addis Ababa road, a few miles north of lake Ashange, is an important market centre. It was the scene of one of the fiercest battles of the 1935-6 war. Cf. *Guida*, 308-9 (map, 304). Cf. ch. 45.

possible care and strength. Dr. Dassios,[15] whom the Ethiopian national Red Cross Society had sent, was never parted from Us. However, from Koräm onwards as far as Maytchäw, there was no other doctor apart from Dr. Mäl'aku Bäyyan[16] who travelled with Us as Our own personal physician. In the neighbourhood of Koräm and Ashange the doctors whom the British Red Cross Society had sent assisted us with much care, while observing Red Cross regulations; We shall never forget this. They had set up their camp at a great distance from the army positions and had spread out very widely on the ground the Red Cross sign as well as the British flag; they had also sewn them on their tents, so that the Italian aeroplanes should see them from far away and recognize that it was a Red Cross camp. But when the Italians in their aeroplanes saw this Red Cross sign, they argued that there would be no-one to question them if they violated Red Cross Society rules and regulations; they therefore dropped bombs upon them with audacity and, breaking their entire medical equipment, made it into a heap of old iron. They made the tents look like old moth-eaten rags. The injured and the sick to whom the doctors were ministering remained buried there when the ground on which they were lying was turned upside down by the bombs. We do not suppose that there are recorded in the annals of any war waged in our contemporary civilization any similar acts of cruelty. We trust that all who read these lines will not fail to observe, when they see such lawless actions, that in Italy the work of civilization is reckoned to be worthless. We must not recoil from repeating this over and over again.

When setting fire to places where the sick and injured are lying in the hope of receiving medical treatment and of recovering there (and in addition to finishing off the injured by crushing their bones anew), the Italians have committed the following deeds of violence which are bound to humiliate and shame them exceedingly in front of all decent men.

After the Italians had obliterated with their bombs the English Red Cross mission, the doctors sought and discovered a cave in the neighbourhood of Koräm which seemed to them a strong

---

[15] Dr. George Dassios of Greece, later head of Menelik II Hospital at Addis Ababa. Cf. Del Boca, 93, 95.

[16] Dr. Mäl'aku Bäyyan was one of the very first Ethiopian physicians (educated in India and the U.S.A.). Cf. Pankhurst, 657, 681.

shelter which the Italians would not be able to reach; they therefore brought all the sick and wounded into that cave and made them lie down there. But the Italian aeroplanes sniffed out this cave like a hunting dog and followed along there; it became therefore impossible to bring further injured people to the cave or indeed to take out those who had entered. The wounded as well as those who carried them had the greatest difficulty in passing in and out. On these grounds the British Red Cross doctors believed that it would be preferable to transport the injured by loading them on to mules which would walk in scattered groups rather then conveying them by lorries which are very clearly visible. It was thus necessary for Dr. Melly,[17] their leader, to go back to Addis Ababa to purchase mules and additional medical equipment. On top of this the doctors also had to take care of their own lives and those of their assistants. Hence Our people, who had hoped that the Red Cross doctors would treat them and look after them, when they saw the kind of attack that was descending upon the doctors as well as such acts of cruelty (which should never be carried out against human beings) being perpetrated against them, felt sure that it was with the devil that they were fighting. Thus their lack of hope and their despair exceeded all bounds.

[17] Dr. John Melly, the greatest of all the Red Cross doctors, was killed at Addis Ababa in 1936. See Del Boca, 95–6; Steer, 388–9.

CHAPTER 44

Our journey from Koräm to the warfront at Maytchäw

WHILE We were at Koräm, enemy aircraft would come over daily, making repeated turns to and fro, from two to nine o'clock (= 8 a.m. to 3 p.m.), dropping many bombs and much poison gas and causing harm to Our army. The army officers who had taken the offensive on the Tämbien front had fought there with valour and discharged their duty; in the end they were defeated by superiority of bombs and weapons and had dispersed; We then

sent for them to join Us. They reached Koräm on 10th Mägabit
(= 19th March, 1936) at eight o'clock at night (= 2 a.m.) and
were reunited with Us. While the principals were H.H. Ras
Kassa Haylu and H.H. Ras Seyum Mängäsha, with them were
Dejazmatch Mängäsha Yelma, Dejazmatch Wand Bäwassän
Kassa, Dejazmatch Abära Kassa, Tsähafe Te'ezaz Afäwarq Bäje-
rond Lätyebälu Gäbre, Qägnazmatch Dähne Waldä Maryam,
Fitawrari Zäwdu Abba Koran, and other officers.

On Thursday,[1] 11th Mägabit (= 20th March 1936), We heard
that the Italians had passed Amba Alage and were encamped at
Maytchäw; We decided, therefore, to take the guard of honour
which had been waiting with Us as rearguard, as well as the army
which had returned from the front, and to go to fight, with
Ourselves as leader. We thus set out from Koräm at two o'clock
in the evening (= 8 p.m.) and proceeded towards the war front at
Hayo.[2] As the night was dark, We directed the army to prepare
torches and we marched by torch-light. And since the road was
narrow, the march took many hours.

Having marched in this fashion, we spent the day of Mägabit
12th (= 21st March) at a place, a little beyond Lake Ashange,
which was suitable for protection against aeroplanes; and marching again that night we reached the district called Hayo (Aya). On
this day enemy aircraft dropped many bombs and were spraying
yperite poison that was flowing like water; thus the terrible death
that came upon man and beast was most distressing.

The day of 13th Mägabit (= 22nd March) We spent encamped
at Hayo (Aya) upon an arid *amba,* a place that was suitable for
observation of aircraft. At two o'clock in the evening (= 8 p.m.)
We assembled all the army officers and chiefs and explained to
them Our plan as regards the battle tactics and the order of muster.
After this We directed them, on their part, to express their views
in what manner the waging of the battle might be improved. The
great officers present on this occasion were H.H. Ras Kassa, H.H.
Ras Seyum, Ras Getatchäw, Dejazmatch Wandirad, Dejazmatch
Waldä Ammanu'el, Dejazmatch Adäfersäw, Ligaba Tassäw,

---

[1] As far as I know, Mägabit 11th (= 20th March 1936) was, in fact, a Friday.
[2] Hayo, i.e. Aya or Aia, is a mountain pass (2910 metres) about half-way
between Amba Alage and Maytchäw. See *Guida,* 308–9 (map, 304); Steer, 302;
Del Boca, 162–3.

Fitawrari Ashänafi[3] as well as other captains and army officers who served under them. The officers consulted and then presented to Us the following unanimous opinion:

'Death is an inheritance that cannot fail to come to all of us. God has assigned to us the day, and if we are victorious, then we shall have saved our independence; and if we die, then it will be for our country, for our death will be reckoned as martyrdom. It is a great good fortune to die having struggled with the enemy. Making the approach to battle overnight, let us meet the enemy at dawn.'

After We had listened to their speech, We said to them: 'Whether We die or live, it is for Our country; all We are concerned about is lest Our country should die.' We then informed them that we would be marching towards the war front to Ba'tawayo.[4]

We spent the day of Mägabit 14th (= 23rd March) on that arid *amba* of Hayo (Aya). On this day the chiefs of Tchärtchär[5] came with rifles and ammunition which they had received from the Italians and expressed to Us the following sentiments of loyalty: 'It is because the Italians had told us "your king is not there" that our hearts were divided; but now that we have seen you with our own eyes, we shall die fighting for our country's freedom with the arms we received from the enemy.' And We warned them, saying: 'Do realize that the lies which the enemy is telling you are apt to destroy you and your country!'

When it was twelve o'clock (= 6 p.m.) on this day We departed from the barren *amba* and, marching through the night, We camped at the Ba'tawayo cave. This place is vis-à-vis the Italian encampment.

When We were at Ba'tawayo on 15th Mägabit (= 24th March), enemy aircraft spent the day going to and fro and dropping many bombs. At six o'clock (= 12 noon) a large aeroplane arrived[6] and, flying low over the place where We were, dropped bombs. From Our side a machine-gun volley was fired and it was

---

[3] Fit. Ashänafi was at one time Minister of the Palace. He died in the battle of Maytchäw in 1936. Cf. *JES*, VII, 2, 249. Photograph in Käbbädä Täsämma, 146.

[4] From what is said in the following, Ba'tawayo is the name of a cave in the Maytchäw area. See also Käbbädä Täsämma, 150.

[5] Tchärtchär in the Wag region (*Guida*, 315), some 40 miles east of Koräm.

[6] Steer, 304.

hit and set on fire; emitting smoke it fell beyond the Dubbar[7] pass. The Italian radio confirmed that the plane was burnt together with its crew of four.

We stayed at Ba'tawayo preparing military plans from the 16th to the 19th Mägabit (= 25th to 28th March). On these days enemy aircraft went to and fro in great numbers and dropped bombs and poison gas; every day, as a result of Our soldiers' fire, these planes were seen to be burning and to emit smoke, going towards the Tchärtchär lowland. On 19th Mägabit in particular one of the aircraft that had come over was hit by an Oerlikon gun and came down near there; after that many aircraft arrived dropping bombs and poison, and as a result many people were killed and injured.

On Saturday, 19th Mägabit (= 28th March), We summoned the army commanders and gave them the following guide-lines:

'It is necessary to be resolute and to eschew vengeance even when going to hunt a wild beast—let alone for this present decisive great battle against our enemy. Young men facing war, you have seen that God has condemned any irresolute soldier in the past, for it is worthless doing things only on instructions and orders fearing that God will condemn one—rather than doing one's duty whole-heartedly.

If one flees, not having acted resolutely, there is only death. Fight fiercely, lest the freedom of your country of Ethiopia and its flag should be obliterated and torn to shreds, for it is to him who acts decisively and intrepidly that God extends his help. If you break the oath, death is surely bound to occur; do not die having ruined the honour of your soul and your body.

To claim: "my officer has fled or has died; I have to carry an injured body" is not really motivated by compassion for the injured but to fabricate a refuge for his frightened heart. When an officer dies, is not a soldier who has been fighting bravely to become an officer?

If God favours us, do not hasten to quarrel over property, for Ethiopia's existence is our property and wealth. If you find a foreigner, a wounded prisoner, do not finish him off with the dagger, pistol or explosives in his hand, except if he tries to harm you, for having him as a prisoner may help us to find out the enemy's secrets.

[7] A mountain pass some 7 or 8 miles west of Aya. *Guida*, 309–10 (map, 304).

If a servant gets separated from his master, troops from their commander, this means the beginning of flight, so recognize it as the enemy of myself and of Ethiopia.'

Anxious that no harm should befall the rest of Our army for lack of precautions, We transmitted to them the orders set out here below and divided into eight paragraphs:

'(1) It is at 2 o'clock in the evening (= 8 p.m.) that you are to depart from your camp to the place to which you have been ordered.

(2) When you march at night to go to the battle front, you are to follow the way which your officer will show you, but you must not shout to your friend and sing war songs, shine a light or blow a trumpet. The reason for this is that, if the enemy were to hear your voice, he would harm you by waiting for you in a state of preparedness; but if you were to launch an unexpected attack upon him, before he hears or knows about it, our enemy would be greatly hurt.

(3) Take care lest our enemy, appearing to be fleeing, should induce you to enter in the midst of his fire where his machine-guns are positioned on all sides. While wary of the enemy's ruses and before you pull back, fall upon your enemy, leaving him when he tries to lead you on and going to his flank.

(4) We have to be dedicated to destroying completely the enemy who has now invaded us, as he has set out to extinguish altogether Ethiopia and her people. By killing just one man before the battle ends and going back exhibiting him as a war trophy before the enemy's defeat is known, is bound to hamper our war effort; for if you return and say "for me alone things have gone well", you are leaving your friend on his own and exposing him to enemy attack; thus the trophy will not be counted in your favour if you return in the morning claiming that you have been successful.

(5) Since for the Ethiopian people the chief possession is freedom, do not hasten to pillage things before you have defeated and put to flight the invading enemy who has come to destroy that freedom and before you have caused him to abandon his position. If you plunder him and he then takes it back, what benefit will you have derived? A man who takes away the enemy's property, in order to ensure for himself the permanence of the possessions he has

taken, has first of all to destroy the enemy to prevent him returning and snatching things back.

(6) Having spent the day fighting and if, perhaps, on one occasion you did not manage to win because the enemy has been too
strong for you, you have to fight fiercely until We send you
support troops; but you are not to turn back until you are told to
withdraw.

(7) A rocket signal[8] will be given on Adimoshash[9] to indicate
"open fire!"

(8) Especially when men of rank are found, they are to be
taken prisoners—to the extent that it is possible for you, since it is
through the evidence of prisoners that the enemy's secrets and
strength are found out—except, of course, if the enemy threatens
you with pistol, hand-grenade or dagger.

19th Mägabit 1928 (= 28th March 1936).'

Afterwards We divided the strategic order, by which we were
going into battle, into four groups and, adding the troops collected
from various offices, We arranged that one group be directly
commanded and led by Ourselves and that the remaining three
groups be led by three commanders, i.e. by H.H. Ras Kassa, by
H.H. Ras Seyum, and by Ras Getatchäw. The part commanded
and led by Ourselves direct was divided as follows:

At the front, the corps of the guard of honour under Qägnazmatch Mäkuriya Bant Yergu and his deputy Grazmatch Kefle
Ergätu.[10]

On the left, the corps of the guard of honour under Grazmatch
Abära Gezaw.[11]

On the right, the corps of palace servants and footmen under
Qägnazmatch Bälhu Däggäfu.

At the rear, the corps of palace guards under Dejazmatch
Adäfersäw.

We directed them to be placed in battle position.

The three groups led by their respective commanders were
divided as follows:

[8] Del Boca, 166: 'two red rockets soared up into the sky'.
[9] A place name, probably of a hill, unknown to me.
[10] Cf. Käbbädä Täsämma, 145. Later Dejazmatch; Minister of the Interior.
[11] Served in the Palace under Emperor Haile Sellassie. Shot by the Italians in
Hararge. Cf. *JES*, VII, 2, 249.

On the centre front

We divided in the following manner the men mustered on the central front under the command of H.H. Ras Kassa Haylu:

Ras Käbbädä Mängäsha with his men.

The *Mähal Säfari* corps commanded by Ligaba Tassäw Walälu.

The army of the Ministry of the Palace commanded by Fitawrari Ashänafi.

The army of Baso and Gola commanded by Dejazmatch Gezaw Jimma.[12]

The army of the Ministry of Agriculture.

Dejazmatch Abära Tädla (attached as direction guide, since he was a native of the district and governor of Maytchäw).

On the right wing

We divided in the following manner the men mustered on the right-wing front under the command of H.H. Ras Seyum Mängäsha:

The corps of Schneider rifle carriers.

The army of Walläga Arjo[13] and of Walläga Gudru.[14]

The cavalry.

The contingent of Liqä Mäkwas Haylä Maryam Waldä Gäbr'el.[15]

The artillery corps commanded by Qägnazmatch Waldä Yohannes Waldä Ab.[16]

Fitawrari Täfäri Tädla[17] (attached as direction guide, since he was a native of the district).

On the left wing

We divided in the following manner the men mustered on the left-wing front under the command of Ras Getatchäw Abätä:

---

[12] Dej. Gezaw Jimma. Died 1959. *JES*, VII, 2, 287.

[13] For the Walläga province in western Ethiopia in general see *Guida*, 506. For the Arjo part of Walläga cf. *Guida*, 503 (main map).

[14] The Gudru highlands, intersected by the Guder river, are in the northern part of Walläga.

[15] Born 1901. Grew up in palace and was one of Emperor Haile Sellassie's favourites. Killed in 1937 during Graziani massacre.

[16] Käbbädä Täsämma, 148.   [17] Käbbädä Täsämma, 148.

The army of Kämbata.[18]
The army of the treasury and stores.
The army of the Ministry of Finance.
The army of the Post and Telephone Ministry[19] commanded by Qägnazmatch Täklä Marqos Waldä Gäbr'el.
The excellent rifle bearers commanded by Qägnazmatch Abäbä Räde.[20]
The army of the Master of the Horse commanded by Qägnazmatch Bäyyänä Bälaynäh.[21]
Dejazmatch Haylu Käbbädä (attached as direction guide).
Other than these, the spiritual fathers who had followed Us to help with prayer and supplication: Abuna Petros, bishop of Wallo, Etchäge Gäbrä Giyorgis,[22] Liqe Gäbrä Krestos[23] and Liqä Liqawent Gäbrä Ab;[24] We arranged that they be mustered, together with their retinue of priests, with the group where We were. Among princes and nobles the following were assigned to be close to Us for consultation and the transaction of essential major affairs: H.H. Ras Kassa Haylu, H.H. Ras Seyum, Fitawrari Berru Waldä Gäbr'el, Dejazmatch Wandirad, Dejazmatch Wand Bäwassän Kassa, Dejazmatch Abära Kassa, and Ato Waldä Giyorgis Waldä Yohannes.[25]
After We had arranged that the organization of the battle order and the strategy of approach be conducted in this manner, a sign was given to Our army that would serve to distinguish our side

[18] Region and population west of the Ethiopian lake district, between the Billate and Omo rivers. See *Guida*, 549 (map, 552).
[19] The various 'armies' of ministries and offices were made up of the employees (and their families) in the capital and elsewhere in the country.
[20] Käbbädä Täsämma, 149.
[21] Emperor Haile Sellassie's master of the stables. Fought at Maytchäw and was killed in 1936. Cf. *JES*, VII, 2, 230.
[22] Later Abuna Baselyos (1891–1970), first Patriarch of Ethiopia. See Mara, chapter VI. Photographs, *op. cit.*, frontispiece; Käbbädä Täsämma, 174.
[23] Photograph in Käbbädä Täsämma, 125.
[24] Later Abuna Fillepos of Jerusalem (information from Dr. Zewde Gabra Sellasse).
[25] Born about 1902. The Emperor's secretary before the war. Chief of the Imperial Secretariat, Minister of the Pen (Tsähafe Te'ezaz), and the most powerful minister after the war until, in 1955, he was sent to become a provincial governor and deprived of effective power. Since 1961 he has lived in retirement and virtual seclusion.

from the enemy forces during the battle and in the course of
communications.

The pass-word was that, when someone said 'to whom do you
belong', the person questioned was to reply to him: 'To Abba
Täqel'.²⁶ If he asked him 'What does Täqel mean?', he could not
be trusted to be in my army. He was to say 'The power is God's'.
If the person questioned replied to him with this pass-word, he
could believe him to be of our side. But if it was impossible for
him to reply thus, then he would know that he belonged to the
enemy army and he was to regard him with hostility.

Besides We issued a precautionary password to the guard
officers who had been ordered to look after the arms and ammunition, equipment and property which remained in the Ba'tawayo
cave: 'If perchance Our army should be defeated, have the arms
and equipment set on fire, lest they should fall into enemy hands,
as soon as We send you the sign.' This message is 'Our God has
not departed from us.'

²⁶ Ras Tafari/Emperor Haile Sellassie's traditional horse name (cf. *JES*, VII, 2,
195–209).

CHAPTER 45

The battle of Maytchäw¹

WHILE We were at the Ba'tawayo camp, on Sunday, 20th
Mägabit 1928 (= 29th March 1936), enemy aircraft, coming and
going continuously, spent the day dropping bombs and poison
gas. We gave orders for the battle to begin on the next day,
Monday, and We set out from Ba'tawayo on Sunday at eleven
o'clock (= 5 p.m.) to approach more closely to the place of the
engagement; We spent the night at Mähan.² On Monday, 21st
Mägabit (= 30th March), as the army which had been grouped
into its various contingents was not yet fully assembled,³ the
joining of battle could not take place on the Monday and We
arranged spending the day at Mähan. At this place there was no

¹ Steer, 306 ff.; Del Boca, chapter 13; *Guida*, 309.
² A mountain pass near Maytchäw (*Guida*, map, 304, Mecan), *Guida*, 309,
311–12; Del Boca, 166, 170.   ³ Steer, 307.

cave adequate for protection against attacks from the air. When they told Us, having found a small cave, that We should go there and that the cave was insufficient for the whole army, I said to them: 'I won't go there leaving my people, for, just as I have shared joy with my people, so I shall inseparably share its tribulations.' So I remained there.

We had determined that the battle be waged on Tuesday, 22nd Mägabit (= 31st March); on the preceding day, on the basis of the prepared plan, We had given orders that the mustered ranks in their various contingents should march that night and get close to the battle area and that the fighting should start at dawn. When the army, in its respective divisions, marched off in accordance with its orders and reached its destination close to the front, it spent the night there. We Ourselves set out from Mähan at ten o'clock at night (= 4 a.m.) and marched towards the battle field.

Our advance troops were marching in the hours of darkness with the intention of approaching the enemy's fortified positions; when the enemy's night patrols sounded the noise of fire in order to wake up their side, Our army, while still on the march, began shooting in the direction in which the sound of firing had been heard. They thus started shooting at a place called Mähan in the Maytchäw area, where the Italian soldiers were firmly entrenched in fortified positions, and since the fighting had been opened by an accidental shot prior to the plan which We had devised, We gave orders for the regular battle to be begun, and so the fighting started to develop.

As Our army moved forward with enthusiasm and reached the enemy's fortifications, the enemy troops abandoned the forward positions and were seen to defend a second more heavily fortified line towards the rear.[4]

Within four or five hours enemy aircraft arrived, dropped bombs, and cut off Our army at the rear preventing it from coming to the aid of the advance troops at the front. At this time the enemy army was recovering once again and began fighting hard to re-enter the strongholds which it had abandoned.

Our forces spent the whole day fighting with an ardent spirit and with daring. The battle did not cease until five o'clock at night (= 11 p.m.). In this day's fighting many nobles and army officers died sacrificing their life for their country.

4 Steer, 312–13.

While We Ourselves were in this kind of struggle and as it became evening, We returned to Mähan where We had spent the night yesterday. Since Our army had greatly suffered in the fighting, most of them marched that night to Ba'tawayo and rested there. Some troops spent the night near the enemy's fortified lines and kept up a running fire throughout the night.

Wednesday, 23rd Mägabit (= 1st April), We spent the day at Mähan and gave orders for the wounded to be carried in and the dead to be buried. Some of the troops, their ardour having been aroused, went to the enemy trenches and spent the day fighting there.

The day of Thursday, 24th Mägabit (= 2nd April), We again spent at Mähan. When on this day We informed the army officers of Our intention of having the battle renewed, all those who had assessed the situation remarked to Us as follows: 'Since our army marched from Tuesday evening till today to the Ba'tawayo camp, we are now very few who are present here; we do not have enough troops for a battle. The place where we are now is a dangerous one, because there is nothing at all here that represents protective cover against aeroplanes. For this reason we went to Ba'tawayo; it would be better if we fought, once we had re-assembled and re-mobilized the army.' We replied to them: 'If we pull out our foothold from here, the renewal of the battle will not take place; hence it is preferable for us here to fight.'

At this time H.H. Ras Kassa and H.H. Ras Seyum were uneasy at Our decision and said: 'To fight before there are sufficient troops for the battle means dying and perishing in vain.' Since they persuaded Us by detailing all the reasons, We left for Ba'tawayo at six o'clock at night (= midnight) following the counsel which the army officers had proffered to Us.

We spent the day of Friday, 25th Mägabit (= 3rd April), at the Ba'tawayo cave. While We were there, it was learnt that the Italians had re-occupied the fortified positions which they had abandoned last Tuesday. In consequence of this We directed that an army contingent guarding the mountain passes be stationed at the places said to be suitable for defending the surroundings of Ba'tawayo, so as to enable us to resist the invading enemy; We then proceeded to devise military plans for the future in consultation with the army commanders.

The places referred to are the other mountain passes at the central camp of Ba'tawayo where We were, and the following are the army commanders who were ordered there for guard duty:

(1) Dejazmatch Haylu Käbbädä, with the army of Säqota,[5] to be stationed at the pass between the Bokra[6] and Mähan mountains;

(2) Ras Getatchäw at the three passes which are situated between the mountain barrier of Hayo and Adbamazu;[7]

(3) From the cave at the rear of the mountain barrier of Hayo up to Mähan: Ras Käbbädä Mängäsha;

(4) It was arranged that the contingent of the Palace Ministry should be encamped at the mountain pass near Hayo Mika'el.[8]

Before the army officers whom We had detailed to guard duties at the passes could reach the places and occupy the passes, the enemy army had come out from its trenches and was seen to enter Mähan where We had rested on the previous day. The place called Mähan is near to Ba'tawayo where We now were.

We had observed the initial stages of the enemy's march and, since he had emerged from his fortified positions, it seemed possible to engage him on the plains, particularly as it was bound to be the beginning of a march towards us. We therefore transmitted orders to the various commanders: 'take up positions for immediate running fire, in order to fight from those positions'. As the enemy aircraft were going to and fro, they hit our camp uninterruptedly, and We Ourselves not excepted were resisting by firing the Oerlikon.

The enemy army which had entered Mähan had abandoned an engagement on the plains or an advance towards us and was engaged in constructing fortifications there; then, firing its guns, it began to hit Our soldiers' camp with long-range artillery. At this time Our troops were fed up, as they had suffered much injury from the bombs and poison gas which the aircraft above were raining upon them as well as from the firing of guns below; thus the army began to dissolve and turned round to march towards Koräm.

---

[5] Main centre of Lasta and Wag. See *Guida*, 326 ff. (map, 304).

[6] Bokra or Bohara, mountain dominating Maytchäw (*Guida*, 309).

[7] This name is not known to me, but from the description it must refer either to the Ezba or the Agumberta pass (*Guida*, 312; map, 304).

[8] This is the name of a cave (Käbbädä Täsämma, 153).

Because in this manner Our entire plan which We had conceived to fight at Ba'tawayo had come to grief, the nobles and army commanders approached Us and proffered to Us the following opinion: 'It would be better if we fought at Ashange after returning to Koräm and assembling the army there. If we fail to succeed there, it would be preferable if we fought taking up position in Lasta, in Yäjju, or in Wallo.' After this We desired that all the army commanders should assemble and reflect about this; all of them, therefore, congregated in front of Us and expressed their counsel in detail. They assured Us on oath that the advice which they had offered sprang from a true conscience.

We cautioned them in these terms: 'Since man is God's tool and, lest I should say that what you have told me is fraudulent, you have assured me on oath that it is absolutely firm, I shall therefore go as far as Alamata;[9] but pray to God and, while suppressing mutual rivalry, reflect on our sins, arouse your servants and your retinue and think what it is that you are dying for rather than being concerned over living.'

After this We directed that the provisions and arms which were at Ba'tawayo should be distributed to the army officers and We gave orders that the remaining weapons and supplies should be set on fire lest they be of service to the enemy; We then departed for Koräm at 3.30 o'clock at night (= 9.30 p.m.).

When We reached Ashange in the morning of Saturday, 26th Mägabit (= 4th April), enemy aeroplanes came in great numbers and hit with bombs Our army marching at Ashange. We Ourselves left Lake Ashange on the left and spent the day near Ashange Maryam[10] which is in the direction towards the right; and that evening We marched on and spent the night at Enda Agafari.[11]

Sunday, the 27th Mägabit (= 5th April) We stayed the day at Enda Agafari. On this day the Italians had sent the army which they had at Qorbata,[12] down in the Tchärtchär[13] lowlands, in

[9] An important centre, some 15 miles south of Lake Ashange, situated at the foot of Amba Wamberät. Cf. Guida, 315 (map, 304).

[10] The church of Enda Maryam at Ashange; see Guida, 313.

[11] Or Addi Agafari, a mountain west of Lake Ashange, near the road to Säqota (Guida, 313).

[12] Qorbata is an important argicultural centre in Azäbo-Galla country, east of Maytchäw, and some 2000 feet lower than the latter (Guida, 310; map, 304).

[13] The plateau of intermediate elevation (some 1500–1700 metres) running east of the line Qorbata to Alamata (Guida, 311).

order to encircle the Ashange region where We had spent the night; We had heard that their army, reaching Koräm and Alamata before Ours, had occupied the place. Our army which was marching along there suffered heavy losses as it was hit by Italian aeroplanes and by worthless country-folk launching attacks upon it. Those who survived scattered and proceeded by way of Lasta; it became thus impossible for Us to carry out Our plan to fight.

CHAPTER 46

Our return to Addis Ababa

OUR army, which had advised that we should fight at Koräm and had taken an oath to this effect, was beginning to disperse claiming they had been told to go on the road to Lasta; they proceeded on their march with mutual recriminations.

The chiefs who had remained with Us observed the condition of the army and remarked to Us that it would be better to retreat to the area behind us and to fight in Lasta or Yäjju. However, as We were convinced that it was not a useful enterprise to do things on Our own without an army, We departed from Edda Agafari on Sunday, 27th Mägabit (= 5th April 1936), at 12 o'clock (= 6 p.m.), marched through that night and then rested at Lat Giyorgis[1] at a cave called Gureza.

We spent the day of Monday, 28th Mägabit (= 6th April), at Lat Giyorgis and then marched at 12 o'clock (= 6 p.m.) to Gura Maryam;[2] there we remained during the day of 29th Mägabit (= 7th April) and departed at 11 o'clock (= 5 p.m.) resting at Märäwa[3] at a place called Maryam Mahdär. On Wednesday, 30th Mägabit (= 8th April), We stayed at Mahdär during the day and left for Azäzge[4] at 10 o'clock (= 4 p.m.). There we remained a little and at 6.30 (= 12.30) we continued the march, reached Lasta Geraretch[4] and rested there.

[1] Lat Giyorgis is a village near the Wamberät mountain range, a little to the north of Märäwa; *Guida*, 314.

[2] The precise position of Gura Maryam is not known to me, but I believe it forms part of the Ammest Addi, the district north of Märäwa.

[3] Important market and caravan centre (*Guida*, 314; map, 304).

[4] Some of these places are too small and insignificant to be marked on maps.

On Saturday, 3rd Miyazya (= 11th April), We crossed the Takazze,[5] and when we had arrived at Telasfärre Sellasse[6] We spent the night at church to celebrate the festival of the Resurrection (Easter).

On Sunday, 4th Miyazya (= 12th April), We spent the day at Telasfärre Sellasse on account of the Easter festival and also remained there overnight. As prior to this day the army, which was on the move, had marched onwards, a journey of three or four days, We transmitted the following order with the intention that no harm should befall either those who had gone ahead or those who had remained behind:

'May it reach you officers and troops who have advanced ahead: the fact that you have gone ahead and got separated from Us has caused harm and, therefore, as soon as this message reaches you, you are to stop and wait at the various places at which you are encamped. If, however, you proceed further after this order has reached you, you will be in the position of enemies towards me and my government.'

After this message had been received, Ras Getatchäw and Ligaba Tassäw stopped and waited in a district called Gemwasha, but other chiefs and troops, having gone ahead, lost many men when the country people attacked them.[7]

On 5th Miyazya (= 13th April), at nine o'clock (= 3 o'clock), We set out from Telasfärre Sellasse and marched to the churches at holy Lalibäla.[8] Among the great notables in Our retinue were Abuna Petros and Etchäge Gäbrä Giyorgis, H.H. Ras Kassa Haylu, Dejazmatch Wand Bäwassän Kassa, Dejazmatch Abära Kassa, Dejazmatch Waldä Ammanu'el Hawwas, and Dejazmatch Adäfersaw Yenadu.

On this day, at four o'clock in the evening (= 10 p.m.), We reached Lalibäla and stayed the night in the house of H.H. Ras Kassa. At ten o'clock during the night (= 4 a.m.) We went to Betä Maryam[9] Church and had mass celebrated there.

---

[5] Here called Tsellari, but the Emperor may, in fact, be at a more southerly point in the area of the Takazze sources.   [6] Playne, 168-9.   [7] Steer, 329.

[8] The famous Lasta town with its medieval rock-hewn churches. See *The Ethiopians*[2] for bibliography of some of the principal works on this subject. See also *Guida*, 317 ff. (map, 304), and Monti della Corte, 16 (for sketch map).

[9] The famous rectangular church (*Guida*, 317).

On Tuesday, 6th Miyazya (= 14th April), We toured and visited all the churches of holy Lalibäla. On this day the American missionaries who were at Lalibäla received Us and offered Us hospitality. Subsequently We went out to visit Ashätän Maryam;[10] later We returned and again spent the night in Ras Kassa's house.

On 7th Miyazya (= 15th April), at eight o'clock at night (= 2 a.m.), We departed and began Our march; in the morning We paid homage from afar to the Church of Holy Nä'akweto Lä'ab[11] and then passed on to Gännätä Maryam.[12] When We arrived there, the priests of Gännätä Maryam said the nəsebho prayer (the *Magnificat*) and received Us with songs. Subsequently We returned to Telasfärre, and arriving there at six o'clock = noon) We spent the night there.

As We had previously heard of some clashes occurring between the army on the march and the country people, We issued the following proclamation, so that troops as well as peasants should stop the quarrel amongst themselves and concentrate only on resisting the enemy.

PROCLAMATION

'The Lion of Judah has prevailed.
Haile Sellassie I
Elect of God
King of Kings of Ethiopia.

Men of my country of Ethiopia: While We are stationed at one place only, together with Our army, our enemy has come upon us not only on one side but distributed over some eight directions. The fighting and mutual enmity between peasants and soldiers has become a source of great harm to Our country and to Our people. As Our attacker has been striving to destroy Ethiopia's independence, setting fire to churches, uprooting inherited land, and debasing our religion, We have sent an army to Tämbien and Mäqälle, and We Ourselves have been toiling, entering into the slaughter to the extent that God has enabled Us. But because it is only by fighting for many days that we shall be able to repulse our enemy's might and because We have become convinced that by

---

[10] The church to the east of Lalibäla (Monti della Corte, *loc. cit.*; plate XXIX).
[11] See Playne, 156–7; about an hour from Lalibäla.
[12] Monti della Corte, 16; plate XXXI ff.; *Guida*, 317.

staying in one place for a long time soldiers and peasants get into mutually hostile positions and fights, on account of looting, which are injurious to Our people, We are now marching towards Shoa to wage the great battle in a province in which there are ample supplies.

Do not believe it to be the truth when the enemy who has now invaded us distributes to you some pamphlets making his message appear agreeable. You have heard with your own ear and seen with your own eye the violence and iniquity he is now committing even upon our churches, priests, monks, and women. As he has come against us determined to extinguish our descendants and to pass our inheritance to his son, it is well known how even a thorn, let alone a human being endowed with intelligence, can cause trouble by hurting him who stumbles upon it at its habitat. So when he enters your land, attack him who camps or marches upon it with all the means at your command; go about your land and fight wherever you are, lest your country and your land be violated. But if it causes you difficulty to work while remaining on your land, then come to where We are and We shall give you your livelihood for yourself and your dependants; so fight in company with Us for your country, your inherited land, and for your religion. Since our enemy has risen up to extinguish Ethiopia's future generation, whether rich or poor, he assembles the people, in whichever district he enters, only to exterminate them with machine-guns; you will be convinced of this if you ask what happened in Tämbien and Adwa. Even the gentry who submitted to his command he arrested and carried away, without any wrongdoing whatever being found against them. Therefore, whether you fight or do not fight, death is bound to come to you. That I tell you this is not to my advantage or to deceive you; it is in fact for your own benefit. As I know for sure that afterwards there will catch up with you contrition that cannot be forgotten and loss that cannot be made good, believe what I tell you without doubting it, for I have made God the witness that I make known to you that which I know myself.

5th Miyazya 1928 (= 13th April 1936), written at Telasfärre in Lasta.'

Subsequently We transmitted the following written orders, in particular to the army marching with Us:

'As it is necessary to observe caution on the journey henceforth, I shall appoint an officer for you who have none, so march without getting separated from him; you who have an officer, see that you are not separated from him during the march. On the march, two-thirds should join the escorts; one-third to join the camp followers. When you are on the march, keep your baggage in the centre; you are to march without leaving your path, taking great care and being in front and at the rear, left and right. If you remain behind the rearguard or if you pass ahead of the Fitawrari, you will be punished. If you are the commander of a marching column, obtain your papers in turn and proceed observing the order you have been assigned, without advancing ahead or straying behind. Ammunition is for you to fight with and is not for you to use for marketing; hence do not sell it.

5th Miyazya 1928 (= 13th April 1936) written at Telasfärre.'

Since Our army had turned back in disarray, it was clearly a useless matter for Us alone to carry on the work together with a few of Our men. The plan which We had conceived, i.e. of going ahead to Yäjju, taking up position there and to fight, had remained unfulfilled. Similarly, all the places which We had intended to be used for fighting had been occupied by the enemy who had got there first, and therefore We had to march being conducted along directions and routes which We had not intended to take. In the districts which We had to traverse We certainly encountered things which were troublesome for Our convoy.

The districts through which We passed on Our way from Maytchäw to Addis Ababa were: Säqota, Lasta, Wadla, Dälanta, Warrähimänu,[13] Tänta,[14] Ali Bet,[15] Abbäy Bet,[16] Lägamba,[17] Lägähida,[18] Jämma,[19] Mida,[20] Märhabete,[21] Sällale, and Fitche.

[13] Warrähimänu (Warrä Haymanot) is the highland region in the Magdala area (Guida, 394). [14] Tänta, in the same area (Guida, 394–5). [15] Ali Bet, in the Wallo province. [16] Abbäy Bet, in the Wallo province. [17] Lägamba: central highland district (AOI map, G-i); Topon. Etiop., 179; Steer, 336. [18] Lägähida (Käbbädä Täsämma, 159–60); region to the south of Lägamba (AOI map, FG-i); Topon. Etiop., 176; Steer, 336. [19] Jämma, river (Guida, 405; Käbbädä Täsämma, 160); Steer, 336–7. Should read 𝔛 rather than 𝔛. [20] Mida: Käbbädä Täsämma, 160; Steer, 337. [21] Märhabete (Guida, 402), the region to the N.E. of the Jämma river (de Coppet Atlas, IV).

We passed all these and entered Addis Ababa at three o'clock (= 9 a.m.) on Thursday, 22nd Miyazya 1928 (= 30th April 1936).[22]

[22] As regards the fighting reported in these chapters, and particularly at May-tchäw, the verdict on the Emperor's own conduct by Col. Konovaloff (and confirmed by Steer) deserves mention (Steer, 316):

'As far as the Emperor himself was concerned, his conduct during the offensive was irreproachable. He was always in the zone of artillery fire and continually exposed himself to danger. In the end he went down into the plain and machine-gunned the enemy himself with terrific effect.'

CHAPTER 47

The decision, on advice, to go abroad

On Thursday, 22nd Miyazya (= 30th April), after We had re-entered Our capital city, Addis Ababa, the ministers and nobles and all the great men assembled in Our palace, and an important council was held. At the council it was decided, on the basis of advice proffered, that it would be well for the Emperor to go to Europe and to inform the League of Nations, by his own voice, of all the violence Italy had perpetrated against us. Hence it was only necessary for Us to choose one of two courses of action and to take a decision.

The first was to cease fighting and to go to Geneva to alert the League of Nations, as had been resolved by the council; the second was to go on fighting with the few soldiers available in the city, irrespective of the death of the aged and of women and children or indeed of the burning of the capital.

While We were still pondering this difficult thought, the news that reached Us hourly was to the effect that the Italians were to set the city on fire with bombs, taking the Emperor's re-entry into Addis Ababa as a pretext.

Furthermore, lest We should fail to believe that the Italians would destroy the city of Addis Ababa with bombs, it ought to be mentioned that We had heard that they had hit with bombs the town of Harar, in which there was no army and no defence equipment, and that they had caused much damage to

Mons. Andreas Jarosseau who lived greatly honoured within the walled city.

As it was in this city of Harar that We had spent most of Our time since Our childhood, the fact of its being hit by bombs and set on fire saddened Our heart very specially. Hence We were convinced that there was nothing at all that would prevent an enemy who had set the city of Harar on fire doing the same to Addis Ababa. Moreover, meaning to make quite sure about this, they had dropped from aeroplanes printed pronouncements, together with black flags, that they would destroy the city. In particular, when We were contemplating fighting at Addis Ababa, there appeared, depicted before Our eyes, Our soldiers on the northern front, numbering many thousands, who were grievously injured and were dying, burnt by poison gas on the mountains and in the plains; and in addition there was the suffering of the country people, women and children, who had perished being burnt with poison gas; it was thus an extremely hard thing for Us to decide whether on Our account an attack of similarly grievous affliction would be made on Addis Ababa. The men who attended the council loved their country and were loyal to Us and thus spoke to Us as follows: 'We now know that we are unable to win fighting with the Italians either at Addis Ababa or outside. For what purpose do we exterminate our peaceful people and have its capital burnt by bombs? Hence, as previously planned, let the government move to Gore and let Bitwaddäd Waldä Tsadeq stay there acting as Regent. But it would be better if the Emperor, accompanied by the necessary assistants, presented his appeal.' Since they had resolved thus, We accepted their advice.

We subsequently issued orders that Bitwaddäd Waldä Tsadeq should conduct all government business from Gore. We also gave instructions that the Käntiba,[1] in command of the municipal guards, should have security safeguarded; and when the Italians reached the outskirts of Addis Ababa, he was to receive them peacefully with the customary white flag.

Afterwards We boarded the train and went down to Dire Dawa during the night of Friday to Saturday. When We reached Dire Dawa in the evening of Saturday, 24th Miyazya (= 2nd May), We heard that panic had broken out at Addis Ababa, that

[1] Mayor, originally mainly of Gondar, nowadays of most of the major towns.

many people had died, that much property had been looted, and that many houses had been set on fire.

As to the cause of the rioting that had occurred, We learnt from the newspapers, after passing through Jibuti, that the Italians had spread the exceedingly shameful and despicable falsehood that it was the departing Emperor who had given instructions that the city be set on fire and property be looted. While We were thinking only of preventing the death at the hands of the enemy of those who were Our people, how could We contemplate that by Our own advice they should exterminate and plunder each other? Furthermore, if We had had such a thought, how could We have gone away leaving to the Italians the new palace which We had built at great expense without setting it on fire?

When We set out on this Our journey, We took down Ras Haylu as far as Dire Dawa; he had been found guilty and was under arrest ever since he had attempted, earlier on in 1924 (= 1932), to create unrest in Ethiopia by deceitfully conspiring with the enemy who had now come to destroy our independence; evidence had been given against him and he was condemned to imprisonment for life. Although he deserved to die for betraying Ethiopia, his country, We released him and set him free, thinking that God should mete out to him what was due for his betrayal.

He himself had confessed all the wrongdoing he had committed in the past and had given his word on oath to safeguard Ethiopia's freedom working for it in future to the utmost extent possible; he then returned to Addis Ababa. We set out from Dire Dawa by train and reached Jibuti on Sunday, 25th Miyazya (= 3rd May), at 4.30 in the morning (= 10.30 a.m.). We shall never forget the welcome of friendship which the governor of the colony, other French government authorities, and the whole population accorded to Us. It was at Government House that preparations for resting had been made for Us, and We went there together with Our family.

When at this hour filled with sorrow We saw the friendly reception given to Us, without anything missing, exactly as on several previous occasions when We had gone down to Jibuti, We can only say that Our heart was greatly encouraged.

CHAPTER 48

From Jibuti to Jerusalem

THE plan upon which We were resolved when We departed from Addis Ababa had been for Us to go to Geneva and to draw the attention of the League of Nations, with Our own voice, to the affliction and suffering brought upon us by the Italian aggressor as well as to seek justice. But We were conscious of the need, first of all, to prepare for the Empress and Our family, and for the many army commanders who had come out into exile with Us, a place at which they could stay, and We therefore decided to go to Jerusalem.

Hence, on Miyazya 25th (= 3rd May) the British warship 'Enterprise'[1] arrived at Jibuti, and the Captain informed Us that We should prepare for embarkation.

The reason why this warship had reached Jibuti so quickly was this: when we were fighting with the Italians at Maytchäw, they had destroyed, by aerial bombardment, Our radio and telephone communications with Addis Ababa; Our ministers were, therefore, unable to get in touch with Us for about a month, and as news from Us was cut off and they were in difficulty over it, they contemplated sending the Empress and Our family to Jerusalem, while they themselves would go to western Ethiopia and set up the government at Gore. They held conversations with the British Minister at Addis Ababa with a view to the British Government sending a warship for the Empress, and the British Government had already notified its willingness to do so.

Some people, however, had gone so far as to spread it about that the reason why We were travelling on a British warship and had decided to come to Europe was that a friendly government had intervened in the matter and had proffered advice to this effect. This is a fairy-tale which is totally false, and there is no truth in it whatever. The main reason is simply as We have expounded it above. Also, since We were going to Jerusalem, in a British mandated territory, no-one can fail to see the propriety of

[1] Photograph on p. 16 of vol. II of the Emperor's autobiography.

travelling in a British warship. Those people who have expressed this idea may not be cognizant of the nature of British hospitality.

On the morrow, Monday 26th Miyazya 1928 (= 4th May 1936), at approximately 10 o'clock (= 4 p.m.) in the afternoon, We boarded the warship. Just before the ship was about to sail, the army commanders who had continued resisting on the Ogaden front, i.e. Dejazmatch Näsibu Zämanel, Dejazmatch Habtä Mika'el Yenadu, Dejazmatch Amde Habtä Sellasse, Dejazmatch Abäbä Damtäw, and Dejazmatch Makonnen Endalkatchäw, came to Us to convey a report on what they had done in the past and to receive orders on what they were to do in future. After submitting their report and receiving instructions for future action, they took their leave with great sorrow. Later, however, with the exception only of Dejazmatch Habtä Mika'el Yenadu, they were to come on another boat.

As the ship set out on her voyage, the Government of the colony of French Somaliland offered Us a farewell salute by firing guns and by having aircraft fly close to the ship in which We were sailing. Our heart was touched with joy at this gesture.

Another five British warships (torpedo-boats) followed at a distance the warship in which We were travelling.

When We reached Port Said, after passing through the Suez Canal, Our consul at Port Said and some other Ethiopians were in a boat with our greatly honoured tricolour flag; as they rowed their boat close to the ship, We saw them wipe off their tears with their handkerchiefs, and thus that great grief of Ours was re-awakened and We were deeply moved. Moreover, the ship was not stopping there, and there was thus much sadness in all our hearts at our passing by without being able to meet each other. On the fifth day We reached the port of Haifa, and our ship anchored there. Other British warships were positioned in formation there to await Our arrival.

At a small distance from the ship in which We were, there was an Italian boat at anchor, called the 'Carnero' and bedecked with flags. There was no doubt that they had done this with malice, thinking that We would be sad at seeing an Italian vessel now at Our arrival as an exile from Our own country.

As We disembarked, the musical band of the 'Enterprise' sounded the Ethiopian national anthem. Stepping on to the shore, We passed along the mustered ranks of the soldiers giving Us a respectful welcome; and here likewise they played the Ethiopian national anthem. Even the Jews and Arabs who had been quarrelling amongst themselves forgot their dispute and, standing together, watched Us with pleasure and respect.

Thence We set out for Jerusalem and when We reached the railway station there, the British Government authorities received Us with honour. First of all We went to Golgotha, and after We had paid homage at the Tomb of our Lord, We went to the King David Hotel.

On the following day We went out to Our monastery called Däbrä Gännät.[2] At Jerusalem there is an extensive monastery which has been firmly established for a long time, and there live in it, entering into holy asylum, monks and nuns who have come from Ethiopia having renounced the world.

Their joy is great, for they live in this monastery conversing in Amharic and celebrating Mass in Ge'ez.

But now when they heard of the entry into Addis Ababa, Our capital city, of our aggressive enemy, and when they saw Our arrival in a foreign country as an exile from Our own, and in particular when We told them that in the Italian war many churches and many books had been burnt and that many monks and priests, women and children as well as the aged had perished through poison gas and bombs, they began bursting into tears.

Later on, in accordance with the plans which We had made when departing from Addis Ababa, We transmitted to the League of Nations at Geneva the following message, in order to explain the reason why We had come here as an exile from Our country.

To the Secretary General of the
League of Nations at Geneva.

We would request you to make known, on Our behalf, the following to member governments:

In leaving for abroad to stop the total extermination of the Ethiopian people, We are resolved to devote Ourselves in peace and in liberty to halting a war of aggression such as has never been seen or heard of in modern times, that is without parallel and is outside the character and nature of man. We also wish to bring about protection from Italian evil deeds and the honouring of

[2] Cerulli, *Etiopi in Palestina*, II, 471.

international obligations[3] as a basis of Ethiopia's ancient independence and, indeed, the peace of the nations of the world.

From the beginning We have done everything possible to prevent peace being disturbed. We faithfully defended our country until Italy began to strike with poison gas like rain and until it became obvious that our resistance could not be continued, for if we did [not] resist[4] the result would only be the extermination of the Ethiopian people.

And now We request that the League of Nations should not cease the strenuous efforts to have the covenant honoured and that it should not recognize claims of sovereignty or of territorial expansion through improper military force in breach of treaty obligations.

Jerusalem, 11th Genbot 1928 (= 19th May 1936)
Haile Sellassie I, Emperor

³ ወ·ጥ ı should almost certainly read ወ·ስ ı here.
⁴ The Amharic text appears to be faulty here: read bə- instead of ba-.

CHAPTER 49

Our journey from Jerusalem to London

W E had requested permission to go from Jerusalem to London, and after it had been granted We arranged for the Empress and Our family and the army commanders who had come with Us to stay at Jerusalem. Accompanied by Our sons, Crown Prince Märed-Azmatch[1] Asfa Wassän and Makonnen, Duke of Harar, and Our daughter Tsähay[2] as well as by Ras Kassa, who had been appointed by Us commander of the northern army, We went from Jerusalem to Haifa on 15th Genbot (= 23rd May). There We embarked in the British warship 'Capetown' and sailed to Gibraltar.

¹ Ancient title of the sovereigns of Shoa (Guidi, *Voc.*, 68; *Suppl.*, 26).

² The Emperor's youngest daughter, who had trained as a nurse in London, was married to Gen. Abiy Abäbä (on the latter see Käbbädä Täsämma, 435; at one time President of the Senate, Governor-General of Eritrea, and Minister of Defence; killed during the events of 23rd November 1974), and died tragically young in 1942. The Princess Tsähay Memorial Hospital at Addis Ababa was named after her.

At Gibraltar We transferred to a passenger ship of the Orient line, disembarked at the British seaport of Southampton, and from there travelled by train to London.

At the railway station in London the British public gave Us a great welcome, and We then departed for the accommodation which had been prepared for Us. The people assembled there demonstrated to Us their participation in Our grief, and We admired the tenderness and kindness of the British people.

A few days later, We went to a meeting at which many people were assembled, and Our daughter Tsähay did the same at a crowded assembly of women: There we laid bare the acts of cruelty which Italy had wrought upon the Christian and innocent Ethiopian people. When We now expounded to them in Our own words the story of our tribulations, of which they had hitherto heard through news bulletins only, the British people, who do not love violence but seek true justice, all manifested to Us their sympathy in Our sadness.

We had, of course, informed the League of Nations of the aggression carried out by Italy against Ethiopia, and We had accepted the conciliation proposals which the League, after due deliberation, had submitted, while Italy had persisted in her refusal to accept these, had crossed the borders and launched her attack. As laid down in article 16 of the League covenant, sanctions had been applied against Italy, but after the sanctions had continued for about ten months, the matter was raised in the British parliament. They debated the problem for a number of days arguing that, although sanctions had been applied against Italy, the latter had merely gone on intensifying her aggressive action against Ethiopia who had not obtained any benefit from those sanctions; it would therefore be better to stop them rather than allow them to impede international trade in vain. Subsequently many on behalf of the people argued that as Italy went on intensifying her aggression, it was necessary to add further sanctions. But whatever the circumstances, government opinion is known to prevail over the people's views, and We thus learnt of the decision to discontinue sanctions.

CHAPTER 50

Our journey to Geneva in quest of justice from the League of Nations

BEFORE the Walwal attack, and even after it, We had not abandoned Our firm faith in the League of Nations. Some people who saw this tried to instil doubts into Our heart by arguing 'if you had given up, earlier on, your faith in the League of Nations and had persisted preparing for war, all this calamity would not have come upon you; the faith which from now onwards you are reposing in the League of Nations will be in vain.' But We were conscious that it was right to have a covenant honoured even between two individuals, let alone a covenant of 52 nations. So We did not change Our mind up to the last, other than adhering firmly to Our intention not to diminish Our faith in the League. That We had come here after leaving Our country was to explain, in person, Our tribulations to the League, in the firm conviction that the League would not fail to give Us a fair judgement.

When We were in London We learnt that the League had arranged a meeting for June 26th 1936 (= 19th Säne 1928) in order to discuss the dispute between Ethiopia and Italy as well as some other smaller matters; We consequently decided to go to Geneva. When there were only some eight days to go before the appointed day, some of Our friends came and said to Us: 'It would be better if Your Majesty were not to go to Geneva; the reason being, if you yourself went and appeared before the Assembly and if, after your speech, you failed to secure justice, your grief would be the greater; hence it would be better if you sent envoys.' Others again gave Us friendly advice to this effect: 'At this time of your great troubles, unless you yourself appeared before the Assembly and explained in your own words any of the matters concerned, or if you merely sent envoys, the problem would not appear sufficiently grave to the Assembly; hence it would be better if you definitely attended.'

The reason why We had left Our country Ethiopia and come here had not been in order to send envoys but to explain in front of the League of Nations, Ourselves and in Our own words, the nature of the aggression committed against us. On 18th Säne (= 25th June), accompanied by H.H. Ras Kassa, Dejazmatch Näsibu, Blattengeta Heruy, Ato Waldä Giyorgis Waldä Yohannes, Ato Lorenso Ta'ezaz,[1] and Ato Efrem Täwaldä Mädhen,[2] We set out from London and went to Geneva by way of Paris, arriving there by train on the following morning. Subsequently, 23rd Säne 1928 (= 30th June 1936) was the day fixed for Us to speak Our mind before the representatives of fifty-two nations assembled there. When We went there on the appointed day and stood by the lectern, the Italians who had come there for news reporting started to whistle continuously with the intention of obstructing Our speech and rendering it inaudible. At this moment, the Rumanian delegate, M. Titulescu,[3] remarked to the President of the Assembly, M. van Zeeland:[4] 'For the sake of justice, silence these beasts!'

The President of the Assembly, seeing the rude behaviour of the Italians in front of so many international representatives, ordered the guards to expel the Italians by force; they then seized them and ejected them.

After this We read Our speech in Amharic, and it was arranged that it should immediately be translated into French and English, so that the whole Assembly could understand it. The text was as follows:

Your Excellency, Mr. President,
Your Excellencies, Envoys of the Nations!

I should have liked to speak to you in French. But as it is in the Amharic language alone that I am able to speak my mind from my heart and with all the force of my spirit, I would beg the

[1] 1900–47; Emperor's private secretary before the war. Of Eritrean birth and educated in France, he was Minister of Foreign Affairs and Ambassador to Russia.

[2] Also of Eritrean birth; served Emperor Haile Sellassie in a variety of posts, including as Minister in London.

[3] Nicola Titulescu; born 1883; Rumanian Foreign Minister, and for many years one of the most active men in the League of Nations. The actual words used by Titulescu were: 'à la porte les sauvages!'

[4] Paul van Zeeland; born 1893; Belgian Prime Minister 1935–7. Subsequently a professor at Louvain University.

forgiveness of the General Assembly of the League of Nations for not speaking in French.

I, Haile Sellassie I, Emperor of Ethiopia, am present here today to ask for the impartial justice due to my people and for the help which fifty-two nations had undertaken to extend to it when they affirmed, eight months ago, that a war of aggression, in violation of international law, was being waged against Ethiopia.

There is no man other than the Emperor to present the appeal of the Ethiopian people to these fifty-two nations.

Perhaps this is the first time that a king or president appears before this assembly and addresses it. But it is truly only today that violence of this kind is seen being committed against a people which is now falling victim to the aggressor.

Furthermore, there has not been seen a previous example of a government that has set out to extinguish methodically and by means of cruelty, the entire stock[5] of another people, in transgression of a covenant which it has honourably and publicly entered into in form of a treaty concluded with the nations of the world, to wit that one government was not to deprive another of its country by means of war and that it was not to exterminate innocent human beings by powerful and toxic poison gas. The reason that I, as Emperor of Ethiopia, have come to Geneva after having fought myself as Commander-in-Chief of my army is to fulfil this highest duty of mine and to defend the Ethiopian people struggling to preserve its independence which has endured for many thousands of years. I pray to God that He may keep the nations of the world from the torment that has been inflicted upon my people and from the nauseating things of which these chiefs who have followed me here have been witnesses and which have, indeed, happened to themselves.

I shall explain in detail to the representatives of the nations assembled in Geneva, who are responsible for the lives of many millions of men, women, and children, about the mortal danger awaiting these creatures and the fate which has overwhelmed Ethiopia.

It is not only upon Ethiopian soldiers that the Italian Government has made war; above all, it has struck at peaceful people far

---

[5] The Amharic words used here by the Emperor correspond exactly to 'genocide'—except, of course, that this term had not yet been coined in English at that time.

removed from the battlefield by killing them with terror raids
and exterminating them altogether.

At the beginning of the war, in 1928 (= 1935), Italian aeroplanes launched tear-gas bombs upon my armies. These bombs
did not harm them very greatly, as the soldiers knew, when these
bombs were being dropped, how to scatter until the wind had
disposed of the gas.

After this, the Italian aeroplanes began to drop yperite gas.
Casks containing yperite fell upon the Ethiopian army; but the
harm which this yperite gas caused was not considerable. The
reason for this was that there were only a few soldiers whom the
yperite liquid affected, and when the casks fell upon the ground
both the soldiers and the population realized that they contained
poison.

When Ethiopian troops had encircled Mäqälle, the Italian army
Commander-in-Chief had good reason to feel anxiety about the
possible dissolution of the Italian army and, therefore, directed
the dropping of yperite in a different manner. It is now my duty
to reveal this action to the world.

A mechanism spraying yperite liquid was installed in the aircraft, and it was arranged that a fine rain bringing death should
descend over vast tracts of country. At one time, nine, fifteen, or
eighteen Italian aeroplanes were going to and fro bringing down
an unceasing rain of yperite. From the end of Ter 1928 (= late
January 1936) onwards this death-dealing rain descended uninterruptedly upon our soldiers, upon women, children, cattle,
streams, stagnant waters as well as pastures. The Italian army
commander made the aeroplanes repeat this work of theirs, in
order to extinguish completely all living creatures and to turn into
poison the waters and the grazing grounds. He made this the
principal means of warfare.

This work of cruelty, carried out with some finesse, annihilated
people in places far removed from the battlefield and made their
country into a desert. The plan was to spread terror and death
over the greater part of Ethiopia.

This most deplorable scheme was eventually accomplished.
Man and beast perished completely. The deadly downpour that
descended from the aircraft made anyone who touched it fly with
torment. Those who drank the water upon which this poisonous
rain had settled or ate the food which the poison had touched

died in dreadful agony. The people who died as a result of the Italian yperite must be reckoned in many thousands. It was to make known to the civilized world the torment inflicted upon the Ethiopian people that I decided to come to Geneva.

There is none better qualified than myself and these men who were in the war with me to provide the League of Nations with this indisputable testimony.

If Europe reckons this matter to be an accomplished fact, then it is proper to consider this fate which awaits it and which is bound to come upon it.

The appeal which my envoys presented to the League of Nations when this whole tribulation descended upon my army and my people has remained without obtaining any reply. My envoys have not been in this war and, as they themselves have not witnessed the afflictions suffered by Ethiopia, I have resolved to come myself to describe the criminal acts perpetrated against my people.

It is not necessary, is it, to remind the General Assembly of the League of Nations meeting here today of what has happened to Ethiopia over this period of time?

For the past twenty years, when working first as Crown Prince and Regent of the Ethiopian realm and later as Emperor and leader of my people, I have not ceased striving to obtain for my country the benefits of modern civilization and, in particular, to establish relations of good neighbourliness with adjacent governments. With Italy especially I concluded a treaty of friendship in 1920 (= 1928) which prohibited the resort to war under any circumstances whatsoever and which provided for any dispute arising between the two governments to be settled amicably and by arbitration, a procedure which the civilized nations of the world have made the basis for the peace of their peoples.

In the declaration which the Committee of thirteen governments presented on 25th Mäskäräm 1928 (= 6th October 1935) it told me expressly that it was aware of the efforts I had made. The text was as follows:

'The nations had considered that, by her entry into the League and by affording her new confidence that her territorial integrity would not be impaired and her independence not be destroyed, Ethiopia would attain a higher level of civilization than she possessed now. In present-day Ethiopia there does not appear to be the lack of security and the condition of lawlessness that could still be seen in 1915 (= 1923).[6] In fact, the country has become more united than before, and the authority of the central government is more respected than in the past.'

If the Italian Government had not created all sorts of troubles for me by pushing some men to raise up revolts in Ethiopia and by giving arms to the rebels, the work I have been doing for my people would have been even more beneficial and have shown better results.

The Rome Government—as indeed it has now openly admitted—has been preparing unceasingly plans to take Ethiopia by means of war. Thus all the treaties with me which it had signed were not sincere. The fact that it had signed this treaty of friendship in particular was intended to serve the purpose of concealing its real plans.

The Italian Government has confirmed its preparations, for the past fourteen years, to undertake what it has now obtained by force. Therefore, it is possible to say that it was doing things to undermine the confidence of the world when it aided and supported the admission of Ethiopia to the League of Nations in 1915 (= 1923), when it concluded the treaty of friendship in 1920 (= 1928), and when it signed the Treaty of Paris to outlaw war. The Ethiopian Government, however, believed to find in all these treaties, concluded with great solemnity, fresh confidence that it was possible to accomplish the work it had initiated with all its heart and strength to lead the country on a peaceful path towards civilization.

The Walwal conflict which occurred in Hedar 1927 (= December 1934) was felt by me like a sudden flash of lightning descended from the sky. But it was obvious that Italy wished this quarrel to take place. I did not delay informing the League of Nations of this incident. I requested, therefore, that the matter be looked at according to the text laid down in the 1920 (= 1928) treaty, on the basis of the League's *raison d'être,* in accord with the arbitration provisions, and all these various procedures.

But it was Ethiopia's misfortune that it appeared absolutely essential to some governments to obtain Italy's friendship by

---

[6] The year in which Ethiopia joined the League.

whatever means on the grounds of the situation in Europe. The price paid for the Italian Government's coercive demands was to hand over Ethiopia's independence. This secretly contrived agreement, rather than the obligations into which the nations of the world had entered under the League covenant, became an awful burden for all the affairs of Ethiopia that arose at that time. On these grounds Ethiopia and the whole world have experienced great difficulties over this calamity; and to this day these problems persist.

This setting aside of the covenant of the League, then occurring for the first time, has not remained a unique occasion. The Rome Government, feeling reinforced in the policy adopted against Ethiopia, initiated preparations for war, just in case the pressure that began to be exerted upon Ethiopia turned out to be insufficient to induce the Ethiopian people to accept Italian rule. Hence it was to Italy's advantage to delay matters. Things were dragged out by many kinds of stratagems and in various ways, so that the arbitrators who had been chosen for conciliation were unable to start their task. All sorts of obstacles were devised to prevent the work of the arbitrators being completed. Some governments sought to prohibit the selection of arbitrators from among their nationals. Once the arbitration procedure had been set up, the arbitrators were subjected to pressure to bring in a verdict favourable to Italy. However, all this effort was in vain. The arbitrators, two of whom were Italians, issued a unanimous judgement to the effect that neither in the Walwal incident nor in any subsequent one was there anything to make Ethiopia responsible before the comity of nations.

After this verdict had been given, the Ethiopian Government was truly confident in supposing that this would usher in a new era of friendship with Italy. I stretched out my hand to the Rome Government in all sincerity.

The Committee of thirteen nations informed the General Assembly, in the report rendered at its meeting on 25th Mäskäräm 1928 (= 6th October 1935), of the details of the entire story in its various stages, beginning with Hedar 1927[7] (= December 1934) until 23rd Mäskäräm 1928 (= 4th October 1935).

From the conclusions reached in this report I would now only remind you of the text in paragraphs 24, 25, and 26:

[7] The Amharic version's '1926' is clearly an error.

It was on 29th Nähase 1927 (= 4th September 1935) that the Italian memorandum was handed to the Council. But the Ethiopian memorandum, its first appeal, is dated 5th Tahsas 1927[7] (= 14th December 1934). Between these two dates the Italian Government insisted that the matter should only be determined according to the wording laid down in the 1920 (=. 1928) treaty between Ethiopia and Italy, meaning to prevent the problem coming before the Council. Throughout this time Italian soldiers were continually being despatched in the direction of East Africa. The Italian Government, concealing its secret intentions, informed the Council that the reason for the despatch of troops was that they were needed for defence, as the Ethiopian Government, by its military preparations, was causing anxiety to the Italian colonies in that area. The Ethiopian Government repeatedly drew attention to the fact that, quite to the contrary, the Italian Government left no doubt as to their hostile intentions—as can indeed be seen from the official speeches delivered in Italy.

From the beginning of the dispute the Ethiopian Government has sought to settle the matter by peaceful means. It has requested that the problem be looked into under the provisions of the League's covenant. As, however, the Italian Government desired that the matter be looked at only under the procedures laid down in the Italo-Ethiopian treaty of 1920 (= 1928), the Ethiopian Government accepted this. The latter also declared that, even if the arbitrators failed to find in its favour, it would carry out the conditions of the verdict with good-will. When Italy remained adamant that she would not allow the arbitrators to look into the question of the ownership of Walwal, Ethiopia accepted this as well. The Ethiopian Government requested the Council to send to the country neutrals who should investigate this matter; and it also declared its preparedness to accept any inquiry upon which the Council may wish to decide. The Italian Government, on its part, presented to the Council, once the Walwal problem had been settled by arbitration, a detailed memorandum to request the freedom to be able to do what it pleased. It asserted that there was nothing appropriate laid down in the League's covenant to settle the whole problem concerning Ethiopia. It further announced that, since this matter was of vital interest to Italy and was a primary requirement for its own security, Italy would be neglecting its most elementary duty, unless it entirely removed its confidence from Ethiopia and obtained full freedom to carry out what was necessary to safeguard its own interests and to protect its colonies.

These then are the terms of the report which the committee of thirteen nations presented. The Council and the General Assembly announced unitedly and openly that 'the Italian Government was the aggressor and was in breach of the League's covenant'.

I have unceasingly made it known, time and time again, that I was not seeking to wage the war that was being imposed upon me. That I was fighting was solely to prevent my people's liberty and Ethiopia's territorial integrity being affected; I was additionally defending in this war the cause of all small nations who are neighbours of powerful states, lest such a neighbour should be able to take their country by force.

In the month of Teqemt 1928 (= October 1935) the fifty-two nations who are listening to me today gave me the following promise: 'The aggressor will not prevail; we shall see that the provisions of the covenant are implemented, so that a lawful government shall be firmly supported and that the perpetrator of force, transgressing the law, shall be destroyed.'

I would remind the nations not to forget this their policy, for it is I who have followed the policy which the fifty-two nations have pursued these last eight months, in which I manifested my faith and upon which I directed my people to defend themselves against a government that had been condemned of aggression by the whole world.

Although my war equipment was so much less than the aggressor's and although I possessed no aeroplanes, artillery, other weapons whatsoever or indeed hospital services for the wounded, my hope rested upon the covenant of the League. I thought it impossible that fifty-two nations, among whom were some of the mightiest in the world, could be defeated by one sole aggressor government. Reposing my trust in the efficacy of treaties—exactly as happened to some small nations in Europe—I had made no preparations for war. When the danger became more pressing and the responsibility towards my people irked my conscience, I tried to obtain arms throughout 1928 (= October 1935–May 1936). Many governments prohibited the export of arms intending to prevent me from obtaining any. The Italian Government, however, was able to transport through the Suez Canal weapons, munitions, and troops, uninterruptedly and without anyone stopping them. On Mäskäräm 23rd (= 4th October) the Italian army invaded my country, and only a few hours after that did I issue a proclamation of mobilization. In the desire to live by maintaining peace, I directed my troops to fall back some 30 kilometres from the frontiers, in order not to provoke a conflict by whatever pretext—exactly as an important nation had done when war was about to break out at the time of the Great War. After that, war continued with great violence, exactly as I have explained to the Council.

In this struggle of unequal rivalry between a government which had at its disposal a people of 42 million inhabitants, which was able to obtain all the necessary weapons and resources, and which possessed all the technical knowledge to make arms of various kinds to extinguish human life and, on the other hand, a small people of 12 million inhabitants which lived by trusting only impartial justice and the covenant of the League of Nations and which possessed neither arms nor money—in this unequal war you yourselves can well assess that there has not been any real help for the Ethiopian Government, even after the Rome Government had been condemned of having violated the League's covenant and after the nations had declared that they would resist the aggressor's triumph.

Is it that every single government in the League has considered the war of aggression exactly as if it had been waged against itself as an individual member, as the signature which it appended to article 17[8] of the League's covenant required it to do?

I had placed all my hopes in the dutiful fulfilment of these obligations. My hopes had obtained support from the declarations made in the League that the aggressor would not gain a reward and that force would be defeated by the law.

In the month of Tahsas 1928 (= December 1935) the Council made it clearly known that it shared the view of many hundreds of million people in the whole world who opposed the plan which had been presented for the partition of Ethiopia.[9] It has been said many times: 'this conflict which has arisen is not only

---

[8] I believe this should read 16.
[9] This is, of course, a reference to the Hoare-Laval plan.

the conflict of Ethiopia and Italy but it is the conflict of the Italian Government and the League of Nations.'

This is why I myself, and my people, replied that I would not accept all the proposals which (the Italians) had submitted to me which were for my own benefit but which would undermine the covenant of the League of Nations. That I had adopted the position of resistance was additionally also for the cause of the small nations exposed to aggression. And where have all the promises of support that were given to me got to?

Ever since Tahsas 1928 (= December 1935) I had noted with much distress that three governments[10] were regarding as entirely valueless the obligations under which they had entered into the League covenant. The relationship which they had with Italy made them unwilling to accept anything to stop the work of aggression which Italy had undertaken.

Moreover, it was the position of some governments that made me very dejected. These governments, while unceasingly declaring the faith which they reposed in the League of Nations, were equally unceasingly striving to prevent the law of the League being carried out. Some governments, when some sound proposal was tabled that would at once arrest the work of the aggressor, were causing delay with many pretexts, so that the matters should not come up for discussion—let alone be carried out. The secret agreements made in the month of Ter 1927[11] (= early January 1935), were they intended to presage this work of obstruction?

The Ethiopian Government did not expect other governments, whose direct interests were not involved, to shed their soldiers' blood for the defence of the League's covenant. What the warriors of Ethiopia did expect was merely the means they required for their defence. I had therefore asked many times to obtain the funds necessary for the purchase of arms. I was denied this assistance. What then is the explanation of the wording of article 16 in the League's covenant or, indeed, of the solemn promises made that the nations would stand together and, by mutual assistance, prevent the extinction of security?

[10] Austria, Hungary, Albania (Hardie, 102).

[11] The Amharic text has 1928, clearly erroneously, for the reference is obviously to the secret Rome talks of early January 1935 held between Mussolini and Laval. Cf. Baer, 73-5.

Many difficulties have been brought up to prevent the transport of arms intended for Ethiopia by the Jibuti-Addis Ababa railway and, equally, to stop the entry by that route of equipment, at the required time, that would be of service to the Ethiopian Government. Yet, for the present this is the principal route of transportation of supplies and arms for the Italian army which has entered Ethiopia illicitly. Even the rules of neutrality should prohibit the loading of equipment of this kind to reach the Italian forces at the places where they are at present. This being so, under the wording of article 16 of the covenant of the League of Nations it is improper for the neutrality clauses to be waived in this case, for all governments who are League-members have to suspend their neutrality if one government attacks another, as it is incumbent upon them to offer help, not to the aggressor but to the victim of the attack. In this manner, has the covenant been observed in the past? And is it possible to say that it is being respected today?

Now, latterly, some great nations who have considerable influence in the League have announced in their parliaments that, since the Italian aggressor had managed to seize part of the Ethiopian territory, there was no need now to continue the preventive measures in the financial sphere that had been set up against Italy.

This is the position in which the General Assembly of the League finds itself today as it meets to examine, at the request of the Argentine Government, the situation brought about by the Italian aggressor.

The issue which is today before the League of Nations' General Assembly is not merely to settle what Italy has done by way of aggression. I would assert that it is something that touches upon all governments of the world. This is a problem of the duty of governments to assist each other to establish world security (what is called collective security); it is a question of the very life of the League of Nations; of the trust which the nations of the world can properly repose in treaties they have concluded; of the value attached to promises which the small nations have received as regards the inviolability of their territorial integrity and independence, so that these values be respected and properly esteemed; it is to assess whether the principle of the equality of nations is to be confirmed or whether the small states will have to accept subjection to the powerful ones. In brief, it is not only Ethiopia that is at stake but the decent way of life of the peoples of the world who have been thus affected and wronged. The signatures appended to a treaty, is it that they attain their value only in so far as they are of use to the signatories in the pursuit of their personal, direct, and immediate interests?

Subtle comparisons cannot change the main problem or lead the discussion in another direction. It is with sincerity of heart that I submit these reflections to the General Assembly of the League.

Apart from the Kingdom of God, there is no human government that possesses greater merit than any other. But on this earth, when a powerful government sets out in the belief that it is right to exterminate another nation against which no offence has been proved, then the hour has come for the injured party to bring the wrongs it has suffered before the League of Nations. God and history will observe as witnesses the judgement you will give.

At a time when my people is close to extinction, when the help of the League may yet be able to save it from that fate, it is proper that I should be permitted to speak the truth, without holding back anything, without reticence, and without prevarication.

I hear it being asserted that the sanctions, which have hitherto been applied and which have remained inadequate, have not produced the expected result. It was well known that sanctions which were intentionally devised to be insufficient and which were also improperly applied could not at any time and in any circumstances stop the aggressor. This has caused our failure to stop the aggressor, but it is not right to say that it was impossible. Ethiopia had previously asked to be given financial aid. She is asking for it now. Was this a matter incapable of implementation?

Yet the League of Nations had given financial assistance—and even in peace-time—to other governments who now refuse to apply sanctions against the aggressor. Despite the fact that the Italian Government had employed cruel means of warfare and had many times and repeatedly transgressed all international laws, I note with a very sad heart that a plan is now being devised to lift sanctions. Is this intended action not tantamount to abandoning Ethiopia and to saying 'let the aggressor government do to her what it pleases'? Does not this initiative, coming as it does just before I appear before the League's General Assembly with this great effort in the defence of my people, cut off one of Ethiopia's last chances of obtaining help and guarantees from the governments who are members of the League? Is it an objective of this kind which the League and its members may confidently expect from the support of the great powers who possess the means to be leaders of the League's actions?

If by the acts of aggression carried out by Italy things have come to such a pass, will the governments who are members of the League have to subordinate their own wishes to the precedent of brute force?

Proposals are assuredly to come before the General Assembly of the League with a view to improving the League covenant and rendering more effective the guarantees of mutual aid. But is it really necessary to change the covenant? Unless those who have signed the covenant have the will to observe its provisions in full, what guarantees are there that the covenant, even if changed, will be safeguarded? It is the determination of the nations of the world that is defective and not the covenant of the League.

In the name of the Ethiopian people which is a member of the League of Nations, I request the Assembly that everything necessary be carried out to have the covenant respected.

I now renew once more the protest which I have previously submitted on the grounds of the transgression of treaties to the detriment of the Ethiopian people and on account of the violence perpetrated against it. I declare before the world that the Emperor of Ethiopia, the Ethiopian Government, and the people will not accept anything done to them by force. I further declare that they will do everything in their power to see international order triumph, to have the League covenant respected, and to have the authority and the territory which is theirs restored to them.

I ask the fifty-two nations who have given a promise to the Ethiopian people that they would come to their aid at the time of the aggression against them, in order to prevent the aggressor from defeating them—I ask these fifty-two nations for their support by upholding their promise. What are you willing to do for Ethiopia?

You, Great Powers, who have promised to give guarantees of collective security, lest small nations be extinguished and the fate which has overtaken Ethiopia should befall them as well, have you considered what kind of assistance to provide, so that Ethiopia's liberty shall not be destroyed and her territorial integrity shall be respected?

You representatives of the world assembled here! I have come to you to Geneva to carry out the saddest duty that has befallen an Emperor. What answer am I to take back to my people?

GENEALOGICAL OUTLINE

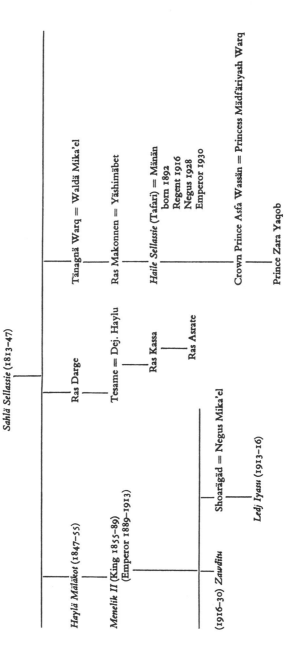

BIBLIOGRAPHICAL NOTES

ABRAHAM DEMOZ, 'Emperor Menelik's phonograph message to Queen Victoria' in *BSOAS*, XXXII, 1969.

ABU SĀLIH, *Churches and monasteries of Egypt and some neighbouring countries* (translated and edited by B. T. A. Evetts, with notes by A. J. Butler); Oxford, 1895.

ACCADEMIA NAZIONALE DEI LINCEI, *IV Congresso Internazionale di Studi Etiopici*, Rome 1974.

AFĀWARQ, *Dagmawi Menilek*, Rome 1909.

L'Africa Orientale, 2 vols., Milan 1936.

ARMBRUSTER, C. H., *Initia Amharica*, Part II, English-Amharic Vocabulary, Cambridge, 1910.

AVON, EARL OF, *Facing the Dictators*, London 1962.

BAER, G. W., *The Coming of the Italian-Ethiopian War*, Cambridge (Mass.) 1967.

BAETEMAN, J., *Dictionnaire amarigna-français*, Dire Daoua, 1929.

BARKER, A. J., *The Civilizing Mission, The Italo-Ethiopian War 1935-6*, London 1968.

BECCARI, C., *Rerum Aethiopicarum Scriptores Occidentales Inediti a Seculo XVI ad XIX*, Rome, 1903-17; Brussels, 1969 (reprint).

BECKINGHAM, C. F. and HUNTINGFORD, G. W. B., *The Prester John of the Indies*, 2 vols., Hakluyt Society, London, 1961.

BERLAN, EDOUARD, *Addis Abeba: La plus haute ville d'Afrique*, Grenoble 1963.

BEZOLD, C., *Kebra Nagast*, Munich, 1909.

BOMBACI, A. and others, *Elementi per la Toponomastica Etiopica*, Napoli 1937 (cited *Toponomastica*).

BRUCE, J., *Travels to discover the Source of the Nile* (1st ed., 5 vols., Edinburgh, 1790; 3rd ed., 8 vols., Edinburgh, 1813).

BUDGE, SIR E. A. WALLIS, *The life and exploits of Alexander the Great*, 2 vols., London, 1896.

——, *The Nile*, London 1910.

——, *A history of Ethiopia*, 2 vols., London, 1928; (cited as Budge).

——, *The Queen of Sheba and her only son Menyelek*, London, 1932.

CAMPBELL, MARGARET, *A Short History of The British Embassy, Addis Ababa*, Addis Ababa 1972.

CERULLI, ENRICO, 'Canti popolari amarici' in *RRAL*, 1916.

——, *Studi Etiopici*:
    I. *La Lingua e la storia di Harar*, Rome 1936.
    II. *La Lingua e la storia dei Sidamo*, Rome, 1938.
    III. *Il Linguaggio dei Giangero, etc.*, Rome, 1938.
    IV. *La Lingua caffina*, Rome, 1951.

CERULLI, ENRICO, *Etiopi in Palestina*, 2 vols, Rome, 1943–7.
——, *Storia della letteratura etiopica*, Rome, 1956; 3rd ed., Milan, 1968.
CHEESMAN, R. E., *Lake Tana and the Blue Nile*, London, 1936.
Chi è dell'Eritrea, see Puglisi, G.
CLAPHAM, C., *Haile Selassie's government*, London 1969.
COFFEY, T. M., *Lion by the Tail*, London 1974.
COHEN, M., *Traité de langue amharique*, Paris 1936.
——, *Nouvelles études d'éthiopien méridional*, Paris 1939 (cited NE).
COMMAND PAPER 2680 of 1926
COMMAND PAPER 2792 of 1927
CONTI ROSSINI, C., 'Note per la storia letteraria abissina', *RRAL*, 1899.
——, *Storia d'Etiopia*, Bergamo 1928.

DÄSTA TÄKLÄ WALD, New Amharic Dictionary (in Amharic), Addis Ababa 1970 (cited DTW).
DE COPPET—see under Guebre Sellassie.
DEBRE QEDDUS ESTIFANOS—see under Pontificio Collegio Etiopico.
DEL BOCA, ANGELO, *The Ethiopian War*, 1935–41, Univ. of Chicago Press, 1969.
DUCHESNE-FOURNET, J., *Mission en Ethiopie* (1901–3), 2 vols. and atlas, Paris 1909.

Encyclopaedia of Islam, 2nd edition, Leiden 1954–.
ERLICH, H., *Biography of Ras Alula* (unpublished London University, SOAS, Ph.D. thesis, 1973).
ETHIOPIA, Constitution, Addis Ababa 1930.
ETHIOPIA, Revised Constitution, Addis Ababa 1955.
Ethiopian Studies: Proceedings of the International Conference of Ethiopian Studies at Manchester University, 1963, edited by E. Ullendorff and C. F. Beckingham, *JSS*, Spring 1964.

FARAGO, L., *Abyssinia on the Eve*, London 1935.
Fetha Nagast—see under Guidi.
FUMAGALLI, G., *Bibliografia etiopica*, Milan, 1893.

GÄBRÄ SELLASSE, History of Menelik II (in Amharic), Addis Ababa 1966/7; see also de Coppet and Guebre Sellassie.
GANKIN, E., *Russian-Amharic: Amharic-Russian dictionary*, Moscow, 1965, 1969.
GÉRARD, A., *Four African literatures: Amharic*, Univ. of California Press, 1971.
GOLDENBERG, G., 'The Amharic tense-system' (Ph.D. thesis, in Hebrew); Jerusalem University, 1966.
GUEBRE SELLASSIE, *Chronique du règne de Ménélik II*, translated from Amharic, 2 vols. and atlas, Paris, 1930–2; annotated by de Coppet and cited as de Coppet.
Guida dell'Africa orientale italiana, Milan, 1938; cited as *Guida*.
GUIDI, I., *Il Fetha Nagast* (Eth. text, Italian translation); 2 vols., Rome, 1897 and 1899.
——, *Vocabolario amarico-italiano*, Rome, 1901.
——, *(Breve) Storia della letteratura etiopica*, Rome, 1932.

GUIDI, I., 'Le Synaxaire éthiopien' (Sane, Hamle, Nahase, Paguemen); in *Patrologia Orientalis*, IX, 4, Paris.
GUIDI, I., and others, *Supplemento al vocabolario amarico-italiano*, Rome 1940.

HABTÄ MARYAM WARQNÄH, *təntawi yä'ityopəya təmhərt*, Addis Ababa 1970.
(HAILE SELLASSIE I) *Academic Honours of H.I.M. Haile Sellassie I*, Addis Ababa 1964.
HARDIE, FRANK, *The Abyssinian Crisis*, London 1974.
HARMSWORTH, GEOFFREY, *Abyssinian Adventure*, London 1935.
HARRIS, BRICE JR., *The United States and the Italo-Ethiopian Crisis*, Stanford, Calif., 1964.
HARRIS, W. CORNWALLIS, *The Highlands of AEthiopia*, 3 vols., London 1844.
HELIODORUS, *AETHIOPICA*, Rome 1938.
HERUY WALDÄ SELLASSIE, *Biographie*, Addis Ababa 1922/3; cited as Heruy.
HEYER, F., *Die Kirche Athiopiens*, Berlin 1971.
HOBEN, ALLAN, *Land Tenure among the Amhara of Ethiopia*, Chicago 1973.
HUNTINGFORD, G. W. B., *The Galla of Ethiopia*, London 1955.
HYATT, H. M., *The Church of Abyssinia*, London 1928.

JENNY, H., *Äthiopien, Land im Aufbruch*, Stuttgart 1957.
Journal of Ethiopian Studies, VII, 2, Addis Ababa 1969.

KÄBBÄDÄ TÄSÄMMA, *yätarik mastawwäsha*, Addis Ababa 1969/70.
KIRKPATRICK, SIR IVONE, *Mussolini, Study of a Demagogue*, London 1964.
KOLMODIN, J. A., 'Meine Studienreise in Abessinien, 1908–10', *MO*, Uppsala, 1910.
——, 'Traditions de Tsazzega et Hazzega, textes tigrigna', Rome, Uppsala, 1912–14 (*Archives d'Etudes Orientales*, vol. 5: 1, 2, 3).

LESLAU, W., *Falasha anthology*, New Haven, 1951.
——, *An annotated bibliography of the Semitic languages of Ethiopia*, The Hague, 1965.
LEVINE, D. N., *Wax and Gold*, University of Chicago Press, 1965.
LEWIS, I. M., *The modern history of Somaliland*, London, 1965.
LITTMANN, E., *Deutsche Aksum Expedition*, Berlin, 1913.
LUDOLF, H., *Historia Aethiopica*, Frankfort, 1681.
——, *Commentarius ad suam Historiam Aethiopicam*, Frankfort, 1691.

MAKONNEN ENDALKATCHÄW, *yähəlm ruǧǧa*, Addis Ababa 1956/7.
MANGESTU LAMMA, *Yalatcha Gabtcha* (*yalaǧǧa gabəǧǧa*), Addis Ababa 1964/5.
MARA, YOLANDE, *The Church of Ethiopia*, Asmara 1972.
MARCUS, HAROLD G., *The Life and Times of Menelik II, Ethiopia 1844–1913*, Clarendon Press, 1975.
MARKHAM, C. R., *A history of the Abyssinian expedition*, London 1869.
MÉRAB, 'Docteur', *Impressions d'Ethiopie (L'Abyssinie sous Ménélik II)*, 3 vols., Paris, 1921, 1922, 1929.
MINISTERO DELL'AFRICA ITALIANA, *Servizio Cartografico*, Rome 1939; cited as AOI map.

MONTI DELLA CORTE, A. A., *Lalibela*, Rome, 1940.
MOSLEY, L., *Haile Selassie*, London, 1964.

NICHOLSON, T. R., *A toy for the lion*, London, 1965.

PANKHURST, R., *Economic history of Ethiopia*, 1800–1935, Addis Ababa, 1968; cited as Pankhurst.
PANKHURST, SYLVIA, *Ethiopia, A Cultural History*, Woodford Green 1955.
PAULOS TZADUA (transl.), *The Fetha Nagast*, Addis Ababa 1968.
PERHAM, M., *The government of Ethiopia*, London, 1948; new ed. 1969.
PÉTRIDÈS, S. P., *Le Héros d'Adoua—Ras Makonnen, Prince d'Ethiopie*, Paris, 1963.
PHILIPPOS, ABUNA, *Know Jerusalem*, Addis Ababa 1971/2.
PLAYNE, B., *St. George for Ethiopia*, London, 1954.
POLLERA, A., *Lo Stato Etiopico e la sua Chiesa*, Rome-Milan, 1926.
——, *Le popolazioni indigene dell'Eritrea*, Bologna, 1935.
——, *L'Abissinia di ieri*, Rome 1940.
PONTIFICIO COLLEGIO ETIOPICO, *Celebrazione del 50 anniversario, 1919–1969*, Città del Vaticano 1971.
PRAETORIUS, F., *Die Amharische Sprache*, Halle, 1879.
PUGLISI, GIUSEPPE, *Chi è dell'Eritrea*, Asmara 1952.

REALE SOCIETÀ GEOGRAFICA ITALIANA, *L'Africa Orientale*, Bologna, 1936.
RENNELL OF RODD, LORD, *British military administration of occupied territories in Africa*, London, 1948.
RICCI, LANFRANCO, *Letterature dell'Etiopia* (Botto, *Storia delle letterature d'Oriente*) Milan, 1969.
ROSEN, F., *Eine deutsche Gesandtschaft in Abessinien*, Leipzig, 1907.

SABELLI, LUCA DEI, *Storia di Abissinia*, Rome, 1936-8.
SANDFORD, C., *The Lion of Judah hath prevailed*, London, 1955.
STARKIE, E., *Arthur Rimbaud in Abyssinia*, Oxford 1937.
STEER, G. L., *Caesar in Abyssinia*, London, 1936; cited as Steer.
——, *Sealed and Delivered*, London 1942.

TADDASA TAMRAT, *Church and State in Ethiopia, 1270–1527*, Oxford, 1972.
TÄSÄMMA HABTÄ MIKA'EL, Amharic Dictionary (in Amharic), Addis Ababa 1959; cited KBT.
Toponomastica Etiopica—see Bombaci, A.
ULLENDORFF, E., *The Semitic Languages of Ethiopia*, London, 1955.
——, *An Amharic Chrestomathy*, London, 1965.
——, 'The 1897 treaty between Great Britain and Ethiopia', in *RSE*, XXII, 1966-68.
——, 'The Anglo-Ethiopian Treaty of 1902', in *BSOAS*, XXX, 1967.
——, *Ethiopia and the Bible*, British Academy and O.U.P., 1968.
——, *The Ethiopians*, 3rd edition, Oxford Paperbacks, 1973; cited as *The Ethiopians*[3] or Ullendorff[3].
ULLENDORFF, E., AND BECKINGHAM, C. F., 'The first Anglo-Ethiopian Treaty' in *JSS*, Spring 1964.

ULLENDORFF, E., AND ABRAHAM DEMOZ, 'Two letters from the Emperor Yohannes of Ethiopia to Queen Victoria and Lord Granville' in *BSOAS*, XXXII, 1969.

VATIKIOTIS, P. J., *The Modern History of Egypt*, London 1969.

WALKER, C. H., *The Abyssinian at home*, London, 1933.
WRIGHT, STEPHEN, *Ethiopian Incunabula*, Addis Ababa 1967.
WRIGHT, W., *Catalogue of Ethiopic MSS in the British Museum*, London, 1877.

ZANDER, WALTER, *Israel and the Holy Places of Christendom*, London 1971.
ZEWDE GABRE-SELLASSIE, *Yohannes IV of Ethiopia, A Political Biography*, Clarendon Press, Oxford 1975; cited as Zewde, biographies.

Index

Šaläqa, 233.
Säläqläqa. 270.
Säläwa (Seloa), 61, 247.
Sällale, 26, 27, 28, 56, 62, 205, 289.
Samre, 247.
Samuel, Abba, 18, 43.
Samuel, Sir Herbert (later Viscount), 85.
Sandford, Christine, xxii, 18, 20, 28, 43, 53, 59, 67.
Säne, 76, 96, 98, 100, 103, 104, 134, 135, 137, 141, 142, 219, 298, 299.
Säqota, 283, 284, 289.
säräz, 144.
Sasäbäne, 241–2.
Savoy, House of, 68.
Sawiros, Abuna (Etchäge Gäbrä Mänfäs Qeddus), 171.
Sayent, 57, 157.
Säyo, 75.
Scheveningen, 221.
Schlee, Ann, xxi.
Schneider (rifle), 267, 278.
Scholefield, Alan, xxi.
School of Oriental and African Studies, xv, 16.
Sedest Kilo, 147.
Sehin, Wayzäro, 42.
Seloa (see Säläwa).
Semien, 56, 84, 157, 204, 270.
Semitic, xvii, xxiv.
Senafe, 247.
Serah Bezu Gäbre, Fitawrari, 58.
ser'atä negs, 57, 172, 176.
Seraye, 230.
Seyum Mängäsha, H.H. Ras (Gov.-Gen. of Tigre), 16, 56, 57, 61–2, 84, 179, 209, 234–5, 247, 249, 257, 265–7, 273, 277–9, 282.
Seyum, Dej. (earlier name of Ras Haylu), 201–2.
Shäfärra (or Shefärraw, Shifärraw), Fitawrari, 268.
shanqella, 80.
Shäwaye, Ato, 54.
Sheba, Queen of, 5, 49, 69, 111, 122.
Shebäshi Bäyan, Dej., 60.
Shebäta, 40.

Shire, 257, 265–9.
Shoa, 5, 13, 14, 18, 51–3, 55, 157, 168, 170, 179, 204, 235, 288, 296.
Shoarägäd (or Shoarägga), 6, 15, 313.
Shola, 87.
Shum Awre, 267.
Sidamo, Sidama, 28, 29, 32, 46, 152, 179, 212, 240, 251, 259–62.
Sirak Heruy, Blatta, 89.
Sixtus IV, Pope, 103.
Sobat (river), 124, 145.
Società Agricola Italo-Somala, 150.
Söderblom, Nathan (Archbishop of Uppsala), 96.
Solomon, King, 5, 49, 111, 112, 122.
Solomon, Star of, 69.
Somali(s), 14, 46–7, 49, 50, 242.
Somalia (Italian Somaliland), xx, 75, 102, 124, 126–7, 129, 131, 133, 140, 150, 210, 213–15, 217, 219, 222–3, 226, 229, 230, 241, 253, 254, 258.
Somaliland, British, 57, 106, 156, 209, 215, 216, 218, 253.
Somaliland, French, 57, 127, 209, 253, 257, 294.
Sophoulis, Themistocles, xxiv, 115.
Southampton, 297.
Spezia, 104.
Starkie, Enid, 48.
Steer, G.L., 113, 214, 220, 235, 238–43, 247–9, 252, 257, 259, 264–5, 269, 270, 272–4, 280–1, 286, 289, 290.
Stockholm, xxxi, 95, 97–8, 207.
Strabo, 117.
Sudan, 16, 106, 126–34, 139, 209, 228.
Sudan, Anglo-Egyptian (Govt. of), 57, 106–7, 124–5, 139, 144–5.
Sudan Interior Mission, 239–40.
Suez, 120.
Suez Canal, 85, 294, 307.
Sweden, Swedish, xxiv, 68, 70, 95–7, 163, 173, 175, 206–12, 240–1, 258–9.
Switzerland, Swiss, 67, 76–7, 79, 80, 112, 163, 211, 238.
Synaxarium, 116.
Syrian, 52.

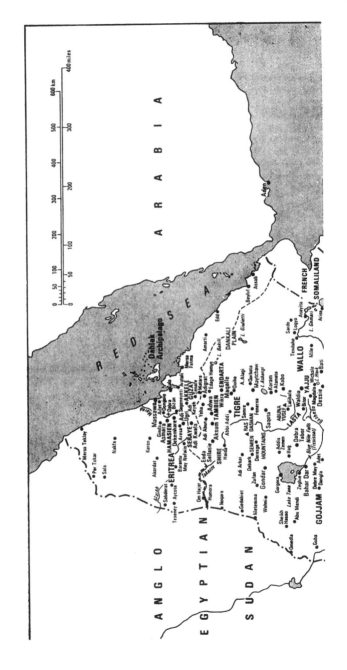

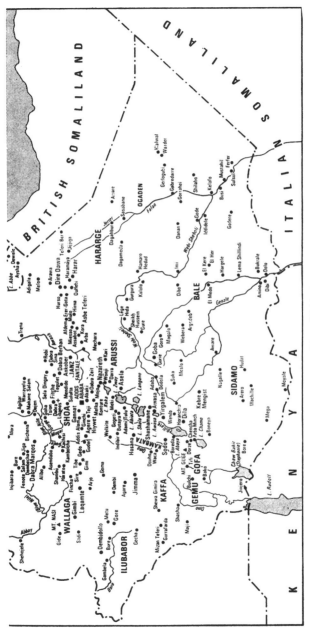

Map of Ethiopia